2015 BOND'S Top 100 FRANCHISES

2015 (6th) EDITION

D1260579

Robert E. Bond, Publisher
Annie Barbarika, Senior Editor
Christopher Buenaventura, Graphic Design

Source Book Publications
Serving the Franchising Industry
1814 Franklin Street, Suite 603
Oakland, CA 94612
(510) 839-5471

ISBN-10: 1-887137-93-9
ISBN-13: 978-1-887137-93-5

DISCLAIMER

Bond's Top 100 Franchises is based on data submitted by the franchisors themselves. Every effort has been made to obtain up-to-date and reliable information. As the information returned has not been independently verified, we assume no responsibility for errors or omissions and reserve the right to include or eliminate listings and otherwise edit and present the data at our discretion and based on our judgment as to what is useful to the readers of this directory. Inclusion in the publication does not imply endorsement by the editors or the publisher. Errors brought to the attention of the publisher and verified to the satisfaction of the publisher will be corrected in future editions. The publisher specifically disclaims all warranties, including the implied warranties of merchantability and fitness for a specific purpose.

This publication is designed to provide its readers with accurate and authoritative information with regard to the subject matter covered. It is sold with the understanding that neither the author nor the publisher is engaged in rendering legal, accounting, or other professional services. If legal advice or other expert assistance is required, the services of a competent professional should be sought.

From a Declaration of Principles jointly adopted by a Committee of the American Bar Association and a Committee of Publishers.

Cover Design by Christopher Buenaventura.

ISBN-10: 1-887137-93-9
ISBN-13: 978-1-887137-93-5
Printed in the United States of America.

10 9 8 7 6 5 4 3 2 1

Bond's Top 100 Franchises is available at special discounts for bulk purchase. Special editions or book excerpts can also be created to specifications. For details, contact Source Book Publications, 1814 Franklin Street, Suite 603, Oakland, CA 94612. Phone: (888) 612-9908; (510) 839-5471; Fax: (510) 839-2104.

This book is dedicated to

FRANdata

For providing over 25 years of exceptional and objective information to franchisors, franchisees, lenders, investors, suppliers, and everyone associated with the franchising industry.

Preface

At its best, purchasing a franchise is a time-tested, paint-by-the-numbers method of starting a new business. Many of the myriad pitfalls normally encountered by someone starting a new business are avoided and the odds of success are vastly improved. Franchising represents an exceptional blend of operating independence with a proven system that includes a detailed blueprint for starting and managing the business, as well as the critical ongoing support. However, purchasing a franchise is clearly not a fool-proof investment that somehow guarantees the investor financial independence.

At its worst, if the evaluation and investment decision is sloppy or haphazard, franchising can be a nightmare. If things don't work out, for whatever reason, you can't simply walk away. You are still responsible for the long-term lease on your retail space, the large bank loan that underwrote your entry into the business and/or the binding, long-term financial obligation to the franchisor. While it is easy to sell a profitable business, an unprofitable business will most likely result in a significant financial loss. If that loss is all equity, that might be an acceptable risk. If, however, you still have obligations to the bank, landlord, and others, your hardship is greatly compounded. This says nothing about the inevitable stress on one's personal life, relationships, and self-esteem.

Your ultimate success as a franchisee will be determined by two factors:

1. The homework you do at the front-end to ensure that you are selecting the optimal franchise for your particular needs, experience, and financial resources.

2. Your commitment to work hard and play by the rules once you have signed a binding, long-term franchise agreement. For most new franchisees, this involves working 60 or more hours per week until you can justify delegating some of the day-to-day responsibilities. It also requires being a team player— not acting as an entrepreneur who does his or her own thing without regard for the system as a whole. A franchise system is only as good as the franchisees make it. This means following the script.

Another harsh reality, unfortunately, is that there is no such thing as the "Top 100 franchises." Similarly, there isn't a list of the "Top 10 colleges," the "Top 5 professional basketball players," or the "Top 3 sports cars." Like everything else in life, the beauty is in the eye of the beholder. Picking the optimal franchise is a good example. What appeals to me, even after exhaustive and, hopefully, well-thought-out research, may not appeal to you or be appropriate for you. Whereas I might be prepared to work 70-hour weeks for the first year my new business is open, you might not. Whereas I might be willing to invest $500,000 in a specific franchise concept, you might feel that the projected rewards do not outweigh the inherent risks. Whereas you might be exceptional at working with minimum wage personnel, I might be unable to communicate effectively with younger, less-educated staff. These are just a few examples of the literally hundreds of weighty considerations that you will have to consider and evaluate before deciding to invest in a specific franchise system.

In short, one prospective franchisee will clearly not have the same life experiences, talents, abilities, and financial wherewithal as the next. Therefore, it is critical that you take what we say only as a best effort on our part to go through literally hundreds of concepts before arriving at those which, we feel, best address our collective needs and experiences as professionals within the franchising industry.

My strong suggestion is that you take the time to carefully read the first two chapters of this book to better understand the industry and the variables you will have to consider in making a long-term investment decision. Even though you may already have a sense as to what type of franchise you want to purchase, maybe even a specific franchise, keep an open mind to the other options available to you. Request marketing information on all of the competing systems and rigorously evaluate each. Be sure to visit the various websites for each franchise. You may be pleasantly surprised to learn that one system offers a range of benefits that better complements your experience and capabilities. Also keep in mind that how successful you will be, in the final analysis, is up to you — not the franchisor.

Remember, this is not a game. I cannot overemphasize the fact that, in most cases, you will be making a once-in-a-lifetime investment decision. It is incumbent on you to do it correctly at the outset. This can only be done by taking your time, properly researching all the options, realistically addressing both the "best case" and "worst case" scenarios, seeking the advice of friends and professionals, and, in general, doing the due diligence required. You want to invest in a system that will take advantage of your unique talents and experiences and not take advantage of you in the process! Don't take short-cuts. Listen carefully to what the franchisor and your advisors tell you. Don't think you are so clever or independent that you can't benefit from the advice of outside professionals. Don't assume that the franchisor's required guidelines regarding the amount of investment, experience, temperament, etc., somehow don't apply to you. Don't accept any promises or "understandings" from the franchisor that are not committed in writing in the franchise agreement. Invest the additional time to talk to and/or meet with as many franchisees in the system as you can. The additional front-end investment you make, both in time and money, will pay off handsomely if it saves you from making a marginal, or poor, investment decision. This is one of the few times in business when second chances are rare. Make the extra effort to do it right the first time.

Good luck, and Godspeed.

ROB BOND

Table of Contents

Introduction

Determining which franchises should be in the Top 100 (and, equally importantly, which ones should not) was a daunting task. It was difficult to choose only 100. Since franchises are so diverse, it was our intention to include at least one franchise from each industry category. Based on our comprehensive research, the 100 in this book are, in our opinion, among the best in the franchising industry.

The franchising industry is a large and sometimes confusing one. There are several industry categories, each with its own characteristics and subcategories. While we will try to provide you with as meaningful an overview as we can, it is your responsibility to aggressively research every aspect of any company you're interested in. Buy a franchise much like you would buy a house. Whereas you can usually sell a house for roughly what you bought it for, you may not be so lucky liquidating a poorly-researched franchise investment. It's a big investment and it takes time.

METHODOLOGY

How did we arrive at our choices? There were several criteria that were taken into consideration. Primary among these were name recognition, product quality, litigation, total investment, ongoing expenses, training programs, ongoing support, and the exclusive territory awarded to new franchisees. Many of the criteria to take into consideration are personal choices. Is the franchise something you're interested in? Will you have the time and passion to manage it like you want to? These are questions that you'll have to answer for yourself. The information in this book will help you once you've decided what you want to do.

We chose both companies that have already established a strong brand name identity as well as those that are in the process of establishing a recognizable identity. ServiceMaster Clean, for example, is known the world over by millions of people. Conversely, companies like The Grounds Guys and The Flame Broiler are less well-known now, but as their concepts become more and more popular, they will undoubtedly increase their name recognition in the near future.

Litigation was a silent factor in determining the Top 100 franchises. We don't have a litigation section in each profile, but while reviewing each franchisor's FDD (Franchise Disclosure Document—a required document containing 23 categories of information that must be provided by the franchisor to the prospective franchisee at the first face-to-face meeting or at least 14 days prior to the execution of the franchise agreement, whichever is sooner), we certainly took into account Item 3, which lists any relevant court cases, past and present, involving the company and tells us volumes about franchisor-franchisee relations. If a franchisor had no legal problems or a few court cases inconsequential to the reputation and operation of the company, then it was certainly a viable candidate for the Top 100.

The total investment is usually a significant determining factor in choosing a franchise. After all, money talks. Initially, investing in a franchise takes considerable patience. You are faced with numerous questions such as "Which items do I finance and which do I purchase?", "Are real estate costs included?", "Will the company help me with financing?", etc. We don't attempt to explore these questions in depth, but we do give you a brief overview of what you will be expected to invest. A Top 100 company may have a low total investment cost, financing assistance, and a detailed account of what each item costs. We looked at all the franchisors and chose the ones which exemplified the best combination of these factors.

Before you open a franchise, one of the most critical steps is the initial training program, during which you will learn the basics about the franchise you choose. Training is usually held at the franchisor's headquarters and can last anywhere from five days to 12 weeks. The companies in this book all have strong, comprehensive training courses that include hours of both classroom and on-site training.

Ongoing expenses are made up of two fees: a royalty fee and an advertising fee. The royalty fee is a portion of your sales (usually four to eight percent) that you give to the franchisor in exchange for its expertise, ongoing support and brand name. The advertising payment (three to five percent of sales) is also paid to the franchisor, and in return you receive advertising, marketing, and promotional assistance. If these fees were within an acceptable range, then a company was a good candidate for the Top 100.

Most companies listed give exceptional ongoing support to their franchisees: continual managerial aid, advertising assistance, access to the operations manual, etc. The basic tenet of franchising is, as Ray Kroc, the founder of McDonald's, said, "to be in business for yourself, not by yourself." Make sure the franchisor is going to support you over the long-term.

Another very important aspect of franchising that often gets overlooked is the franchisor's exclusive territory policy. An exclusive territory awarded by the franchisor describes the specific area or market in which you can operate your business. Why is this so important? By giving you an exclusive territory of, say, a three-mile radius surrounding your location, the franchisor is agreeing that it will not establish another location within that three-mile radius. So, logically, your business will have less competition. Most of the companies in the Top 100 have some sort of exclusive area policy.

All of these factors are important by themselves. Many companies exhibit some of them. But it's the rare few that combine the majority of these characteristics into one fluid franchising system. From those companies, we chose the Top 100.

ADDITIONAL FACTORS TO CONSIDER

Three additional areas that clearly require serious examination before investing are 1) outstanding legal/litigation issues; 2) the current financial status of the franchisor; and 3) issues regarding renewal, termination, transfer, and dispute resolution. Because the first two areas can change on a daily basis, coupled with the fact that we lack the necessary expertise to comment authoritatively on either, we have intentionally left these important responsibilities to the investor.

If there is any reason to think that an outstanding legal issue may impact the company's ability to prosper or support the franchise system, you will most likely require the interpretation of a qualified and experienced franchise attorney. Prior to signing a franchise agreement, be confident that no new or potential litigation has come up since the publication of the FDD. The franchisor is obligated to give you an accurate status report.

Similarly, the franchisor's financial health is critical to your own success. How does one determine that health? Each franchisor is required to include detailed financial statements in its FDD. Depending upon the date of the FDD, the information may be very current. Most likely, however, it will be outdated by 6 – 12 months. If this is the case, request current financials from the franchisor. If the company is publicly traded, there are numerous sources of detailed information. Go to the firm's website. If you don't have the expertise to judge the financial information, seek the advice of an accountant or financial consultant. As all of the companies included in the Top 100 have in excess of 50 operating units, they most likely are enjoying a positive cash flow from operations and, therefore, are in a much stronger financial position than smaller franchisors. However, this is not an excuse to avoid an investigation.

Item 17 of the FDD covers "Renewal, Termination, Transfer and Dispute Resolution." These are critical areas that should be fully understood before you find out that, after you have developed a profitable business, the franchisor has the unilateral right to terminate your franchise or capriciously deny a sale to a qualified buyer. Don't get blind-sided because you were too lazy or frugal to get a legal interpretation. Again, this is the province of a qualified attorney.

THE FOOD-SERVICE INDUSTRY

The franchising industry contains over 3,500 different concepts. Food-service constitutes roughly one-third of the entire industry—by far the largest. Within the food-service industry, there are several different themes: bakery/coffee, fast-food or quick-service, ice cream, sit-down, subs and sandwiches, and other miscellaneous categories. Frequently, concepts are further subdivided. For example, in the fast-food industry, there are various different segments such as pizza, hamburgers, chicken, Asian, seafood, and Mexican, to name just a few. What does all of this mean? Simply that food-service is a large, dominant, and sometimes confusing industry that has to be fully researched before settling in on a specific franchise concept.

The following table lists the 17 food-service franchises featured in Chapter 3.

Company Name	Franchise Fee	Total Investment	Royalty	Total Units
Auntie Anne's Hand-Rolled Soft Pretzels	$30,000	$194,900 – $367,600	7%	1,163
Big Apple Bagels	$25,000	$254,300 – $379,600	5%	85
Charleys Philly Cheesesteaks	$24,500	$152,193 – $451,236	6% / $300/wk.	534
Checkers Drive-In Restaurants	$30,000	$453,000 – $627,000	4%	792
Church's Chicken	$25,000	$413,300 – $1,336,600	5%	1,188
CiCi's Pizza	$30,000	$444,000 – $717,000	4%	470
Cousins Subs	$25,000	$106,700 – $288,300	6%	144
Denny's	$40,000	$1.178 – $2.621 million	4.5%	1,692
Doc Popcorn	$37,500	$72,000 – $378,000	6%	97
Famous Famiglia	$35,000	$265,750 – $530,800	6%	111
The Flame Broiler	$25,000	$205,400 – $341,800	5%	170
Little Caesars	$20,000	$265,000 – $681,500	6%	undis-closed
Papa Murphy's Take 'N' Bake Pizza	$25,000	$215,905 – $378,421	5%	1,430
Port of Subs	$16,000	$199,300 – $328,300	5.5%	156
Rita's Italian Ice	$30,000	$140,200 – $413,900	6.5%	555
Schlotzsky's Deli	$30,000	$461,700 – $774,000	6%	335

Company Name	Franchise Fee	Total Investment	Royalty	Total Units
Tropical Smoothie Café	$25,000	$165,000 – $424,000	6%	425

THE RETAIL INDUSTRY

Of the 3,500 different franchise concepts, over 400 are retail franchises. There are several different types of retail companies: specialty retailers, clothing, athletic wear, art supplies, convenience stores, home improvement, pet products, photographic products, and electronics/computer products. Like the food-service and service-based franchises, the retail industry is large and needs to be fully researched before settling in on a specific franchise concept.

The following table lists the 9 retail franchises featured in Chapter 4.

Company Name	Franchise Fee	Total Investment	Royalty	Total Units
7-Eleven	Varies	Varies	Gross Profit Split	7,220
Clothes Mentor	$20,000	$155,000 – $235,000	4%	130
Floor Coverings International	$49,500	$137,500 – $310,000	5%	116
Gateway Newsstands	$15,000 – $150,000	$55,900 – $501,800	3.5% – 5% / 10%	127
The HoneyBaked Ham Co. & Café	$30,000	$281,800 – $431,900	5 – 6%	420
Miracle-Ear	$20,000	$122,500 – $450,000	$48.80	1,290

Company Name	Franchise Fee	Total Investment	Royalty	Total Units
Snap-on Tools	$7,500 – $15,000	$152,700 – $319,000	$110	4,795
Wild Birds Unlimited	$18,000	$99,000 – $157,000	4%	280
Wireless Zone	$30,000	$65,250 – $228,500	10%	475

THE SERVICE-BASED INDUSTRY

Service-based franchises make up most of the remaining chunk of the franchising industry. There are several different types of service-based companies: automotive services, child development, real estate, travel, etc. The industry is large and needs to be fully researched before settling in on a specific franchise concept.

The following table lists the 74 service-based franchises featured in Chapter 5.

Company Name	Franchise Fee	Total Investment	Royalty	Total Units
1-800-Got-Junk?	$12,000	$125,000 – $250,000	8%	163
Aire Serv Heating & Air Conditioning	$30,000+	$64,300 – $183,900	5 – 7%	179
Always Best Care Senior Services	$44,900	$60,200 – $109,400	6%	185
Anago Cleaning Systems	$49,000	$7,000 – $33,000	10%	2,456
Anytime Fitness	$29,900	$78,599 – $345,499	$499/mo.	2,040
Archadeck	$49,500	$80,000 – $100,000	2.5 – 5.5%	56

Company Name	Franchise Fee	Total Investment	Royalty	Total Units
Bricks 4 Kidz	$25,900	$33,800 – $51,100	7%	429
BrightStar Care	$48,000	$93,000 – $172,000	5%	284
Brightway Insurance	$60,000	$150,000 – $175,000	15 – 45%	113
Caring Transitions	$39,900	$52,900 – $81,500	6% or $300	166
CMIT Solutions	$49,500	$129,200 – $171,500	6 – 0%	146
Color Glo International	$30,000	$51,000 – $54,800	4% or $300	126
ComForcare Senior Services	$42,000	$77,800 – $141,800	5 – 3%	197
Comfort Keepers	$45,000	$83,060 – $114,390	5%	686
Coverall Health-Based Cleaning System	$11,300 – $37,000	$14,100 – $47,700	5%	8,045
Crestcom International	$69,500	$85,300 – $104,000	35.5%	192
CruiseOne	$9,800	$4,600 – $26,300	3%	945
Cruise Planners – American Express	$495 – $9,995	$2,095 – $21,990	1 – 3%	1,499
Discovery Map International	$25,000	$35,000 – $45,000	10%	124
Express Oil Change	$35,000	$1.3 million – $1.6 million	5%	201

Company Name	Franchise Fee	Total Investment	Royalty	Total Units
Eye Level Learning Centers	$20,000	$68,100 –$135,100	$36-$29 / subject-student	1,209
Fantastic Sams	$25,000 – $40,000	$136,100 – $246,100	Fixed Fee	1,150
FASTSIGNS	$37,500	$178,200 – $289,500	6%	571
FirstLight HomeCare	$38,000	$85,200 – $128,600	5%	124
Five Star Painting	$20,000 – $40,000	$25,000 – $70,000	5%	67
Fresh Coat	$39,900 – $45,900	$44,400 – $71,000	6%	116
Furniture Medic	$29,900	$54,100 – $70,400	7% / $250 min	334
Glass Doctor	$28,000+	$108,000+	5 – 7%	174
Griswold Home Care	$49,500	$95,000 – $121,000	4%	244
The Grounds Guys	$28,500+	$50,000 – $140,000	7%	149
The Growth Coach	$39,900 – $45,900	$52,125 – $82,025	10%	120
Hand & Stone Massage and Facial Spa	$39,000	$393,500 – $488,600	5%	180
Home Helpers	$44,900	$64,500 – $104,900	6 – 3%	655
HouseMaster Home Inspections	$42,500	$60,100 – $107,900	7.5%	325

Company Name	Franchise Fee	Total Investment	Royalty	Total Units
Intelligent Office	$59,000	$314,500 – $524,250	5%	63
The Interface Financial Group – IFG 50/50	$34,500	$50,000 – $100,000	8%	54
Jani-King International	$8,000 – $33,000	$8,200 – $74,000	10%	10,022
Jan-Pro Cleaning Systems	$1,000 – $30,000	$2,800 – $44,000	10%	10,842
Kiddie Academy	$120,000	$372,000 – $702,000	7%	125
KidzArt	$32,000	$17,800 – $39,300	8% / $250 min.	74
Kinderdance International	$12,000 – $40,000	$15,000 – $46,000	6 – 15%	127
Kitchen Tune-Up	$25,000	$83,000 – $91,000	Varies	104
Kumon North America	$1,000, $1,000	$72,200 – $149,300	$32-36 / subj / month	2,000
LearningRX	$25,000 – $35,000	$109,000 – $209,000	10%	93
Liberty Tax Service	$40,000	$57,800 – $71,900	14%	4,438
Liquid Capital	$50,000	$200,000 – $1 million	8%	83
The Little Gym	$29,500 – $49,500	$145,750 – $366,000	8%	294

Company Name	Franchise Fee	Total Investment	Royalty	Total Units
Maaco Collision Repair and Auto Painting	$35,000	$250,000 – $300,000	8%	463
Maids, The	$12,500 + $.95 per QHH	$97,000 – $123,000	3.9 – 6.9%	1,149
Massage Heights	$42,000	$235,100 – $595,900	5%	121
Mathnasium Learning Centers	$40,000	$99,750 – $139,375	10%	535
Meineke Car Care Centers	$30,000	$200,000 – $250,000	5 – 8%	979
Molly Maid	$14,900	$150,000 – $175,000	3 – 6.5%	455
Money Mailer	$50,000	$58,000	$250	237
Mosquito Squad	$25,000	$35,000 – $75,000	$400 – $1,900	142
Mr. Appliance Corporation	$27,000+	$47,400 – $99,100+	7%	185
Mr. Electric Corp.	$28,000+	$73,400 – $171,000+	6 – 8%	174
Mr. Rooter	$30,000+	$68,400 – $162,600+	5 – 7%	241
Padgett Business Services	$38,000 + $18,000 Training	$100,000	9 – 4.5%	385
Pillar to Post Home Inspectors	$16,900	$31,500 – $36,500	7%	435

Company Name	Franchise Fee	Total Investment	Royalty	Total Units
Pop-A-Lock	$62,000 minimum	$99,800 – $133,400 + $15,500/add. franchise	6%	302
Pridestaff	$12,500	$80,400 – $126,900	65%	43
Pronto Insurance	$15,000 – $25,000	$60,000 – $100,000	0%	131
Rainbow International Restoration & Cleaning	$28,000+	$115,700 – $189,100	3 – 7%	309
ServiceMaster Clean	$24,900 – $67,000	$49,600 – $180,600	5 – 10%	4,450
SERVPRO	$44,000	$138,600 – $187,200	3 – 10%	1,649
ShelfGenie	$45,000	$80,000 – $128,000	5%	154
Snip-its	$25,000	$120,300 – $255,400	6%	65
Spherion Staffing Services	$25,000	$98,000 – $164,000	3 – 6% / 25%	146
Sport Clips	$25,000 – $59,500	$158,300 – $316,500	6%	1,207
Spring-Green Lawn Care	$30,000	$82,900 – $94,200	10 – 8%	120
Tutor Doctor	From $39,700	$62,500 – $100,700	8% or $300	400
Vanguard Cleaning Systems	$7,200 – $34,200	$8,500 – $37,900	10%	2,821
Window Genie	$32,000	$85,000 – $150,000	7%	168

In closing, I'd like to emphasize that the 100 companies included in this book are here as the result of many months of intensive research and independent evaluation. We did not draw names out of a hat. We did not necessarily choose the industry "heavyweights." We did, however, pour over countless FDDS, confer with many franchise directors and staff members, and view numerous websites. In addition to studying each company's FDD and marketing materials, we took full advantage of recent articles about each company we evaluated. We sought the opinion of friends, industry experts, and existing franchisees. As we do not allow advertising in any of our publications, we do not have a built-in bias toward any of the companies selected. Nor do we have any financial or other hidden agendas.

It is our hope that, as a potential franchisee, you will benefit from these efforts. In designing the format, we decided the best way to present the information would be to ask the same questions you would: "How much?", "Why are they better than their competitors?", and "What do I get out of it?" These questions and more are answered as we present what we feel are among the 100 best franchises.

30-Minute Overview 1

In presenting this data, we have made some unilateral assumptions about our readers. The first is that you purchased the book because of the depth and accuracy of the data provided—not as a how-to manual. Clearly, dedication to hard work, adequate financing, commitment, good business sense, and access to trusted professional counsel will determine your ultimate success as a franchisee. A strong working knowledge of the industry, however, will help ensure that you have made the best choice of franchise opportunities. I advise you to acquaint yourself with the dynamics of the industry before you initiate the evaluation and negotiation phases of selecting a franchise.

The second assumption is that you have already devoted the time necessary to conduct a detailed personal inventory. This self-assessment should result in a clear understanding of your skills, aptitudes, weaknesses, long-term personal goals, commitment to succeed, and financial capabilities.

ℜ

There are three primary stages to the franchise selection process: 1) the investigation stage, 2) the evaluation stage, and 3) the negotiation stage. This book is intended primarily to assist the reader in the investigation stage by providing a thorough list of the options available. Chapters One and Two include various observations based on our over 20 years of involvement with the franchising industry. Hopefully, they will provide some insights that you will find of value.

Understand at the outset that the entire process will take many months and involve a great deal of frustration. I suggest that you set up a realistic timeline for signing a franchise agreement and that you stick with that schedule. There will be a lot of pressure on you to prematurely complete the selection and negotiation phases. Resist that temptation. The penalties are too severe for a seat-of-the-pants attitude. A decision of this magnitude clearly deserves your full attention. Do your homework!

Before starting the selection process, you would be well advised to briefly review the areas that follow.

FRANCHISE INDUSTRY STRUCTURE

The franchising industry is made up of two distinct types of franchises. The first, and by far the larger, encompasses product and trade name franchising. Automotive and truck dealers, soft drink bottlers, and gasoline service stations are included in this group. For the most part, these are essentially distributorships.

The second group encompasses business format franchisors. This book only includes information on this latter category.

LAYMAN'S DEFINITION OF FRANCHISING

Business format franchising is a method of market expansion by which one business entity expands the distribution of its products and/or services through independent, third-party operators. Franchising occurs when the operator of a concept or system (the **franchisor**) grants

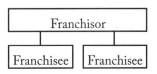

Classic Business Format Model

an independent businessperson (the **franchisee**) the right to duplicate its entire business format at a particular location and for a specified time period, under terms and conditions set forth in a contract (the **franchise agreement**). The franchisee has full access to all of the trademarks, logos, marketing techniques, controls, and systems that have made the franchisor successful. In effect, the franchisee acts as a surrogate for a company-owned store in the distribution of the franchisor's goods and/or services. It is important to keep in mind that the franchisor and the franchisee are separate legal entities.

In return for a front-end **franchise fee**—which usually ranges from $15,000 to $35,000—the franchisor is obligated to "set up" the franchisee in business. This generally includes assistance in selecting a location, negotiating a lease, obtaining financing, building and equipping a site, and providing the necessary training, operating manuals, etc. Once the training is completed and the store is open, the new franchisee should have a carbon copy of other units in the system and enjoy the same benefits they do, whether they are company-owned or not.

Business format franchising is unique because it is a long-term relationship characterized by an ongoing, mutually beneficial partnership. Ongoing services include research and development, marketing strategies, advertising campaigns, group buying, periodic field visits, training updates, and whatever else is required to make the franchisee competitive and profitable. In effect, the franchisor acts as the franchisee's "back office" support organization. To reimburse the franchisor for this support, the franchisee pays the franchisor an ongoing **royalty fee,** generally four to eight percent of gross sales or income. In many cases, franchisees also contribute an **advertising fee** to reimburse the franchisor for expenses incurred in maintaining a national or regional advertising campaign.

For the maximum advantage, both the franchisor and the franchisees should share common objectives and goals. Both parties must accept the premise that their fortunes are mutually intertwined and that they are each better off working in a cooperative effort, rather than toward any self-serving goals. Unlike the parent/child relationship that has dominated franchising over much of the past 30 years, franchising is now becoming a true and productive relationship of partners.

LEGAL DEFINITION OF FRANCHISING

The Federal Trade Commission (FTC) has its own definition of franchising. So do each of the 15 states that have separate franchise registration statutes. The State of California's definition, which is the model for the FTC's definition, follows:

Franchise means a contract or agreement, express or implied, whether oral or written, between two or more persons by which:

A franchisee is granted the right to engage in the business of offering, selling, or distributing goods or services under a marketing plan or system prescribed in substantial part by a franchisor;

The operation of the franchisee's business pursuant to that plan or system as substantially associated with the franchisor's trademark, service mark, trade name, logotype, advertising, or other commercial symbol designating the franchisor or its affiliates; and

The franchisee is required to pay, directly or indirectly, a franchise fee.

MULTI-LEVEL FRANCHISING

With franchisors continually exploring new ways to expand their distribution, the classic business format model shown above has evolved over the years. Modifications have allowed franchisors to grow more rapidly and at less cost than might have otherwise been possible.

If a franchisor wishes to expand at a faster rate than its financial resources or staff levels allow, it might choose to sell development rights in an area (state, national, or international) and let the new entity do the development work. No matter which development method is chosen, the franchisee should still receive the same benefits and support provided under the standard model. The major difference is that the entity providing the training and ongoing support and receiving the franchise and royalty fees changes.

Three variations of the master franchising model include: 1) master (or regional) franchising, 2) sub-franchising and 3) area development franchising.

In **master (or regional) franchising,** the franchisor sells the development rights in a particular market to a master franchisee who, in turn, sells individual franchises within the territory. In return for a front-end master franchise fee, the master franchisee has sole responsibility for developing that area under a mutually agreed upon schedule. This includes attracting, screening, signing, and training all new franchisees within the territory. Once established, ongoing support is generally provided by the parent franchisor.

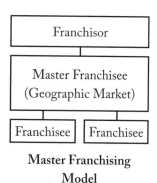

Master Franchising Model

The master franchisee is rewarded by sharing in the franchise fees and the ongoing royalties paid to the parent franchisor by the franchisees within the territory.

Sub-franchising is similar to master franchising in that the franchisor grants development rights in a specified territory to a sub-franchisor. After the agreement is signed, however, the parent franchisor has no ongoing involvement with the individual franchisees in the territory. Instead, the sub-franchisor becomes the focal point. All fees and royalties are paid directly to the sub-franchisor, who is solely responsible for all recruiting, training, and ongoing support. An agreed upon percentage of all incoming fees and royalties is passed on to the parent franchisor.

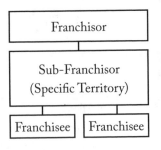

Sub-Franchising Model

In a sub-franchising relationship, the potential franchisee has to be doubly careful in his or her investigation. He or she must first make sure that the sub-franchisor has the necessary financial, managerial, and marketing skills to make the program work. Secondarily, the potential franchisee has to feel comfortable that the parent franchisor can be relied upon to come to his or her rescue if the sub-franchisor should fail.

The third variation is an **area development agreement.** Here again, the franchisor grants exclusive development rights for a particular geographic area to an area development investment group. Within its territory, the area developer may either develop individual franchise units for its own account or find independent franchisees to develop units. In the latter case, the area developer has a residual equity position in the profits of its "area franchisees."

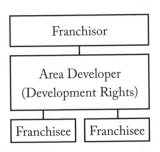

Area Development Model

In return for the rights to an exclusive territory, the area developer pays the franchisor a front-end development fee and commits to develop a certain number of units within a specified time period. (The front-end fee is generally significantly less than the sum of the individual unit fees.) Individual franchisees within the territory pay all contractual franchise, royalty, and advertising fees directly to the parent franchisor. The area developer shares in neither the franchise fee nor in ongoing royalty or advertising fees. Instead, the area developer shares only in the profitability of the individual franchises that it "owns." In essence, the area developer is buying multiple locations over time at a discount, since the franchise fee and (frequently) the royalty fee are less than the per unit rate.

FRANCHISING'S ROLE IN THE ECONOMY

The IFA's Educational Foundation recently released the third volume of the *Economic Impact of Franchised Businesses*. This report, which was prepared by PricewaterhouseCoopers for the IFA's Educational Foundation, documents the important role the franchising industry continues to play in the U.S. economy.

In 2007, more than 828,000 franchised establishments generated over $802 billion of direct economic output, or over 2.8 percent of the private sector economy in the United States. The franchising industry provided jobs for more than 9 million American workers, or 6.2 percent of all U.S. private sector employment. Including the additional economic activity that occurs outside of franchised businesses because of franchising activities, the overall economic contribution of franchised businesses was $2.1 trillion in 2007, or 9 percent of the U.S. economy.

These economic activities provided more than 17 million jobs for American workers, almost 12 percent of all U.S. private sector employment. From 2001 to 2007, the franchising sector of the economy grew at a faster pace than many other sectors of the economy. Franchising now provides more jobs than many other sectors of the U.S. economy. For example, franchising provides more jobs than the financial activities and insurance sector, as well as the real estate sector of the economy. The franchising sector expanded by over 18 percent from 2001 to 2005, adding more than 140,000 new establishments and creating more than 1.2 million new jobs. Direct economic output increased by more than 40 percent from 2001 to 2005, from $624.6 billion to $880.9 billion. Including the impact of additional economic activity that occurs outside of franchised businesses because of franchising activities, the franchising industry added nearly 3 million jobs and over $780 billion of economic output to the U.S. economy. Much more detailed information can be found in the full 600-plus page report, published on the IFA's website www.franchise.org.

THE PLAYERS

Franchisors

After extensive research, we have selected 100 of what we think are among the best franchises the industry has to offer.

Selecting the most appropriate franchisor for your needs is crucial to becoming a successful franchisee. By providing general information, in addition to a detailed analysis of each company's identity, financial requirements, training, support, and territory offering, we hope to aid the prospective franchisee in making the right choice.

The Regulatory Agencies

The offer and sale of franchises are regulated at both the federal and state levels. Federal requirements cover all 50 states. In addition, certain states have adopted their own requirements.

In 1979, after many years of debate, the Federal Trade Commission (FTC) implemented Rule 436. The Rule required that franchisors provide prospective franchisees with a disclosure statement (then called an offering circular) containing specific information about a company's franchise offering. The Rule has two objectives: to ensure that the potential franchisee has sufficient background information to make an educated investment decision and to provide him or her with adequate time to do so.

The Franchise Rule was substantially updated (and improved) on July 1, 2008 as the FTC tried to make the disclosure document more consistent with various state regulations. Among other things, the Uniform Franchise Offering Circular (UFOC) became the Franchise Disclosure Document (FDD) and Item 19 of the new FDD morphed from an Earnings Claims Statement to a Financial Performance Representation. Overall the revisions were positive and resulted in considerably more and better information being available to the prospective franchisee. Unfortunately, the revisions did not require all franchisors to provide a Financial Performance Representation from which potential franchisees could better determine the overall profitability of their potential investments.

Certain "registration states" require additional safeguards to protect potential franchisees. Their requirements are generally more stringent than the FTC's requirements. These states include California, Florida, Illinois, Indiana, Maryland, Michigan, Minnesota, New York, North Dakota, Oregon, Rhode Island, South Dakota, Virginia, Washington and Wisconsin. Separate registration is also required in the provinces of Alberta, Ontario and Prince Edward Island, Canada.

The regulations require that the franchisor provide a prospective franchisee with the required information at their first face-to-face meeting or at least 14 days prior to the signing of the franchise agreement, whichever is earlier. Required information includes:

1. The franchisor and any predecessors.
2. Identity and business experience of persons affiliated with the franchisor.
3. Litigation.
4. Bankruptcy.
5. Franchisee's initial fee or other payments.
6. Other fees.
7. Franchisee's estimated initial investment.
8. Obligations of franchisee to purchase or lease from designated sources.
9. Obligations of franchisee to purchase or lease in accordance with specifications or from approved suppliers.
10. Financing arrangements.
11. Obligations of franchisor; other supervision, assistance, or services.
12. Exclusive area or territory.
13. Trademarks, service marks, trade names, logos, and commercial symbols.
14. Patents and copyrights.
15. Obligations of the participant in the actual operation of the franchise business.
16. Restrictions on goods and services offered by franchisee.
17. Renewal, termination, repurchase, modification, and assignment of the franchise agreement and related information.
18. Arrangements with public figures.
19. Actual, average, projected, or forecasted franchise sales, profits, or earnings.
20. Information regarding franchises of the franchisor.
21. Financial statements.
22. Contracts.
23. Acknowledgement of receipt by respective franchisee.

If you live in a registration state, make sure that the franchisor you are evaluating is, in fact, registered to sell franchises there. If not, and the franchisor has no near-term plans to register in your state, you should consider other options.

Keep in mind that neither the FTC nor any of the states has reviewed the FDD to determine whether the information submitted is true or not. They merely require that the franchisor make representations based upon a prescribed format. If the information provided is false, franchisors are subject to civil penalties. However, this may not help a franchisee who cannot undo a very expensive mistake.

It is up to you to read thoroughly and fully understand all elements of the FDD. There is no question that it is tedious reading. Know exactly what you can expect from the franchisor and what your own obligations are. Ask yourself: under what circumstances can the relationship be unilaterally terminated by the franchisor? What is your protected territory? Specifically, what front-end assistance will the franchisor provide? You should have a professional review the FDD. It would be a shame not to take full advantage of the documentation that is available to you.

The Trade Associations

The **International Franchise Association** (IFA) was established as a non-profit trade association to promote franchising as a responsible method of doing business. The IFA currently represents over 1,200 franchisors in the U.S. and around the world. It is recognized as the leading spokesperson for responsible franchising. For most of its 50+ years, the IFA has represented the interests of franchisors only. In recent years, however, it has initiated an aggressive campaign to recruit franchisees into its membership and represent their interests as well. The IFA's address is 1501 K Street, NW, Suite 350, Washington, DC 20005. TEL (202) 628-8000; FAX (202) 628-0812, www.franchise.org.

The **Canadian Franchise Association** (CFA), which has some 250+ members, is the Canadian equivalent of the IFA. Information on the CFA can be obtained from its offices at 5399 Eglinton Avenue W, Suite 116, Toronto, ON M9C 5K6 Canada. TEL (416) 695-2896; (800) 665-4232; FAX (416) 695-1950, www.cfa.ca.

The **American Association of Franchisees and Dealers** (AAFD) represents the rights and interests of franchisees and independent dealers. Formed in 1992 with the mission of "Bringing Fairness to Franchising," the AAFD represents thousands of franchised businesses, representing over 250 different franchise systems. It provides a broad range of services designed to help franchisees build market power, create legislative support, provide legal and financial support, and provide a wide range of general member benefits. P.O. Box 81887, San Diego, CA 92138. TEL (619) 209-3775; FAX: (619) 209-3777, www.aafd.org.

ADDITIONAL RESOURCES

During your due diligence effort, there are several other sources of information that are invaluable.

1. www.bluemaumau.com – the industry's premier community of franchise research, news, blogs, and management insights. This website is the most open-ended site for in-depth information about franchising in general and individual franchise systems in particular. Through both in-house investigative reporting and third-party blogs, the site provides an excellent snapshot of the industry at any point in time.

2. www.worldfranchising.com – the industry's pre-eminent source of current, up-to-date and detailed information about individual franchises. The site has detailed profiles on over 700 individual franchises and over 100 suppliers. Updates on the franchisor profiles in this book can be found on the site.

3. www.franchisedisclosures.com – the site provides access to both historical UFOCs and current FDDs and has over 30,000 current and archived FDDs/UFOCs in inventory. Additionally, industry packages of historical Item 19s and individual Item 19s for the majority of companies that produce them are available on its sister site, www.Item19s.com. To the extent that you wish to streamline the investigative process, it might make sense to purchase a company's FDD well before you spend a great deal of time researching a franchisor. Having access to a company's litigation history and information about their financial strength before you make a significant time commitment could save you many hours of effort.

4. www.FRANdata.com – unquestionably the leader in third-party research on the franchising industry. Their president, Darrell Johnson, is the most widely-quoted independent spokesman for the industry.

5. www.franchise.org – the website for the International Franchising Association and the voice of the industry in representing the interests of franchising to the public.

An invaluable gauge on historical franchisee success has to do with how various franchise systems have performed in connection with SBA (Small Business Administration) loans. Although the report is not made available to the general public, one can nevertheless gain access to the report through www.bluemaumau.com. The report is called the SBA Failure Rates by Franchise Brand and can be found at http://www.bluemaumau.org/sba_franchisee_failure_rates_brand_2012.

The report lists all the franchise systems that have received SBA 7(a) and 504 loans between 10/1/2001 and 9/30/2011. It lists the number of loans that were disbursed to that franchisor, the total dollar amount of the loans, the percentage failure rate (number of loans in liquidation or charged off divided by the number of loans disbursed) and, most importantly, the percentage rate that the SBA had to charge off as bad debt (dollar amount charged off divided by the dollar amount disbursed). You can download the report and sort it both alphabetically and by the amount of the charge off percentage. If a company has an above-average charge off percentage, that should certainly raise some red flags. What is not shown, however, is what has happened during the eight-year period. If the franchisor can demonstrate to your satisfaction that the problems occurred years ago and are no longer relevant, that is a good sign. If the franchisor avoids the question, that may well mean that the poor franchisee problems are still prevalent.

FRANCHISE SURVIVAL/FAILURE RATE

In order to promote the industry's attractiveness, most literature on franchising includes the same often-quoted, but very misleading, statistics that leave the impression that franchising is a near risk-free investment.

In the 1970s, the Small Business Administration produced a poorly documented report that 38% of all small businesses fail within their first year of operation and 77% fail within their first five years. With franchising, however, comparative failure rates miraculously drop to only three percent after the first year and eight percent after five years. No effort was made to define failure. Instead, "success" was defined as an operating unit still in business under the same name at the same location.

While most people would agree that the failure rates for franchised businesses are substantially lower than those of independent businesses, this assumption is not substantiated by reliable statistics. Part of the problem is definitional. Part is the fact that the industry has a vested interest in perpetuating the myth rather than debunking it.

FRANdata, the industry's pre-eminent research firm, conducted a review several years ago of franchise terminations and renewals. It found that 4.4% of all franchisees left their franchise system each year for a variety of reasons, excluding sales to third parties (to be fully meaningful, the data should include sales to third parties and the reasons behind a sale).

The critical issue is to properly define failure and success, and then require franchisors to report changes in ownership based on these universally accepted definitions. A logical starting point in defining success should be whether the franchisee can "make an honest living" as a franchisee. A "success" would occur when the franchisee prefers to continue as a franchisee rather than sell the business. A "failure" would occur when the franchisee is forced to sell his or her business at a loss.

A reasonable measure of franchise success would be to ask franchisees "would you do it again?" If a legitimate survey were conducted of all franchisees of all systems, my guess is that the answer to this question would indicate a "success rate" well under 70% after a five-year period. Alternatively, one could ask the question "has the franchise investment met your expectations?" I estimate that fewer than 50% would say "yes" after a five-year period. These are just educated guesses.

The failure rate is unquestionably lower for larger, more mature companies in the industry that have proven their systems and carefully chosen their franchisees. It is substantially higher for smaller, newer companies that have unproven products and are less demanding in whom they accept as a franchisee.

As it now stands, the Franchise Disclosure Document (FDD) only requires the franchisor to provide the potential franchisee with the names of owners who have left the system within the past 12 months. In my opinion, this is a severe shortcoming of the regulatory process. Unless required, franchisors will not willingly provide information about failures to prospective franchisees. There is no question in my mind, however, that franchisors are fully aware of when and why past failures have occurred.

It is patently unfair that a potential investor should not have access to this critical information. To ensure its availability, I propose that the FDD be amended to require that franchisors provide franchisee turn-over information for the most recent five-year period. Underlying reasons for a change in ownership would be provided by a departing franchisee on a universal, industry-approved questionnaire filled out during an "exit" interview. The questionnaire would then be returned to some central clearing house.

The only way to make up for this lack of information is to aggressively seek out as many previous and current franchisees as possible. Request past FDDs to get the names of previous owners, and then contact them. Whether successful or not, these owners are an invaluable resource. Try to determine the reason for their failure and/or disenchantment. Most failures are the result of poor management or inadequate finances on the part of the departing franchisee. But people do give up franchises for other reasons.

Current franchisees are even better sources of meaningful information. For systems with under 25 units, I strongly encourage you to contact all franchisees. For those having between 25 and 100 units, I recommend talking to at least half. For all others, interview a minimum of 50.

WHAT MAKES A WINNING FRANCHISE

Virtually every writer on the subject of franchising has his or her own idea of what determines a winning franchise. I maintain that there are five primary factors:

1. A product or service with a clear advantage over the competition. The advantage may be in brand recognition, a unique, proprietary product, or 30 years of proven experience.

2. A standardized franchise system that has been time-tested. Look for a com-

pany in which most of the bugs in the system have been worked out through the cumulative experience of both company-owned and franchised units. By the time a system has 30 or more operating units, it should be thoroughly tested.

3. Exceptional franchisee support. This includes not only the initial training program, but the ongoing support (research and development, refresher training, [800] help-lines, field representatives and on-site training, annual meetings, advertising and promotion, central purchasing, etc.).

4. The financial wherewithal and management experience to carry out any announced growth plans without short-changing its franchisees. Sufficient depth of management is often lacking in high-growth franchises.

5. A strong mutuality of interest between a franchisor and its franchisees. Unless both parties realize that their relationship is one of long-term partners, it is unlikely that the system will ever achieve its full potential. Whether they have the necessary rapport is easily determined by a few telephone calls to existing franchisees.

FINANCIAL PROJECTIONS

The single most important factor in buying a franchise—or any business for that matter—is having a realistic projection of sales, expenses, and profits. Specifically, how much can you expect to make after working 65 hours a week for 52 weeks a year? No one is in a better position to supply accurate information (subject to caveats) about a franchise opportunity than the franchisor itself. A potential franchisee often does not have the experience to sit down and project what his or her sales and profits will be over the next five years. This is especially true if he or she has no applied experience in that particular field.

Financial performance representations (Item 19 of the FDD) present franchisor-supplied sales, expense, and/or profit summaries based on actual operating results for company-owned and/or franchised units. Since no format is prescribed, however, the data may be cursory or detailed. The only constraint is that the franchisor must be able to substantiate the data presented. Further complicating the process is the fact that providing a financial performance representation is strictly optional. Accordingly, only around 67% of franchisors provide one.

Virtually everyone agrees that the information included in a financial performance representation can be exceedingly helpful to a potential franchisee. Unfortunately, there are many reasons why franchisors might not willingly choose to make their actual results available to the public. Many franchisors feel that a prospective investor would be turned off if he or she had access to actual operating results. Others may not want to go to the trouble and expense of collecting the data.

Some franchisors are legitimately afraid of being sued for "misrepresentation." There is considerable risk to a franchisor if a published financial performance representation is interpreted in any way as a "guarantee" of sales or income for new units. Given today's highly litigious society, and the propensity of courts to award large settlements to the underdog, it's not surprising that so few franchisors provide this information.

As an assist to prospective franchisees, Source Book Publications has recently published the fourteenth edition of *"How Much Can I Make?"* It includes 84 financial performance representations covering a diverse group of industries. It is the only publication that contains current financial performance representations submitted by the franchisors themselves. Given the scarcity of industry projections, this is an invaluable resource for potential franchisees and investors in determining what he or she might make by investing in a franchise or similar business. The book is $34.95, plus $8.50 shipping. See the inside rear cover of this book for additional details on *"How Much Can I Make?"* and the companies included. The book can be obtained from Source Book Publications, 1814 Franklin Street, Suite 603, Oakland, CA 94612, by calling (888) 612-9908 or (510) 839-5471, faxing a request to (510) 839-2104, or visiting our online bookstore at www.bookstore.worldfranchising.com.

NEW VERSUS USED

As a potential franchisee, you have the option of becoming a franchisee in a new facility at a new location or purchasing an existing franchise. This is not an easy decision. Your success in making this choice will depend upon your business acumen and your insight into people.

Purchasing a new franchise unit will mean that everything is current, clean, and under warranty. Purchasing an existing franchise may involve a smaller investment and allow greater financial leverage. However, you will have to assess the seller's reason for selling. Is the business not performing to expectations because of poor management, poor location, poor support from the franchisor, an indifferent staff, obsolete equipment and/or facilities, etc.? The decision is further clouded because you may be working through a business broker who may or may not be giving you good information. Regardless of the obstacles, considering a "used" franchise merits your consideration. Apply the same analytical tools you would to a new franchise. Do your homework. Be thorough. Be unrelenting.

THE NEGOTIATION PROCESS

Once you have narrowed your options down to your top two or three choices, you must negotiate the best deal you can with the franchisor. In most cases, the franchisor will tell you that the franchise agreement cannot be changed. Do not accept this explanation. Notwithstanding the legal requirement that all of a franchisor's agreements be substantially the same at any point in time, there are usually a number of variables in the equation. If the franchisor truly wants you as a franchisee, it may be willing to make concessions not available to the next applicant.

Will the franchisor take a short-term note for all or part of the franchise fee? Can you expand from your initial unit after you have proven yourself? If so, can the franchise fee be eliminated or reduced on a second unit? Can you get a right of first refusal on adjacent territories? Can the term of the agreement be extended from ten to fifteen years? Can you include a franchise cancellation right if the training and/or initial support don't meet your expectations or the franchisor's promises? The list goes on ad infinitum.

To successfully negotiate, you must have a thorough knowledge of the industry, the franchise agreement you are negotiating (and agreements of competitive franchise opportunities) and access to experienced professional advice. This can be a lawyer, an accountant, or a franchise consultant. Above all else, they should have proven experience in negotiating franchise agreements. Franchising is a unique method of doing business. Don't pay someone $300+ per hour to learn the industry. Make them demonstrate that they have been through the process several times before. Negotiating a long-term agreement of this type is extremely tricky and fraught with pitfalls. The risks are extremely high. Don't be so smug as to think that you can handle the negotiations yourself. Don't be so frugal as to think you can't afford outside counsel. In point of fact, you can't afford not to employ an experienced professional advisor.

THE FOUR Rs OF FRANCHISING

We are told as children that the three Rs of reading, 'riting, and 'rithmetic are critical to our scholastic success. Success in franchising depends on four Rs — realism, research, reserves, and resolve.

Realism

At the outset of your investigation, it is important that you be realistic about your strengths and weaknesses, your goals and your capabilities. I strongly recommend that you take the time necessary to do a personal audit—possibly with the help of outside professionals—before investing your life's savings in a franchise.

Franchising is not a money machine. It involves hard work, dedication, set-backs, and long hours. Be realistic about the nature of the business you are buying. What traits will ultimately determine your success? Do you possess them? If it is a service-oriented business, will you be able to keep smiling when you know the client is a fool? If it is a fast-food business, will you be able to properly manage a minimum-wage staff? How well will you handle the uncertainties that will inevitably arise? Can you make day-to-day decisions based on imperfect information? Can you count on the support of loved ones after you have gone through all of your working capital reserves, and the future looks cloudy and uncertain?

Be equally realistic about your franchise selection process. Have you thoroughly evaluated all of the alternatives? Have you talked with everyone you can to ensure that you have left no stone unturned? Have you carefully and realistically assessed the advantages and disadvantages of the system offered, the unique demographics of your territory, near-term market trends, the financial projections, etc.? The selection process can be tiring. It is easy to convince yourself that the franchise opportunity in your hand is really the best one for you. The penalties for doing so, however, are extreme.

Research

There is no substitute for exhaustive research!

It is up to you to spend the time required to come up with an optimal selection. At a minimum, you will probably be in that business for five years. More likely, you will be in it ten years or more. Given the long-term commitment, allow yourself the necessary time to ensure you don't regret having made a hasty decision. Research can be a tedious and boring process. But doing it carefully and thoroughly can greatly reduce your risk and exposure. The benefits of this kind of research are considerable.

Based on personal experience, you may feel you already know the best franchise. Step back. Assume there is a competing franchise out there with a comparable product or service, comparable management, etc., that charges a royalty fee two percent of sales less than your intuitive choice. Over a ten-year period, that could add up to a great deal of money. It certainly justifies your requesting initial information.

A thorough analysis of the literature you receive should allow you to reduce the list of prime candidates down to six to eight companies. Aggressively evaluate each firm. Talking with current and former franchisees is the single best source of information you can get. When possible, site visits are invaluable. My experience is that franchisees tend to be candid in their level of satisfaction with the franchisor. However, since they don't know you, they may be less upfront about their sales, expenses, and income. Go to the library and review studies that forecast industry growth, market saturation, industry problems, technical breakthroughs, etc. Don't find out a year after becoming a franchisee of a coffee company that earlier reports suggested that the coffee market was over-saturated or that coffee was linked to some form of terminal disease.

Reserves

As a new business, franchising is replete with uncertainty, uneven cash flows, and unforeseen problems. It is an imperfect world that might not bear any relation to the clean pro formas you prepared to justify getting into the business. Any one of these unforeseen contingencies could cause a severe drain on your cash reserves. At the same time, you will have fixed and/or contractual payments that must be met on a current basis regardless of sales: rent, employee salaries, insurance, etc. Adequate back-up reserves may be in the form of savings, commitments from relatives, bank loans, etc. Just make certain that the funds are available when, and if, you need them. To be absolutely safe, I suggest you double the level of reserves recommended by the franchisor.

Keep in mind that the most common cause of business failure is an inadequate amount of working capital. Plan properly so you don't become a statistic.

Resolve

Let's assume for the time being that you have demonstrated exceptional levels of realism, research, and reserves. You have picked an optimal franchise that takes full advantage of your strengths. You are in business and bringing in enough money to achieve a positive cash flow. The future looks bright. Now the fourth R—resolve—comes into play. Remember why you chose franchising in the first place: to take full advantage of a system that has been time-tested in the marketplace. Remember what makes franchising work so well: the franchisor and franchisees maximize their respective success by working within the system for the common good. Invariably, two obstacles arise.

The first is the physical pain associated with writing that monthly royalty check. Annual sales of $250,000 and a six percent royalty fee result in a monthly royalty check of $1,250 that must be sent to the franchisor. Every month. As a franchisee, you may look for any justification to reduce this sizable monthly outflow. Resist the temptation. Accept the fact that royalty fees are simply another cost of doing business in the franchising industry. They are also a legal obligation that you willingly agreed to pay when you signed the franchise agreement. Look at them as the dues you agreed to pay when you joined the club.

Although at times there may seem to be an incentive, don't look for loopholes in the franchise contract that might allow you to sue the franchisor or get out of the relationship. Don't report lower sales than you actually had in an effort to reduce monthly royalties. If you have received the support that you were promised, continue to play by the rules and honor your commitment. Let the franchisor enjoy the rewards and benefits it has earned as a result of your own success as one of its franchisees.

The second obstacle is the desire to change the system. You need to honor your commitment to be a "franchisee" and to live within the franchise system. What makes franchising successful as far as your customers are concerned is uniformity and consistency of appearance, product/service quality, and corporate image. The most damaging thing an individual franchisee can do is to suddenly and unilaterally introduce changes to the proven system. While these modifications may work in one market, they also serve to diminish the value of the system as a whole. Imagine what would happen to the national perception of your franchise if every franchisee had the latitude to make unilateral changes in his or her operations. Accordingly, any ideas you have on improving the system should be submitted directly to the franchisor for evaluation. Accept the franchisor's decision on whether or not to pursue an idea.

If you think you might be a closet entrepreneur, prone to unrestrained experimenting and tinkering, you are probably not cut out to be a franchisee. Seriously consider this before you get into such a relationship, instead of waiting until you are locked into an untenable situation.

SUMMARY

I hope that I have been clear in suggesting that the selection of an optimal franchise is both very time- and energy-consuming. If done properly, the process may take six to nine months and involve the expenditure of several thousand dollars. However, the difference between a hasty, gut-feel investigation and an exhaustive, well-thought out investigation may mean the difference between finding a poorly-conceived, or even fraudulent, franchise, and an exceptional one.

Chapter 1

My sense is that there is a strong correlation between the effort you put into the investigative process and the ultimate degree of success you enjoy as a franchisee. The process is to investigate, evaluate, and negotiate. Don't try to bypass any one of these critical elements.

How to Use the Data 2

The data at the beginning of each company profile is the result of a 48-point questionnaire that we send out annually to the franchising community. This information is intended as a brief overview of the company; the text that follows provides a more in-depth analysis of the company's requirements and advantages.

In some cases, an answer has been abbreviated to conserve room and to make the profiles more directly comparable. All of the data is displayed with the objective of providing as much background data as possible. In cases where no answer was provided to a particular question, an "N/A" is used to signify "Not Available."

Please take 20 minutes to acquaint yourself with the composition of the sample questionnaire data. Supplementary comments have been added where some interpretation of the franchisor's response is required.

ও

FASTSIGNS has been selected to illustrate how this book uses the collected data.

FASTSIGNS

2542 Highlander Way
Carrollton, TX 75006
Tel: (800) 827-7446; (214) 346-5679
Fax: (866) 422-4927
Email: mark.jameson@fastsigns.com
Website: www.fastsigns.com
Mark Jameson, Executive Vice President, Franchise Support & Development

Signage has never been more important. Right now, businesses are looking for new and better ways to compete. Industries are revamping to meet compliance standards and advertisers are expanding their reach into new media, like digital signage, QR codes and mobile websites. Join the franchise that's leading the next generation of business communication. Now more than ever, businesses look to FASTSIGNS® for innovative ways to connect with customers in a highly competitive marketplace. Our high standards for quality and customer service have made FASTSIGNS the most recognized brand in the industry, driving significantly more traffic to the Web than any other sign company.

BACKGROUND:	IFA MEMBER
Established: 1985;	1st Franchised: 1986
Franchised Units:	571
Company-Owned Units	0
Total Units:	571
Dist.:	US-507; CAN-26; O'seas-40
North America:	50 States, 8 Provinces

Density:	58 in TX, 45 in CA, 36 in FL	Space Needs:	1,200-1,500 SF
Projected New Units (12 Months):	45		
Qualifications:	5, 5, 1, 3, 4, 5	**SUPPORT & TRAINING:**	
		Financial Assistance Provided:	Yes (I)
FINANCIAL/TERMS:		Site Selection Assistance:	Yes
Cash Investment:	$80K	Lease Negotiation Assistance:	Yes
Total Investment:	$178.2 – 289.5K	Co-Operative Advertising:	No
Minimum Net Worth:	$250K	Franchisee Assoc./Member:	Yes/Yes
Fees: Franchise —	$37.5K	Size Of Corporate Staff:	110
Royalty — 6%;	Ad. — 2%	Ongoing Support:	C,D,E,G,H,I
Financial Performance Representation:	Yes	Training:	1 Week Local Center;
Term of Contract (Years):	20/20		2 Weeks in Dallas, TX; 1 Week On-Site
Avg. # Of Employees:	2-3 FT, 0 PT		
Passive Ownership:	Discouraged	**SPECIFIC EXPANSION PLANS:**	
Encourage Conversions:	Yes	US:	All United States
Area Develop. Agreements:	Yes	Canada:	All Canada Except Quebec as
Sub-Franchising Contracts:	No		Master/Area Developer Only
Expand In Territory:	Yes	Overseas:	UK, South America, Africa, Europe,
			Asia, New Zealand, Mexico

ADDRESS/CONTACT

1. **Company name, address, telephone and fax numbers.**

All of the data published in this book were current at the time the completed questionnaire was received or upon subsequent verification by phone. Over the period between annual publications, 10–15% of the addresses and/or telephone numbers become obsolete for various reasons. If you are unable to contact a franchisor at the address/telephone number listed, please call Source Book Publications at (510) 839-5471 or fax us at (510) 839-2104 and we will provide you with the current address and/or telephone number.

2. **(800) 827-7446, (214) 346-5679.** In many cases, you may find that you cannot access the (800) number from your area. Do not conclude that the company has gone out of business. Simply call the local number.

An (800) number serves two important functions. The first is to provide an efficient, no-cost way for potential franchisees to contact the franchisor. Making the prospective franchisee foot the bill artificially limits the number of people who might otherwise make the initial contact. The second function is to demonstrate to existing franchisees that the franchisor is doing everything it can to efficiently respond to problems in the field as they occur. Many companies have a restricted (800) line for their franchisees that the general public cannot access. Since you will undoubtedly be talking with the franchisor's staff on a periodic basis, determine whether an (800) line is available to franchisees.

3. **Contact.** You should honor the wishes of the franchisor and address all initial correspondence to the contact listed. It would be counter-productive to try to reach the president directly if the designated contact is the director of franchising.

The president is the designated contact in many of the company profiles in this book. The reason for this varies among franchisors. The president is the best spokesperson for his or her operation, and no doubt it flatters the franchisee to talk directly with the president, or perhaps there is no one else around. Regardless of the justification, it is important to determine if the operation is a one-man show in which the president does everything or if the president merely feels that having an open line to potential franchisees is the best way for him or her to sense the "pulse" of the company and the market. Convinced that the president can only do so many things effectively, I would want assurances that, by taking all incoming calls, he or she is not neglecting the day-to-day responsibilities of managing the business.

DESCRIPTION OF BUSINESS

4. **Description of Business.** The questionnaire provides franchisors with adequate room to differentiate their franchise from the competition. In a minor number of cases, some editing was required for length.

In instances where franchisors show no initiative or imagination in describing their operations, you must decide whether this is symptomatic of the company or simply a reflection on the individual who responded to the questionnaire.

BACKGROUND

5. **IFA.** There are two primary affinity groups associated with the franchising industry—the International Franchise Association (IFA) and the Canadian

Franchise Association (CFA). Both the IFA and the CFA are described in Chapter One.

6. **Established: 1985.** FASTSIGNS was founded in 1985, and, accordingly, has 29 years of experience in its primary business. It should be intuitively obvious that a firm that has been in existence for over 29 years has a greater likelihood of being around five years from now than a firm that was founded only last year.

7. **1st Franchised: 1986.** 1986 was the year that FASTSIGNS' first franchised unit(s) were established.

Over ten years of continuous operation, both as an operator and as a franchisor, is compelling evidence that a firm has staying power. The number of years a franchisor has been in business is one of the key variables to consider in choosing a franchise. This is not to say that a new franchise should not receive your full attention. Every company has to start from scratch. Ultimately, a prospective franchisee has to be convinced that the franchise has 1) been in operation long enough, or 2) its key management personnel have adequate industry experience to have worked out the bugs normally associated with a new business. In most cases, this experience can only be gained through on-the-job training. Don't be the guinea pig that provides the franchisor with the experience it needs to develop a smoothly running operation.

8. **Franchised Units: 571.** As of 2/15/15, FASTSIGNS had 571 franchisee-owned and operated units.

9. **Company-Owned Units: 0.** As of 2/15/15, FASTSIGNS had no company-owned or operated units.

A younger franchise should prove that its concept has worked successfully in several company-owned units before it markets its "system" to an inexperienced franchisee. Without company-owned prototype stores, the new franchisee may well end up being the "testing kitchen" for the franchise concept itself.

If a franchise concept is truly exceptional, why doesn't the franchisor commit some of its resources to take advantage of the investment opportunity? Clearly a financial decision on the part of the franchisor, the absence of company-owned units should not be a negative in and of itself. This is especially true of proven franchises, which may have previously sold their company-owned operations to franchisees.

Try to determine if there is a noticeable trend in the percentage of company-owned units. If the franchisor is buying back units from franchisees, it may be doing so to preclude litigation. Some firms also "churn" their operating units with some regularity. If the sales pitch is compelling, but the follow-through is not competitive, a franchisor may sell a unit to a new franchisee, wait for him or her to fail, buy it back for $0.60 cents on the dollar, and then sell that same unit to the next unsuspecting franchisee. Each time the unit is resold, the franchisor collects a franchise fee, plus the negotiated discount from the previous franchisee.

Alternatively, an increasing or high percentage of company-owned units may well mean the company is convinced of the long-term profitability of such an approach. The key is to determine whether a franchisor is building new units from scratch or buying them from failing and/or unhappy franchisees.

10. **Total Units: 571.** As of 2/15/15, FASTSIGNS had a total of 571 operating units.

Like a franchisor's longevity, its experience in operating multiple units offers considerable comfort. Those franchisors with over 15–25 operating units have proven that their system works and have probably encountered and overcome most of the problems that plague a new operation. Alternatively, the management of franchises with less than 15 operating units may have gained considerable industry experience before joining the current franchise. It is up to the franchisor to convince you that it is providing you with as risk-free an operation as possible. You don't want to be the first to provide a company with basic experience in the business.

11. **Distribution: US-507; CAN-26; O'seas-40.** As of 2/15/15, FASTSIGNS had 507 operating units in the U.S., 26 in Canada, and 40 overseas.

12. **Distribution: North America: 50 States, 8 Provinces.** As of 2/15/15, FAST-SIGNS had operations in 50 states and 8 Canadian provinces.

It should go without saying that the wider the geographic distribution, the greater the franchisor's level of success. For the most part, such distribution can only come from a large number of operating units. If, however, the franchisor has operations in 15 states, but only 18 total operating units, it is unlikely that it can efficiently service these accounts because of geographic constraints. Other things being equal, a prospective franchisee should vastly prefer a franchisor with 15 units in New York to one with 15 units scattered throughout the U.S., Canada, and overseas.

13. **Distribution: Density: TX, CA, FL.** The franchisor was asked which three states/provinces have the largest number of operating units. As of 2/15/15, FASTSIGNS had the largest number of units in Texas, California, and Florida.

For smaller, regional franchises, geographic distribution could be a key variable in deciding whether or not to buy. If the franchisor has a concentration of units in your immediate geographic area, it is likely you will be well-served.

For those far-removed geographically from the franchisor's current areas of operation, however, there can be problems. It is both time consuming and expensive to support a franchisee 2,000 miles away from company headquarters. To the extent that a franchisor can visit four franchisees in one area on one trip, there is no problem. If, however, your operation is the only one west of the Mississippi, you may not receive the on-site assistance you would like. Don't be a missionary who has to rely on his or her own devices to survive. Don't accept a franchisor's idle promises of support. If on-site assistance is important to your ultimate success, get assurances in writing that the necessary support will be forthcoming. Remember, you are buying into a system, and the availability of day-to-day support is one of the key ingredients of any successful franchise system.

14. **Projected New Units (12 Months): 45.** FASTSIGNS plans to establish 45 new units over the course of the next 12 months.

In business, growth has become a highly visible symbol of success. Rapid growth is generally perceived as preferable to slower, more controlled growth. I maintain, however, that the opposite is frequently the case. For a company of FASTSIGNS' size, adding 45 new units over a 12-month period is both reasonable and achievable. It is highly unlikely, however, that a new franchise with only five operating units can successfully attract, screen, train, and bring multiple new units on-stream in a 12-month period. If it suggests that it can, or even wants to, be properly wary. You must be confident a company has the financial and management resources necessary to pull off such a Herculean feat. If management is already thin, concentrating on attracting new units will clearly diminish the time it can and should spend supporting you. It takes many months, if not years, to develop and train a second level of management. You don't want to depend upon new hires teaching you systems and procedures they themselves know little or nothing about.

15. **Qualifications: 5, 5, 1, 3, 4, 5.** This question was posed to determine which specific evaluation criteria were important to the franchisor. The franchisor was asked the following: "In qualifying a potential franchisee, please rank the following criteria from Unimportant (1) to Very Important (5)."The responses should be self-explanatory:

Financial Net Worth (Rank from 1–5)
General Business Experience (Rank from 1–5)
Specific Industry Experience (Rank from 1–5)
Formal Education (Rank from 1–5)
Psychological Profile (Rank from 1–5)
Personal Interview(s) (Rank from 1–5)

CAPITAL REQUIREMENTS/RIGHTS

16. **Cash Investment: $80K.** On average, a FASTSIGNS franchisee will have made a cash investment of $80,000 by the time he or she finally opens the initial operating unit.

It is important that you be realistic about the amount of cash you can comfortably invest in a business. Stretching beyond your means can have grave and far-reaching consequences. Assume that you will encounter periodic set-backs and that you will have to draw on your reserves. The demands of starting a new business are harsh enough without the added pressures of uncertainties associated with inadequate working capital. Trust the franchisor's recommendations regarding the suggested minimum cash investment. If anything, there is an incentive for setting the recommended level of investment too low, rather than too high. The franchisor will want to qualify you to the extent that you have adequate financing. No legitimate franchisor wants you to invest if there is a chance that you might fail due to a shortage of funds.

Keep in mind that you will probably not achieve a positive cash flow before you've been in business more than six months. In your discussions with the franchisor, be absolutely certain that its calculations include an adequate working capital reserve.

17. **Total Investment: $178.2 – 289.5K.** On average, FASTSIGNS franchisees will invest a total of $178,200 to $289,500, including both cash and debt, by the time the franchise opens its doors.

The total investment should be the cash investment noted above plus any debt that you will incur in starting up the new business. Debt could be a note to the franchisor for all or part of the franchise fee, an equipment lease, building and facilities leases, etc. Make sure that the total includes all of the obligations that you assume, especially any long-term lease obligations.

Be conservative in assessing what your real exposure is. If you are leasing highly specialized equipment or if you are leasing a single-purpose building, it is naive to think that you will recoup your investment if you have to sell or sub-lease those assets in a buyer's market. If there is any specialized equipment that may have been manufactured to the franchisor's specifications, determine if the franchisor has any form of buy-back provision.

18. **Minimum Net Worth: $250K.** FASTSIGNS feels that a potential franchisee should have a minimum net worth of $250,000. Although net worth can be defined in vastly different ways, the franchisor's response should suggest a minimum level of equity that the prospective franchisee should possess. Net worth is the combination of both liquid and illiquid assets. Again, don't think that franchisor-determined guidelines somehow don't apply to you

19. **Fees (Franchise): $37.5K.** FASTSIGNS requires a front-end, one-time-only payment of $37,500 to grant a franchise for a single location. As noted in Chapter One, the franchise fee is a payment to reimburse the franchisor for the incurred costs of setting the franchisee up in business—from recruiting

through training and manuals. The fee usually ranges from $15,000–30,000. It is a function of competitive franchise fees and the actual out-of-pocket costs incurred by the franchisor.

Depending on the franchisee's particular circumstances and how well the franchisor thinks he or she might fit into the system, the franchisor may finance all or part of the franchise fee. (See Section 32 below to see if a franchisor provides any direct or indirect financial assistance.)

The franchise fee is one area in which the franchisor frequently provides either direct or indirect financial support.

Ideally, the franchisor should do no more than recover its costs on the initial franchise fee. Profits come later in the form of royalty fees, which are a function of the franchisee's sales. Whether the franchise fee is $5,000 or $35,000, the total should be carefully evaluated. What are competitive fees and are they financed? How much training will you actually receive? Are the fees reflective of the franchisor's expenses? If the fees appear to be non-competitive, address your concerns with the franchisor.

Realize that a $5,000 differential in the one-time franchise fee is a secondary consideration in the overall scheme of things. You are in this relationship for the long-term.

By the same token, don't get suckered in by an extremely low fee if there is any doubt about the franchisor's ability to follow through. Franchisors need to collect reasonable fees to cover their actual costs. If they don't recoup these costs, they cannot recruit and train new franchisees on whom your own future success partially depends.

20. **Fees (Royalty): 6%.** Six percent of gross sales (or other measure, as defined in the franchise agreement) must be periodically paid directly to the franchisor in the form of royalties. This ongoing expense is your cost for being part of the larger franchise system and for all of the "back-office" support you receive. In a few cases, the amount of the royalty fee is fixed rather than variable. In others, the fee decreases as the volume of sales (or other measure) increases (i.e., 8%

on the first $200,000 of sales, 7% on the next $100,000, and so on). In others, the fee is held at artificially low levels during the start-up phase of the franchisee's business, then increases once the franchisee is better able to afford it.

Royalty fees represent the mechanism by which the franchisor finally recoups the costs it has incurred in developing its business. It may take many years and many operating units before the franchisor is able to make a true operating profit.

Consider a typical franchisor who might have been in business for three years. With a staff of five, rent, travel, operating expenses, etc., assume it has annual operating costs of $300,000 (including reasonable owner's salaries). Assume also that there are 25 franchised units with average annual sales of $250,000. Each franchise is required to pay a 6% royalty fee. Total annual royalties under this scenario would total only $375,000. The franchisor is making a $75,000 profit. Then consider the personal risk the franchisor took in developing a new business and the initial years of negative cash flows. Alternatively, evaluate what it would cost you, as a sole proprietor, to provide the myriad services included in the royalty payment.

In assessing various alternative investments, the amount of the royalty percentage is a major ongoing expense. Assuming average annual sales of $250,000 per annum over a 15 year period, the total royalties at 5% would be $187,500. At 6%, the cumulative fees would be $225,000. You have to be fully convinced that the $37,500 differential is justified. While this is clearly a meaningful number, what you are really evaluating is the quality of management and the competitive advantages of the goods and/or services offered by the franchisor.

21. **Fees (Advertising): 2%.** Most national or regional franchisors require their franchisees to contribute a certain percentage of their sales (or other measure, as determined in the franchise agreement) into a corporate advertising fund. These individual advertising fees are pooled to develop a corporate advertising/marketing effort that produces great economies of scale. The end result is a national or regional advertising program that promotes the franchisor's products and services. Depending upon the nature of the business, this percentage usually ranges from 2–6% and is in addition to the royalty fee.

One of the greatest advantages of a franchised system is its ability to promote, on a national or regional basis, its products and services. The promotions may be through television, radio, print medias, or direct mail. The objective is name recognition and, over time, the assumption that the product and/or service has been "time-tested." An individual business owner could never justify the expense of mounting a major advertising program at the local level. For a smaller franchise that may not yet have an advertising program or fee, it is important to know when an advertising program will start, how it will be monitored and its expected cost.

22. **Financial Performance Representation: Yes.** This means FASTSIGNS provides a financial performance representation to potential franchisees. Unfortunately, only approximately 67% of franchisors provide a financial performance representation in their Franchise Disclosure Document (FDD). The franchising industry's failure to require financial performance representations does a serious disservice to the potential franchisee. See Chapter One for comments on financial performance representations.

23. **Term of Contract (Years): 20/20.** FASTSIGNS' initial franchise period runs for twenty years. The first renewal period runs for an additional twenty years. Assuming that the franchisee operates within the terms of the franchise agreement, he or she has forty years within which to develop and, ultimately, sell the business.

The potential (discounted) value of any business (or investment) is the sum of the operating income that is generated each year plus its value upon liquidation. Given this truth, the length of the franchise agreement and any renewals are extremely important to the franchisee. It is essential that he or she has adequate time to develop the business to its full potential. At that time, he or she will have maximized the value of the business as an ongoing concern. The value of the business to a potential buyer, however, is largely a function of how long the franchise agreement runs. If there are only two years remaining before the agreement expires, or if the terms of an extension(s) are vague, the business will be worth only a fraction of the value assigned to a business with 15 years to go. For the most part, the longer the agreement and the subsequent extension, the better. (The same logic applies to a lease. If your sales are largely a function of your location and traffic count, then it is important that you have options to extend the lease under known terms. Your lease should never be longer than the remaining term of your franchise agreement, however.)

Assuming the length of the agreement is acceptable, be clear on the circumstances under which renewals might not be granted. Similarly, know the circumstances under which a franchise agreement might be prematurely and unilaterally canceled by the franchisor. I strongly recommend you have an experienced lawyer review this section of the franchise agreement. It would be devastating if, after spending years developing your business, there was a loophole in the contract that allowed the franchisor to arbitrarily cancel the relationship.

24. **Avg. # of Employees: 2-3 FT.** The questionnaire asked, "Including the owner/operator, how many employees are recommended to properly staff the average franchised unit?" In FASTSIGNS' case, two to three full-time employees are required.

Most entrepreneurs start a new business based on their intuitive feel that it will be "fun" and that their talents and experience will be put to good use. They will be doing what they enjoy as well as something they are good at. Times change. Your business prospers. The number of employees increases. You are spending an increasing percentage of your time taking care of personnel problems and less and less on the fun parts of the business. In Chapter One, the importance of conducting a realistic self-appraisal was stressed. If you found that you really are not good at managing people, or you don't have the patience to manage a large minimum wage staff, cut your losses before you are locked into doing just that.

25. **Passive Ownership: Discouraged.** Depending on the nature of the business, many franchisors are indifferent as to whether you manage the business directly or hire a full-time manager. Others are insistent that, at least for the initial franchise, the franchisee be a full-time owner/operator. FASTSIGNS allows, but discourages, franchisees to hire full-time managers to run their outlets.

Unless you have a great deal of experience in the business you have chosen or in managing similar businesses, I feel strongly that you should initially commit your personal time and energies to make the system work. After you have developed a full understanding of the business and have competent, trusted staff members who can assume day-to-day operations, then consider delegating these responsibilities. Running the business through a manager can be fraught with peril unless you have mastered all aspects of the business and there are strong economic incentives and sufficient safeguards to ensure the manager will perform as desired.

26. **Encourages Conversions: Yes.** This section pertains primarily to sole proprietorships or "mom and pop" operations. To the extent that there truly are centralized operating savings associated with the franchise, the most logical people to join a franchise system are sole practitioners who are working hard but only eking out a living. The implementation of proven systems and marketing clout could significantly reduce operating costs and increase profits.

The franchisor has the option of 1) actively encouraging such independent operators to become members of the franchise team, 2) seeking out franchisees with limited or no applied experience, or 3) going after both groups. Concerned that it will be very difficult to break independent operators of the bad habits they have picked up over the years, many only choose course two. "They will continue to do things their way. They won't, or can't, accept corporate direction," they might say to themselves. Others are simply selective in the conversions they allow. In many cases, the franchise fee is reduced or eliminated for conversions.

27. **Area Development Agreements: Yes.** FASTSIGNS offers an area development agreement for two years. Area development agreements are more fully described in Chapter One. Essentially, area development agreements allow an investor or investment group to develop an entire area or region. The schedule for development is clearly spelled out in the area development agreement.

Area development agreements represent an opportunity for the franchisor to choose a single franchisee or investment group to develop an entire area. The franchisee's qualifications should be strong and include proven business experience and the financial depth to pull it off. An area development agreement represents a great opportunity for an investor to tie up a large geographical area and develop a concept that may not have proven itself on a national basis. Keep in mind that this is a quantum leap from making an investment in a single franchise and is relevant only to those with development experience and deep pockets.

28. **Sub-Franchising Contracts: No.** FASTSIGNS does not grant sub-franchising agreements. (See Chapter One for a more thorough explanation.) Like area

development agreements, sub-franchising allows an investor or investment group to develop an entire area or region. The difference is that the sub-franchisor becomes a self-contained business, responsible for all relations with franchisees within its area, from initial training to ongoing support. Franchisees pay their royalties to the sub-franchisor, who in turn pays a portion to the master franchisor.

Sub-franchising is used primarily by smaller franchisors who have a relatively easy concept and who are prepared to sell a portion of the future growth of their business to someone for some front-end cash and a percentage of the future royalties they receive from their franchisees.

29. **Expand in Territory: Yes.** Under conditions spelled out in the franchise agreement, FASTSIGNS will allow its franchisees to expand within their exclusive territory.

Some franchisors define the franchisee's exclusive territory so tightly that there would never be room to open additional outlets within an area. Others provide a larger area in the hopes that the franchisee will do well and have the incentive to open additional units. There are clearly economic benefits to both parties from having franchisees with multiple units. There is no question that it is in your best interest to have the option to expand once you have proven to both yourself and the franchisor that you can manage the business successfully. Many would concur that the real profits in franchising come from managing multiple units rather than being locked into a single franchise in a single location. Additional fees may or may not be required with these additional units.

30. **Space Needs: 1,200-1,500 SF.** The average FASTSIGNS retail outlet will require 1,200-1,500 square feet.

Armed with the rough space requirements, you can better project your annual occupancy costs. It should be relatively easy to get comparable rental rates for the type of space required. As annual rent and related expenses can be as high as 15% of your annual sales, be as accurate as possible in your projections.

FRANCHISOR SUPPORT AND TRAINING PROVIDED

31. **Financial Assistance Provided: Yes (I).** FASTSIGNS provides indirect financial assistance. Indirect (I) assistance might include making introductions to the franchisor's financial contacts, providing financial templates for preparing a business plan, or actually assisting in the loan application process. In some cases, the franchisor becomes a co-signer on a financial obligation (such as equipment or space lease). Other franchisors are directly (D) involved in the process. In this case, the assistance may include a lease or loan made directly by the franchisor. Any loan would generally be secured by some form of collateral. A very common form of assistance is a note for all or part of the initial franchise fee. The level of assistance will generally depend upon the relative strengths of the franchisee.

The best of all possible worlds is one in which the franchisor has enough confidence in the business and in you to co-sign notes on the building and equipment leases and allow you to pay off the franchise fee over a specified period of time. Depending upon your qualifications, this could happen. Most likely, however, the franchisor will only give you some assistance in raising the necessary capital to start the business. Increasingly, franchisors are testing a franchisee's business acumen by letting him or her assume an increasing level of personal responsibility in securing financing. The objective is to find out early on how competent a franchisee really is.

32. **Site Selection Assistance: Yes.** This means that FASTSIGNS will assist the franchisee in selecting a site location. While the phrase "location, location, location" may be hackneyed, its importance should not be discounted, especially when a business depends upon retail traffic counts and accessibility. If a business is home- or warehouse-based, assistance in this area is of negligible or minor importance.

Since you will be locked into a lease for a minimum of three, and probably five, years, optimal site selection is absolutely essential. Even if you were somehow able to sub-lease and extricate yourself from a bad lease or bad location, the franchise agreement may not allow you to move to another location. Accordingly, it is imperative that you get it right the first time.

If a franchisor is truly interested in your success, it should treat your choice of a site with the same care it would use in choosing a company-owned site. Keep in mind that many firms provide excellent demographic data on existing locations at a very reasonable cost.

33. **Lease Negotiation Assistance: Yes.** Once a site is selected, FASTSIGNS will be actively involved in negotiating the terms of the lease.

Given the complexity of negotiating a lease, an increasing number of franchisors are taking an active role in lease negotiations. There are far too many trade-offs that must be considered—terms, percentage rents, tenant improvements, pass-throughs, kick-out clauses, etc. This responsibility is best left to the professionals. If the franchisor doesn't have the capacity to support you directly, enlist the help of a well-recommended broker. The penalties for signing a bad long-term lease are very severe.

34. **Co-operative Advertising: No.** This refers to the existence of a joint advertising program in which the franchisor and franchisees each contribute to promote the company's products and/or services (usually within the franchisee's specific territory).

Co-op advertising is a common and mutually-beneficial effort. By agreeing to split part of the advertising costs, whether for television, radio, or direct mail, the franchisor is not only supporting the franchisee, but guaranteeing itself royalties from the incremental sales. A franchisor that is not intimately involved with the advertising campaign—particularly when it is an important part of the business—may not be fully committed to your overall success.

35. **Franchisee Assoc./Member: Yes, Yes.** This response notes that the FASTSIGNS system includes an active association made up of FASTSIGNS franchisees and that, consequently, the franchisor is a member of such franchisee association.

The empowerment of franchisees has become a major rallying cry within the industry over the past several years. Various states have recently passed laws favoring franchisee rights, and the subject has been widely discussed in congressional staff hearings. Political groups even represent franchisee rights on a national basis.

Similarly, the IFA is now actively courting franchisees to become active members. Whether they are equal members remains to be seen.

Franchisees have also significantly increased their clout with respect to the franchisor. If a franchise is to grow and be successful in the long term, it is critical that the franchisor and its franchisees mutually agree they are partners rather than adversaries.

36. **Size of Corporate Staff: 110.** FASTSIGNS has 110 full-time employees on its staff to support its 550 operating units.

There are no magic ratios that tell you whether the franchisor has enough staff to provide the proper level of support. It would appear, however, that FASTSIGNS' staff of 110 is adequate to support 550 operating units. Less clear is whether a staff of three, including the company president and his wife, can adequately support 15 fledgling franchisees in the field.

Many younger franchises may be managed by a skeleton staff, assisted by outside consultants who perform various management functions during the start-up phase. From the perspective of the franchisee, it is essential that the franchisor have actual in-house franchising experience, and that the franchisee not be forced to rely on outside consultants to make the system work. Whereas a full-time, salaried employee will probably have the franchisee's objectives in mind, an outside consultant may easily not have the same priorities. Franchising is a unique form of business that requires specific skills and experience—skills and experience that are markedly different from those required to manage a non-franchised business. If you are thinking about establishing a long-term relationship with a firm just starting out in franchising, you should insist that the franchisor prove that it has an experienced, professional team on board and in place to provide the necessary levels of support to all concerned.

37. **Ongoing Support: C,D,E,G,H,I.** Like initial training, the ongoing support services provided by the franchisor are of paramount importance. Having a solid and responsive team behind you can certainly make your life much easier and allow you to concentrate your energies on other areas. As is noted below, the franchisors were asked to indicate their support for nine separate ongoing services:

Service Provided	Included in Fees	At Add'l. Cost	N/A
Central Data Processing	A	a	N/A
Central Purchasing	B	b	N/A
Field Operations Evaluation	C	c	N/A
Field Training	D	d	N/A
Initial Store Opening	E	e	N/A
Inventory Control	F	f	N/A
Franchisee Newsletter	G	g	N/A
Regional or National Meetings	H	h	N/A
800 Telephone Hotline	I	i	N/A

If the franchisor provides the service at no additional cost to the franchisee (as indicated by letters A–I), a capital letter was used to indicate this. If the service is provided, but only at an additional cost, a lower case letter was used. If the franchisor responded with a N/A, or failed to note an answer for a particular service, the corresponding letter was omitted from the data sheet.

38. Training: 1 Week Local Center; 2 Weeks Dallas, TX; 1 Week On-Site.

Assuming that the underlying business concept is sound and competitive, adequate training and ongoing support are among the most important determinants of your success as a franchisee. The initial training should be as lengthy and as "hands-on" as necessary to allow the franchisee to operate alone and with confidence. Obviously, every potential situation cannot be covered in any training program, but the franchisee should come away with at least a basic understanding of how the business operates and where to go to resolve problems when they come up. Depending on the business, there should be operating manuals, procedural manuals, company policies, training videos, (800) help-lines, etc. It may be helpful at the outset to establish how satisfied recent franchisees are with a company's training. I would also have a clear understanding about how often the company updates its manuals and training programs, the cost of sending additional employees through training, etc.

Remember, you are part of an organization that you are paying (in the form of a franchise fee and ongoing royalties) to support you. Training is the first step. Ongoing support is the second step.

SPECIFIC EXPANSION PLANS

39. **U.S.: All United States.** FASTSIGNS is currently focusing its growth on the entire United States. Alternatively, the franchisor could have listed particular states or regions into which it wished to expand.

40. **Canada: All Canada Except Quebec as Master/Area Developer Only.** FAST-SIGNS is currently seeking additional franchisees in all Canadian provinces except for Quebec, where it is only seeking Master Franchisees and Area Developers. Specific markets or provinces could have also been indicated.

41. **Overseas: UK, South America, Africa, Europe, Asia, New Zealand, Mexico.** FASTSIGNS is currently expanding overseas with a focus on the United Kingdom, South America, Africa, Europe, Asia, New Zealand, and Mexico.

You will note that many smaller companies with less than 15 operating units suggest that they will concurrently expand throughout the U.S., Canada, and internationally. In many cases, these are the same companies that foresee a 50+ percent growth rate in operating units over the next 12 months. The chances of this happening are negligible. As a prospective franchisee, you should be wary of any company that thinks it can expand throughout the world without a solid base of experience, staff, and financial resources. Even if adequate financing is available, the demands on existing management will be extreme. New management cannot adequately fill the void until they are able to fully understand the system and absorb the corporate culture. If management's end objective is expansion for its own sake rather than by design, the existing franchisees will suffer.

Note: The statistics noted in the profiles preceding each company's analysis are the result of data provided by the franchisors themselves by way of a detailed questionnaire. Similarly, the data in the summary comparisons in the Introduction Chapter were taken from the company profile data. The figures used throughout each company's analysis, however, were generally taken from the franchisor's FDD filed in 2014. In some cases, the data was taken from an FDD filed in 2013. The FDDs, which are only printed annually, may in some cases contain information that is somewhat out of date. This is especially true with regard to the number of operating units and the current level of investment. A visit to our website at www.world-franchising.com should provide current data.

You will note that several of the companies listed in this book have the "World-Class Franchise®" seal, along with the franchisees' ratings of their franchisors in several categories. The degree of satisfaction existing franchisees experience with their franchisor should be a fundamental consideration in making an optimal franchise investment decision. The World Franchising Network is collaborating with the Franchise Research Institute to determine which franchisors excel in several areas critical to the franchise selection process. The Franchise Research Institute confidentially contacts every existing franchisee within various franchise systems to determine their general level of happiness with their investment decision. Please visit www.franchiseresearchinstitute.com for additional information on this highly beneficial program, and for detailed reports on certified "World-Class" franchisors.

If you have not already done so, please invest some modest time to read Chapter One, 30-Minute Overview.

The Franchise Bookstore
Order Form

Call (888) 612-9908 or (510) 839-5471; or Fax (510) 839-2104

Item #	Title	Price	Qty.	Total

	Total
Basic postage (1 book)	$8.50
Each additional book add $4.00	
California tax @ 9.75% (if CA resident)	
Total due in U.S. dollars	
Deduct 15% if total due is over $100.00	
Net amount due in U.S. dollars	

Please include credit card number, expiration date, and security code for all charge card orders! Checks should be made payable to Source Book Publications. All prices are in U.S. dollars.

Mailing Information: All books are shipped by USPS Priority Mail (2nd Day Air). Please print clearly and include your phone number in case we need to contact you. Postage and handling rates are for shipping within the U.S. For international rates, please call (888) 612-9908.

☐ **Check enclosed or**

Charge my:

☐ American Express   ☐ MasterCard   ☐ VISA

Card #:_____

Expiration Date:_____

Security Code: _____

Signature: _____

Name:_____

Company:_____

Address:_____

City: _____

Title:_____

Telephone No.: (_____)_____

State/Prov.:_____ Zip:_____

Special Offer — Save 15%

If your total order above exceeds $100.00, deduct 15% from your bill.

Please send order to:
Source Book Publications
1814 Franklin St., Ste. 603, Oakland, CA
94612 **Satisfaction Guaranteed.** If not fully satisfied, return for a prompt, 100% refund.

Food Service *3*

Auntie Anne's Hand-Rolled Soft Pretzels

Auntie Anne's

48-50 W. Chestnut St., # 200
Lancaster, PA 17603
Tel: (717) 435-1479
Fax: (717) 442-1471
Email: lengels@auntieannesinc.com
Website: www.auntieannes.com
Linda Engels, Franchise Development Specialist

Auntie Anne's, Inc. is a franchise organization with a commitment to exceeding our customers' expectations. We've built our company on the quality of our products and strong support for our franchisees, nurturing relationships for the long-term growth of the franchise system. That approach continues to drive our growth. We provide our customers with pretzels, dips, and drinks which are mixed, twisted, and baked to a golden brown in full view of our customers. Each and every one of our pretzels comes with the Pretzel Perfect Guarantee - we guarantee you'll love your pretzel or we'll replace it with one that you do.

BACKGROUND: IFA Member
Established: 1988; First Franchised: 1991
Franchised Units: 1,146
Company-Owned Units: 17
Total Units: 1,163

Dist.:	US-1,163; CAN-0; O'seas-471
North America:	48 States
Density:	68 in CA, 74 in NY, 117 in PA
Projected New Units (12 Months):	125
Qualifications:	4, 2, 2, 2, 3, 5

FINANCIAL/TERMS:

Cash Investment:	Varies
Total Investment:	$194.9 – 367.6K
Minimum Net Worth:	$400K
Fees: Franchise -	$30K
Royalty - 7%;	Ad. - 1%
Financial Performance Representation:	Yes
Term of Contract (Years):	20/Variable
Avg. # of Employees:	4 FT, 4 PT
Passive Ownership:	Allowed
Encourage Conversions:	N/A
Area Develop. Agreements:	No
Sub-Franchising Contracts:	No
Expand in Territory:	Yes
Space Needs:	400-600 SF

SUPPORT & TRAINING:

Financial Assistance Provided:	Yes (I)
Site Selection Assistance:	Yes
Lease Negotiation Assistance:	Yes
Co-operative Advertising:	Yes
Franchisee Assoc./Member:	Yes/Yes
Size of Corporate Staff:	150
Ongoing Support:	C,D,E,G,H,I
Training:	3 weeks Lancaster, PA

SPECIFIC EXPANSION PLANS:

US:	All United States
Canada:	Yes
Overseas:	All Countries

Since its franchising start in 1989, Auntie Anne's has provided customers with a delicious line-up of pretzels and more from its more than 1,150 locations worldwide. Auntie Anne's franchise success leads back to a three-pronged philosophy: to provide premium products and friendly, courteous service in a sparkling clean store. As one of the most popular franchises in the industry, Auntie Anne's provides franchisees with all the necessary tools and support to develop the Auntie Anne's concept including training for franchisees and staff at Auntie Anne's Pretzel University, ongoing field support, and access to Auntie Anne's confidential manuals, training videos, and marketing materials.

Operating Units	12/31/2011	12/31/2012	12/31/2013
Franchised	785	885	962
% Change	--	12.74%	8.7%
Company-Owned	13	14	15
% Change	--	7.69%	7.14%
Total	798	899	977
% Change	--	12.66%	8.68%
Franchised as % of Total	98.37%	98.44%	98.46%

Investment Required

The initial fee for an Auntie Anne's franchise is $30,000. Auntie Anne's provides the following range of investments required to open your initial franchise. The range assumes that all items are paid for in cash. To the extent that you choose to finance any of these expense items, your front-end investment could be substantially reduced.

Item	Established Low Range	Established High Range
Initial Franchise Fee	$27,000	$30,000
Leasehold Improvements, Furniture and Fixtures	$90,000	$175,000

Equipment & Smallwares	$35,000	$45,000
Business Licenses and Permits	$175	$600
Initial Inventory	$3,300	$4,000
Insurance	$400	$2,500
Training Expenses	$1,000	$7,500
Grand Opening Advertising	$1,000	$5,000
Signage	$4,000	$12,000
POS Equipment	$8,000	$15,000
Office Equipment and Supplies	$5,000	$10,000
Professional Fees	$5,000	$10,000
Additional Funds (3 Months)	$15,000	$51,000
Total Initial Investment	$194,875	$367,600

Ongoing Expenses

Auntie Anne's franchisees pay royalty fees equal to 7% of net sales and an advertising and marketing fund contribution equal to 1% of net sales.

Franchisee Satisfaction

A critical component of the due diligence process is that you, as a prospective franchisee, have a strong sense of existing franchisee satisfaction. Please review the franchisor's ratings below for this extremely important information.

How do you rate Auntie Anne's in terms of:	Rating*
Overall Quality of the Franchisor	99%

Initial Training Supplied by the Franchisor	100%
Ongoing Training and Support Supplied by Franchisor	97%

* Independent Audit of Existing Franchisees Who Rated Auntie Anne's as Excellent, Very Good, or Good

What You Get: Training and Support

All franchisees go through up to 3 weeks of complete store operations training, with 1 to 2 weeks in a classroom setting and 1 to 8 days in a store setting. At least two days of on-site training are available once a store opens. Auntie Anne's continually provides ongoing training and support for franchisees and their employees, boasting approximately one corporate employee for every three franchisees.

Territory

Auntie Anne's does not grant exclusive territories.

Big Apple Bagels

500 Lake Cook Rd., # 475
Deerfield, IL 60015
Tel: (800) 251-6101, (847) 948-7520
Fax: (847) 405-8140
Email: tcervini@babcorp.com
Website: www.babcorp.com
Anthony S. Cervini, Director of Development

Bakery-cafe featuring three brands, fresh-from-scratch Big Apple Bagels and My Favorite Muffin, and freshly roasted Brewster's specialty coffee. Our product offering covers many day parts with a delicious assortment of made-to-order gourmet sandwiches, salads, soups, espresso beverages, and fruit smoothies. Franchisees can develop beyond their stores with corporate catering and gift basket opportunities, as well as wholesaling opportunities within their market area.

BACKGROUND:

Established: 1992;	First Franchised: 1993
Franchised Units:	85
Company-Owned Units:	0
Total Units:	85
Dist.:	US-85; CAN-0; O'seas-0
North America:	25 States

Density:	24 in MI, 12 in WI, 6 in CO	Expand in Territory:	Yes
Projected New Units (12 Months):	8	Space Needs:	1,600-1,900 SF
Qualifications:	3, 4, 3, 3, 3, 5		
		SUPPORT & TRAINING:	
FINANCIAL/TERMS:		Financial Assistance Provided:	No
Cash Investment:	$100K	Site Selection Assistance:	Yes
Total Investment:	$254.3 – 379.6K	Lease Negotiation Assistance:	Yes
Minimum Net Worth:	$300K	Co-operative Advertising:	No
Fees: Franchise -	$25K	Franchisee Assoc./Member:	No
Royalty - 5%;	Ad. - 3%	Size of Corporate Staff:	14
Financial Performance Representation:	No	Ongoing Support:	C,D,E,F,G,H,I
Term of Contract (Years):	10/10	Training:	Varies 3-10 Days IL and MI
Avg. # of Employees:	3 FT, 11 PT		
Passive Ownership:	Allowed	**SPECIFIC EXPANSION PLANS:**	
Encourage Conversions:	Yes	US:	All United States
Area Develop. Agreements:	Yes	Canada:	All Canada
Sub-Franchising Contracts:	No	Overseas:	All Countries

BAB, Inc. offers customers a wide range of high quality foods through its three brands, My Favorite Muffin, Brewsters Coffee, and Big Apple Bagels. Each of the restaurants offers a casual yet comfortable atmosphere in which customers can order to-go or linger in the dining area with a wide assortment of breakfast and lunch items, treats, and beverages. On the menu, BAB restaurants offer freshly baked bagels, fresh deli sandwiches, cake-like muffins prepared with soybean oil, as well as salads, soups, and specialty drinks made to order. BAB recognizes that today's consumer wants to make informed choices about the foods they eat, so restaurants serve a wide range of meal options that can easily fit into a healthy, balanced diet. Additionally, the restaurant is not only a retail destination, but also a wholesale distributorship from which franchisees' baked-from-scratch bagels and muffins can be sold in bulk to corporate clients, restaurants, convenience stores, and other businesses for resale.

Operating Units	12/31/2011	12/31/2012	12/31/2013
Franchised	101	100	95
% Change	--	-0.99%	-5.0%
Company-Owned	0	0	0
% Change	--	--	--
Total	101	100	95

% Change	--	-0.99%	-5.0%
Franchised as % of Total	100%	100%	100%

Investment Required

The initial franchise fee for a BAB Production Store is $25,000 and $15,000 for a satellite store. BAB, Inc. provides the following range of investments required to open your initial franchise. The range assumes that all items are paid for in cash. To the extent that you choose to finance any of these expense items, your front-end investment could be substantially reduced. Please note that the figures below represent expenses for a BAB production store.

Item	Established Low Range	Established High Range
Initial Franchise Fee	$25,000	$25,000
Training	$2,500	$3,500
Leasehold Improvements	$87,000	$145,000
Furniture, Fixtures, Equipment, Signage and Display	$125,000	$155,000
Opening Inventory and Supplies	$10,000	$12,000
First Month's Rent and Security Deposit	$4,000	$10,500
Marketing Deposit	$7,500	$7,500
Insurance	$5,200	$7,200
Prepaid Expenses, Deposits	$500	$2,000
Professional Fees	$2,500	$7,000
Additional Funds (3 Months)	$7,500	$22,100
Total Initial Investment	$276,700	$396,800

Ongoing Expenses

BAB franchisees pay a royalty fee equal to 5% of gross revenues plus a marketing fund contribution equal to 3% of gross revenues which is subject to increase by BAB but not to exceed 5% of gross revenues.

What You Get: Training and Support

Pre-opening support for BAB franchisees includes site selection assistance, restaurant layout and design, a Grand Opening marketing campaign, full seasonal marketing strategies, and a password-protected BAB Franchisee Intranet featuring a download center, on-line sales reporting, resource center, and trading post. Additionally, franchisees undergo BAB Inc.'s initial training program comprised of 10 to 18 days of hands-on learning in our company-owned location and classroom instruction. This training details day-to-day restaurant operations, hiring, training and retaining good employees, and maintaining financial controls.

Territory

BAB, Inc. does not grant exclusive territories.

Charleys Philly Steaks

2500 Farmers Dr., # 140
Columbus, OH 43235
Tel: (800) 437-8325, (614) 923-4700
Fax: (614) 923-4701
Email: jwoo@charleys.com
Website: www.charleys.com
John Woo, Vice President of Development

CHARLEYS is the world's #1 Philly Cheese Steak brand. In 1986, Charleys redefined the Philly Cheese Steak. Today, more than 520 locations in 47 states and 20 countries serve up the world's number one Philly Cheese Steak. Made with fresh, quality ingredients grilled-to-order the Charleys way. Also known for its gourmet fries smothered in deliciousness and refreshing natural lemonades, the restaurant franchise is quickly expanding to serve the world's favorite Cheese Steaks across the globe. (*Please note: all Charley's Grilled Subs locations will transition to Charleys Philly Steaks by the end of 2015*).

BACKGROUND:	IFA Member
Established: 1986;	First Franchised: 1991
Franchised Units:	487
Company-Owned Units:	47
Total Units:	534
Dist.:	US-445; CAN-4; O'seas-89
North America:	47 States, 1 Province

71

Density:	57 in CA, 38 in FL, 33 in OH
Projected New Units (12 Months):	50
Qualifications:	4, 5, 2, 2, 2, 5
FINANCIAL/TERMS:	
Cash Investment:	$100K
Total Investment:	$152.2 – 451.2K
Minimum Net Worth:	$300K
Fees: Franchise -	$24.5K
Royalty - 6% or $300/wk.;	Ad.- 0.25%
Financial Performance Representation:	No
Term of Contract (Years):	10/10
Avg. # of Employees:	12-15 PT
Passive Ownership:	Not Allowed
Encourage Conversions:	Yes
Area Develop. Agreements:	No
Sub-Franchising Contracts:	No

Expand in Territory:	Yes
Space Needs:	N/A
SUPPORT & TRAINING:	
Financial Assistance Provided:	Yes (I)
Site Selection Assistance:	Yes
Lease Negotiation Assistance:	Yes
Co-operative Advertising:	No
Franchisee Assoc./Member:	Yes/Yes
Size of Corporate Staff:	75
Ongoing Support:	C,D,e,G,h
Training:	3 Weeks Columbus, OH
SPECIFIC EXPANSION PLANS:	
US:	All United States
Canada:	Yes
Overseas:	All Countries

At Charleys, we know that opening a franchise is a tremendous opportunity. Our family has grown from that first restaurant in Columbus, Ohio to a network that spans the globe. Charleys began franchising in 1991, and soon locations began popping up all over the world, including mall food courts, strip centers, airports, and even Army and Air Force Bases. For almost thirty years, we've built a base of knowledge, experience, and resources that we extend to our franchise partners. From location selection to day-to-day marketing activities, we'll do everything we can to make your business a success. You can count on our passion and support to guide you throughout your career as a business owner and franchise partner.

Operating Units	12/31/2011	12/31/2012	12/31/2013
Franchised	357	371	386
% Change	--	3.92%	4.04%
Company-Owned	41	43	42
% Change	--	4.88%	-2.33%
Total	398	414	428
% Change	--	4.02%	3.38%
Franchised as % of Total	89.70%	89.61%	90.02%

Investment Required

The initial fee for a Charleys Restaurant franchise is $24,500. Charleys provides the following range of investments required to open your initial franchise. The range assumes that all items are paid for in cash. To the extent that you choose to finance any of the expense items, your front-end investment could be substantially reduced.

Item	Established Low Range	Established High Range
Franchise Fee	$24,500	$24,500
Leasehold Improvements	$52,551	$252,909
Equipment/Furniture/Fixtures	$30,900	$90,600
POS System	$5,242	$13,260
Signage	$5,000	$13,000
Architect	$5,000	$15,000
Expenses while Training	$4,000	$6,000
Insurance	$3,500	$10,000
Miscellaneous Deposits	$1,500	$8,000
Additional Funds (3 months)	$20,000	$30,000
Total Initial Investment	$152,193	$451,236

Ongoing Expenses

Franchisees are required to pay ongoing royalty fees equal to the greater of $300 or 6% of gross sales per week, an advertising fund equal to 0.25% of gross sales, and an advertising expenditure requirement of 3% of gross sales.

What You Get: Training and Support

Franchisees will participate in a three-week initial training program to take place in Columbus, OH, which will cover food safety, crew certifications, administrative duties, operational standards, and customer service. New franchisees will also receive on-site opening assistance in beginning operations. Charleys will continue to provide guidance and support regarding day-to-day operations, as well as offer additional training programs when deemed necessary.

Territory

Charleys does not grant exclusive territories.

Checkers Drive-In Restaurants

4300 W. Cypress St., # 600
Tampa, FL 33607
Tel: (888) 913-9135, (813) 283-7069
Fax: (813) 936-6201
Email: mercksont@checkers.com
Website: www.checkersfranchise.com
Tena Merckson, Franchise Administration Manager

Quick-service, fast-food restaurant (double drive-thru). Total below reflect ownership of both CHECKERS and RALLY'S brands.

BACKGROUND: IFA Member
Established: 1986; First Franchised: 1989
Franchised Units: 455
Company-Owned Units: 337
Total Units: 792
Dist.: US-776; CAN-0; O'seas-1
North America: 40 States
  Density: 191 in FL, 85 in GA, 32 in AL
Projected New Units (12 Months): 35
Qualifications: 5, 4, 5, 4, 4, 4

FINANCIAL/TERMS:
Cash Investment: N/A
Total Investment: $453 – 627K
Minimum Net Worth: $750K
Fees: Franchise - $30K
  Royalty - 4%; Ad. - 3-5%
Financial Performance Representation: Yes
Term of Contract (Years): 20
Avg. # of Employees: 4 FT, 20 PT
Passive Ownership: Discouraged
Encourage Conversions: Yes
Area Develop. Agreements: Yes
Sub-Franchising Contracts: No
Expand in Territory: Yes
Space Needs: 15,000 – 25,000 SF

SUPPORT & TRAINING:
Financial Assistance Provided: No
Site Selection Assistance: Yes
Lease Negotiation Assistance: N/A
Co-operative Advertising: Yes
Franchisee Assoc./Member: Yes/Yes
Size of Corporate Staff: N/A
Ongoing Support: A,B,C,D,E,F,G,H,I
Training: 5 Weeks FL

SPECIFIC EXPANSION PLANS:
US: All United States
Canada: All Canada
Overseas: All Countries

From the day we first opened our doors in 1986, Checkers Drive-In Restaurants has become a market leader in the rapidly growing QSR burger business. Today, we stand as one of the fastest growing restaurants in our industry with more than 500 locations across the country. As part of the Checkers family, you'll benefit from this brand history and be instantly connected to our comprehensive support structure and one of the industry's most unparalleled operating systems. With a strong brand identity, excellent franchisee relationships and an outstanding executive leadership team firmly in place, Checkers is well positioned for development across the country.

Operating Units	12/31/2011	12/31/2012	12/31/2013
Franchised	317	315	314
% Change	--	-0.63%	-0.32%
Company-Owned	168	174	184
% Change	--	3.57%	5.75%
Total	485	489	498
% Change	--	0.82%	1.84%
Franchised as % of Total	65.36%	64.42%	63.05%

Investment Required

The initial fee for a Checkers franchise is $30,000. Checkers provides the following range of investments required to open your initial franchise. The range assumes that all items are paid for in cash. To the extent that you choose to finance any of these expense items, your front-end investment could be substantially reduced. Please note that the figures below represent expenses for a Traditional Double Drive-Thru Modular Restaurant.

Item	Established Low Range	Established High Range
Initial Franchise Fee	$15,000	$30,000
Initial Advertising Deposit	$10,000	$10,000
Equipped Restaurant Building	$159,000	$1,039,700

Signage, Menuboards	$15,000	$60,700
Inventory	$1,000	$5,000
Additional Funds (3 months)	$40,000	$90,000
Total Initial Investment	$240,000	$1,235,400

Ongoing Expenses

Franchisees pay ongoing royalty fees equal to 4% of net sales and an advertising expenditure of 5% of net sales. Additional fees include a National Production Fund contribution of up to 3% of net sales and other local and regional marketing and advertising fees.

What You Get: Training and Support

As a Checkers franchisee, you'll benefit from a robust, hands-on training program and support system designed to increase business value and operational efficiency. You will participate in a 5-week intensive in-restaurant training program that will cover a vast array of topics including food preparation, equipment operation and maintenance, and inventory control. A field-based franchise business team will also be assigned to support each franchisee in their respective markets, and training managers, field marketing managers, and operational support professionals may be available upon request.

Territory

Checkers does not grant exclusive territories.

Church's Chicken

980 Hammond Dr., Bldg. # 2, # 1100
Atlanta, GA 30328-6161
Tel: (800) 639-3495, (770) 350-3876
Fax: (770) 512-3924
Email: jfraser@churchs.com
Website: www.churchs.com
Jodi Fraser, Franchise Sales Manager

Founded in San Antonio, Texas, in 1952, Church's Chicken is a highly recognized brand name in the Quick Service Restaurant sector and is one of the largest quick service chicken concepts in the world. Church's serves up a rich tradition of gracious Southern hospitality and freshly prepared, high quality, authentic Southern-style fare, to help people provide affordable, complete meals for their families. Church's menu includes flavorful chicken both Original and Spicy, Tender Strips™ and chicken sandwiches with classic sides and hand-made from scratch honey butter biscuits. The Church's system consists of more than 1,675 locations in 24 countries. For more information on Church's Chicken, visit www.churchs.com.

BACKGROUND: IFA Member
Established: 1952;   First Franchised: 1967
Franchised Units: 924
Company-Owned Units: 264
Total Units: 1,188

Dist.:	US-1,321; CAN-16; O'seas-338
North America:	29 States, 2 Provinces
Density:	490 in TX, 86 in GA, 75 in CA
Projected New Units (12 Months):	120
Qualifications:	5, 5, 5, 3, 4, 5

FINANCIAL/TERMS:

Cash Investment:	$650K
Total Investment:	$413.3 – 1,336.6K
Minimum Net Worth:	$1.5M
Fees: Franchise -	$25K
Royalty - 5%;	Ad. - 5%
Financial Performance Representation:	Yes
Term of Contract (Years):	20/10
Avg. # of Employees:	15 FT, 6 PT
Passive Ownership:	Not Allowed
Encourage Conversions:	Yes
Area Develop. Agreements:	Yes
Sub-Franchising Contracts:	No
Expand in Territory:	Yes
Space Needs:	850 - 2,200 SF

SUPPORT & TRAINING:

Financial Assistance Provided:	No
Site Selection Assistance:	Yes
Lease Negotiation Assistance:	No
Co-operative Advertising:	Yes
Franchisee Assoc./Member:	Yes/Yes
Size of Corporate Staff:	163
Ongoing Support:	C,D,E,G,H,I
Training:	5 weeks regional

SPECIFIC EXPANSION PLANS:

US:	All United States
Canada:	Selected provinces
Overseas:	ME, Mexico, Brazil, Ecuador, Peru, Colombia, Panama, Caribbean, N. Africa, China, Thailand, E. Europe, Australia

As one of the largest quick-service chicken concepts in the world, Church's Chicken has been serving freshly cooked original and spicy fried chicken since 1952. Church's Chicken is an international brand with over $1.2 billion in sales per year that serves three million customers every week. Church's menu appeals to a diverse audience: while the famous chicken franchise is best known for both its original and spicy fried chicken, Church's also serves other specialties including fried okra, coleslaw, mashed potatoes, jalapeno peppers, French fries, corn on the cob and Church's unique Honey Butter Biscuits. Church's Chicken provides remarkable franchisee support via its purchasing and supply chain as well as strategic marketing campaigns and product development.

Operating Units	12/31/2011	12/31/2012	12/31/2013
Franchised	1,072	1,063	1,062
% Change	--	-0.84%	-0.09%
Company-Owned	259	258	258
% Change	--	-0.39%	0.0%
Total	1,331	1,321	1,320
% Change	--	-0.75%	-0.08%
Franchised as % of Total	80.54%	80.47%	80.45%

Investment Required

The initial fee for a Church's franchise is $15,000 with a $10,000 development fee. Church's provides the following range of investments required to open your initial franchise. The range assumes that all items are paid for in cash. To the extent that you choose to finance any of these expense items, your front-end investment could be substantially reduced. Please note that the figures below represent expenses for an "1850" Prototype Restaurant.

Item	Established Low Range	Established High Range
Initial Franchise Fee	$15,000	$15,000
Development Fee	$10,000	$10,000
Site work	$110,000	$270,000
Building and Improvements	$315,000	$485,000
Equipment and Signs	$215,000	$265,000
Fees, Misc., A&E Services, Deposits	$65,000	$105,000

Initial Training	$0	$23,000
Opening Supplies	$4,500	$10,000
Insurance	$7,500	$10,000
Utility Deposits	$1,000	$3,000
Business Licenses	$300	$600
Additional Funds (3 Months)	$10,000	$20,000
Total Initial Investment	$753,300	$1,216,600

Ongoing Expenses

Franchisees pay ongoing royalty fees equal to 5% of gross sales plus an advertising fund contribution equal to 5% of gross sales.

What You Get: Training and Support

Franchisees are enrolled in a two-day orientation conducted at our corporate offices in Atlanta, GA and are provided with ongoing assistance in the operation of the restaurant either in person or by email. Church's field operations team has extensive experience in working through business strategies and challenges and is always available to share that knowledge. Franchise restaurant managers also attend a structured three-week in-depth management training program that is designed to ensure optimum effectiveness and preparedness for Church's restaurant systems and operations. Ongoing training support is provided including training procedures for new product rollouts.

Territory

Church's Chicken does not grant exclusive territories.

CiCi's Pizza

1080 W. Bethel Rd.
Coppell, TX 75019
Tel: (972) 745-9313
Fax: (469) 675-6405
Email: miglesias@cicispizza.com
Website: www.cicispizza.com
Michael Iglesias, Director, Franchise Development

Declared America's Favorite Pizza Chain*, CiCi's Pizza is the nation's largest pizza buffet concept with approximately 500 restaurants in 33 states. The leading brand is now baking fresh franchise opportunities in the Southeast and across the country. With no significant direct competitors in the pizza buffet segment, now is the time to invest in CiCi's Pizza. Franchisees benefit from 29 years of brand heritage, a 2-to-1 sales-to-investment ratio and four distinct revenue streams: the custom buffet, catering, to-go orders and a game room. Learn more about CiCi's Pizza financing and incentive programs at cicispizza.com/franchising. (*CiCi's Pizza ranked No. 1 in 2012 Market Force consumer study.)

BACKGROUND:

	IFA Member
Established: 1985;	First Franchised: 1988
Franchised Units:	453
Company-Owned Units:	17
Total Units:	470

Dist.:	US-470; CAN-0; O'seas-0
North America:	33 States
Density:	N/A
Projected New Units (12 Months):	N/A
Qualifications:	5, 4, 1, 1, 3, 5

FINANCIAL/TERMS:

Cash Investment:	$250K
Total Investment:	$444 – 717K
Minimum Net Worth:	$750K
Fees: Franchise -	$30K
Royalty - 4% w/ ranges;	Ad.- 5%
Financial Performance Representation:	Yes
Term of Contract (Years):	10/1 – 10
Avg. # of Employees:	8 FT, 15 PT
Passive Ownership:	Allowed
Encourage Conversions:	No
Area Develop. Agreements:	Yes
Sub-Franchising Contracts:	No
Expand in Territory:	Yes
Space Needs:	3,000 – 3,600 SF

SUPPORT & TRAINING:

Financial Assistance Provided:	Yes (D)
Site Selection Assistance:	Yes
Lease Negotiation Assistance:	Yes
Co-operative Advertising:	No
Franchisee Assoc./Member:	No
Size of Corporate Staff:	40
Ongoing Support:	C,D,E,F,G,H
Training:	8-12 Weeks Dallas, TX

SPECIFIC EXPANSION PLANS:

US:	South, S. East, N. Central, Midwest, S. West
Canada:	Yes
Overseas:	No

Declared America's Favorite Pizza Chain*, CiCi's Pizza is the nation's largest pizza buffet concept with almost 500 restaurants in 33 states. The leading brand is now baking fresh franchise opportunities in the Southeast and across the country. With no significant direct competitors in the pizza buffet segment, now is the time to invest in CiCi's Pizza. Franchisees benefit from 29 years of brand heritage, a 2-to-1 sales-to-investment ratio and four distinct revenue streams: the custom buffet, catering, to-go orders and a game room. Learn more about CiCi's Pizza financing and incentive programs at cicispizza.com/franchising. (*CiCi's Pizza ranked No. 1 in 2012 Market Force consumer study.)

Operating Units	12/31/2011	12/31/2012	12/31/2013
Franchised	562	508	462
% Change	--	-9.61%	-9.06%
Company-Owned	11	11	13
% Change	--	0.0%	18.18%
Total	573	519	475
% Change	--	-9.42%	-8.48%
Franchised as % of Total	98.08%	97.88%	97.26%

Investment Required

The initial fee for a CiCi's Pizza franchise is $30,000 for your first restaurant and $25,000 for each additional restaurant. CiCi's Pizza provides the following range of investments required to open your initial franchise. The range assumes that all items are paid for in cash. To the extent that you choose to finance any of these expense items, your front-end investment could be substantially reduced. Please note that the figures below represent expenses for a restaurant unit.

Item	Established Low Range	Established High Range
Initial Franchise Fee	$15,000	$30,000
Leasehold Improvements	$200,000	$340,000
Impact Fees	$0	$10,000
Fixtures	$144,567	$169,900
Signage	$7,500	$25,000
Insurance	$500	$2,000
Business Licenses	$1,000	$5,000

Opening Inventory/Supplies	$25,234	$28,180
Promotional Expenses	$5,000	$7,000
Training Costs	$11,500	$20,500
Deposits/Pre-Opening Costs	$8,500	$34,000
Additional Funds (3 months)	$25,000	$45,000
Total Initial Investment	$443,801	$716,580

Ongoing Expenses

Franchisees pay an ongoing royalty fee ranging from 4% of the first $28,850 of weekly sales to 6% of the incremental weekly net sales in excess of $38,450. Additional fees include an Advertising Fund of the greater of $2,500 or 5% of net sales and other local advertising costs.

What You Get: Training and Support

Franchisees receive comprehensive training in all aspects of operating a CiCi's Pizza. This includes a required 4-12 weeks, based on relative experience, of on-site training at a CiCi's Dallas training restaurant. The company also provides a wide range of ongoing training opportunities for franchisees, as well as employees, of both company-owned and franchised operations. Additionally, each CiCi's Pizza franchisee is assigned a Corporate Brand Excellence Manager who provides operational and business consultation to assist the franchisee in all aspects of operating his or her restaurant.

Territory

CiCi's Pizza does not grant exclusive territories.

Cousins Subs

N83 W13400 Leon Rd.
Menomonee Falls, WI 53051
Tel: (800) 238-9736, (262) 825-8418
Fax: (262) 364-2984
Email: mcairns@cousinssubs.com
Website: www.cousinssubs.com
Mark Cairns, Director of Franchise Sales

Over 33 years of excellence describes our Eastern-Style submarine sandwich concept. Our COUSINS SUBS niche is offering a quality submarine sandwich 25% larger than most of our competitiors. Hot and cold subs are highlighted by our freshly baked bread, delicious soups and garden salads made to order! The value and portability of our products promote leveraging outside sales to bottom line profitability. We have high expectations for 2009 and invite you to learn more about our exciting franchise opportunities. We offer single unit and multi-unit franchises.

BACKGROUND: IFA Member
Established: 1972;   First Franchised: 1985
Franchised Units: 133
Company-Owned Units: 11
Total Units: 144
Dist.:   US-144; CAN-0; O'seas-0
  North America: 6 States

Density:	128 in WI, 6 in MN, 11 in AZ
Projected New Units (12 Months):	15
Qualifications:	5, 4, 3, 3, 3, 4

FINANCIAL/TERMS:

Cash Investment:	$80-100K
Total Investment:	$106.7-288.3K
Minimum Net Worth:	$300K
Fees: Franchise -	$25K
Royalty - 6%;	Ad. - 2%
Financial Performance Representation:	Yes
Term of Contract (Years):	10/10
Avg. # of Employees:	2 FT, 12 PT
Passive Ownership:	Discouraged
Encourage Conversions:	Yes
Area Develop. Agreements:	Yes
Sub-Franchising Contracts:	Yes
Expand in Territory:	Yes
Space Needs:	1,250-1,600 SF

SUPPORT & TRAINING:

Financial Assistance Provided:	Yes (D)
Site Selection Assistance:	Yes
Lease Negotiation Assistance:	Yes
Co-operative Advertising:	Yes
Franchisee Assoc./Member:	No
Size of Corporate Staff:	40
Ongoing Support:	C,D,E,h,I
Training:	10 days franchisee store;
	30 days training store; 3 days headquarters

SPECIFIC EXPANSION PLANS:

US:	IL, MI, MN, WI, AZ
Canada:	No
Overseas:	No

After 40 years in the business, Cousins Subs has this sub sandwich thing figured out. Cousins Subs doesn't take shortcuts on taste, using only the freshest, highest quality ingredients and loading them all on our signature fresh baked bread. It's a proven recipe for a delicious sandwich. Using the same recipe that our founders Bill Specht and Jim Sheppard developed with the help of a local baker back in 1972, you'll still find us baking bread in every store – two or three times a day. Consumers have a taste for subs in a big way. So big that subs are the Number Two QSR category in the nation. Better yet, the submarine sandwich category is growing, and we're poised to clean up in it.

Operating Units	12/31/2011	12/31/2012	12/31/2013
Franchised	127	121	115
% Change	--	-4.72%	-4.96%
Company-Owned	16	16	16
% Change	--	0.0%	0.0%
Total	143	137	131
% Change	--	-4.2%	-4.38%
Franchised as % of Total	88.81%	88.32%	87.79%

Investment Required

The initial fee for a Cousins Subs franchise is $25,000. Cousins Subs provides the following range of investments required to open your initial franchise. The range assumes that all items are paid for in cash. To the extent that you choose to finance any of these expense items, your front-end investment could be substantially reduced.

Item	Established Low Range	Established High Range
Franchise Fee	$25,000	$25,000
Leasehold Improvements	$20,000	$88,000
Equipment and Small Wares	$15,000	$75,000
Seating Package/Millwork	$7,500	$60,000
Initial Inventory and Supplies	$2,500	$6,500
POS System/Technology	$10,000	$15,000
Architectural Fees	$2,500	$6,000
Rent	$1,000	$6,000

Lease and Utility Security Deposits	$0	$6,000
Insurance	$700	$1,500
Training	$2,500	$5,500
Store Marketing Fee	$10,000	$10,000
Signage	$2,500	$10,000
Additional Funds (3 months)	$20,000	$30,000
Total Initial Investment	$119,200	$344,500

Ongoing Expenses

Franchisees are required to pay continuing service fees equal to 6% of gross receipts, and an advertising and development fund contribution of 2% of gross receipts. Additional fees include local advertising costs of 3% of gross receipts and contributions to a cooperative advertising program of up to 3% of gross receipts.

What You Get: Training and Support

Cousins Subs will provide at least 21 days of initial training for up to four employees, to take place at corporate headquarters in Menomonee Falls, WI or at other designated training facilities in the surrounding area. Training will cover food safety, management of daily operations, guest services, baking, and local store advertising. Franchisees will also be provided with a training representative to assist in on-site operations training for at least ten days within the first 30 days of operation of your shop. Cousins Subs will continue to provide advice and guidance regarding the operation of the store and may make periodic visits as well.

Territory

Cousins Subs grants limited exclusive territories.

Denny's

203 E. Main St.
Spartanburg, SC 29319
Tel: (800) 304-0222, (770) 777-0796
Fax: (864) 597-7708
Email: dwong@dennys.com
Website: www.dennysfranchising.com
Doug Wong, Senior Director Franchise Recruiting

For over 60 years, Denny's has been the trusted leader in family dining. Today, Denny's is a true icon, with brand awareness of almost 100%. Having grown to almost 1,700 restaurants and system-wide sales of over $2.5 billion, Denny's is one of the largest and most recognized full-service family restaurant chains in the United States. We rank in the top 100 Chains in Food Service Sales in Nation's Restaurant News, Bond's Top 100 Franchises and are ranked #1 in category by Entrepreneur Magazine's Franchise 500. If you are an experienced restaurateur or businessman, we invite you to contact us and learn more about growth opportunities within our great brand.

BACKGROUND: IFA Member
Established: 1953; First Franchised: 1963
Franchised Units: 1,532
Company-Owned Units: 160
Total Units: 1,692
Dist.: US-1,589; CAN-65; O'seas-38

North America:	50 States, 5 Provinces
Density:	345 in CA, 174 in TX, 127 in FL
Projected New Units (12 Months):	40
Qualifications:	5, 5, 5, 3, 1, 5

FINANCIAL/TERMS:

Cash Investment:	$350-$400K
Total Investment:	$1.178-2.621M
Minimum Net Worth:	$1M
Fees: Franchise -	$40K
Royalty - 4.5%;	Ad. - 3%
Financial Performance Representation:	Yes
Term of Contract (Years):	20/10 or 20
Avg. # of Employees:	50 FT, 25 PT
Passive Ownership:	Discouraged
Encourage Conversions:	Yes
Area Develop. Agreements:	Yes
Sub-Franchising Contracts:	No
Expand in Territory:	Yes
Space Needs:	4,550 SF

SUPPORT & TRAINING:

Financial Assistance Provided:	Yes (I)
Site Selection Assistance:	Yes
Lease Negotiation Assistance:	Yes
Co-operative Advertising:	Yes
Franchisee Assoc./Member:	Yes/Yes
Size of Corporate Staff:	250
Ongoing Support:	C,D,e,G,H,I
Training:	10 – 13 weeks at nearest certified training restaurant

SPECIFIC EXPANSION PLANS:

US:	All United States
Canada:	All Canada
Overseas:	India, China, UK, Caribbean, Central America, Indonesia

For 60 years Denny's has provided the quintessential family dining experience with modestly priced meals. Denny's is committed to being the go-to restaurant for America's best breakfast and prides itself on continuously pursuing innovation to enhance its quality menu and service platform. In addition to its reputation for its breakfast items and late-night dining, Denny's has also seen substantial success with its updated lunch and dinner menus that include a variety of health-conscious choices. With almost 1,700 restaurants worldwide and annual sales of more than $2 billion, Denny's boasts nearly 100% brand recognition as one of the largest full-service family restaurant chains in the United States.

Operating Units	12/31/2011	12/31/2012	12/31/2013
Franchised	1,386	1,426	1,436
% Change	--	2.89%	0.7%
Company-Owned	206	164	163
% Change	--	-20.39%	-0.61%
Total	1,592	1,590	1,599
% Change	--	-0.13%	0.57%
Franchised as % of Total	87.06%	89.69%	89.81%

Investment Required

The fee for a Denny's franchise is $40,000. Denny's provides the following range of investments required to open your initial franchise. The range assumes that all items are paid for in cash. To the extent that you choose to finance any of these expense items, your front-end investment could be substantially reduced.

Item	Established Low Range	Established High Range
Initial Franchise Fee	$0	$40,000
Building and Improvements	$740,000	$1,600,000
Architectural Design	$13,000	$40,000
Equipment, Fixtures, Furnishings	$400,000	$475,000
Signs	$15,000	$90,000
D.I.N.E POS Systems	$20,000	$40,000
Opening Costs	$20,608	$51,428
Security Deposits	$10,000	$15,000

Insurance	$15,000	$20,000
Permits	$5,000	$100,000
Additional Funds (3 Months)	$80,000	$150,000
Total Initial Investment (does not include land)	$1,318,608	$2,621,428

Ongoing Expenses

Denny's franchisees pay royalties equal to 4.5% of gross sales and advertising fees equal to 3% or 4% of gross sales. Other fees payable by the franchisee include a local advertising co-op fee and semi-annual menu costs.

What You Get: Training and Support

Denny's franchisees spend 10 to 13 weeks at a nearby certified training restaurant for hands-on training, with complete instruction in all aspects of restaurant operation, from management to food safety. Denny's commitment to franchisee support extends to field-based real estate assistance, an industry-leading supply chain to deliver high-quality food, and ongoing advertising and field support. Additionally, Denny's continually seeks out new and innovative ways to make operations more efficient and help franchisees operate more effectively.

Territory

Denny's grants nonexclusive territories. Denny's may grant exclusive territories only through its Market Growth Incentive Plan.

Doc Popcorn

5680 Logan Ct.
Denver, CO 80216
Tel: (866) 559-9744
Email: hannah@docpopcorn.com
Website: www.docpopcornfranchising.com
Hannah MacKay, Development Coordinator

Doc Popcorn (DP) is the largest franchised retailer of fresh-popped kettle-cooked popcorn offering a fun, simple and affordable business opportunity. With several different models from which to choose, we offer flexible options from which to grow.

BACKGROUND: IFA Member
Established: 2003; First Franchised: 2009
Franchised Units: 96
Company-Owned Units: 1
Total Units: 97
Dist.: US-91; CAN-0; O'seas-6
  North America: 26 States
  Density: N/A
Projected New Units (12 Months): 30
Qualifications: 4, 2, 1, 3, 4, 5

FINANCIAL/TERMS:
Cash Investment: $72K
Total Investment: $72 – 378K
Minimum Net Worth: $250K
Fees: Franchise - $37.5K
  Royalty - 6%; Ad. - 0%
Financial Performance Representation: Yes
Term of Contract (Years): 10/10
Avg. # of Employees: 0 FT, 2 – 3 PT
Passive Ownership: Discouraged
Encourage Conversions: Yes
Area Develop. Agreements: Yes
Sub-Franchising Contracts: Yes
Expand in Territory: Yes
Space Needs: 120 SF

SUPPORT & TRAINING:
Financial Assistance Provided: No
Site Selection Assistance: Yes
Lease Negotiation Assistance: Yes
Co-operative Advertising: Yes
Franchisee Assoc./Member: No
Size of Corporate Staff: 10
Ongoing Support: A,B,C,D,E,H,I
Training: 5 Days Boulder, CO; 2 Days On-Site

SPECIFIC EXPANSION PLANS:
US: Yes
Canada: Yes
Overseas: Yes

Doc Popcorn is the first fresh popped branded all-natural popcorn franchise system. They are leaders in the healthy and happy snack revolution. Doc Popcorn offers delicious flavor varieties including sweet butter, klassic kettle, cheesy cheddar, better butter, triple white cheddar, salt-n-pepper, caramel kettle, hoppin' jalapeno, and sinfully cinnamon.

Operating Units	12/31/2011	12/31/2012	12/31/2013
Franchised	43	85	86
% Change	--	97.67%	1.18%
Company-Owned	0	0	5

% Change	--	--	--
Total	43	85	91
% Change	--	97.67%	7.06%
Franchised as % of Total	100%	100%	94.51%

Investment Required

The initial fee for a Doc Popcorn franchise varies depending on the type of franchise being opened. For a single unit franchise, the fee is $37,500; for a standard franchise, the fee is $49,500; and for an Empire Builder Franchise, the fee is $69,500. Doc Popcorn provides the following range of investments required for your initial franchise. The range assumes that all items are paid for in cash. To the extent that you choose to finance any of these expense items, your front-end investment could be substantially reduced. Please note that the figures below represent expenses for a fixed POPKIOSK or POPSHOP unit.

Item	Established Low Range	Established High Range
Initial Franchise Fee	$37,500	$69,500
Expenses While Training	$1,000	$3,550
Real Estate Lease	$1,000	$32,000
Equipment/Décor	$15,000	$45,000
Construction	$10,000	$130,000
Store Creation Fee	$10,000	$10,000
Architect's Fee	$0	$14,000
Opening Inventory	$4,000	$10,000
Signage	$3,500	$12,000
Computer System	$3,000	$6,000
Store Camera System	$1,000	$3,500
Misc. Opening Costs	$3,000	$12,500
Additional Funds (3 months)	$5,000	$40,000

Total Initial Investment	$97,300	$378,050

Ongoing Expenses

Franchisees are required to pay a royalty fee equal to 6% of the weekly gross revenue. Other fees include a local advertising fee of 2% of monthly gross revenue, a monthly technology fee of $65 and a store camera fee of $35 per month.

What You Get: Training and Support

Doc Popcorn will provide training for up to 2 people which will last between 4-10 days depending on the type of franchise being opened. Topics to be covered include marketing, ordering products and supplies, customer service, and sales training. Doc Popcorn will continue to provide ongoing consultation via phone and internet, as well as national, regional, and local conferences and additional training when needed.

Territory

Doc Popcorn does not grant exclusive territories for Fixed Poperating Units.

Famous Famiglia

245 Main St., # 620
White Plains, NY 10601
Tel: (914) 328-4444
Fax: (914) 328-4479
Email: giorgio@famousfamiglia.com
Website: www.famousfamiglia.com
Giorgio Kolaj, Co-Founder/President

FAMOUS FAMIGLIA is an award-winning international pizza brand with leading sales in the pizza segment. Operating worldwide, FAMOUS FAMIGLIA has earned several leading industry awards for its unsurpassed product quality and customer service. Expansion plans include high-profile markets and locations such as: leading airports, shopping plazas, universities, casinos, military bases, cinemas, etc. With a successful franchise program in place, a number of high-caliber locations internationally are available.

BACKGROUND:		Encourage Conversions:	Yes
Established: 1986;	First Franchised: 2001	Area Develop. Agreements:	Yes
Franchised Units:	100	Sub-Franchising Contracts:	Yes
Company-Owned Units:	11	Expand in Territory:	Yes
Total Units:	111	Space Needs:	600-1,200 SF
Dist.:	US-106; CAN-2; O'seas-4		
North America:	26 States, 1 Province	**SUPPORT & TRAINING:**	
Density:	33 in NY, 17 in MA, 8 in PA	Financial Assistance Provided:	No
Projected New Units (12 Months):	8	Site Selection Assistance:	Yes
Qualifications:	4, 4, 3, 1, 4, 5	Lease Negotiation Assistance:	Yes
		Co-operative Advertising:	Yes
FINANCIAL/TERMS:		Franchisee Assoc./Member:	No
Cash Investment:	$200K	Size of Corporate Staff:	12
Total Investment:	$265.8 – 530.8K	Ongoing Support:	A,B,C,D,E,F,G,H,I
Minimum Net Worth:	$500K	Training:	2-4 Weeks Corporate Headquarters, NY
Fees: Franchise -	$35K		and surrounding region
Royalty - 6%;	Ad. - 1%		
Financial Performance Representation:	No	**SPECIFIC EXPANSION PLANS:**	
Term of Contract (Years):	10/5 – 10	US:	All United States
Avg. # of Employees:	4 FT, 8 PT	Canada:	All Canada
Passive Ownership:	Discouraged	Overseas:	UAE

Famous Famiglia, established in New York City in 1986, is an award-winning national pizza brand with leading sales in the QSR pizza segment. Dubbed "New York's Favorite Pizza"™, the pizzeria has earned several leading industry awards that herald its unsurpassed product quality and customer service. Famous Famiglia serves a wide variety of pizzas, pastas, calzones, strombolis, salads and desserts. Famous Famiglia's expansion program revolves around building strong and meaningful partnerships with market-leading operators and landlords. Currently the company is focusing on expanding to high-profile markets and locations, such as leading theme parks, airports, universities, travel plazas, shopping centers, sporting stadiums, casinos, arenas and more. Additionally, Famous Famiglia makes a point of giving back to the community that it serves; the franchisor is engaged in various charitable programs and projects, e.g. donating funds to local children's charities.

Operating Units	12/31/2011	12/31/2012	12/31/2013
Franchised	36	34	35
% Change	--	-5.56%	2.94%
Company-Owned	18	17	17

% Change	--	-5.56%	0.0%
Total	54	51	52
% Change	--	-5.56%	1.96%
Franchised as % of Total	66.67%	66.67%	67.31%

Investment Required

The fee for a Famous Famiglia franchise is $35,000 for a Standard Unit (e.g. a restaurant with 700-2,000 square feet) and $10,000 for an Express Unit (e.g. a restaurant with 200-600 square feet and a limited menu). Famous Famiglia provides the following range of investments required to open a Famous Famiglia franchise. The range assumes that all items are paid for in cash. To the extent that you choose to finance any of these expense items, your front-end investment could be substantially reduced.

Item	Established Low Range	Established High Range
Initial Franchise Fee	$35,000	$35,000
Leasehold Improvements	$100,000	$250,000
Rent	$5,000	$20,000
Equipment, Furniture and Fixtures	$60,000	$85,000
Signage	$5,000	$15,000
Initial Inventory	$5,000	$12,500
Architectural/Engineering	$10,000	$25,000
Computer and POS System	$10,000	$18,500
Travel and Living Expenses During Initial Training	$2,500	$5,000
Office Supplies	$1,500	$2,500
Business Licenses and Permits (for first year)	$250	$1,000

Insurance Premiums (for first year)	$1,500	$2,500
Grand Opening Advertising	$5,000	$5,000
Delivery or Catering	$0	$3,800
Additional Funds (3 Months)	$25,000	$50,000
Total Initial Investment	$265,750	$530,800

Ongoing Expenses

Famous Famiglia franchisees pay royalty fees equal to 6% of gross sales for the first 5 restaurants and 5% for each additional restaurant, an advertising fee ranging from 0% to 2% of gross sales, and a cooperative advertising fee ranging from 0% to 2% of gross sales.

What You Get: Training and Support

A franchisee, a general manager and two employees are required to attend a one to three week initial training session conducted at the Famous Famiglia corporate headquarters and a designated company-owned restaurant in White Plains, NY. Training programs cover topics on restaurant operation, management, marketing and accounting. Supplementary training sessions are offered throughout the year.

Territory

Famous Famiglia does not grant exclusive territories.

The Flame Broiler

3525 Hyland Ave., # 270
Costa Mesa, CA 92626
Tel: (714) 424-0223
Email: ylee@flamebroilerusa.com
Website: www.flamebroilerusa.com
Young Lee, President

The Flame Broiler restaurant serves simple, delicious, healthful, Korean style fast food all without dairy, trans-fat, frying, skin, HFCS, or added MSG.	

BACKGROUND: IFA Member
Established: 1996; First Franchised: 1999
Franchised Units: 168
Company-Owned Units: 2
Total Units: 170
Dist.: US-170; CAN-0; O'seas-0
North America: 4 States
 Density: 164 in CA, 3 in FL, 2 in AZ
Projected New Units (12 Months): 21
Qualifications: N/A

FINANCIAL/TERMS:
Cash Investment: N/A
Total Investment: $205.4 – 341.8K
Minimum Net Worth: N/A
Fees: Franchise - $25K
 Royalty - 5%; Ad. - 3%
Financial Performance Representation: Yes
Term of Contract (Years): 10/10

Avg. # of Employees: N/A
Passive Ownership: Allowed
Encourage Conversions: Yes
Area Develop. Agreements: Yes
Sub-Franchising Contracts: No
Expand in Territory: Yes
Space Needs: 1,200+ SF

SUPPORT & TRAINING:
Financial Assistance Provided: No
Site Selection Assistance: Yes
Lease Negotiation Assistance: Yes
Co-operative Advertising: No
Franchisee Assoc./Member: Yes/Yes
Size of Corporate Staff: 8
Ongoing Support: A,B,C,D,E,F,G,H
Training: N/A

SPECIFIC EXPANSION PLANS:
US: Yes
Canada: No
Overseas: Yes

With his own proprietary Flame Broiler sauce and beef marinade, the first The Flame Broiler The Rice Bowl King restaurant opened in 1995 in Fullerton, California. After graduating from UCLA and joining the workforce, Young Lee set out to create a better, healthier alternative to the fast food he had to choose from on the road. This led him to open the first Flame Broiler restaurant, which served simple, delicious, healthful, Korean style fast food all without dairy, trans-fat, frying, skin, HFCS, or added MSG. The The Flame Broiler The Rice Bowl King had become so popular on the West Coast that Lee decided to franchise in 1999. Lee saw franchising as a way to provide even more customers with a better, healthy alternative to fast food while maintaining the high level of service and food quality for which The Flame Broiler The Rice Bowl King is so well known. Currently there are almost 150 The Flame Broiler The Rice Bowl King restaurants operating in four different states, and we are continuing to expand.

Operating Units	12/31/2011	12/31/2012	12/31/2013
Franchised	94	123	148
% Change	--	30.85%	20.33%

Company-Owned	3	3	1
% Change	--	0.0%	-66.6%
Total	97	126	149
% Change	--	29.9%	18.25%
Franchised as % of Total	96.91%	97.62%	99.33%

Investment Required

The initial fee to purchase a Flame Broiler franchise is $25,000. The Flame Broiler provides the following range of investments required to open your initial franchise. The range assumes that all items are paid for in cash. To the extent that you choose to finance any of these expense items, your front-end investment could be substantially reduced.

Item	Established Low Range	Established High Range
Initial Franchise Fee	$25,000	$25,000
Rent Deposit and 3 Months Rent	$8,000	$24,000
Utility Security Deposits	$0	$1,500
Leasehold Improvements	$110,000	$195,000
Furniture, Fixtures, & Equipment	$26,000	$35,000
Initial Inventory	$2,000	$3,400
Insurance	$2,400	$3,400
Expenses while Training	$4,500	$7,500
Grand Opening Advertising	$1,000	$3,500
Signage	$4,000	$10,000
Office Equipment/Supplies	$1,000	$2,500
Additional Funds (3 months)	$20,000	$26,000
Professional Fees, License, & Permits	$1,500	$5,000
Total Initial Investment	$205,400	$341,800

Ongoing Expenses

Franchisees are required to pay ongoing royalty fees equal to 5% of net sales, and an advertising fee equal to 3% of net sales.

What You Get: Training and Support

Franchisees will be enrolled in an initial training program that will last up to four weeks and will take place at a company-owned or franchised restaurant in Southern California. The Flame Broiler will also provide a representative at your franchise location for up to one week immediately before, during, or following the opening of your franchise. The Flame Broiler will continue to offer ongoing advice and guidance as well as additional training courses when deemed necessary.

Territory

The Flame Broiler does not grant exclusive territories.

Little Caesars

2211 Woodward Ave., Fox Office Center
Detroit, MI 48201
Tel: (800) 553-5776, (313) 471-6327
Fax: (313) 471-6435
Email: ed.ader@lcecorp.com
Website: www.littlecaesars.com
Ed Ader, Director of Franchise Development

Little Caesars is growing in markets across the country! As the fastest growing pizza chain in America*,

Little Caesars provides strong franchisee candidates an opportunity for independence with a time-tested system and a simple operating model. Named "Best Value in America"** of all quick-serve restaurant chains for the seventh year in a row, Little Caesars franchisees benefit from a comprehensive training program that focuses on all aspects of the business. And they continue to receive support, expert analysis and consultation from corporate as their business grows. This unique franchise opportunity is for goal-oriented, focused, dedicated and energetic candidates. For more information, visit LittleCaesars.com.

*"Fastest growing pizza chain in America" based on 2013 U.S. store growth

** "Highest-Rated Chain – Value for the Money" based on a nationwide survey of quick-service restaurant consumers conducted by Sandelman & Associates, 2007-2013.

BACKGROUND:	IFA Member	Area Develop. Agreements:	Yes
Established: 1959;	First Franchised: 1962	Sub-Franchising Contracts:	No
		Expand in Territory:	Yes
Unfortunately, Little Caesars does not permit the publication of any detail about the number of operating units it has.		Space Needs:	1,400 SF
		SUPPORT & TRAINING:	
		Financial Assistance Provided:	Yes (I)
Qualifications:	4, 2, 2, 2, 4, 5	Site Selection Assistance:	Yes
		Lease Negotiation Assistance:	Yes
FINANCIAL/TERMS:		Co-operative Advertising:	Yes
Cash Investment:	$100K	Franchisee Assoc./Member:	Yes/No
Total Investment:	$265 - 681.5K	Size of Corporate Staff:	N/A
Minimum Net Worth:	$250K	Ongoing Support:	B,C,D,E,F,G,H,I
Fees: Franchise -	$20K	Training:	6 weeks Detroit, MI
Royalty - 6%;	Ad. - 4%		
Financial Performance Representation:	No	**SPECIFIC EXPANSION PLANS:**	
Term of Contract (Years):	10/10	US:	All United States
Avg. # of Employees:	N/A	Canada:	All Canada
Passive Ownership:	Not Allowed	Overseas: China, India, Caribbean, Latin America,	
Encourage Conversions:	Yes		Philippines

Founded in 1959 and with a franchising history dating back to 1962, Little Caesars has become the largest carry-out pizza chain in America and the fastest growing pizza chain in the world*. Little Caesars products are made with quality ingredients, like fresh, never frozen, mozzarella and muenster cheese, dough made fresh daily in-store, and sauce made from fresh California vice-ripened tomatoes. Little Caesars is also known for innovation product, offering its Crazy Bread® and Hot-N-Ready® products. Little Caesars was named "Best Value in America"** for seven consecutive years in Sandelman & Associates' Quick-Track® research study. Little Caesars is also devoted to giving back to the community. Established in 1985, the company's pizza kitchen on wheels, the "Love Kitchen," has served more than 2.5 million people, meeting the needs of the hungry, the homeless, and disaster services.

*Based on the net number of stores added 2008-2013.

**"Highest-Rated Chain – Value for the Money" based on a nationwide survey of quick-service restaurant consumers conducted by Sandelman & Associates, 2007-2013.

Investment Required

The fee for a Little Caesars franchise is $20,000, with a $5,000 reduction for existing franchisees and for veterans (service-disabled veterans do not have to pay the fee). Little Caesars provides the following range of investments required to open your initial franchise. The range assumes that all items are paid for in cash. To the extent that you choose to finance any of these expense items, your front-end investment could be substantially reduced.

Item	Established Low Range	Established High Range
Initial Franchise Fee	$0	$20,000
Rent	$1,500	$7,000
Leasehold Improvements	$50,000	$300,000
Fixtures, Equipment, and Signage	$150,000	$225,000
Grand Opening Advertising	$11,000	$20,000
Expenses While Training	$8,000	$11,000
Start-up Inventory and Supplies	$25,000	$35,000
Insurance	$500	$1,500
Utility Expenses	$1,000	$5,000
Licenses and Permits	$1,000	$10,000
Additional Funds (3 Months)	$17,000	$47,000
Total Initial Investment	$265,000	$681,500

Ongoing Expenses

Little Caesars franchisees pay royalty fees equal to the greater of 6% of gross sales or $100 for each one-week period, as well as advertising contributions of up to 7% of gross sales.

What You Get: Training and Support

Little Caesars has a strong belief in supporting its franchisees. Initial training, a comprehensive program lasting six weeks at corporate headquarters and company-owned restaurants in Detroit, Michigan, covers topics such as store operations, cash management, human resources, customer service, marketing and quality assurance. A two-day real estate/architecture/equipment training program is completed before franchisees continue the rest of the training. Little Caesars supports franchisees with the tools of a proven system, including ongoing training, architectural services to help with design and construction, preferred lenders to assist with financing, ongoing research and development of new products, and continuing, effective marketing programs and support.

Territory

Little Caesars grants protected territories with a radius equal to one mile, except under certain circumstances (e.g. in highly populated urban areas).

Papa Murphy's

8000 N.E. Parkway Dr., # 350
Vancouver, WA 98662
Tel: (800) 257-7272, (360) 260-7272
Fax: (360) 260-0500
Email: rhonda.mcgrew@papamurphys.com
Website: www.papamurphys.com
Rhonda McGrew, Manager Business Development

Papa Murphy's is the largest take-and-bake pizza company in the world with over 1,400 locations in the U.S. and Canada. The entire concept is built around the idea of take 'n' bake menu options. By baking Papa Murphy's pizzas at home, customers get to experience the home-baked aroma of a convenient, delicious meal that the brand is known for. To franchise owners, Papa Murphy's offers an opportunity that is attractive with a simplistic business model at a great investment price.

BACKGROUND: IFA Member
Established: 1981; First Franchised: 1982
Franchised Units: 1,362
Company-Owned Units: 68
Total Units: 1,430
Dist.: US-1,407; CAN-19 O'seas-4
  North America: 38 States, 3 Provinces
  Density: 180 in CA, 145 in WA, 98 in OR
Projected New Units (12 Months): 100
Qualifications: 4, 3, 2, 3, 2, 5

FINANCIAL/TERMS:
Cash Investment: $80K
Total Investment: $215.9 – 378.4K
Minimum Net Worth: $270K
Fees: Franchise - $25K
  Royalty - 5%; Ad. - 2%
Financial Performance Representation: Yes
Term of Contract (Years): 10/5
Avg. # of Employees: 2 FT, 8-10 PT
Passive Ownership: Allowed
Encourage Conversions: Yes

Area Develop. Agreements:	Yes	Franchisee Assoc./Member:	Yes/Yes
Sub-Franchising Contracts:	No	Size of Corporate Staff:	150
Expand in Territory:	Yes	Ongoing Support:	C,D,E,G,H,I
Space Needs:	1,200-1,400 SF	Training:	5 days owners class at corp.; 23 days certified training store; 2 days POS training
SUPPORT & TRAINING:			
Financial Assistance Provided:	Yes (I)	**SPECIFIC EXPANSION PLANS:**	
Site Selection Assistance:	Yes	US:	Midwest, Central, South
Lease Negotiation Assistance:	Yes	Canada:	Yes
Co-operative Advertising:	Yes	Overseas:	No

Papa Murphy's is the fifth-largest pizza chain in the country and is undeniably the leader of the take 'n' bake pizza segment. Every store offers custom-made pizzas featuring high-quality, fresh toppings generously layered on a pizza dough that is made fresh every morning in each store. Because our entire concept is take 'n' bake, our owners do not hassle with the complications that other restaurants have. There is no expensive delivery operation. There are no commercial ovens, eliminating cooking and the special requirements and costs that go along with it. And with no cooking, there is no sit-down dining, which reduces space requirements and lease costs.

Operating Units	12/31/2011	12/31/2012	12/31/2013
Franchised	1,232	1,270	1,327
% Change	--	3.08%	4.49%
Company-Owned	51	59	69
% Change	--	15.69%	16.95%
Total	1,283	1,329	1,396
% Change	--	3.59%	5.04%
Franchised as % of Total	96.02%	95.56%	95.06%

Investment Required

The initial fee for a Papa Murphy's franchise is $25,000. Papa Murphy's provides the following range of investments required to open your initial franchise. The range assumes that all items are paid for in cash. To the extent that you choose to finance any of these expense items, your front-end investment could be substantially reduced.

Item	Established Low Range	Established High Range
Initial Franchise Fee	$15,000	$25,000
Lease and Utility Deposits and Payments	$2,500	$6,000
Leasehold Improvements	$50,000	$130,000
Signs	$5,000	$10,000
Stamped Architectural Drawings	$2,800	$5,250
Opening Package	$95,000	$150,000
Inventory	$5,000	$7,000
Initial Advertising Fees and Expenses	$30,000	$30,000
Franchise Premises Rent (3 months)	$3,450	$12,186
Materials and Supplies	$500	$2,000
Phase 2 (ServSafe Manager Certification	$106	$300
Phase 2 (Profit Mastery Online Course)	$0	$50
Phase 4 Training	$400	$400
Expenses While Training	$3,880	$11,860
Employee Training	$500	$1,500
Insurance (3 months)	$375	$1,175
Bookkeeping/Payroll Service (3 months)	$1,500	$1,600
Additional Funds (3 months)	$10,000	$20,000
Total Initial Investment	$226,011	$414,321

Ongoing Expenses

Franchisees are required to pay ongoing royalty fees equal to 5% of weekly net sales, a advertising fee equal to 2% of weekly net sales, and local marketing and promotion, as well as regional cooperative advertising fees equal to the greater of 5% of net sales or $2,000 during each four-week period.

What You Get: Training and Support

Franchisees must complete a four-phase, month-long training program: Phase 1 consists of a 3 day in-store orientation; Phase 2 goes over pizza preparation and administrative/management duties; Phase 3 covers marketing, human resources, administration, and operations; and Phase 4 is PMI Enterprise Solution Training. Papa Murphy's will continue to provide advice and assistance regarding the operation of the franchise, as well as administer the advertising program and hold franchise conventions.

Territory

Papa Murphy's does not grant exclusive territories.

Port of Subs

5365 Mae Anne Ave., # A-29
Reno, NV 89523
Tel: (800) 245-0245 x1324, (775) 747-0555 x1324
Fax: (775) 747-1510
Email: jlarsen@portofsubs.com
Website: www.portofsubs.com
John R. Larsen, Chief Executive Officer

Port of Subs is an established fast-casual submarine sandwich chain with over 30 years of proven operating systems. Port of Subs specializes in fresh, quality, deli-style products and sandwiches. We serve breakfast, lunch and dinner, and offer catering and special event planning. We offer an assortment of made-to-order submarine type sandwiches, hot sandwiches, salads, pastries, party platters, beverages and other quick service food items for the on-premises consumption or take-out.

BACKGROUND:		IFA Member
Established: 1972;		1st Franchised: 1984
Franchised Units:		130
Company-Owned Units:		26
Total Units:		156
Dist.:		US-156; CAN-0; O'seas-0
North America:		5 States
Density:		69 in NV, 45 in CA, 11 in AZ
Projected New Units (12 Months):		25
Qualifications:		N/A

FINANCIAL/TERMS:

Cash Investment:	$80K	**SUPPORT & TRAINING**:	
Total Investment:	$199.3 – 328.3K	Financial Assistance Provided:	No
Minimum Net Worth:	$250K	Site Selection Assistance:	Yes
Fees: Franchise -	$16K	Lease Negotiation Assistance:	Yes
Royalty - 5.5%;	Ad. - 1%	Co-Operative Advertising:	No
Financial Performance Representation:	No	Franchisee Assoc./Member:	Yes/Yes
Term of Contract (Years):	10/10	Size Of Corporate Staff:	27
Avg. # Of Employees:	2-3 FT, 6-7 PT	Ongoing Support:	A,B,C,D,E,F,G,H,I
Passive Ownership:	Not Allowed	Training:	3 Weeks Reno, NV
Encourage Conversions:	Yes		
Area Develop. Agreements:	Yes	**SPECIFIC EXPANSION PLANS:**	
Sub-Franchising Contracts:	No	US:	West, Northwest, Southwest
Expand In Territory:	Yes	Canada:	No
Space Needs:	1,200 – 1,500 SF	Overseas:	No

For over 40 years, Port of Subs® has been preparing fresh, great-tasting sandwiches and the brand has become synonymous with quality sandwich making and superior customer service. Made-fresh-to-order sandwiches are prepared while the customer looks on and the unique taste comes from freshly-sliced, top quality meats and cheeses, freshly baked breads, and zesty dressings and spices. Port of Subs® also offers a breakfast sandwich, hot sandwiches, fresh salads, chips, an extensive line of party trays, desserts, and a variety of refreshing beverages. With over 130 restaurants in operation and 35 years of corporate support, Port of Subs® has developed a proven, effective system of operation that will give you the edge necessary to create a thriving business.

Operating Units	12/31/2011	12/31/2012	12/31/2013
Franchised	113	111	109
% Change	--	-1.77%	-1.8%
Company-Owned	26	27	27
% Change	--	3.85%	0.0%
Total	139	138	136
% Change	--	-0.72%	-1.45%
Franchised as % of Total	81.29%	80.43%	80.15%

Investment Required

The initial fee for a single Port of Subs franchise varies from $12,000 to $17,500 depending on the type of restaurant. Port of Subs provides the following range of investments required to open your initial franchise. The range assumes that all items are paid for in cash. To the extent that you choose to finance any of these expense items, your front-end investment could be substantially reduced. Please note that the figures below represent expenses for a Traditional Restaurant.

Item	Established Low Range	Established High Range
Initial Franchise Fee	$12,000	$17,500
Rent	$2,000	$5,500
Utility & Security Deposits	$2,500	$6,500
Leasehold Improvements	$55,000	$115,000
Equipment	$57,000	$80,000
POS System & Electronics	$7,000	$13,000
Fixtures	$17,500	$23,000
Initial Inventory & Supplies	$3,500	$5,000
Insurance	$600	$1,000
Training	$2,500	$6,000
Grand Opening Advertising	$3,000	$5,000
Signage	$4,500	$14,000
Working Capital	$12,000	$20,000
Tax, License, Insurance Deposit	$1,000	$2,500
Plans & Specifications, Professional and Legal Services	$4,000	$6,000
Municipal Permits	$1,000	$13,000
Lease Review	$0	$3,000
Additional Funds	$2,000	$4,000
Total Initial Investment	$192,600	$340,000

Ongoing Expenses

Port of Subs franchisees pay ongoing royalty fees equal to 5.5% of gross sales and contribute to an advertising and development fund that ranges from 1-3% of gross sales per month. Additional fees include local and regional advertising.

What You Get: Training and Support

Franchisees are enrolled in a four-week training program that includes both classroom and in-restaurant training in an existing Port of Subs restaurant. Franchisees will also be assigned a local Franchise Field Consultant and a Field Marketing Consultant who will offer up to ten days of opening support, in addition to ongoing in person assistance in the operation and marketing of your restaurant.

Territory

Port of Subs grants exclusive territories to traditional restaurant locations.

Rita's Italian Ice

Rita's is the largest Italian Ice chain in the nation. With a 30 year proven business model, Rita's offers a variety of frozen treats including its famous Italian Ice, Old Fashioned Frozen Custard, and layered Gelati as well as its signature Misto and Blendini creations.

1210 NorthBrook Dr., # 310
Trevose, PA 19053
Tel: (800) 677-7482, (215) 876-9300
Fax: (866) 449-0974
Email: e.taylor@ritascorp.com
Website: www.ritasice.com
Eric Taylor, SVP & Chief Development Officer

BACKGROUND:	IFA Member
Established: 1984;	First Franchised: 1989
Franchised Units:	555
Company-Owned Units:	0
Total Units:	555
Dist.:	US-555; CAN-0; O'seas-0
North America:	22 States
Density:	196 in PA, 120 in NJ, 82 in MD
Projected New Units (12 Months):	66

Qualifications:	3, 3, 3, 3, 3, 5	Space Needs:	800-1,200 SF
FINANCIAL/TERMS:		**SUPPORT & TRAINING:**	
Cash Investment:	$100K	Financial Assistance Provided:	Yes (I)
Total Investment:	$140.2 – 413.9K	Site Selection Assistance:	Yes
Minimum Net Worth:	$300K	Lease Negotiation Assistance:	Yes
Fees: Franchise -	$30K	Co-operative Advertising:	Yes
Royalty - 6.5%;	Ad. - 3%	Franchisee Assoc./Member:	No
Financial Performance Representation:	Yes	Size of Corporate Staff:	60
Term of Contract (Years):	10/10	Ongoing Support:	C,D,E,F,G,H,I
Avg. # of Employees:	2 FT, 15 PT	Training:	4 days on-site; 5 days corporate office
Passive Ownership:	Discouraged		
Encourage Conversions:	No	**SPECIFIC EXPANSION PLANS:**	
Area Develop. Agreements:	Yes	US:	All United States
Sub-Franchising Contracts:	No	Canada:	Yes
Expand in Territory:	Yes	Overseas:	Yes

Since 1984, when Bob Tumolo and his mother Elizabeth began experimenting with Italian ice recipes, Rita's Italian Ice has experienced enormous growth. Today, the Italian Ice franchise has more than 500 stores in 20 states, serving guests with one of the best-tasting, highest-quality Italian Ice around - made with real fruit and available in more than 30 flavors. With its adherence to the "RITA" values—Respect, Integrity, Trust and Accountability, Rita's has received top rankings by highly regarded industry publications, such as Entrepreneur magazine and The Wall Street Journal's StartupJournal.com.

Operating Units	12/31/2011	12/31/2012	12/31/2013
Franchised	545	552	555
% Change	--	1.28%	0.54%
Company Owned	1	0	0
% Change	--	-100%	--
Total	546	552	555
% Change	--	1.1%	0.54%
Franchised as % of Total	99.82%	100%	100%

Investment Required

The fee for a Rita's Italian Ice franchise is $30,000. Rita's provides the following range of investments required to open your initial franchise. The range assumes that all items are paid for in cash. To the extent that you choose to finance any of these expense items, your front-end investment could be substantially reduced. Please note that the figures below represent expenses for a standard Rita's store.

Item	Established Low Range	Established High Range
Initial Franchise Fee	$0	$30,000
Lease Deposit	$1,000	$15,000
Leasehold Improvements	$60,000	$160,000
Equipment	$35,000	$105,000
Computer	$600	$600
Permits & Licenses	$100	$1,800
Signs & Awnings	$5,000	$20,000
Prepaid Insurance Premium	$1,500	$1,500
Initial Order	$8,000	$13,000
Grand Opening Advertising	$0	$20,000
Training	$500	$5,000
Architect and Attorney Fees	$8,500	$12,000
Working Capital (3 months)	$20,000	$30,000
Total Initial Investment	$140,200	$413,900

Ongoing Expenses

Rita's Italian Ice franchisees pay a royalty fee equal to 6.5% of estimated and/or gross sales, an advertising fee equal to 3% of estimated and/or gross sales, and minimum weekly advertising expenditures equal to 2% of gross sales.

What You Get: Training and Support

Training takes place at Rita's Cool University in Trevose, PA, where franchisees learn how to successfully operate their store through a series of intensive workshops. A dedicated team of Rita's Education Specialists teaches franchisees how to make Rita's famous treats, as well as how to uphold company standards, program registers, train staff, and other essential operating procedures. Following this workshop, franchisees train at specially designated Rita's locations, working alongside seasoned franchisees to gain hands-on experience in a store environment. Rita's assists with store setup, staff development, and grand opening marketing. Following store opening, franchisees have access to support via the "Cool Support Center," Rita's corporate headquarters that is home to 80 staff members dedicated to supporting franchisees, ensuring the best quality products, and building the Rita's brand. Rita's online support website, the "CoolNet," provides franchisees easy access to all resources and information that is required to operate their Rita's Store. Franchisees continue to benefit from one-on-one field support and ongoing local marketing support throughout their relationship with Rita's.

Territory

Rita's Italian Ice grants exclusive territories.

Schlotzsky's Deli

200 Glenridge Point Pkwy., # 200
Atlanta, GA 30342
Tel: (404) 255-3250, (404) 705-4412
Fax: (404) 257-7073
Email: spando@schlotzskys.com
Website: www.schlotzskys.com

Sofia Pando, Vice President of Franchise Sales

Since 1971, Schlotzsky's has been the home of The Original toasted sandwich. The menu has evolved with customers' tastes to include the highest quality sandwiches, pizzas, salads, and soups available today. With approximately 365 locations worldwide, Schlotzsky's is the fast-casual choice for a quick, healthful, and fresh dining experience.

BACKGROUND:		IFA Member
Established: 1971;	First Franchised:	1977
Franchised Units:		297
Company-Owned Units:		38

Total Units:	335	Sub-Franchising Contracts:	No
Dist.:	US-341; CAN-0; O'seas-17	Expand in Territory:	Yes
North America:	35 States	Space Needs:	2,800 SF +/-
Density:	N/A		
Projected New Units (12 Months):	N/A	**SUPPORT & TRAINING:**	
Qualifications:	5, 5, 4, 3, 3, 5	Financial Assistance Provided:	No
		Site Selection Assistance:	Yes
FINANCIAL/TERMS:		Lease Negotiation Assistance:	Yes
Cash Investment:	$650K	Co-operative Advertising:	Yes
Total Investment:	$ 461.7 – 774K	Franchisee Assoc./Member:	Yes/No
Minimum Net Worth:	$2.2M	Size of Corporate Staff:	0
Fees: Franchise -	$30K	Ongoing Support:	C,D,E,F,G,H,I
Royalty - 6%;	Ad. - 4%	Training:	3 Weeks Austin, TX
Financial Performance Representation:	Yes		
Term of Contract (Years):	20/10	**SPECIFIC EXPANSION PLANS:**	
Avg. # of Employees:	5 FT, 20 PT	US:	Yes
Passive Ownership:	Not Allowed	Canada:	No
Encourage Conversions:	Yes	Overseas:	No
Area Develop. Agreements:	No		

Founded in 1971, Schlotzsky's is a pioneer in the fast casual restaurant category, priding itself on its fun, unique, and quirky atmosphere. Schlotzsky's has created a passionate following amongst customers with over 350 locations in 35 states and four foreign countries. With features including the Lotz Better Table Service unique to this market segment, and new Lotz Better restaurant design, Schlotzsky's is primed for aggressive, responsible growth. Schlotzksy's franchisees have the opportunity to create lasting memories for their guests, as well as becoming an integral part of the community in which they serve.

Operating Units	12/31/2011	12/31/2012	12/31/2013
Franchised	297	299	298
% Change	--	0.67%	-0.33%
Company-Owned	40	41	39
% Change	--	2.5%	-4.88%
Total	337	340	337
% Change	--	0.89%	-0.88%
Franchised as % of Total	88.13%	87.94%	88.43%

Investment Required

The initial fee for a Schlotzsky's franchise is $30,000. Schlotzsky's provides the following range of investments required to open your initial franchise. The range assumes that all items are paid for in cash. To the extent that you choose to finance any of these expense items, your front-end investment could be substantially reduced.

Item	Established Low Range	Established High Range
Initial Franchise Fee	$30,000	$30,000
Leasehold Improvements	$173,350	$309,000
Furniture, Equipment, Equipment, Graphics, POS, etc.	$148,400	$216,000
Exterior Signage	$9,000	$18,000
Licenses and Permits	$1,000	$3,000
Lease Acquisition / Professional Fees	$10,000	$25,000
Supplies and Inventory	$18,000	$25,000
Insurance	$7,000	$12,000
Deposits	$3,000	$5,000
Expenses While Training	$21,000	$35,000
Grand Opening Advertising and Promotions Expenditure	$15,000	$15,000
Additional Funds (3 Months)	$39,000	$48,000
Cinnabon Express Bakery Initial Franchise Fee	$7,500	$7,500
Cinnabon Express Bakery	$17,064	$24,484
Total Initial Investment	$499,314	$773,484

Ongoing Expenses

Schlotzsky's franchisees pay a monthly royalty fee of 6% of net sales as well as an advertising contribution fee of 4% of net sales. Additional fees include promotions and additional local advertising and promotions.

Franchisee Satisfaction

A critical component of the due diligence process is that you, as a prospective franchisee, have a strong sense of existing franchisee satisfaction. Please review the franchisor's ratings below for this extremely important information.

How do you rate Schlotzsky's Deli in terms of:	Rating*
Initial Training Supplied by the Franchisor	94%
Opening Support Supplied by the Franchisor	92%
Quality of the Products and/or Services Received from the Franchisor	89%

* Independent Audit of Existing Franchisees Who Rated Schlotzsky's Deli as Excellent, Very Good, or Good

What You Get: Training and Support

Schlotzsky's comprehensive training program includes continuing corporate training and on-site restaurant training, online access to Franchise Partner training tools and development support, and an in-depth operations manual. The initial management training is followed up with ongoing business consultation including business review and performance analysis by the corporate management team and up to four regular consultation visits per year. Schlotzsky's helps franchisees stay competitive with provided marketing campaigns and continuing product development. Their innovative, targeted local and national marketing plans are designed to increase customer frequency.

Territory

Schlotzsky's does not grant exclusive territories.

Tropical Smoothie Café

eat better. feel better.

1117 Perimeter Center W., # W200
Atlanta, GA 30338
Tel: (770) 821-1900
Fax: (770) 821-1895
Email: cwatson@tropicalsmoothie.com
Website: www.tropicalsmoothiefranchise.com
Charles Watson, Vice President of Franchise Development

Tropical Smoothie Café's business model is unique, as we offer both real fruit smoothies and a variety of fresh, flavorful food. We are two franchises in one! Our initial store development costs are lower because we do not utilize deep fryers, grills, or hooding systems (healthier too!) and our balanced business model of 50% Food Sales and 50% Smoothie sales allow us to drive higher gross sales and service all dayparts: breakfast, lunch, dinner, snack times, and dessert. In fact, for full year 2012, the top 50% of our Cafes had average gross sales over $669,000*! Get the franchisee solutions, strength, and support you need at Tropical Smoothie Café.
*Based on Calendar year 2013, 61 of 283 or 21.6% of the Cafes gained or surpassed this sales level. Your results may differ. There is no assurance you will do as well. Offer made by prospectus only.

BACKGROUND:

	IFA Member
Established: 1997;	First Franchised: 1998
Franchised Units:	424

Company-Owned Units:	1
Total Units:	425
Dist.:	US-425; CAN-0; O'seas-0
North America:	36 States
Density:	110 in FL, 75 in VA, 20 in NV
Projected New Units (12 Months):	100
Qualifications:	3, 5, 4, 2, 1, 5

FINANCIAL/TERMS:

Cash Investment:	$100 – 125K
Total Investment:	$165 – 424K
Minimum Net Worth:	$300K
Fees: Franchise -	$25K
Royalty - 6%;	Ad. - 4%
Financial Performance Representation:	Yes
Term of Contract (Years):	15/10
Avg. # of Employees:	1 FT, 10-12 PT
Passive Ownership:	Not Allowed
Encourage Conversions:	Yes
Area Develop. Agreements:	No
Sub-Franchising Contracts:	No
Expand in Territory:	Yes
Space Needs:	1,200 – 1,600 SF

SUPPORT & TRAINING:

Financial Assistance Provided:	Yes (D)
Site Selection Assistance:	Yes
Lease Negotiation Assistance:	Yes
Co-operative Advertising:	Yes
Franchisee Assoc./Member:	No
Size of Corporate Staff:	25
Ongoing Support:	A,B,C,D,E,F,G,H,I
Training:	1 week corporate office; 2 weeks local stores; 1 week store opening

SPECIFIC EXPANSION PLANS:

US:	All United States
Canada:	No
Overseas:	No

Tropical Smoothie Café is a healthy quick casual restaurant chain with over 400 Cafés in the United States. We offer delicious real fruit smoothies and healthier, flavorful food including sandwiches, wraps, salads, and flatbreads. Our business is balanced with 50% of our sales in food and 50% in smoothies which allows us to service all day-parts and drive higher gross sales. Our development costs are lessened by the fact that we go not utilize grills, deep-fryers, or hooding systems, also great for our healthy consumer appeal. Tropical Smoothie Cafe is expanding rapidly as a category killer offering two brands in one!

Operating Units	12/31/2011	12/31/2012	12/31/2013
Franchised	301	329	359
% Change	--	9.3%	9.12%
Company-Owned	4	0	1
% Change	--	-100%	--
Total	305	329	360
% Change	--	7.87%	9.42%
Franchised as % of Total	98.69%	100%	99.72%

Investment Required

The initial fee for a Tropical Smoothie Café franchise is $25,000. Tropical Smoothie Cafe provides the following range of investments required to open your initial franchise. The range assumes that all items are paid for in cash. To the extent that you choose to finance any of these expense items, your front-end investment could be substantially reduced.

Item	Established Low Range	Established High Range
Initial Franchise Fee	$25,000	$25,000
Real Estate Broker	$0	$4,000
Architect	$4,500	$10,000
Store Fixtures, Furniture and Equipment	$57,000	$115,000

Leasehold Improvements	$50,500	$140,000
Signage	$4,000	$10,335
Uniforms	$350	$4,800
Initial Inventory	$5,000	$10,500
Initial Training Expenses	$5,000	$10,100
Insurance Deposits	$500	$3,000
Initial Deposits	$725	$7,650
Licenses, Bonding & Permits	$1,000	$11,000
Legal/Accounting	$365	$6,000
Grand Opening Marketing	$2,000	$7,300
Additional Funds (3-6 months)	$10,000	$50,000
Total Initial Investment	$165,940	$414,685

Ongoing Expenses

Franchisees are responsible for paying royalty fees equal to 6% of weekly gross sales, a national marketing fee at a maximum of 2% of weekly gross sales, and additional advertising fees such as a local advertising cooperative contribution of 2% of gross sales.

What You Get: Training and Support

Tropical Smoothie Cafe provides an initial training program: Weeks 1 and 2 consist of on-the-job training at an existing franchise location covering marketing, equipment review, and work station maintenance; approximately 60 days before opening there is one week of classroom instruction. Tropical Smoothie Cafe will also provide one week of on-site pre-opening and opening supervision and assistance. Franchisees will continue to receive advice and guidance regarding the operations of the franchise, along with updates and revisions to the manuals and periodic inspections.

Territory

Tropical Smoothie Cafe grants protected territories consisting of a one-half mile radius.

Retail 4

7-Eleven

7-ELEVEN
franchisease℠

1722 Routh St., # 1000
Dallas, TX 75227
Tel: (800) 782-0711, (972) 828-7011
Fax: (972) 828-8997
Email: franchise.inquiries@7-11.com
Website: www.franchise.7-eleven.com
Dorian Cunion, Manager of Franchise Recruiting
& Marketing

7-ELEVEN stores were born from the simple concept of giving people "what they want, when and where they want it." This idea gave rise to the entire convenience store industry. While this formula still works today, customers' needs are changing at an accelerating pace. We are meeting this challenge with an infrastructure of daily distribution of fresh foods, pasties and time-sensitive products, and an information system that greatly improves ordering and merchandising decisions.

BACKGROUND:

		IFA Member
Established: 1927;		First Franchised: 1964
Franchised Units:		6,220
Company-Owned Units:		1,000
Total Units:		7,220
Dist.:	US-8,160; CAN-489; O'seas-44,400	
North America:		32 States, 5 Provinces

Density:	1,587 in CA, 855 in FL, 727 in VA
Projected New Units (12 Months):	N/A
Qualifications:	4, 4, 4, 3, 5, 5

FINANCIAL/TERMS:

Cash Investment:	Varies by Store
Total Investment:	Varies
Minimum Net Worth:	$50K
Fees: Franchise -	Varies by Store
Royalty - Gross Profit Split;	Ad. - N/A
Financial Performance Representation:	Yes
Term of Contract (Years):	10/10
Avg. # of Employees:	8 FT, 5 PT
Passive Ownership:	Discouraged
Encourage Conversions:	Yes
Area Develop. Agreements:	No
Sub-Franchising Contracts:	No
Expand in Territory:	Yes
Space Needs:	2,400 SF

SUPPORT & TRAINING:

Financial Assistance Provided:	Yes (D)
Site Selection Assistance:	N/A
Lease Negotiation Assistance:	N/A
Co-operative Advertising:	No
Franchisee Assoc./Member:	Yes/Yes
Size of Corporate Staff:	1,000
Ongoing Support:	A,B,C,D,E,F,G,H,I
Training:	1 week Dallas, TX; 5-8 weeks various training stores throughout US

SPECIFIC EXPANSION PLANS:

US:	NW,SW,MW,NE, Great Lakes, SE
Canada:	Western Canada
Overseas:	Select Countries

For 85 years, 7-Eleven has been both a leader and an innovator in the convenience store industry. Today, as the world's largest convenience retailer with a widely recognized brand name, 7-Eleven continues to thrive. 7-Eleven operates, franchises and licenses more than 40,000 stores in 17 countries. This exposure has made 7-Eleven an industry giant and an unshakable statue of fast, reliable and convenient service, while its focus on community and people has preserved its reputation as "the friendly little store that's just around the corner." 7-Eleven has a multi-faceted relationship with franchisees: it serves as landlord, financing source and record-keeper. 7-Eleven takes an active role in the franchisee's business, investing directly in their success in an effort to ensure a profitable and beneficial relationship between the franchisee and 7-Eleven.

Operating Units	12/31/2011	12/31/2012	12/31/2013
Franchised	5,438	5,870	6,219
% Change	--	7.94%	5.95%
Company-Owned	1,063	1,532	1,587
% Change	--	44.12%	3.59%
Total	6,501	7,402	7,806
% Change	--	13.86%	5.46%
Franchised as % of Total	83.65%	79.30%	79.67%

Investment Required

The franchise fee for a 7-Eleven store depends on the franchised store's gross profits for the past year; i.e. the fee is higher for locations that generate more revenue. Fees for brand new store locations are determined by the average combined gross profits of nearby locations. The fee can be reduced or waived depending on a franchisee's experience. Financing is available. Veterans receive a 20% discount on the franchise fee for their first 7-Eleven store. 7-Eleven provides the following range of investments required to open your initial franchise. The range assumes that all items are paid for in cash. To the extent that you choose to finance any of these expense items, your front-end investment could be substantially reduced. The below fees vary based upon the store selected.

Item	Established Low Range	Established High Range
Initial Franchise Fee	$0	$1,500,000
Expenses While Training	$0	$9,000
Opening Inventory	$30,350	$75,700
Cash Register Fund	$100	$10,000
Store Supplies	$250	$2,000
Licenses and Permits	$6,500	$8,500
Additional Funds (3 Months)	$0	$30,000
Total Initial Investment	$37,200	$1,635,200

Ongoing Expenses

Franchisees pay a monthly 7-Eleven charge in the amount of a variable percentage of the store's gross profit for the month. There is also an advertising fee ranging from 0.5% to 1.5% that varies based on total gross profit.

What You Get: Training and Support

Prior to store opening, franchisees undergo approximately 300 hours of initial training, with 24 hours in the 7-Eleven Store Support Center in Dallas TX, followed by training in a designated 7-Eleven Training Store. 7-Eleven also provides ongoing training opportunities, including in-store computer-based training programs for employees. 7-Eleven continues to support franchisees after store opening with a field consultant who meets with the franchisee regularly to help maximize store performance and profitability. 7-Eleven provides exceptional support services to its franchisees, including record keeping, bill paying, payroll services for store operations, as well as financing for all normal store operating expenses.

Territory

7-Eleven does not grant exclusive territories.

Clothes Mentor

 CLOTHES MENTOR

4350 Baker Rd., # 350
Minnetonka, MN 55343
Tel: (866) 261-2030, (952) 923-1223
Fax: (952) 923-1224
Email: jwollman@clothesmentor.com
Website: www.clothesmentor.com
James Wollman, Franchise Contact

Our women's fashions resale business creates loyal repeat customers who love these stores for their: tremendous value on a wide variety of better brands, in "gently-used" "like-new" condition, at about 70% off mall store pricing, available every day; great shopping experience in a well lit, organized, beautifully designed environment; dynamic, ever-changing inventory bargains; resale business model (not consignment); immediacy and convenience of getting cash, on the spot for selling us their fashions, which we buy right over-the-counter. (No waiting for months to get paid, and no worrying about missing items as in a consignment shop.); and opportunity to take this cash and update their wardrobes on a regular basis...for a lot less!

BACKGROUND:

	IFA Member
Established: 2001;	First Franchised: 2007
Franchised Units:	129
Company-Owned Units:	1
Total Units:	130
Dist.:	US-130; CAN-0; O'seas-0

North America:	25 States
Density:	13 in TX, 12 in OH, 8 in MN
Projected New Units (12 Months):	70
Qualifications:	5, 3, 2, 3, 2, 5

FINANCIAL/TERMS:

Cash Investment:	$75K
Total Investment:	$155 – 235K
Minimum Net Worth:	$300K
Fees: Franchise -	$20K
Royalty - 4%;	Ad. - $1,500
Financial Performance Representation:	Yes
Term of Contract (Years):	10/10
Avg. # of Employees:	2 FT, 8 PT
Passive Ownership:	Not Allowed
Encourage Conversions:	Yes
Area Develop. Agreements:	No
Sub-Franchising Contracts:	No
Expand in Territory:	No
Space Needs:	3,500 SF

SUPPORT & TRAINING:

Financial Assistance Provided:	No
Site Selection Assistance:	Yes
Lease Negotiation Assistance:	Yes
Co-operative Advertising:	Yes
Franchisee Assoc./Member:	No
Size of Corporate Staff:	10
Ongoing Support:	a,C,D,E,F,G,h,I
Training:	2 week Minneapolis, MN

SPECIFIC EXPANSION PLANS:

US:	All United States
Canada:	No
Overseas:	No

Clothes Mentor resale stores are excelling in this economy. While delivering tremendous values on women's fashions to customers, Clothes Mentor's established franchise store owners have attained over 60% gross profit margins. In essence, this means that the stores have 60 cents out of every sales dollar to cover overhead/expenses before the net profit line. These are far superior gross profit margins compared to traditional retailing. Clothes Mentor franchisees achieve these results by utilizing a proven business model, a proprietary point-of-sale computer system, highly-effective advertising materials, training, and follow-up guidance from the support staff.

Operating Units	12/31/2011	12/31/2012	12/31/2013
Franchised	48	75	92
% Change	--	56.25%	22.67%
Company-Owned	1	1	1
% Change	--	0.0%	0.0%
Total	49	76	93
% Change	--	55.1%	22.37%
Franchised as % of Total	97.96%	98.68%	98.92%

Investment Required

The initial franchise fee for a Clothes Mentor franchise is $20,000. Clothes Mentor provides the following range of investments required to open your initial franchise. The range assumes that all items are paid for in cash. To the extent that you choose to finance any of these expense items, your front-end investment could be substantially reduced.

Item	Established Low Range	Established High Range
Initial Franchise Fee	$15,000	$20,000
Leasehold Improvements	$10,000	$20,000
Fixtures and Supplies	$40,000	$59,000
Signs	$4,000	$10,000
Inventory	$40,000	$50,000
Deposits and Business Licenses	$2,000	$9,000
POS System	$16,000	$22,000
Miscellaneous Pre-Opening Expenses	$8,000	$20,000
Additional Funds (3 Months)	$28,000	$48,000
Total Initial Investment	$163,000	$258,000

Ongoing Expenses

Clothes Mentor Franchisees pay a weekly royalty fee of 4% of total gross sales, as well as national marketing and promotional fees, income and sales taxes, and local advertising fees, among others.

What You Get: Training and Support

Franchisees undergo an initial training program that is split into two separate sessions and lasts approximately two weeks. Topics covered include management and operation of a privately-owned retail business, instruction on sales and marketing, merchandising, computer operation and others. While the first session of training occurs over the phone or online, the second session of the training program takes place at Clothes Mentor's training center in Minnetonka, MN. A field consultant will also be made available to assist in opening and initial operations of the store. Clothes Mentor will continue to provide advisory services relating to store operations, marketing assistance, administrative procedures and more.

Territory

Clothes Mentor grants exclusive territories.

Floor Coverings International

FLOOR COVERINGS
international

5250 Triangle Pkwy., # 100
Norcross, GA 30092

Tel: (800) 955-4324, (770) 874-7600
Fax: (770) 874-7605
Email: djames@floorcoveringsinternational.com
Website: www.flooring-franchise.com
Denise James, Franchise Administator

FLOOR COVERINGS INTERNATIONAL is the 'Flooring Store at your Door.' FCI is the first and leading mobile 'shop at home' flooring store. Customers can select from over 3,000 styles and colors of flooring right in their own home! All the right ingredients are there to simplify a buying decision. We offer all the brand names you and your customers will be familiar with. We carry all types of flooring.

BACKGROUND: IFA Member
Established: 1988; First Franchised: 1989
Franchised Units: 116
Company-Owned Units: 0
Total Units: 116
Dist.: US-105; CAN-11; O'seas-0
North America: 43 States, 5 Provinces
Density: 10 in CA, 7 in NY, 6 in MN
Projected New Units (12 Months): 36
Qualifications: 5, 5, 4, 3, 4, 4

FINANCIAL/TERMS:
Cash Investment: $60K
Total Investment: $137.5 – 310K
Minimum Net Worth: $75K
Fees: Franchise - $49.5K
Royalty - 5%; Ad. - 2%/Mo.

Financial Performance Representation:	Yes
Term of Contract (Years):	10/5/5
Avg. # of Employees:	1 FT, 1 PT
Passive Ownership:	Discouraged
Encourage Conversions:	Yes
Area Develop. Agreements:	No
Sub-Franchising Contracts:	No
Expand in Territory:	Yes
Space Needs:	1,200 – 1,500 SF

SUPPORT & TRAINING:
Financial Assistance Provided:	Yes (D)
Site Selection Assistance:	Yes
Lease Negotiation Assistance:	Yes
Co-operative Advertising:	Yes
Franchisee Assoc./Member:	Yes/Yes
Size of Corporate Staff:	15
Ongoing Support:	A,B,C,D,E,G,H,I
Training:	1 Week Atlanta, GA

SPECIFIC EXPANSION PLANS:
US:	All United States
Canada:	All Canada
Overseas:	No

Floor Coverings International is the leader in the mobile flooring industry, bringing homeowners an international showcase in the comfort of their own home, inspiring their homes to be everything they can be. Whether it is stone from Turkey, cork from Portugal, wood from the forests of Brazil, or wool from New Zealand - our flooring business Design Associates help homeowners navigate the sea of confusing options offering the perfect blend of products and services personalized to suit the tastes and style of their homes. Our flooring franchise's personalized process makes choosing the right flooring simple, convenient, and enjoyable. With a powerful home improvement business model in an enormous marketplace, estimated to be $100 billion and growing, Floor Coverings International is an outstanding flooring franchise opportunity for entrepreneurs to build a large business that can maximize their potential.

Operating Units	12/31/2011	12/31/2012	12/31/2013
Franchised	94	87	93
% Change	--	-7.45%	6.9%

Company-Owned	0	0	0
% Change	--	--	--
Total	94	87	93
% Change	--	-7.45%	6.9%
Franchised as % of Total	100%	100%	100%

Investment Required

The initial fee for a Floor Coverings International franchise is $49,500 for a designated marketing area (DMA) of between 50,000 to 100,000 single family dwellings. For larger territories, an additional $0.25 per single family dwelling over 100,000 will be added to this initial fee. Floor Coverings International provides the following range of investments required for your initial franchise. The range assumes that all items are paid for in cash. To the extent that you choose to finance any of these expense items, your front-end investment could be substantially reduced.

Item	Established Low Range	Established High Range
Initial Franchise Fee	$49,500	$49,500 plus $0.25 per single family dwelling over 100,000 in DMA
Inspirenet Software	$5,000	$5,000
Training Related Expenses	$5,000	$7,500
Opening Package	$20,000	$45,000
Personnel/Staffing	$0	$24,000
Initial Advertising Expenses	$40,000	$60,000
Insurance-Liability/Vehicle	$1,500	$6,000
Miscellaneous Opening Costs	$2,000	$15,000
FCI Vehicle	$0	$38,000
Office Equipment	$2,000	$10,000

Real Estate and Improvements	$5,000	$30,000
Additional Funds (6 months)	$7,500	$20,000
Total Initial Investment	$137,500	$310,000

Ongoing Expenses

Franchisees are required to pay continuing royalty fees equal to the greater of 5% of gross sales, or $750 in the first 12 months of operation or $2,000 per month thereafter. Additional fees include a brand fund contribution of up to 3% of gross sales (currently 2%) and local advertising of at least 6% of gross sales.

What You Get: Training and Support

Franchisees will receive initial training in the form of a home study program, as well as three weeks of classroom training at company headquarters in Atlanta, GA, covering hardwood and vinyl flooring, ceramic tile, carpet construction, marketing, and business management. Franchisees will also spend up to five days in post-training consultation with a Regional Manager. Floor Coverings International will continue to provide support regarding technical advice, product information, and marketing assistance, as well as additional training when deemed necessary.

Territory

Floor Coverings International grants protected licenses for territories of 50,000 to 100,000 single family dwellings.

Gateway Newstands

240 Chrislea Rd.
Woodbridge, ON L4L 8V1
Tel: (905) 851-9652
Email: michael@gatewaynewstands.com
Website: www.gatewaynewstands.com
Michael Aychental, Chief Executive Officer

Gateway Newstands' business is to serve the daily merchandise needs of premier commercial, retail, and transit developments. The merchandise mix is formulated specifically to cater to the everyday needs and impulse sales of today's busy consumers.

BACKGROUND:

Established: 1989;	First Franchised: 1991
Franchised Units:	127
Company-Owned Units:	0
Total Units:	127
Dist.:	US-127; CAN-0; O'seas-0
North America:	16 States
Density:	40 in IL, 34 in NY, 11 in TX
Projected New Units (12 Months):	N/A
Qualifications:	N/A

FINANCIAL/TERMS:

Cash Investment:	N/A
Total Investment:	$55.9 – 501.8K
Minimum Net Worth:	N/A
Fees: Franchise -	$15 – 150K
Royalty - 3.5-5%/10%;	Ad.- 0%
Financial Performance Representation:	No
Term of Contract (Years):	N/A
Avg. # of Employees:	N/A
Passive Ownership:	Allowed
Encourage Conversions:	Yes
Area Develop. Agreements:	No
Sub-Franchising Contracts:	No
Expand in Territory:	No
Space Needs:	N/A

SUPPORT & TRAINING:

Financial Assistance Provided:	Yes (D)
Site Selection Assistance:	Yes
Lease Negotiation Assistance:	Yes
Co-operative Advertising:	No
Franchisee Assoc./Member:	Yes/Yes
Size of Corporate Staff:	N/A
Ongoing Support:	A,B,C,D,E,F,G,H,I
Training:	N/A

SPECIFIC EXPANSION PLANS:

US:	No
Canada:	No
Overseas:	No

Gateway Newstands are specialists; their only business is to serve the daily merchandise needs of premier commercial, retail, and transit developments. Gateway Newstands has established itself as the leading national tobacco/news store specialist. The principals of the company have an aggregate sum of 43 years of experience in the industry. The Service Store Concept developed as a direct result of the company's analysis of traffic count studies and its identification and emphasis on the daily needs of a diverse variety of shoppers. The merchandise mix is formulated specifically to cater to the everyday needs and impulse sales of today's busy consumers.

Operating Units	12/31/2011	12/31/2012	12/31/2013
Franchised	131	126	123

% Change	--	-3.82%	-2.38%
Company-Owned	0	0	0
% Change	--	--	--
Total	131	126	123
% Change	--	-3.82%	-2.38%
Franchised as % of Total	100%	100%	100%

Investment Required

The initial fee to open a Gateway Newstand franchise ranges from $15,000 to $150,000, based on the size of the building density of tenants, percentage of building leased, and other variables. Gateway Newstands provides the following range of investments required to open your initial franchise. The range assumes that all items are paid for in cash. To the extent that you choose to finance any of these expense items, your front-end investment could be substantially reduced.

Item	Established Low Range	Established High Range
Initial Franchise Fee	$15,000	$150,000
Lease or Sublease of Real Property or Concession Rights (per month)	$500	$10,000
Equipment, fixtures, other fixed assets, construction, remodeling, leasehold improvements, and decoration costs	$25,000	$250,000
Initial Inventory	$10,000	$40,000
Security Deposits and other prepaid expenses	$2,000	$30,000
Additional Funds (3 Months)	$3,375	$21,750
Total Initial Investment	$55,875	$501,750

Ongoing Expenses

Franchisees are required to pay monthly royalty fees equal to 3.5-5% of gross sales and 10% of commissions.

What You Get: Training and Support

No formal training program is required, however Gateway Newstands will in most cases provide up to one week of on-site training for new franchisees to be conducted by a field representative. Franchisees will continue to receive ongoing advice and guidance regarding the operation of the franchise, inventory, hiring, implementation of advertising, and administrative procedures.

Territory

Gateway Newstands does not grant exclusive territories.

The HoneyBaked Ham Co. & Café

HONEYBAKED.

••••••••••••••••••••••••

3875 Mansell Rd.
Alpharetta, GA 30022
Tel: (866) 968-7424, (678) 966-3224
Fax: (678) 966-3134
Email: mdemis@hbham.com
Website: www.honeybakedfranchising.com
Mark Demis, Franchise Development Department

The HONEYBAKED HAM CO. & CAFE is a truly exciting franchise opportunity with 50 years of experience building a strong brand. We are the original (and the world's largest) specialty retailer of high quality spiral-sliced glazed hams, turkeys and other special occasion center-of-the-table products complemented by a full service café.

BACKGROUND:	IFA Member
Established: 1957;	First Franchised: 1998
Franchised Units:	186
Company-Owned Units:	234
Total Units:	420
Dist.:	US-420; CAN-0; O'seas-0

North America:	39 States
Density:	41 in FL, 41 in GA, 37 in CA
Projected New Units (12 Months):	N/A
Qualifications:	4, 3, 4, 3, 2, 4

FINANCIAL/TERMS:

Cash Investment:	$100 – 125K
Total Investment:	$281.8 – 431.9K
Minimum Net Worth:	$350K
Fees: Franchise -	$30K
Royalty - 5-6%;	Ad. - 2%
Financial Performance Representation:	Yes
Term of Contract (Years):	10/10
Avg. # of Employees:	2-3 FT, 7 PT
Passive Ownership:	Not Allowed
Encourage Conversions:	Yes
Area Develop. Agreements:	Yes
Sub-Franchising Contracts:	No

Expand in Territory:	Yes
Space Needs:	2,000 SF

SUPPORT & TRAINING:

Financial Assistance Provided:	No
Site Selection Assistance:	Yes
Lease Negotiation Assistance:	Yes
Co-operative Advertising:	No
Franchisee Assoc./Member:	No
Size of Corporate Staff:	110
Ongoing Support:	C,D,E,F,G,h,I
Training:	1 Week Franchise Location;
	2 Weeks Atlanta, GA

SPECIFIC EXPANSION PLANS:

US:	Yes, 25 States
Canada:	No
Overseas:	No

More than 50 years ago, HoneyBaked Ham began with one store in Detroit, Michigan. Our founder, Harry J. Hoenselaar, selected the finest quality bone-in hams, which he'd smoke for hours over a unique blend of hardwood chips to add extra flavor and tenderness. The final touch was a sweet glaze and, of course, the process of slicing it in a single, continuous spiral. Since that beginning in a single store with a single product, HoneyBaked has grown into a premium brand featuring a wide assortment of fresh and interesting products such as smoked and roasted turkey breasts, roasts, BBQ, fresh deli sides, and delectable desserts. To maintain relevance with today's consumers as well as increase market share, we are focused on preserving our innovative product development history by introducing new product ideas, all of which can be sold through various revenue channels: over-the-counter retail, lunch, catering, and business-to-business gifting.

Operating Units	12/31/2011	12/31/2012	12/31/2013
Franchised	183	188	184
% Change	--	2.73%	-2.13%
Company-Owned	251	240	234
% Change	--	-4.38%	-2.5%
Total	434	428	418

% Change	--	-1.38%	-2.34%
Franchised as % of Total	42.17%	43.93%	44.02%

Investment Required

The initial fee for a HoneyBaked Ham Franchise is $30,000. HoneyBaked Ham provides the following range of investments required to open your initial franchise. The range assumes that all items are paid for in cash. To the extent that you choose to finance any of these expense items, your front-end investment could be substantially reduced.

Item	Established Low Range	Established High Range
Franchise Fee	$30,000	$30,000
Deposit Fee	$5,000	$5,000
Area Development Fee	$10,000	$10,000
Expenses while Training	$2,000	$4,000
Real Estate and Improvements	$93,000	$165,000
Architectural Fees	$3,000	$12,000
Equipment, Decor, and Fixtures	$62,500	$110,000
Rent	$8,100	$13,800
Security Deposit	$2,000	$4,000
Other Deposits and Licenses	$2,700	$4,600
Signs	$3,500	$10,000
Opening Advertising Costs	$10,000	$10,000
Opening Inventory	$10,000	$12,000
CMS/Point-of-Sale System	$5,000	$6,500
Additional Funds	$50,000	$50,000
Total Initial Investment	$281,800	$431,900

Ongoing Expenses

Franchisees are required to pay ongoing royalty fees equal to 5% of net sales for the first year, 5.5% of net sales for the second year, and 6% for all subsequent years. Additional fees include an advertising fund contribution of 2% of net sales and local advertising expenses of 2.25% of net sales.

What You Get: Training and Support

HoneyBaked Ham provides and initial training program divided into three phases: phase one consists of 25 hours of preparatory self-studying; phase two is a two-week in-store hands-on training program conducted at an existing HoneyBaked Ham store; and phase three consists of 30 to 40 hours of on-site consulting and assistance during your grand opening. Franchisees will continue to receive advice and consultation regarding the day-to-day operations of the store, marketing, and refresher training courses when needed.

Territory

HoneyBaked Ham grants protected territories.

Miracle-Ear

5000 Cheshire Lane N.
Plymouth, MN 55446
Tel: (800) 761-3103, (763) 268-4259
Fax: (763) 268-4295
Email: charlie.bever@amplifon.com

Website: www.miracle-ear.com
Charlie Bever, Senior Business Development Manager

Established in 1948, Miracle-Ear, Inc. is a network of over 1,200 retail outlets that distribute hearing aids manufactured by M-E Manufacturing and Services Inc. ("MEMSI"), a subsidiaryof Siemens Medical Solutions. Miracle-Ear is a subsidiary of Amplifon S.p. A, a worldwide distributor of hearing aids based in Italy.

BACKGROUND:	IFA Member
Established: 1948;	First Franchised: 1984
Franchised Units:	1,282
Company-Owned Units:	8
Total Units:	1,290
Dist.:	US-1,290; CAN-0; O'seas-0
North America:	50 States
Density:	83 in CA, 51 in FL, 43 in MD
Projected New Units (12 Months):	50
Qualifications:	4, 4, 3, 2, 1, 5

FINANCIAL/TERMS:

Cash Investment:	$75 – 100K
Total Investment:	$122.5 – 450K
Minimum Net Worth:	$100K
Fees: Franchise -	$20K
Royalty - $48.80/Unit;	Ad. - N/A
Financial Performance Representation:	Yes
Term of Contract (Years):	5/5
Avg. # of Employees:	2 FT
Passive Ownership:	Not Allowed

Encourage Conversions:	Yes
Area Develop. Agreements:	Yes
Sub-Franchising Contracts:	No
Expand in Territory:	Yes
Space Needs:	750 SF

SUPPORT & TRAINING:

Financial Assistance Provided:	Yes (D)
Site Selection Assistance:	Yes
Lease Negotiation Assistance:	Yes
Co-operative Advertising:	No
Franchisee Assoc./Member:	No
Size of Corporate Staff:	16
Ongoing Support:	A,C,D,E,f,G,h,I
Training:	1 Week Corp. HQ; 1 Week In-Field; Ongoing Field Staff Training

SPECIFIC EXPANSION PLANS:

US:	West, Midwest, SE, NE
Canada:	No
Overseas:	No

Miracle-Ear offers technological advancement that allows us to customize a hearing solution to your individual hearing loss profile with products that are more discreet and comfortable than ever. We understand how important your hearing is and our hearing care experts are there to help you through each step of the way. We want you to be fully satisfied with your experience and your hearing. By building a strong national presence, we're able to be right where you are. No one matches Miracle-Ear for convenience: we can be found in over 900 locations across the U.S., many in Sears stores. Our association with Sears means even greater access and assurance for you. Miracle-Ear is your trusted resource for the hearing solutions, outstanding service, and convenient locations you expect from a leader for over 60 years.

Operating Units	12/31/2011	12/31/2012	12/31/2013
Franchised	893	913	1,157
% Change	--	2.24%	26.73%
Company-Owned	9	6	8
% Change	--	-33.33%	33.33%
Total	902	919	1,165

% Change	--	1.88%	26.77%
Franchised as % of Total	99.0%	99.35%	99.31%

Investment Required

The fee for a Miracle-Ear franchise is based on the population in your exclusive territory. The minimum initial franchise fee will equal a license fee of $20,000, plus a territory fee of $4,000 per 100,000 population (prorated to a percent per year per 100,000 population) in your territory, provided, however, that the minimum territory fee required will be $10,000 for any exclusive territory with a population of up to 250,000 persons. Miracle-Ear provides the following range of investments required to open your initial franchise. The range assumes that all items are paid for in cash. To the extent that you choose to finance any of these expense items, your front-end investment could be substantially reduced.

Item	Established Low Range	Established High Range
Initial Franchise Fee	$30,000	$30,000
Prepaid Expenses	$1,000	$7,500
Expenses While Training	$1,500	$5,000
Real Property, Build Out Costs	$10,000	$85,000
Furniture, Fixtures, and Equipment	$40,000	$60,000
Signage	$1,500	$10,000
Inventory	$5,000	$10,000
Additional Funds (3 Months)	$30,000	$80,000
Total Initial Investment	$119,000	$287,500

Ongoing Expenses

Miracle-Ear franchisees pay royalty fees equal to $48.80 for each Miracle Ear hearing aid and $30.15 for each AudioTune Pro, as well as Sycle.net software access fees of $80 per month, and at least 10% of net sales for general advertising expenditures, among others.

What You Get: Training and Support

Franchisees will receive one week of classroom training that will cover marketing, human resources, business and financial management, and technical and sales training. Miracle-Ear will also provide opening assistance before and during the initial opening of your center. Ongoing support includes site evaluation assistance for additional centers, refresher product courses, business management and operational consultations, marketing materials and services, and more.

Territory

Miracle-Ear grants exclusive territories.

Snap-on Tools

2801 80th St., P.O. Box 1410
Kenosha, WI 53141
Tel: (800) 786-6600, (877) 476-2766
Fax: (262) 656-5635
Email: thomas.j.kasbohm@snapon.com
Website: www.snaponfranchise.com
Tom Kasbohm, Director of Franchising

The premier solutions provider to the vehicle service industry. Premium quality products, delivered and sold with premium service. We are proud of our heritage and are boldly addressing the future needs of our customers with improved efficiency, creating products and services from hand tools to data and management systems. Contact us today for discussion.

BACKGROUND:	
	IFA Member
Established: 1920;	First Franchised: 1991
Franchised Units:	4,581
Company-Owned Units:	214
Total Units:	4,795
Dist.:	US-3,458; CAN-361; O'seas-976
North America:	50 States, 10 Provinces
Density:	364 in CA, 244 in TX, 193 in NY
Projected New Units (12 Months):	N/A
Qualifications:	3, 4, 2, 2, 3, 5
FINANCIAL/TERMS:	
Cash Investment:	$30.2 – 80.3K
Total Investment:	$152.7 – 319K
Minimum Net Worth:	$30K
Fees: Franchise -	$7.5 – 15K
Royalty - $110/Mo.;	Ad. - 0%
Financial Performance Representation:	Yes
Term of Contract (Years):	10/5
Avg. # of Employees:	1 FT, 0 PT

Passive Ownership:	Allowed	Franchisee Assoc./Member:	No
Encourage Conversions:	Yes	Size of Corporate Staff:	0
Area Develop. Agreements:	No	Ongoing Support:	A,B,C,D,E,F,G,h,I
Sub-Franchising Contracts:	No	Training:	Minimum of 3 weeks On-The-Job;
Expand in Territory:	Yes		6 Days National Training Facility
Space Needs:	N/A		
		SPECIFIC EXPANSION PLANS:	
SUPPORT & TRAINING:		US:	All United States
Financial Assistance Provided:	Yes (D)	Canada:	All Canada
Site Selection Assistance:	N/A	Overseas: Australia, Benelux, Germany, Japan, New	
Lease Negotiation Assistance:	N/A		Zealand, S. Africa, UK
Co-operative Advertising:	No		

Founded in 1920, Snap-on has over 94 years of experience in the tool industry. Today it has become a $3.1 billion S&P 500 Company that is universally recognized by professionals as providing the highest-quality products in the industry. As the #1 professional tool brand in the world, Snap-on produces over 33,000 products and operates more than 4,800 locations in over 130 countries. Snap-on offers a variety of products, including hand tools, tool storage solutions, diagnostic equipment, information and management systems, and "under-car" shop implements, such as hydraulic lifts and tire changers. Snap-on serves the auto, marine, and aviation industries, as well as government, utilities, and industrial organizations. Snap-on commands tremendous brand name recognition and an exemplary reputation within the industry. Snap-on is driven by a determination to provide the best quality, practical, original, and innovative solutions to customers. In joining the Snap-on Tools team, franchisees enjoy this impeccable reputation, as well as the benefit of selling the most demanded product in the market.

Operating Units	12/31/2011	12/31/2012	12/31/2013
Franchised	3,064	3,103	3,186
% Change	--	1.27%	2.67%
Gateway	152	136	80
% Change	--	-10.53%	-41.18%
Company-Owned	195	173	157
% Change	--	-11.28%	-9.25%

Total	3,411	3,412	3,423
% Change	--	0.52%	2.05%
Franchised as % of Total	89.83%	90.94%	93.08%

Investment Required

The initial license fee for a Snap-on Tools ranges from $7,500 - $15,000. Snap-on provides the following range of investments required to open your initial standard franchise. The range assumes that all items are paid for in cash.

Item	Established Low Range	Established High Range
License Fee	$7,500	$15,000
Initial Inventory	$85,000	$95,000
Technology Package	$0	$2,400
Supplies	$0	$400
Uniforms	$0	$400
Van	$55,000	$105,000
Van Insurance (3 months)	$250	$1,250
Van Delivery Charge	$180	$4,100
License	$200	$2,400
Acquisition/Development of Revolving Accounts	$0	$52,500
Other Equipment, Fixtures, and Expenses	$150	$750
Computer Software License Fee	$770	$770
Invoice Line of Credit Repayment	$0	$20,000
Van Merchandising Displays and Safety Equipment	$0	$4,000

| Additional Funds (3 months) | $3,642 | $15,009 |
| Total Initial Investment | $152,692 | $318,979 |

Ongoing Expenses

Franchise owners operating a Standard Franchise pay a monthly license fee equal to $110 and a monthly computer software maintenance fee equal to $26, among other fees.

What You Get: Training and Support

Snap-on is dedicated to providing franchisees with considerable training and support. Franchisees attend an initial training program that involves approximately 135 hours (45 hours/week) of on-site training and over 50 hours of classroom instruction at the Snap-on training facility in Ft. Worth, TX. The classroom training covers a range of topics including selling skills, computer training, business management, and product knowledge regarding hand tools, tool storage, trade-ins, diagnostics, power tools, and safety. Snap-on offers ongoing training and support, including assistance with bookkeeping and operational methods, inventory control methods, product knowledge, and sales and marketing. Assistance is available to franchisees through visits from field representatives, over the phone, in meetings, and through Internet communication. Snap-on conducts national advertising campaigns and may opt to administer specialized, regional advertising programs as deemed appropriate. Furthermore, Snap-on arranges and distributes promotional materials.

Territory

Snap-on does not grant exclusive territories.

Wild Birds Unlimited

11711 N. College Ave., # 146
Carmel, IN 46032
Tel: (888) 730-7108, (317) 571-7100
Fax: (317) 208-4050
Email: pickettp@wbu.com
Website: www.wbu.com
Paul Pickett, VP of Franchise Development

WILD BIRDS UNLIMITED is North America's original and largest group of retail stores catering to the backyard birdfeeding and nature enthusiast. We currently have over 280 stores in the U. S. and Canada. Stores provide birdseed, feeders, houses, optics and nature-related gifts. Additionally, stores provide extensive educational programs regarding backyard birdfeeding. Franchisees are provided an all-inclusive support system.

BACKGROUND: IFA Member
Established: 1981;   First Franchised: 1983
Franchised Units: 280
Company-Owned Units: 0
Total Units: 280
Dist.:   US-260; CAN-15; O'seas-0
North America: 42 States, 3 Provinces
Density: 17 in MI, 16 in OH, 17 in NC

Projected New Units (12 Months):	15
Qualifications:	5, 5, 1, 3, 2, 5

FINANCIAL/TERMS:
Cash Investment:	$25 – 35K
Total Investment:	$99 – 157K
Minimum Net Worth:	$200K
Fees: Franchise -	$18K
Royalty - 4%;	Ad. - .5%
Financial Performance Representation:	Yes
Term of Contract (Years):	10/5
Avg. # of Employees:	2 (including owner) FT, 3 PT
Passive Ownership:	Allowed
Encourage Conversions:	Yes
Area Develop. Agreements:	No
Sub-Franchising Contracts:	No
Expand in Territory:	Yes
Space Needs:	1,400-1,700 SF

SUPPORT & TRAINING:
Financial Assistance Provided:	Yes (I)
Site Selection Assistance:	Yes
Lease Negotiation Assistance:	Yes
Co-operative Advertising:	No
Franchisee Assoc./Member:	Yes/Yes
Size of Corporate Staff:	39
Ongoing Support:	C,D,E,F,G,H,I
Training:	5 days Carmel, IN; 5 days store site

SPECIFIC EXPANSION PLANS:
US:	All United States
Canada:	All Canada
Overseas:	No

Wild Birds Unlimited operates over 280 stores in North America, offering superior bird feeding/watching and nature hobby products. Wild Birds Unlimited offers a number of goods tailored to nature enthusiasts, including bird feeders, birdhouses, birdbaths, bird food, decorative lawn and garden accessories, and unique nature gifts. Wild Birds' certified bird feeding specialists help customers transform their yards into beautiful bird feeding habitats that benefit both wild birds and the environment. Backyard bird feeding and watching represents a surprisingly profitable industry: over 55.5 million people participate in backyard bird feeding, and bird feeding/watching is a $5.4 billion industry. Thus, Wild Birds Unlimited offers prospective franchisees the opportunity to combine their business ambitions with their love for nature, and gives them access to over 25 years of experience and the highest quality of nature hobby products and services available.

Operating Units	12/31/2011	12/31/2012	12/31/2013
Franchised	275	279	285
% Change	--	1.45%	2.15%
Company-Owned	0	0	0
% Change	--	--	--
Total	275	279	285
% Change	--	1.45%	2.15%
Franchised as % of Total	100%	100%	100%

Investment Required

The initial fee for a Wild Birds Unlimited franchise is $22,000. Wild Birds Unlimited provides the following range of investments required to open your initial franchise. The range assumes that all items are paid for in cash. To the extent that you choose to finance any of these expense items, your front-end investment could be substantially reduced.

Item	Established Low Range	Established High Range
Initial Franchise Fee	$22,000	$22,000
Training	$3,000	$3,000
Travel, Meals, Lodging	$983	$5,253
Lease Deposit	$2,500	$5,500
First Month's Rent	$2,500	$5,500
Leasehold Improvements	$6,333	$29,360
Insurance (first quarter)	$125	$580
Legal/Accounting	$500	$7,380

Office Equipment	$9,309	$9,395
Signs	$2,492	$8,270
Advertising	$6,048	$10,218
Retail Fixtures	$10,699	$13,897
Opening Inventory	$22,974	$25,805
Gift Card Fee	$104	$104
Annual Conference Fee	$500	$500
Misc. Expenses	$4,095	$5,749
Additional Funds (3 months)	$10,000	$20,000
Total Initial Investment	$104,162	$172,511

Ongoing Expenses

Wild Birds Unlimited franchisees pay a royalty fee equal to 4% of gross sales, a minimum local advertising fee equal to 2% of gross sales, a regional/local advertising cooperative fee equal to a maximum of 2% of gross sales, and an annual fee for point-of-sale software.

What You Get: Training and Support

Wild Birds Unlimited assists franchisees throughout the entirety of the franchise relationship to ensure the success of franchised locations. Before opening a franchised location, franchisees must complete a training program at Wild Birds Unlimited's corporate headquarters in Carmel, Indiana. The initial training program includes approximately 10 days of classroom instruction and on-the-job training, covering a number of topics, including visual merchandising, store layout, store tours, purchasing strategies, inventory management, POS systems, seed strategies, product and hobby education, marketing strategies, human resources, customer services, sales skills and strategies, and financial management.Following the store opening, Wild Birds Unlimited conducts regular additional training programs on selected topics, as well as periodic evaluations to provide constructive feedback.

Territory

Wild Birds Unlimited grants exclusive territories.

Wireless Zone

34 Industrial Park Place
Middletown, CT 06457
Tel: (866) 994-3577, (860) 798-4473
Fax: (860) 632-9343
Email: clayn@wirelesszone.com
Website: www.wirelesszone.com
Clay Neff, National Vice President of Franchise Growth

WIRELESS ZONE stores are primarily retail, with strong emphasis on local ownership, networking and community involvement. Franchise provides local field support staff, centralized advertising and purchasing, initial and ongoing training and strong commissions and residual income from Verizon Wireless phones, service, accessories, wireless email, etc. Join a winning team!

Projected New Units (12 Months):	65
Qualifications:	2, 4, 3, 2, 1, 5

FINANCIAL/TERMS:

Cash Investment:	$100 – 150K
Total Investment:	$65.3 – 228.5K
Minimum Net Worth:	N/A
Fees: Franchise -	$30K
Royalty - 10%;	Ad. - $800/Mo.
Financial Performances Representation:	No
Term of Contract (Years):	7/7
Avg. # of Employees:	2 FT, 1 PT
Passive Ownership:	Not Allowed
Encourage Conversions:	Yes
Area Develop. Agreements:	Yes
Sub-Franchising Contracts:	Yes
Expand in Territory:	Yes
Space Needs:	1,000 SF

SUPPORT & TRAINING:

Financial Assistance Provided:	Yes (D)
Site Selection Assistance:	Yes
Lease Negotiation Assistance:	Yes
Co-operative Advertising:	No
Franchisee Assoc./Member:	Yes/Yes
Size of Corporate Staff:	64
Ongoing Support:	B,C,D,E,G,H
Training:	2 Days 3rd Party Trainer New Store; Up to 1 Week Executive Trainer

BACKGROUND:

	IFA Member	
Established: 1988;	First Franchised: 1989	
Franchised Units:		452
Company-Owned Units:		23
Total Units:		475
Dist.:	US-475; CAN-0; O'seas-0	
North America:		13 States
Density:	46 in CT, 38 in PA, 23 in NY	

SPECIFIC EXPANSION PLANS:

US:	FL and VA to ME
Canada:	No
Overseas:	No

At the dawn of the cell phone age, Wireless Zone founder Russ Weldon started an instantly successful business called "The Car Phone Store" in

Wethersfield, CT, in 1988. At that time, few people knew what cellular was all about and a stand-alone wireless store was truly a unique idea. We changed our name to Wireless Zone in 1999 in order to convey more clearly the products that we sold then and still offer. Today we sell all the latest cellular/wireless phones, GPS navigation, wireless accessories, Verizon FIOS High Speed Fiber Optic Network, Wireless Data Devices, and pre-paid cellular services. As a leader in the wireless communications franchise industry, we can help you to establish a successful and fulfilling business opportunity.

Operating Units	12/31/2011	12/31/2012	12/31/2013
Franchised	423	397	375
% Change	--	-6.15%	-5.54%
Company-Owned	22	20	29
% Change	--	-9.09%	45.0%
Total	445	417	404
% Change	--	-6.29%	-3.12%
Franchised as % of Total	95.06%	95.20%	92.82%

Investment Required

The initial fee for a Wireless Zone franchise ranges from $1,000 to $30,000 depending on your level of experience in the wireless and wireline sales industry and location of your store. Wireless Zone provides the following range of investments required to open your initial franchise. The range assumes that all items are paid for in cash. To the extent that you choose to finance any of these expense items, your front-end investment could be substantially reduced.

Item	Established Low Range	Established High Range
Initial Franchise Fee	$1,000	$30,000
Training Expenses (per person)	$1,250	$5,000
Real Estate Improvements	$10,000	$30,000

Business Equipment & Supplies	$9,000	$15,000
Computer Equipment	$5,000	$10,000
Signs, Fixtures, Kiosks, Displays	$15,000	$95,000
Miscellaneous Opening Costs	$2,000	$13,500
Initial Product Inventory	$50,000	$150,000
Initial Marketing Program	$5,000	$5,000
Sales Tax, Use Tax, Other Similar Tax, Freight and Delivery Charges	$3,000	$38,000
Additional Funds (3 months)	$1,000	$25,000
Total Initial Investment	$102,250	$416,500

Ongoing Expenses

Franchisees pay ongoing royalties based on 10% of commissions received from providers, 20% of residuals, and 5% of gross sales. Additional fees include an advertising contribution of 5% of gross sales and your portion of commissions, and a Global Fund Contribution of currently $200 per month.

What You Get: Training and Support

Franchisees are enrolled in an initial training program of approximately four weeks, which includes both in-classroom training at corporate headquarters in Middletown, CT and on-the-job training at franchised store locations and your own store. Training will cover all aspects of operating a successful franchise, including store management, carrier relations, product training, and sales and marketing strategies. Throughout the year, Wireless Zone will offer new product training classes and provide ongoing assistance and supervision of operations either in-person, via telephone, or other electronic means.

Territory

Wireless Zone does not grant exclusive territories.

Service-Based 5

1-800-Got-Junk?

1-800-GOT-JUNK?®
THE WORLD'S LARGEST JUNK REMOVAL SERVICE

887 Great Northern Way, # 301
Vancouver, BC V5T 4T5
Tel: (866) 475-6842, (800) 468-5865
Fax: (514) 370-4625
Email: jason.isley@1800gotjunk.com
Website: www.1800gotjunk.com
Jason Isley, Franchise Developement Director

1-800-GOT-JUNK? has revolutionized customer service in junk removal for 25 years. By setting the mark for service standards and professionalism, an industry that once operated without set rates, price lists or receipts, now has top service standards. You will have the expert advice and support that is key to success. Our intensive training program will get you on track; our ongoing support and continuing education will keep you there. Centralized call center allows you to focus on your business.

BACKGROUND: IFA Member
Established: 1989;   First Franchised: 1998
Franchised Units: 163
Company-Owned Units: 0
Total Units: 163
Dist.:   US-136; CAN-21; O'seas-6
  North America: 44 States, 9 Provinces
  Density: 45 in CA, 20 in FL, 13 in NY

Projected New Units (12 Months):   1
Qualifications: 5, 5, 1, 2, 4, 5

FINANCIAL/TERMS:
Cash Investment: $70 – 100K
Total Investment: $125 – 250K
Minimum Net Worth: $250K
Fees: Franchise - $12K
  Royalty - 8%;   Ad. - 1%
Financial Performance Representation: Yes
Term of Contract (Years):   5/15
Avg. # of Employees: 2 FT, 2 PT
Passive Ownership: Not Allowed
Encourage Conversions: No
Area Develop. Agreements: No
Sub-Franchising Contracts: No
Expand in Territory: Yes
Space Needs: N/A

SUPPORT & TRAINING:
Financial Assistance Provided: Yes (D)
Site Selection Assistance: N/A
Lease Negotiation Assistance: N/A
Co-operative Advertising: Yes
Franchisee Assoc./Member: Yes/Yes
Size of Corporate Staff: 68
Ongoing Support: a,B,C,D,G,H,I
Training: 5 Days Vancouver, BC

SPECIFIC EXPANSION PLANS:
US: All United States
Canada: Yes
Overseas: No

1-800-GOT-JUNK? has revolutionized customer service in junk removal for over 25 years. By setting the mark for service standards and professionalism, an industry that once operated without set rates, price lists or receipts, now has top service standards. You will have the expert advice and support that is key to success. Our intensive training program will get you on track; our ongoing support and continuing education will keep you there. Centralized call center allows you to focus on your business.

Operating Units	12/31/2011	12/31/2012	12/31/2013
Franchised	147	145	136
% Change	--	-1.36%	-6.21%
Company-Owned	0	0	0
% Change	--	--	--
Total	147	145	136
% Change	--	-1.36%	-6.21%
Franchised as % of Total	100%	100%	100%

Investment Required

The initial franchise fee for a 1-800-GOT-JUNK? franchise is $12,000 for a single subterritory, plus $6,000 for each additional subterritory to be developed. 1-800-GOT-JUNK? provides the following range of investments required to open your initial franchise. The range assumes that all items are paid for in cash. To the extent that you choose to finance any of these expense items, your front-end investment could be substantially reduced.

Item	Established Low Range	Established High Range
Initial Franchise Fee	$30,000	$30,000
Initial Marketing Fee	$12,000	$12,000
Computer Hardware and Software	$1,500	$3,000
Miscellaneous Opening Costs	$5,000	$10,000

Equipment (Vehicle Lease with Dump Box)	$0	$10,000
Real Estate/Rent	$1,200	$1,200
Local Marketing (3 Months)	$3,600	$3,600
Insurance	$800	$800
Additional Funds (6 months)	$56,200	$70,000
Training Expenses	$1,500	$3,000
Total Initial Investment	$111,800	$143,600

Ongoing Expenses

1-800-GOT-JUNK? franchisees pay semi-monthly royalty fees equal to 8% of gross revenues, sales center fees equal to 7% of gross revenues, and marketing fund fees equal to 1% of gross revenues. Additional fees include branding cooperative fees and training fees.

What You Get: Training and Support

1-800-GOT-JUNK? provides an extensive training program which covers all aspects of the business operating system, consisting of both in-class and in-field training. The initial training session generally includes 4 days of classroom instruction and 1 day of field training. All training takes place at the company's main offices in Vancouver, British Columbia, or at franchised businesses in the Vancouver area. Topics covered during the training session include: company culture, brand and marketing philosophy, onsite sales systems, schedule management, and truck loading and dumping. 1-800-GOT-JUNK? will continue to provide ongoing general advice, assistance, and field support as needed, as well as administer and maintain the marketing fund.

Territory

1-800-GOT-JUNK? does not grant exclusive territories.

Aire Serv Heating & Air Conditioning

1020 N. University Parks Dr.
Waco, TX 76707
Tel: (800) 583-2662, (254) 745-2404
Email: bruce.knudson@dwyergroup.com
Website: www.aireserv.com
Bruce Knudson, Director of Franchise Development

Established in 1992, Aire Serv is a global franchise organization providing installation, maintenance and repair of heating, ventilation, air conditioning and indoor air quality systems. Recognized by Entrepreneur magazine among its "Franchise 500," Aire Serv franchisees provide these services to both residential and commercial customers at more than 100 locations worldwide. Aire Serv is part of The Dwyer Group family of companies, which also includes Rainbow International, Mr. Rooter, Mr. Electric, Mr. Appliance, The Grounds Guys, and Glass Doctor.

BACKGROUND:

	IFA Member
Established: 1992;	First Franchised: 1992
Franchised Units:	179
Company-Owned Units:	0
Total Units:	179
Dist.:	US-161; CAN-11; O'seas-7
North America:	31 States, 2 Provinces
Density:	16 in CA, 15 in TX, 8 in FL

Projected New Units (12 Months):	59
Qualifications:	4, 3, 5, 3, 3, 5

FINANCIAL/TERMS:

Cash Investment:	$75K+
Total Investment:	$64.3 – 183.9K
Minimum Net Worth:	$200K
Fees: Franchise -	$30K/100K pop.
Royalty - 5-7%;	Ad. - 2%
Financial Performance Representation:	Yes
Term of Contract (Years):	10/5
Avg. # of Employees:	Varies
Passive Ownership:	Not Allowed
Encourage Conversions:	Yes
Area Develop. Agreements:	No
Sub-Franchising Contracts:	No
Expand in Territory:	Yes
Space Needs:	N/A

SUPPORT & TRAINING:

Financial Assistance Provided:	Yes (D)
Site Selection Assistance:	N/A
Lease Negotiation Assistance:	N/A
Co-operative Advertising:	Yes
Franchisee Assoc./Member:	Yes/Yes
Size of Corporate Staff:	20
Ongoing Support:	A,B,C,D,E,F,G,H,I
Training:	2 Days Classroom Corporate Office; 11 Days + Ongoing On-site

SPECIFIC EXPANSION PLANS:

US:	All United States
Canada:	No
Overseas:	No

Aire Serv Heating and Air Conditioning has more than 170 HVAC franchise locations in the United States and Canada ready to provide heating and air conditioning repair services. These services range from maximizing heating and air conditioning equipment with service and repair, to indoor air quality products that keep rooms comfortable year round. With Aire Serv's proprietary franchise management systems, our franchisees can learn how to find new customers, gain market share over local competition, and operate a profitable and sustainable HVAC repair franchise. Aire Serv's portfolio of services includes services for residential air conditioning repair and installation, heating repair installation, and air quality and duct cleaning. Each of our Aire Serv franchisees are unique and they decide on which of the areas they would like to concentrate.

Operating Units	12/31/2011	12/31/2012	12/31/2013
Franchised	157	145	152
% Change	--	-7.64%	4.83%
Company-Owned	0	0	0
% Change	--	--	--
Total	157	145	152
% Change	--	-7.46%	4.83%
Franchised as % of Total	100%	100%	100%

Investment Required

The initial fee to purchase an Aire Serv franchise is $30,000 plus $300 per 1,000 population for additional territory. Aire Serv provides the following range of investments required to open your initial franchise. The range assumes that all items are paid for in cash. To the extent that you choose to finance any of these expense items, your front-end investment could be substantially reduced.

Item	Established Low Range	Established High Range
Initial Franchise Fee	$30,000	$30,000 + $300 per add'l 1,000 pop.
Vehicle	$2,500	$25,000
Equipment, Supplies, & Inventory	$5,100	$25,000
Insurance	$3,000	$6,000
Advertising & Promotional	$15,000	$50,000

Expenses while Training	$4,000	$8,000
Deposits, Permits, & Licenses	$0	$1,400
Professional Fees	$0	$5,000
Real Estate	$3,000	$6,000
Additional Funds (3 months)	$15,000	$45,000
Local Marketing Spending for Marketing Start-up Phase	$7,500	$15,000
Total Initial Investment	$85,100	$216,400 + add'l franchise fee

Ongoing Expenses

Franchisees are required to pay ongoing license fees ranging from 5% to 7% of gross sales, a MAP fee equal to 2% of gross sales, and various advertising and marketing spending.

What You Get: Training and Support

Franchisees will be enrolled in an initial training program that includes a webinar-based two-day Phase I training, as well as a 10-day Phase II training program that consists of both business and systems training which will take place at company headquarters in Waco, TX or another location. Additionally, franchisees will be required to complete one to five days of field training at a franchised business. Aire Serv will continue to offer advice and assistance regarding the day-to-day operations of the franchise, as well as refresher training courses when deemed necessary.

Territory

Aire Serv does not grant exclusive territories.

Always Best Care Senior Services

1406 Blue Oaks Rd.
Roseville, CA 95747
Tel: (855) 430-2273, (916) 596-1822
Fax: (916) 722-8780
Email: jbrown@abc-seniors.com
Website: www.franchisewithalwaysbestcare.com
Jake Brown, Chief Operating Officer

Always Best Care Senior Services offers three distinct revenue streams: Assisted living finder and referral assistance, non-medical in-home care, and skilled home health care. We have been in business since 1996, and have contracts with companies representing more than 2,000 assisted living communities. We provide the following: 63 hours of classroom training plus on-the-job training, national contracts, 24/7 call center so franchisees never miss a lead, award-winning national advertising support, and a virtual office (all-in-one web-based software system).

BACKGROUND:

	IFA Member
Established: 1996;	First Franchised: 2007
Franchised Units:	185
Company-Owned Units:	0
Total Units:	185
Dist.:	US-185; CAN-0; O'seas-0
North America:	30 States
Density:	44 in CA, 26 in NJ, 18 in NC

Projected New Units (12 Months):	50
Qualifications:	5, 5, 3, 2, 3, 4

FINANCIAL/TERMS:

Cash Investment:	$60.2 – 109.4K
Total Investment:	$60.2 – 109.4K
Minimum Net Worth:	$200K
Fees: Franchise -	$44.9K
Royalty - 6%;	Ad. - 2%
Financial Performance Representation:	Yes
Term of Contract (Years):	10/5
Avg. # of Employees:	3 FT, 0 PT
Passive Ownership:	Allowed
Encourage Conversions:	Yes
Area Develop. Agreements:	Yes
Sub-Franchising Contracts:	No
Expand in Territory:	Yes
Space Needs:	N/A

SUPPORT & TRAINING:

Financial Assistance Provided:	Yes (I)
Site Selection Assistance:	N/A
Lease Negotiation Assistance:	N/A
Co-operative Advertising:	Yes
Franchisee Assoc./Member:	Yes/Yes
Size of Corporate Staff:	17
Ongoing Support:	C,D,G,H,I
Training:	One-on-one with sales trainer takes about 90 days pre and post training modules; 7 days corporate office; 2 weeks at franchise location

SPECIFIC EXPANSION PLANS:

US:	All United States
Canada:	Yes
Overseas:	Germany, UK, Australia

Always Best Care combines national strength, standards, and stability with local accessibility and personal service. We provide warm, compassionate and professional care for seniors and others when they need it most. We're local experts in senior care, providing a resource for aging and senior living delivered through locally owned and operated offices. Since 1996, Always Best Care has helped families with non-medical in-home care and assisted living placement services. Now, we're adding skilled home health care in select markets, too. Always Best Care offers two types of franchises: the traditional operation of a non-medical in-home personal care, nursing services, and assisted living services, or as an Area Representative franchise who recruits Always Best Care franchisees and provides training and support to these franchisees. Between in-home care, assisted living placement, and skilled home health care, franchisees tap into three sectors of the healthcare industry that serve seniors in the community by providing trusted care, compassionate support and professional advice, and all have the same basic sources of business.

Operating Units	12/31/2011	12/31/2012	12/31/2013
Franchised	165	171	169
% Change	--	3.64%	-1.17%
Company-Owned	0	0	0
% Change	--	--	--
Total	165	171	169
% Change	--	3.64%	-1.17%
Franchised as % of Total	100%	100%	100%

Investment Required

The fee for an Always Best Care franchise is $44,900. The fee for an Area Representative Franchise ranges from $200,000 to $1,200,000 (with a minimum of 2,500,000 people per territory). Always Best Care provides the following range of investments required to open your initial franchise. The range assumes that all items are paid for in cash. To the extent that you choose to finance any of these expense items, your front-end investment could be substantially reduced.

Item	Established Low Range	Established High Range
Initial Franchise Fee	$44,900	$44,900
Expenses While Training	$1,000	$3,000
Rent (3 Months)	$0	$3,000

Furniture & Fixtures	$0	$1,500
Signage	$0	$500
Office Equipment	$1,000	$7,000
Insurance Premium (1 Year)	$3,000	$6,500
Micellaneous Opening Costs	$200	$1,000
Grand Opening Inventory	$0	$500
Advertising	$1,500	$1,500
Computer Equipment, Software and Printer	$1,000	$5,000
Permits/Licenses	$125	$18,000
Professional Fees	$2,500	$5,000
Additional Funds (3 months)	$5,000	$12,000
Total Initial Investment (Traditional Franchise)	$60,225	$109,400

Ongoing Expenses

Always Best Care franchisees pay ongoing royalty fees equal to 6% of gross monthly sales plus a franchisee advertising fund contribution equal to the greater of 2% of gross monthly sales or $300. Additional expenses include local advertising expenditures and training for additional and new employees.

What You Get: Training and Support

Always Best Care's training program includes 3 weeks of online pre-training, 1 1/2 weeks of classroom training, and 1 1/2 weeks of onsite activities which includes 3 days of physical field training provided by an Area Representative or corporate field trainer. From day-to-day operations to sales and marketing, Always Best Care's comprehensive training program equips a franchisee from any professional background to run a successful Always Best Care franchise. In addition, there is an experienced Area Representative assigned to each franchisee to provide local support.

Territory

Always Best Care grants exclusive territories under Area Representative and Developer agreements.

Anago Cleaning Systems

CLEANING SYSTEMS

5203 NW 33rd Ave.
Fort Lauderdale, FL 33309
Tel: (800) 213-5857, (954) 752-3111
Fax: (954) 752-1200
Email: judy@anagocleaning.com
Website: www.anagocleaning.com
Judy Walker, Vice President Marketing

Anago is a franchised commercial cleaning company, with both Master and Unit Franchises available across the U.S. and internationally. The Master has the exclusive developmental rights to sell Unit Franchises in a defined territory, and simultaneously sells cleaning contracts, business to business within the territory, and assigns them to those who purchased a Unit Franchise. This is a huge industry, estimated at over $100 billion annually, with projected double-digit growth.

BACKGROUND:

	IFA Member
Established: 1989;	First Franchised: 1991
Franchised Units:	2,456
Company-Owned Units:	0
Total Units:	2,456
Dist.:	US-2,438; CAN-4; O'seas-5
North America:	15 States, 1 Province
Density:	N/A

Projected New Units (12 Months):	200
Qualifications:	3, 3, 3, 2, 2, 2

FINANCIAL/TERMS:

Cash Investment:	$1 – 24K
Total Investment:	$7 – 33K
Minimum Net Worth:	$1 – 24K
Fees: Franchise -	$49K
Royalty - 10%;	Ad. - Varies
Financial Performance Representation:	No
Term of Contract (Years):	10/10
Avg. # of Employees:	1-2 FT, Varies PT
Passive Ownership:	Not Allowed
Encourage Conversions:	N/A
Area Develop. Agreements:	No
Sub-Franchising Contracts:	No
Expand in Territory:	Yes
Space Needs:	N/A

SUPPORT & TRAINING:

Financial Assistance Provided:	Yes (D)
Site Selection Assistance:	N/A
Lease Negotiation Assistance:	N/A
Co-operative Advertising:	Yes
Franchisee Assoc./Member:	No
Size of Corporate Staff:	25
Ongoing Support:	A,C,D,G,H,I
Training:	56-66 Hours Unit Franchise - Master Office

SPECIFIC EXPANSION PLANS:

US:	All United States
Canada:	All Canada
Overseas:	All Countries

In 1974 in Detroit, Michigan, four brothers began a small cleaning business that built its name on attention to detail and well-organized, focused work teams, and evolved into one of the fastest growing franchise organizations in America. Anago, from the Greek-Latin word meaning to guide or uplift, is a franchised commercial cleaning company, with both Master and Unit Franchises available across the U.S. and internationally. The Master has the exclusive developmental rights to sell Unit Franchises in a defined territory, and simultaneously sells cleaning contracts, business to business within the territory, and assigns them to those who purchased a Unit Franchise. This is a huge industry, estimated at over $100 billion annually, with projected double-digit growth.

Operating Units	12/31/2011	12/31/2012	12/31/2013
Franchised	2,239	2,427	2,438
% Change	--	8.40%	0.45%
Company-Owned	0	0	0
% Change	--	--	--
Total	2,239	2,427	2,438
% Change	--	8.40%	0.45%
Franchised as % of Total	100%	100%	100%

Investment Required

The initial fee to purchase an Anago Cleaning Systems unit franchise ranges from $4,590 to over $32,348.32. Anago provides the following range of investments required to purchase your initial franchise. The range assumes that all items are paid for in cash. To the extent that you choose to finance any of these expense items, your front-end investment could be substantially reduced.

Item	Established Low Range	Established High Range
Initial Fee	$4,590	$32,348.32
Major Equipment	$1,270	$2,610

Vehicle	$0	$20,000
Cleaning Supplies	$0	$105.43
Minor Equipment	$0	$571.43
Insurance*	$3,158	$3,158
Fictitious Name Registration, Incorporation, Legal Review	$500	$1,200
Expenses While Training	$0	$200
Miscellaneous Start-up Costs	$0	$500
Additional Funds (3 months)	$1,000	$5,000
Total Initial Investment	$10,518	$65,693.57

*or 8% of monthly gross revenues

Ongoing Expenses

Unit franchisees are required to pay ongoing royalty fees equal to 10% of gross revenues, an administration fee equal to 3% of gross revenues, and advertising contributions to the marketing fund of 2% of gross revenues, among others.

What You Get: Training and Support

Unit franchisees will participate in an initial orientation program that consists of seven classroom sessions (six hours each) and three on-site sessions (up to eight hours) to take place at an existing account building. Topics to be covered include general office cleaning, restroom cleaning, floor maintenance, and customer relations. Anago will continue to offer ongoing assistance and support in the form of invoicing and accounting services, periodic visits, business development, and continuing education, if needed.

Territory

Anago Cleaning Systems does not grant exclusive territories for unit franchisees.

Anytime Fitness

12181 Margo Ave. S.
Hastings, MN 55033
Tel: (800) 704-5004 (651) 438-5000
Fax: (651) 438-5099
Email: cathyw@anytimefitness.com
Website: www.anytimefitness.com
Cathy Wandmacher, Franchise Sales

Anytime Fitness is the #1 co-ed fitness club chain in the world. We've boiled our business model down to the core essentials which members expect. Our loyal family of preferred vendors supply our franchisees with quality products at the best available prices. Financial and real estate support available. More than half of our franchisees own multiple clubs. Enjoy the freedom of spending time with your friends and family - and the knowledge that you're making your community a better place to live.

BACKGROUND: IFA Member
Established: 2002;   First Franchised: 2002
Franchised Units: 2,015
Company-Owned Units: 25
Total Units: 2,040
Dist.:   US-1,682; CAN-59; O'seas-274
North America: 49 States, 4 Provinces
 Density: 112 in LA, 119 in MN, 156 in TX
Projected New Units (12 Months):   400
Qualifications: 3, 2, 2, 2, 3, 4

FINANCIAL/TERMS:
Cash Investment: $80K
Total Investment: $78.6 – 345.5K
Minimum Net Worth: $250K
Fees: Franchise - $29.9K
 Royalty - $499/mo;   Ad. - $300/mo
Financial Performance Representation: Yes
Term of Contract (Years):   5/5
Avg. # of Employees: 1 FT, 2 PT
Passive Ownership: Discouraged
Encourage Conversions: Yes
Area Develop. Agreements: Yes
Sub-Franchising Contracts: Yes
Expand in Territory: Yes
Space Needs: 4,000 SF

SUPPORT & TRAINING:
Financial Assistance Provided: Yes (D)
Site Selection Assistance: Yes
Lease Negotiation Assistance: Yes
Co-operative Advertising: Yes
Franchisee Assoc./Member: Yes/Yes
Size of Corporate Staff: 162
Ongoing Support: A,B,C,D,E,F,G,H,I
Training: 1 week Hastings, MN

SPECIFIC EXPANSION PLANS:
US: All States
Canada: All Provinces
Overseas: Mexico, Aus., NZ, England, Scotland,
     Grand Cayman, Poland, Netherlands, Spain,
                  Qatar, Japan, India

Anytime Fitness, the #1 co-ed fitness chain club in the world, is a great investment for any franchisee. Their motto is helping real people overcome the barriers to healthier lives. Anytime Fitness has been franchising since 2002 and has continued growing and expanding their brand undeterred by the recession. Hailed by franchising accolades, Anytime Fitness is a low-investment, high return franchise for all.

Operating Units	12/31/2011	12/31/2012	12/31/2013
Franchised	1,538	1,684	1,805

% Change	--	9.49%	7.19%
Company-Owned	14	23	29
% Change	--	64.29%	26.09%
Total	1,552	1,707	1,834
% Change	--	9.99%	7.44%
Franchised as % of Total	99.10%	98.56%	98.42%

Investment Required

The initial fee for an Anytime Fitness franchise is $32,500 for a standard center and $18,000 for an express center. Anytime Fitness provides the following range of investments required for your initial franchise. The range assumes that all items are paid for in cash. To the extent that you choose to finance any of these expense items, your front-end investment could be substantially reduced. Please note that the figures below represent expenses for a standard fitness center.

Item	Established Low Range	Established High Range
Initial Franchise Fee	$18,000	$32,500
Expenses While Training	$1,000	$2,300
Real Estate and Improvements	$14,650	$246,000
Fitness Equipment	$10,350	$16,650
Tanning Equipment	$0	$1,700
Fitness on Request	$0	$1,425
Operating System	$3,500	$14,800
First Aid Equipment	$1,000	$1,600
Interior Signs	$1,200	$1,200
Outside Signs	$400	$1,000
Misc. Opening Costs	$1,900	$2,700
Grand Opening Advertising	$4,000	$6,000
Insurance	$2,500	$2,700

Supplies and Furniture	$1,000	$6,500
Legal and Accounting Expenses	$500	$4,500
Additional Funds (3 months)	$18,700	$29,600
Total Initial Investment	$78,700	$371,175

Ongoing Expenses

Anytime Fitness has a monthly royalty fee of $549. There is also a general advertising fee of $300 per month as well as a voluntary monthly charitable contribution of $100.

What You Get: Training and Support

Anytime Fitness provides a training program during which they will instruct franchisees on Anytime Health, Corporate Sales, General Marketing, Personal Training, Software Security, and more. There is roughly 34 hours of classroom training at the Anytime Fitness offices in Minnesota. Franchisees will also receive ongoing support by phone and electronically as needed.

Territory

Anytime Fitness grants protected territories.

Archadeck

archadeck®

outdoor living

2924 Emerywood Parkway, # 101
Richmond, VA 23294

Tel: (800) 722-4668, (804) 353-6999 x102
Fax: (804) 358-1878
Email: spucel@outdoorlivingbrands.com
Website: www.archadeck.com
Shemar Pucel, Franchise Recruiting Consultant

ARCHADECK, founded in 1980, started the nation's first network specializing in custom-designed and built decks, porches, and other outdoor products.

Because construction experience is not required, our franchisees come from a variety of professional backgrounds.	

BACKGROUND:
Established: 1980; First Franchised: 1984
Franchised Units: 56
Company-Owned Units: 0
Total Units: 56
Dist.: US-55; CAN-1; O'seas-0
North America: 20 States
Density: 6 in NC, 5 in TX
Projected New Units (12 Months): 25
Qualifications: 5, 5, 1, 3, 4, 5

FINANCIAL/TERMS:
Cash Investment: $80 – 100K
Total Investment: $80 – 100K
Minimum Net Worth: $250K
Fees: Franchise - $49.5K
Royalty - 2.5-5.5; Ad. - 1%
Financial Performance Representation: Yes
Term of Contract (Years): 8/8

Avg. # of Employees: 1 FT, 1 PT
Passive Ownership: Not Allowed
Encourage Conversions: Yes
Area Develop. Agreements: Yes
Sub-Franchising Contracts: No
Expand in Territory: Yes
Space Needs: N/A

SUPPORT & TRAINING:
Financial Assistance Provided: Yes (D)
Site Selection Assistance: N/A
Lease Negotiation Assistance: N/A
Co-operative Advertising: No
Franchisee Assoc./Member: Yes/Yes
Size of Corporate Staff: 35
Ongoing Support: C,D,G,H,I
Training: 9 Days On-Site; 20 Business Days Richmond, VA

SPECIFIC EXPANSION PLANS:
US: All United States
Canada: All Canada
Overseas: Europe

Archadeck is part of the Outdoor Living Brands family of franchise brands, a corporation dedicated to the outdoor living category. Our mission at Archadeck is to celebrate outdoor living by enriching lives through our proven franchise brand. For our valued clients, we do this by designing and delivering beautiful, functional, and innovative outdoor living environments that meet their lifestyle needs. You'll soon discover that your growth potential with Archadeck can be as vast as the great outdoors itself. Since our inception, we have designed and built outdoor living projects for well over 100,000 clients across North America. Our business model is focused on much more than just decks! In fact, screened porches, sunrooms, three-season rooms, patios, hardscapes, outdoor kitchens, shade structures, pergolas, gazebos and other categories of outdoor living structures are all important parts of our business mix.

Operating Units	12/31/2011	12/31/2012	12/31/2013
Franchised	57	54	55
% Change	--	-5.26%	1.85%

Company-Owned	0	0	0
% Change	--	--	--
Total	57	54	55
% Change	--	-5.26%	1.85%
Franchised as % of Total	100%	100%	100%

Investment Required

The initial fee to purchase an Archadeck franchise depends on the number of qualified households in your territory: $24,500 for a micro market territory (less than 30,000 qualified households) or $49,500 for a standard territory (between 30,000 and 40,000 qualified households). Archadeck provides the following range of investments required to purchase your initial franchise. The range assumes that all items are paid for in cash. To the extent that you choose to finance any of these expense items, your front-end investment could be substantially reduced. Please note that the figures below represent expense for a standard territory.

Item	Established Low Range	Established High Range
Initial Franchise Fee	$4,950	$49,500
Guarantee Fund Initial Payment	$3,000	$3,000
Tools and Equipment	$1,000	$2,500
Expenses While Training	$2,500	$4,500
Computer Hardware and Software	$3,900	$4,800
Start-Up Advertising for First 3 months	$7,500	$15,000
Start-Up Expenses and Working Capital (3 months)	$6,550	$12,250
Total Initial Investment	$29,400	$91,550

Ongoing Expenses

Franchisees are required to pay ongoing royalty fees ranging from 2.5% to 5.5% of gross receipts for a standard territory, or $700 per month for the first year, $900 per month for the second year, and $1,100 per month thereafter for a micro market territory. Other fees include a marketing royalty equal to 1% of gross receipts and local marketing fees of at least $25,000 a year for standard territory or $15,000 for a micro market territory.

Franchisee Satisfaction

A critical component of the due diligence process is that you, as a prospective franchisee, have a strong sense of existing franchisee satisfaction. Please review the franchisor's ratings below for this extremely important information.

How do you rate Archadeck in terms of:	Rating*
Overall Communication Between Home Office Personnel and Franchisees	95%
Franchisor understands that if I am successful, they will be successful	95%
Franchisor encourages high standards of quality performance throughout the organization	95%

* Independent Audit of Existing Franchisees Who Rated Archadeck as Excellent, Very Good, or Good

What You Get: Training and Support

Franchisees will participate in an initial training program of up to 15 days to take place at company headquarters in Richmond, VA or another specified location. Topics to be covered include product knowladge/design, sales techniques, marketing, and software. Archadeck may also provide up to 5 days of additional on-site assistance during the first year of operation. Franchisees will continue to receive advice and guidance regarding the daily operations of the franchise, as well as marketing assistance.

Territory

Archadeck grants protected territories.

Bricks 4 Kidz

701 Market St., # 113
St. Agustine, FL 32095
Tel: (904) 825-0873
Email: bpappas@bricks4kidz.com
Website: www.bricks4kidz.com
Brian Pappas, Managing Director

Bricks 4 Kidz classes provide an extraordinary atmosphere for children to learn, build, and play with LEGO® bricks. Programs are built around proprietary model plans, designed by engineers and architects, with exciting themes such as space, construction, and amusement parks. Specially designed project kits and theme-based models provide the building blocks for the Bricks 4 Kidz approach to educational play.

BACKGROUND:

Established: 2009;	First Franchised: 2009
Franchised Units:	428
Company-Owned Units:	1
Total Units:	429
Dist.:	US360; CAN-37; O'seas-31
North America:	41 States, 8 Provinces
Density:	37 in CA,33 in FL, 32 in TX

Projected New Units (12 Months):	N/A
Qualifications:	N/A

FINANCIAL/TERMS:

Cash Investment:	N/A
Total Investment:	$33.8 – 51.1K
Minimum Net Worth:	N/A
Fees: Franchise -	$25.9K
Royalty - 7%;	Ad. - 2%
Financial Performance Representation:	No
Term of Contract (Years):	N/A
Avg. # of Employees:	N/A
Passive Ownership:	Allowed
Encourage Conversions:	Yes
Area Develop. Agreements:	No
Sub-Franchising Contracts:	No
Expand in Territory:	No
Space Needs:	N/A

SUPPORT & TRAINING:

Financial Assistance Provided:	Yes (D)
Site Selection Assistance:	Yes
Lease Negotiation Assistance:	Yes
Co-operative Advertising:	No
Franchisee Assoc./Member:	Yes/Yes
Size of Corporate Staff:	N/A
Ongoing Support:	A,B,C,D,E,F,G,H,I
Training:	N/A

SPECIFIC EXPANSION PLANS:

US:	No
Canada:	No
Overseas:	No

Bricks 4 Kidz classes provide an extraordinary atmosphere for children, where we learn, we build, we play... with LEGO® bricks. Programs are built around our proprietary model plans, designed by engineers and architects, with exciting themes such as space, construction, and amusement parks. Our specially designed project kits and theme-based models provide the building blocks for the Bricks 4 Kidz approach to educational play. At Bricks 4 Kidz, we believe that kids learn best through activities that engage their curiosity and creativity. Today BRICKS 4 KIDZ® has over 100 franchises throughout the world, making it one of the fastest growing franchises in the US and Canada (and possibly the world).

Operating Units	12/31/2011	12/31/2012	12/31/2013
Franchised	99	228	428
% Change	--	130.3%	87.72%
Company-Owned	1	1	1
% Change	--	0.0%	0.0%
Total	100	229	429
% Change	--	129.0%	87.34%
Franchised as % of Total	99.0%	99.56%	99.77%

Investment Required

The fee to purchase a Bricks 4 Kidz franchise is $25,900. Bricks 4 Kidz provides the following range of investments required to open your initial franchise. The range assumes that all items are paid for in cash. To the extent that you choose to finance any of these expense items, your front-end investment could be substantially reduced.

Item	Established Low Range	Established High Range
Franchise Fee	$25,900	$25,900
Equipment	$1,000	$2,000
Product/Supplies	$200	$1,000

Insurance Premium	$200	$2,000
Office and Printing Supplies	$200	$200
Professional Fees	$500	$2,000
Training Expenses	$500	$2,000
Marketing Materials	$0	$500
Business License	$50	$200
Additional Funds (3 months)	$4,000	$10,000
Initial Marketing Plan	$1,000	$5,000
Franchise Management Tool (FMT)	$250	$250
Total Initial Investment	$33,800	$51,050

Ongoing Expenses

Franchisees are required to pay ongoing royalty fees equal to 7% of gross weekly receipts, with a minimum of $1,500 every 12 accounting periods. Other fees include a franchise management tool (FMT) of $75 per month and marketing fees equal to 2% of gross weekly receipts.

What You Get: Training and Support

Franchisees will be enrolled in a four-day initial training program at corporate headquarters in St. Augustine, FL, that will cover sales, marketing, business management, and systems and procedures for operating the business. Bricks 4 Kidz will also provide one day on on-site assistance at no additional cost. Franchisees will continue to receive advice and assistance regarding the operation of the business, as well as periodic inspections and additional training when needed.

Territory

Bricks 4 Kidz grants protected territories with a population of at least 50,000 people, encompassing 15 elementary and 3 middle schools.

BrightStar Care

HOME CARE | MEDICAL STAFFING

1125 Tri-State Pkwy., # 700
Gurnee, IL 60031
Tel: (877) 689-6898, (847) 693-2033
Fax: (866) 360-0393
Email: franchise@brightstarcare.com
Website: www.brightstarfranchise.com
Son Kim, Franchise Director

Are you ready to build a business you can feel great about? At BrightStar, we are in the business of providing the full continuum of homecare, childcare, staffing and support services for individuals, families and healthcare facilities. We help keep parents and grandparents out of nursing facilities and in the comfort of their own homes, as well as assisting parents with their childcare needs. BrightStar also provides healthcare staffing solutions to businesses. We have received several awards recognizing our rapid growth, advanced systems technology and senior leadership.

BACKGROUND: IFA Member
Established: 2002;   First Franchised: 2005
Franchised Units: 282
Company-Owned Units: 2
Total Units: 284
Dist.:   US-282; CAN-0; O'seas-0
    North America: 38 States

Density:	26 in FL, 24 in TX, 31 in CA
Projected New Units (12 Months):	60
Qualifications:	4, 4, 2, 4, 4, 5

FINANCIAL/TERMS:

Cash Investment:	$100K
Total Investment:	$93 – 172K
Minimum Net Worth:	$500K
Fees: Franchise -	$48K
Royalty - 5%;	Ad. - 2%, capped ar 3%
Financial Performance Representation:	Yes
Term of Contract (Years):	10/10
Avg. # of Employees:	3 FT, 2 PT
Passive Ownership:	Not Allowed
Encourage Conversions:	Yes
Area Develop. Agreements:	No
Sub-Franchising Contracts:	No
Expand in Territory:	No
Space Needs:	400-800 SF

SUPPORT & TRAINING:

Financial Assistance Provided:	Yes (I)
Site Selection Assistance:	Yes
Lease Negotiation Assistance:	Yes
Co-operative Advertising:	Yes
Franchisee Assoc./Member:	Yes/Yes
Size of Corporate Staff:	70
Ongoing Support:	a,C,D,E,G,h,I
Training:	5 days Gurnee, IL; 5 days Gurnee, IL

SPECIFIC EXPANSION PLANS:

US:	All United States
Canada:	BC, AB, SK, MB
Overseas:	UK, Australia

With national healthcare needs on the rise, BrightStar provides extensive LifeCare, KidCare, and Staffing services. BrightStar is one of the few companies that serves multiple market segments, including care for adults and seniors in their homes, well and sick childcare, and a full range of medical staffing assistance. This broad range of services enables franchisees to draw from a large, established, and rapidly growing customer base. In addition to offering the full range of medical and non-medical home healthcare, BrightStar also provides medical staffing solutions to businesses and private patients, providing personnel to hospitals, nursing homes, doctors' offices, labs, and patients' own homes.

Operating Units	12/31/2011	12/31/2012	12/31/2013
Franchised	237	248	255
% Change	--	4.64%	2.82%
Company-Owned	1	2	3
% Change	--	100%	50.0%
Total	238	250	258
% Change	--	5.04%	3.2%
Franchised as % of Total	99.58%	99.2%	98.84%

Investment Required

The fee for a BrightStar Care franchise is $48,000 for the first 200,000 to 250,000 in population in your territory, plus $400 for each additional 1,000 individuals in your territory above 250,000. BrightStar Care provides the following range of investments required to open your initial franchise. The range assumes that all items are paid for in cash. To the extent that you choose to finance any of these expense items, your front-end investment could be substantially reduced.

Item	Established Low Range	Established High Range
Initial Franchise Fee	$48,000	$48,000
Leased Space for Agency	$3,200	$7,200
Furnishings	$1,500	$3,000
Computer Infrastructure Package	$3,500	$5,500
Signage	$300	$1,000
Utility Deposits	$100	$500
Marketing Materials	$1,800	$2,600

Business Licenses & Home Health Agency License	$200	$7,400
Joint Commission Accreditation Application Fee & Membership	$0	$4,250
Consultants and/or Director of Nursing (Hired as Needed)	$0	$9,000
CPA to Certify Licensure Submission	$0	$1,000
Insurance	$3,422	$3,820
Workers Comp Insurance	$1,558	$8,761
CSA Training & Certification	$0	$1,595
Various Dues and Memberships	$0	$1,000
Loan Packaging Fee	$0	$2,500
Expenses While Training	$3,360	$4,260
Legal Fees	$1,000	$5,000
Additional Fund (3 Months)	$25,337	$53,135
Total Initial Investment	$93,277	$172,521

Ongoing Expenses

BrightStar Care franchisees pay royalty fees equal to 5% of net billings for non-national accounts and 6% of net billings for national accounts. Additional fees payable by the franchisee include general advertising and marketing fees.

Franchisee Satisfaction

A critical component of the due diligence process is that you, as a prospective franchisee, have a strong sense of existing franchisee satisfaction. Please review the franchisor's ratings below for this extremely important information.

How do you rate BrightStar Care in terms of:	Rating*
Encourages High Standards of Quality Performance Throughout the Organization	95%
Overall Communication between Home Office Personnel and Franchisees	93%
Overall Quality of the Franchisor	94%

* Independent Audit of Existing Franchisees Who Rated BrightStar Care as Excellent, Very Good, or Good

What You Get: Training and Support

Training with BrightStar Care begins with 5 days of pre-opening training at company headquarters, followed by a five-day training boot-camp that covers every aspect of the business from how to find clients, how to answer the phones, talk to potential staff, and the Athena Business System. In addition to this training session, BrightStar Care has implemented a business learning management system and online training center in 2010 to deliver online learning to all franchisees and their teams to facilitate continuous learning and improvement. Franchisees have access to a centralized Support Center as well as a BrightStart Coach initially and a Regional Director of Field Support thereafter for support, information, and answers to any questions.

Territory

BrightStar Care grants protected territories.

Brightway Insurance

3733 W. University Blvd.
Jacksonville, FL 32217
Tel: (888) 254-5014, (904) 764-9554
Fax: (904) 482-0739
Email: matt.flagler@brightway.com
Website: www.brightway.com
Matt Flagler, Director of Franchise Development

Brightway Insurance is a Property & Casualty Insurance franchise that offers the look and feel of a direct writer agency with the selection, service and pricing options of a leading independent agency. Our business model enables our offices to consistently produce a substantially higher volume of new business than a traditional captive or independent agency, as well as achieve higher overall quality and retention. We achieve this by handling all of the policy servicing functions in our centralized customer service center, thus allowing our agencies to focus on new business development.

BACKGROUND:

	IFA Member
Established: 2003;	First Franchised: 2007
Franchised Units:	111
Company-Owned Units:	2
Total Units:	113
Dist.:	US-113; CAN-0; O'seas-0

North America:	7 States
Density:	102 in FL, 4 in GA, 3 in TX
Projected New Units (12 Months):	30
Qualifications:	5, 5, 2, 2, 5, 5

FINANCIAL/TERMS:

Cash Investment:	$150 – 175K
Total Investment:	$150 – 175K
Minimum Net Worth:	$250K
Fees: Franchise -	$60K
Royalty - 15-45%;	Ad. - 0%
Financial Performance Representation:	No
Term of Contract (Years):	5/5
Avg. # of Employees:	3-5 FT, 0 PT
Passive Ownership:	Discouraged
Encourage Conversions:	Yes
Area Develop. Agreements:	No
Sub-Franchising Contracts:	No
Expand in Territory:	Yes
Space Needs:	1,000 SF

SUPPORT & TRAINING:

Financial Assistance Provided:	Yes (I)
Site Selection Assistance:	Yes
Lease Negotiation Assistance:	No
Co-operative Advertising:	No
Franchisee Assoc./Member:	No
Size of Corporate Staff:	130
Ongoing Support:	A,C,D,E,G,H,I
Training:	3 Weeks Jacksonville, FL

SPECIFIC EXPANSION PLANS:

US:	South East
Canada:	No
Overseas:	No

Brightway Insurance understands the value of brand identity in presenting a consistent, high quality experience for our customers. It begins with the look and feel of our offices and communications, and extends much further to the way we do business and treat our customers. The Brightway Insurance brand is that of a forward-thinking, service-oriented company. Using our expertise and technology as tools, we provide brilliant service and the right products, creating the best client experience possible.

Operating Units	12/31/2011	12/31/2012	12/31/2013
Franchised	80	102	108
% Change	--	27.5%	5.88%
Company-Owned	2	2	1
% Change	--	0.0%	-50.0%
Total	82	104	109
% Change	--	26.83%	4.81%
Franchised as % of Total	97.56%	98.08%	99.08%

Investment Required

The initial fee for a Brightway Insurance franchise is $60,000. Brightway provides the following range of investments required to open your initial franchise. The range assumes that all items are paid for in cash. To the extent you choose to finance any of these expense items, your front-end investment could be substantially reduced.

Item	Established Low Range	Established High Range
Franchise Fee	$30,000	$60,000
Lease Deposits	$1,500	$2,500
Real Property Lease	$3,000	$10,800
Leasehold Improvements	$5,000	$10,000
Utility and Internet Service Deposits	$500	$1,000
Furniture, Furnishings, and Fixtures	$3,700	$15,000
Equipment	$3,500	$8,000
Telephone System and Installation	$2,000	$3,000
Signage	$4,000	$7,000
Professional Fees	$2,000	$4,500

Initial Training Expenses	$0	$7,500
Grand Opening Advertising	$0	$3,000
Insurance Policies	$3,000	$4,700
Licensing Fees	$0	$2,000
Additional Funds (6 months)	$42,000	$42,000
Total Initial Investment	$100,200	$181,000

Ongoing Expenses

Franchisees are not required to pay royalties, however Brightway Insurance will retain 15% of sales commissions on new businesses, and 45% of sales commissions on renewal businesses. Advertising fees may also apply.

What You Get: Training and Support

Franchisees will participate in a two-week initial training program at company headquarters in Jacksonville, FL, covering insurance products, sales and marketing, sales processing, management systems, office procedures, and computer software. Additional classroom, web-based, pre-recorded, and side-by-side training may be available when deemed necessary, as well as on-premises pre-opening assistance. Brightway will also continue to provide ongoing assistance regarding sales and marketing, purchasing, and operating procedures.

Territory

Brightway Insurance does not grant exclusive territories.

Caring Transitions

Senior Moving • Downsizing • Estate Sales

10700 Montgomery Rd., # 300
Cincinnati, OH 45242
Tel: (800) 647-0766
Email: bboecker@franchisesupport.net
Website: www.caringtransitions.net
Beth Boecker, Dir. Franchise Sales Administration

Ranked "Top 50 New Franchises" by Entrepreneur, 2013, this is a rewarding, home-based business helping Seniors and their families transition from their homes to retirement communities. You'll work with bank trustees, Realtors, moving companies and other professionals to help ease relocation. Five days of extensive, on-site training on operating and growing a successful business. With six revenue streams and the Senior population expected to double by 2030, this is the next big wave in Senior Care.

BACKGROUND: IFA Member
Established: 2006; First Franchised: 2006
Franchised Units: 166
Company-Owned Units: 0
Total Units: 166
Dist.: US-166; CAN-0; O'seas-0
  North America: 30 States
  Density: 11 in VA, 12 in OH, 12 in IL

Projected New Units (12 Months): 30
Qualifications: 3, 3, 1, 2, 3, 4

FINANCIAL/TERMS:
Cash Investment: $20K
Total Investment: $52.9 – 81.5K
Minimum Net Worth: $20K
Fees: Franchise - $39.9K
  Royalty - 6% or $300; Ad. - $350/month
Financial Performance Representation: No
Term of Contract (Years): 10/10
Avg. # of Employees: 1 FT, 1 PT
Passive Ownership: Discouraged
Encourage Conversions: N/A
Area Develop. Agreements: No
Sub-Franchising Contracts: No
Expand in Territory: No
Space Needs: N/A

SUPPORT & TRAINING:
Financial Assistance Provided: Yes (I)
Site Selection Assistance: N/A
Lease Negotiation Assistance: N/A
Co-operative Advertising: Yes
Franchisee Assoc./Member: No
Size of Corporate Staff: 50
Ongoing Support: C, D, H, I
Training: 5 business days Cincinnati, OH

SPECIFIC EXPANSION PLANS:
US: All United States
Canada: All Canada
Overseas: All Countries

With its comprehensive approach to senior transitions services–senior moving, downsizing, and estate sales–Caring Transitions is a leader in this niche market within the senior care industry. Caring Transitions is devoted to being an advocate for seniors and their families throughout transition periods, making it a trusted provider by families, attorneys, bank trustees, real estate professionals, and funeral directors. Caring Transitions keeps the individual and their family's interests at heart, helping seniors to minimize stress and maximize returns throughout the transition process. With the rapid expansion of the elderly population, more than 100 million individuals and their parents are poised to need relocation and home liquidation services. Caring Transitions dominates this industry, and thus possesses potential for significant growth in the upcoming years. With over 20 years of franchise experience, Caring Transitions offers prospective franchisees a financially and personally rewarding business opportunity.

Operating Units	12/31/2011	12/31/2012	12/31/2013
Franchised	98	98	133
% Change	--	0.0%	35.71%
Company-Owned	0	0	0
% Change	--	--	--
Total	98	98	133
% Change	--	0.0%	35.71%
Franchised as % of Total	100%	100%	100%

Investment Required

The initial fee for a Caring Transitions franchise is $39,900 ($45,900 with financing) for an area with a population of up to 175,000. For territory populations exceeding 175,000, franchisees pay an additional $500 for every 1,000 additional people. Caring Transitions provides the following range of investments required to open your initial franchise. The range assumes that all items are paid for in cash. To the extent that you choose to finance any of these expense items, your front-end investment could be substantially reduced.

Item	Established Low Range	Established High Range
Initial Franchise Fee	$39,900	$45,900
Furniture and Equipment	$500	$1,000
Computer System	$1,000	$3,000
Expenses While Training	$750	$1,500

Initial Deposits (Rent, Telephone, Bank)	$350	$2,000
Additional Funds (6 Months)	$4,000	$18,000
Pre-opening Promotion	$3,000	$4,000
Technology/Software Licensing Fee & Web Hosting Fee	$700	$700
Monthly Office Rental Payment	$200	$1,000
Insurance	$1,000	$3,000
Certified Relocation Transition Specialist Training	$850	$850
Membership & Associations fees	$500	$500
Estatesales.net	$80	$80
Total Initial Investment	$52,850	$81,530

Ongoing Expenses

Caring Transitions franchisees pay a monthly royalty fee equal to the greater of 5% of gross revenues or $300, a monthly national branding fee equal to the greater of 2% of gross revenue or $350. Additional fees include a local cooperative advertising fee of up to 3% of monthly gross revenues, among others.

What You Get: Training and Support

Caring Transitions is committed to ensuring franchising success and provides training and support throughout the franchise relationship. Franchisees complete an extensive initial training program at the Caring Transitions corporate headquarters in Cincinnati, Ohio. Topics covered in the training program include the Caring Transitions business model, services, financial management, database management, administration, marketing, and promotion. Following the opening of a franchised location, Caring Transitions offers ongoing support in the form of telephone and e-mail assistance. Furthermore, Caring Transitions provides additional materials, information, training and assistance as deemed necessary.

Territory

Caring Transitions grants exclusive territories.

CMIT Solutions

500 N. Capital of TX Highway, Bldg. 6, # 200
Austin, TX 78746
Tel: (800) 710-2648, (512) 879-4524
Fax: (512) 692-3711
Email: lmontanio@cmitsolutions.com
Website: www.cmitfranchise.com
Lisa Montanio, Franchise Development Manager

CMIT Solutions offers IT-managed services and computer support to small businesses. Franchise can be home-based, as we service the clients remotely or at their place of business.

BACKGROUND: IFA Member
Established: 1996;   First Franchised: 1998
Franchised Units: 146
Company-Owned Units: 0
Total Units: 146
Dist.:   US-145; CAN-1; O'seas-0
  North America: 32 States, 1 Province
  Density: N/A
Projected New Units (12 Months):   20
Qualifications: 2, 3, 4, 2, 4, 4

FINANCIAL/TERMS:

Cash Investment:	$70 – 100K
Total Investment:	$129.2 – 171.5K
Minimum Net Worth:	$350K
Fees: Franchise -	$49.5K
Royalty - 6-0%;	Ad. - 2%
Financial Performance Representation:	Yes
Term of Contract (Years):	10/10
Avg. # of Employees:	1-2 FT, 1-2 PT
Passive Ownership:	Allowed
Encourage Conversions:	Yes
Area Develop. Agreements:	Yes
Sub-Franchising Contracts:	No
Expand in Territory:	No
Space Needs:	N/A

SUPPORT & TRAINING:

Financial Assistance Provided:	No
Site Selection Assistance:	N/A
Lease Negotiation Assistance:	N/A
Co-operative Advertising:	No
Franchisee Assoc./Member:	No
Size of Corporate Staff:	17
Ongoing Support:	A,B,C,d,G,H,I
Training:	2 Weeks Austin, TX; 2 Weeks JumpStart

SPECIFIC EXPANSION PLANS:

US:	All United States
Canada:	Yes
Overseas:	No

CMIT Solutions started as a small computer support company in Austin, Texas in 1996. Over the past decade and a half, we have grown into a leading provider of managed services and other computer consulting services tailored to the unique needs of small business. We're able to combine personalized local service with all the technical resources of a large national company, offering our small business clients the products, partnerships, and around-the-clock technical support that standalone locals can't always provide. CMIT Solutions offers a broad menu of technical support and IT services that all point toward one goal: helping your small business run smoothly and be prepared for anything. With approximately 145 locally owned and operated locations nationwide, our technical support experts will meet with you to understand your business and your IT needs, so that we can find the solution that's right for you.

Operating Units	2/9/2011	12/31/2012	12/31/2013
Franchised	132	136	139
% Change	--	3.03%	2.21%
Company-Owned	0	0	0
% Change	--	--	--
Total	132	136	139
% Change	--	3.03%	2.21%
Franchised as % of Total	100%	100%	100%

Investment Required

The initial fee for a CMIT Solutions franchise is $49,950. CMIT Solutions provides the following range of investments required to open your initial franchise. The range assumes that all items are paid for in cash. To the extent that you choose to finance any of these expense items, your front-end investment could be substantially reduced.

Item	Established Low Range	Established High Range
Initial Franchise Fee	$49,950	$49,950
Territory Fee	$4,000	$20,000
Business Licenses	$550	$1,500

Travel, Food, and Lodging while Training	$2,200	$2,500
Furniture and Equipment	$0	$2,500
Advertising & Marketing (6 months)	$14,000	$14,000
Technical Staffing (6 months)	$18,000	$30,000
Start-up Supplies	$500	$1,000
Additional Funds (6 Months)	$40,000	$50,000
Total Initial Investment	$129,200	$171,450

Ongoing Expenses

CMIT Solutions franchisees pay a royalty fee on a sliding scale of 6% to 0% of gross professional services revenue or a minimum royalty, whichever is greater. There is also a marketing development fund on a sliding scale of 2% to 0% of the gross professional services revenue, or the minimum marketing development fund contribution, whichever is greater, and additional marketing and advertising fees.

Franchisee Satisfaction

A critical component of the due diligence process is that you, as a prospective franchisee, have a strong sense of existing franchisee satisfaction. Please review the franchisor's ratings below for this extremely important information.

How do you rate CMIT Solutions in terms of:	Rating*
Collaboration Between Fellow Franchisees	99%
Quality of Marketing Collateral Provided by the Franchisor	96%

Service-Based

Overall Communication Between Home Office Personnel and Franchisees	100%

* Independent Audit of Existing Franchisees Who Rated CMIT Solutions as Excellent, Very Good, or Good

What You Get: Training and Support

CMIT Solutions provides a pre-training Jump Start program, followed by a comprehensive two-week initial in-person training program conducted at headquarters in Austin, TX. This training program will cover all aspects of the CMIT Solutions business model, including history, business strategy, operations, lead generation, and sales. Ongoing support includes one-on-one business coaching, an annual national convention, an on-line professional development center, monthly web meetings, a centralized intranet with more than 2,000 business documents and templates, and extensive marketing and business development assistance.

Territory

CMIT Solutions grants exclusive territories that typically contain 2,000 to 2,909 small business establishments.

Color Glo International

Specialists in **COLOR RESTORATION & REPAIR**
7111-7115 Ohms Ln.
Minneapolis, MN 55439
Tel: (800) 333-8523, (952) 835-1338
Fax: (952) 835-1395
Email: scott@colorglo.com
Website: www.colorglo.com

Scott L. Smith, VP Franchise Sales

The leader in the leather and fabric restoration and repair industry. From automotive to marine to aircraft to all-leather furniture, COLOR-GLO leads the way with innovative products and protected application techniques. We serve all US and foreign car manufacturers. We were also recently awarded a Top 100 Franchise by Franchise Gator and a Top 50 Franchise by Franchise Business Review.

BACKGROUND:	IFA Member	Encourage Conversions:	N/A
Established: 1976;	First Franchised: 1984	Area Develop. Agreements:	Yes
Franchised Units:	126	Sub-Franchising Contracts:	Yes
Company-Owned Units:	0	Expand in Territory:	Yes
Total Units:	126	Space Needs:	N/A
Dist.:	US-90; CAN-1; O'seas-32		
North America:	30 States, 1 Province	**SUPPORT & TRAINING:**	
Density:	12 in FL, 8 in WA, 7 in OR	Financial Assistance Provided:	Yes (D)
Projected New Units (12 Months):	12	Site Selection Assistance:	Yes
Qualifications:	4, 4, 3, 4, 3, 3	Lease Negotiation Assistance:	N/A
		Co-operative Advertising:	No
FINANCIAL/TERMS:		Franchisee Assoc./Member:	Yes/Yes
Cash Investment:	$44.9K	Size of Corporate Staff:	15
Total Investment:	$51 – 54.8K	Ongoing Support:	B,C,D,G,H,I
Minimum Net Worth:	$50K	Training:	2 Weeks headquarters, MN;
Fees: Franchise -	$30K		1 Week franchisee's territory
Royalty - 4% or $300 monthly;	Ad. - 0%		
Financial Performance Representation:	Yes	**SPECIFIC EXPANSION PLANS:**	
Term of Contract (Years):	10/10	US:	All United States
Avg. # of Employees:	1 FT, 0 PT	Canada:	All Canada
Passive Ownership:	Discouraged	Overseas:	All Countries

Since its beginning in 1976, Color Glo has become the recognized leader in the mobile automotive reconditioning industry. Color Glo International franchisees restore and repair leather, vinyl, velour, cloth and hard plastics. In the last 35 plus years, the company has grown from an idea to an international operation, and has been recognized repeatedly by national and international publications for the excellent products, value, and quality of services that they offer.

Operating Units	12/31/2011	12/31/2012	12/31/2013
Franchised	123	122	125
% Change	--	-0.81%	2.46%
Company-Owned	0	0	0
% Change	--	--	--
Total	123	122	125
% Change	--	-0.81%	2.46%
Franchised as % of Total	100%	100%	100%

Investment Required

The initial franchise fee for a Color Glo franchise is $30,000. For each 10,000 population exceeding 500,000 you will pay an additional $500. Color Glo provides the following range of investments required to open your initial franchise. The range assumes that all items are paid for in cash. To the extent that you choose to finance any of these expense items, your front-end investment could be substantially reduced.

Item	Established Low Range	Established High Range
Franchise Fee	$30,000	$30,000
Start-Up Fee	$19,500	$19,500
Travel Expenses While Training	$500	$2,500
Equipment and Supplies	$200	$300
Additional Funds	$500	$1,500
Additional Funds (3 months)	$300	$1,000
Total Investment	$51,000	$54,800

Ongoing Expenses

Color Glo franchisees pay a maintenance fee equal to 4% of gross sales or $150.00 per month, whichever is greater, $200.00 for the second full year or $300.00 a month following a full year of business. Other ongoing fees include an annual license fee and product purchases of $2,500 and insurance ($1,500-$3,000).

Franchisee Satisfaction

A critical component of the due diligence process is that you, as a prospective franchisee, have a strong sense of existing franchisee satisfaction. Please review the franchisor's ratings below for this extremely important information.

How do you rate Color Glo International in terms of:	Rating*
Overall Quality of Franchisor	98%
Overall Communication Between Home Office Personnel and Franchisees	100%
Quality of Products and/or Services Received From Franchisor	100%

* Independent Audit of Existing Franchisees Who Rated Color Glo International as Excellent, Very Good, or Good

What You Get: Training and Support

Color Glo offers a comprehensive 3-week training course to take place in Minneapolis, MN, that will cover equipment, repair instruction, sales and marketing, and inventory. Refresher training and additional training is conducted during regional and annual seminars in Minneapolis. Color Glo provides additional training for new products and services introduced at the annual International Seminar. During the operation of the franchise business, Color Glo will provide certain advertising production materials, business inspections, and supplements and modifications to the operating manuals.

Territory

Color Glo grants exclusive territories.

ComForcare Senior Services

2520 Telegraph Rd., # 201
Bloomfield Hills, MI 48302
Tel: (800) 886-4044, (248) 745-9700
Fax: (248) 745-9763
Email: pleblanc@comforcare.com
Website: www.comforcarefranchise.com
Phil LeBlanc, Vice President of Franchise Development

ComForcare Senior Services franchise members provide non-medical home care (assistance with the activities of daily living via companion and personal care services) and skilled nursing services to all members of the community, but primarily to the exploding market of those over the age of 65. ComForcare franchise members provide the increasingly-needed services that support individuals' independence, dignity, and quality of life.

BACKGROUND:

	IFA Member
Established: 1996;	First Franchised: 2001
Franchised Units:	197
Company-Owned Units:	0
Total Units:	197
Dist.:	US-193; CAN-3; O'seas-1
North America:	32 States, 1 Province
Density:	13 in MI, 19 in NJ, 29 in CA

Projected New Units (12 Months):	40
Qualifications:	5, 5, 2, 4, 3, 5

FINANCIAL/TERMS:

Cash Investment:	$50 – 75K
Total Investment:	$77.8 – 141.8K
Minimum Net Worth:	$300K
Fees: Franchise -	$42K
Royalty - 5-3%;	Ad. - 0%
Financial Performance Representation:	Yes
Term of Contract (Years):	10/10
Avg. # of Employees:	2 FT, Varies PT
Passive Ownership:	Not Allowed
Encourage Conversions:	No
Area Develop. Agreements:	No
Sub-Franchising Contracts:	No
Expand in Territory:	Yes
Space Needs:	500 SF (avg)

SUPPORT & TRAINING:

Financial Assistance Provided:	Yes (I)
Site Selection Assistance:	Yes
Lease Negotiation Assistance:	Yes
Co-operative Advertising:	No
Franchisee Assoc./Member:	No
Size of Corporate Staff:	30
Ongoing Support:	A,B,C,D,E,G,H,I
Training:	1 week at home; 1 week at franchise location; 2 weeks Bloomfield Hills, MI

SPECIFIC EXPANSION PLANS:

US:	All United States
Canada:	All Canada
Overseas:	Australia/New Zealand, Europe, Asia, South America

ComForcare Senior Services began in Bloomfield Hills, Michigan in 1996 as a company dedicated to establishing a new standard in the quality of non-medical home care. After perfecting the winning formula, ComForcare began franchising in 2001. Today ComForcare has more than 170 franchise members operating almost 200 territories in the United States, Canada, and the U.K. ComForcare has been ranked in the Entrepreneur Franchise 500 and received the FranSurvey's World Class Franchise Designation by the Franchise Research Institute every year since 2008.

Operating Units	12/31/2011	12/31/2012	12/31/2013
Franchised	149	160	176
% Change	--	7.38%	10.0%
Company-Owned	1	1	1
% Change	0.00%	0.00%	0.00%
Total	150	161	177
% Change	--	7.33%	9.94%
Franchised as % of Total	99.33%	99.38%	99.44%

Investment Required

The initial fee for a ComForcare franchise is $42,000. ComForcare provides the following range of investments required to open your initial franchise. The range assumes that all items are paid for in cash. To the extent that you choose to finance any of these expense items, your front-end investment could be substantially reduced.

Item	Established Low Range	Established High Range
Initial Franchise Fee	$42,000	$42,000
Travel Expenses for Training	$2,100	$2,600
Real Estate and Expenses (3 months)	$1,800	$2,700
Office Equipment, Backup, and Access Fees	$1,700	$2,900
Signs	$100	$500
Miscellaneous Opening Costs	$1,200	$5,000
Licensing and Accreditation Fees	$0	$23,000
Insurance (3 months)	$2,000	$3,500
Office Supplies	$1,000	$2,000

Local Marketing and Advertising (3 months)	$4,500	$7,500
Recruiting Expenses (3 months)	$600	$2,000
Additional Funds (3-6 months)	$20,800	$48,100
Total Initial Investment	$77,800	$141,800

Ongoing Expenses

Franchisees pay a royalty and service fee equal to 3-5% of gross sales with a minimum royalty fee per 2-week billing period after 9 months. Additional fees include general marketing, local advertising, and health manager service fees.

Franchisee Satisfaction

A critical component of the due diligence process is that you, as a prospective franchisee, have a strong sense of existing franchisee satisfaction. Please review the franchisor's ratings below for this extremely important information.

How do you rate ComForcare Senior Services in terms of:	Rating*
Overall Communication Between Home Office Personnel and Franchiees	98%
Franchisor Encourages High Standards of Quality Performance	95%
Initial Training Supplied by Franchisor	98%

* Independent Audit of Existing Franchisees Who Rated ComForcare Senior Services as Excellent, Very Good, or Good

What You Get: Training and Support

ComForcare provides a four-phase initial training program for new franchisees that includes online, classroom, and on-the-job training at your location. Franchisees will also receive ongoing support in the form of e-mail and telephone consultation, regular web-based conferences, an annual national franchise conference and regional meetings, a website for each franchise location (maintained by the franchise support team), and access to a public relations agency that specializes in promoting franchise businesses. ComForcare also provides the following: proprietary operational software, a time-saving software that manages all aspects of the ComForcare business including caregiver and client scheduling, billing, payroll, etc.; national strategic alliances that can create instant networking and referral possibilities for all our franchisees, offering the potential of increased revenue; and a variety of print and electronic materials for use in your marketing plan.

Territory

ComForcare grants exclusive territories with an approximate population of between 25,000 and 32,000 people over the age of 65 years.

Comfort Keepers

a *sodexo* brand

6640 Poe Ave., # 200
Dayton, OH 45414-2600
Tel: (888) 836-7488, (937) 665-1320
Fax: (937) 665-1360
Email: larryfrance@comfortkeepers.com

Website: www.comfortkeepersfranchise.com
Larry France, Manager, Franchise Development

COMFORT KEEPERS is the service leader with 95% client satisfaction. We provide in-home care, such as companionship, meal preparation, light housekeeping, grocery and clothing shopping, grooming and assistance with recreational activities for the elderly and others who need assistance in daily living.

BACKGROUND:			Encourage Conversions:	Yes

BACKGROUND: IFA Member
Established: 1998; First Franchised: 1999
Franchised Units: 669
Company-Owned Units: 17
Total Units: 686
Dist.: US-686; CAN-58; O'seas-40
  North America: 47 States, 5 Provinces
  Density: 45 in OH, 58 in FL, 88 in CA
Projected New Units (12 Months): 30
Qualifications: 5, 5, 2, 3, 3, 4

FINANCIAL/TERMS:
Cash Investment: $83K
Total Investment: $83.1 – 114.4K
Minimum Net Worth: $300K
Fees: Franchise - $45K
  Royalty - 5%; Ad. - 2%
Financial Performance Representations: Yes
Term of Contract (Years): 10/10
Avg. # of Employees: 2 FT, 4 – 5 PT
Passive Ownership: Allowed

Encourage Conversions: Yes
Area Develop. Agreements: No
Sub-Franchising Contracts: No
Expand in Territory: Yes
Space Needs: 400 – 700 SF

SUPPORT & TRAINING:
Financial Assistance Provided: Yes (D)
Site Selection Assistance: No
Lease Negotiation Assistance: No
Co-operative Advertising: Yes
Franchisee Assoc./Member: Yes/Yes
Size of Corporate Staff: 65
Ongoing Support: C,D,G,h,I
Training: 5 weeks and ongoing in Dayton, OH

SPECIFIC EXPANSION PLANS:
US: All United States
Canada: Yes
Overseas: Yes

There are basic human needs that transcend age, the most notable being physical and mental health, companionship, independence, peace of mind, security, and—perhaps most importantly—respect and dignity. Comfort Keepers identifies such needs for the senior population and the highly selective Comfort Keepers staff strives to make sure that these basic needs are met with love and compassion. Since its founding more than a decade ago, Comfort Keepers has been providing first-rate in-home care to thousands of seniors and is consistently recognized as a top franchise system in its field. The senior care industry is in its infancy while the American population continues to gray: the population over age 65 is expected to exceed 86 million over the next 40 years, more than doubling the current figure. A Comfort Keepers franchise represents a golden opportunity that promises both business achievement and community contribution.

Operating Units	12/31/2011	12/31/2012	12/31/2013
Franchised	611	629	649
% Change	--	2.95%	3.18%
Company-Owned	8	15	15

% Change	--	87.5%	0.0%
Total	619	644	664
% Change	--	4.04%	3.11%
Franchised as % of Total	98.71%%	98.67%	97.74%

Investment Required

The fee for a Comfort Keepers franchise is $45,000. Comfort Keepers provides the following range of investments required to open your initial franchise. The range assumes that all items are paid for in cash. To the extent that you choose to finance any of these expense items, your front-end investment could be substantially reduced.

Item	Established Low Range	Established High Range
Combined Deposit Fee and Franchise Fee	$45,000	$45,000
Professional Fees	$600	$5,000
Business Premises	$3,400	$5,100
Furniture and Equipment	$2,650	$3,700
Insurance	$2,280	$4,180
Expenses While Training	$3,470	$5,010
Organizational Expenses, Supplies, Printing	$630	$1,240
Telephone, Utility Deposits	$470	$580
Advertising, Marketing and Promotion	$1,000	$2,000
Licensure	$0	$4,200
Caregiver Training	$1,700	$3,410
Background Screening	$320	$560
Additional Funds (3 Months)	$21,540	$34,410
Total Initial Investment	$83,060	$114,390

Ongoing Expenses

Comfort Keepers franchisees pay a royalty fee equal to the greater of $300 per month or 5% of gross revenue. Other fees include a national branding fund equal to the lesser of $600 per month or 2% of monthly gross revenue, and local advertising expenditures equal to a minimum of $1,000 per month or 2% of gross revenue, whichever is greater.

Franchisee Satisfaction

A critical component of the due diligence process is that you, as a prospective franchisee, have a strong sense of existing franchisee satisfaction. Please review the franchisor's ratings below for this extremely important information.

How do you rate Comfort Keepers in terms of:	Rating*
Overall Quality of the Franchisor	96%
Overall Communcation Between Home Office Personnel and Franchisees	93%
Encourages High Standards of Performance Throughout the Organization	96%

* Independent Audit of Existing Franchisees Who Rated Comfort Keepers as Excellent, Very Good, or Good

What You Get: Training and Support

Franchisees complete a comprehensive training course that helps them jump-start their business operations. New franchisees will be assigned to a new franchisee coach who will help to complete the pre-training, which includes approximately 60 hours of study and training activities via web and phone, followed by a five-day corporate training class at our Franchisee Support Center in Dayton, OH. This dynamic and interactive training class is where you receive comprehensive training on sales and networking techniques, human resource training, client care instruction, sales, operations, and management of your business. Corporate headquarters provides ongoing support, and gives hands-on assistance to increase business growth. Franchisees can exchange ideas with one another at state, regional and national meetings. Comfort Keepers also maintains a franchisee website, which offers a library, training resources, news, information and online communication opportunities with other owners.

Territory

While Comfort Keepers does not grant exclusive territories, it does grant territories with limited protection.

Coverall Health-Based Cleaning System

350 SW 12th. Ave.
Deerfield Beach, FL 33442
Tel: (800) 537-3371, (561) 922-2500
Fax: (561) 922-2424
Email: diane.emo@coverall.com
Website: www.coverall.com
Diane Emo, Senior Vice President

As a COVERALL Franchised Business Owner, you will be fully trained and certified in the Health-Based Cleaning System Program, and prepared to help your customers improve the cleanliness, health and wellness of their facilities. COVERALL is recognized as a leading brand in the commercial cleaning industry. The COVERALL® Program removes the maximum amount of dirt as quickly as possible, kills germs that can cause illness, and improves air quality. For over 28 years we've helped thousands entrepreneurs build commercial cleaning franchised businesses by implementing our program. Are you ready to start your business today?

Service-Based

BACKGROUND:	IFA Member
Established: 1985;	First Franchised: 1985
Franchised Units:	8,045
Company-Owned Units:	0
Total Units:	8,045
Dist.:	US-7,652; CAN-295; O'seas-98
North America:	40 States, 3 Provinces
Density:	1,111 in CA, 1,030 in FL, 531 in OH
Projected New Units (12 Months):	1
Qualifications:	3, 3, 2, 2, 3, 5

FINANCIAL/TERMS:	
Cash Investment:	$3.9 – 21.9K
Total Investment:	$14.1 – 47.7K
Minimum Net Worth:	$12.2K
Fees: Franchise -	$11.3 – 37K
Royalty - 5%;	Ad. - 0%
Financial Performance Representation:	No
Term of Contract (Years):	20/20
Avg. # of Employees:	1-2 FT, 2-3 PT
Passive Ownership:	Discouraged

Encourage Conversions:	Yes
Area Develop. Agreements:	No
Sub-Franchising Contracts:	Yes
Expand in Territory:	Yes
Space Needs:	N/A

SUPPORT & TRAINING:	
Financial Assistance Provided:	Yes (D)
Site Selection Assistance:	N/A
Lease Negotiation Assistance:	N/A
Co-operative Advertising:	No
Franchisee Assoc./Member:	No
Size of Corporate Staff:	62
Ongoing Support:	A,B,D,G,H,I
Training:	32-48 hours local regional support center

SPECIFIC EXPANSION PLANS:	
US:	All United States
Canada:	No
Overseas:	No

The Coverall Brand represents a better way to clean. As a Coverall Franchised Business Owner, you will be fully trained and certified in the Health-Based Cleaning System® Program and prepared to help your customers improve the cleanliness, health, and wellness of their facilities. Financing available; Initial customer base with all franchise packages; Excellent business development support services; Training and Professional Certification Programs. Coverall is recognized as a leading brand in the commercial cleaning industry. The Coverall® Program removes the maximum amount of dirt as quickly as possible, kills germs that can cause illness, and improves air quality. For over 28 years we've helped thousands of entrepreneurs build commercial cleaning franchised businesses by implementing our program. Are you ready to start your business today?

Operating Units	12/31/2011	12/31/2012	12/31/2013
Franchised	5,219	5,015	4,596
% Change	--	-3.91%	-8.35%
Company-Owned	0	0	0
% Change	--	--	--

Total	5,219	5,015	4,596
% Change	--	-3.91%	-8.35%
Franchised as % of Total	100%	100%	100%

Investment Required

Coverall offers entry level, mid-level, and executive level franchise packages, depending on your business and investment goals. The fee to purchase a Coverall Franchised Business ranges from $11,250 to $37,000. Coverall also offers financing options that will help you to start, maintain, and grow your franchised business. Coverall will provide financing for the following items: Initial Franchise Fee, New Equipment, Additional Business, Apparel or other business supply purchases. The following details the range of investments required to open your initial franchised business. The range assumes that all items are paid for in cash.

Item	Established Low Range	Established High Range
Initial Franchise Fee	$11,250	$37,000
Initial Equipment and Supply Package	$890	$1,890
Corporate Filings, Banking, Business License, and Permits	$175	$475
Office Supplies and Equipment	$0	$100
Apparel	$0	$100
Miscellaneous Pre-Opening Costs	$0	$200
Additional Funds (4 Months)	$314	$3,400
General Liability Insurance (monthly)	$58	$351
Automobile Insurance	$1,200	$3,000
Workers' Compensation Insurance (per $100 of payroll)	$12	$23

Vehicle	$225	$900
Total Initial Investment	$14,148	$47,656

Ongoing Expenses

Coverall Franchise Owners pay ongoing royalty fees equal to 5% of Gross Monthly Dollar Volume and support fees equal to 10% of Gross Monthly Dollar volume.

What You Get: Training and Support

Coverall offers the most advanced training program in the industry with a comprehensive classroom, online and a hands-on approach to training. Our Franchised Business Owners and their employees are trained and certified to become Health-Based Cleaning System Professionals. The Coverall Training Program also includes small business ownership education, strategies for growth, and further professional certification programs that can help further your expertise as an independent franchised business owner. With a network of 90 Support Centers, Coverall Franchised Business Owners are part of a larger System that is available to provide valuable support and advice as needed. Additional benefits include billing and collections services and a Cash Flow Protection Program to help with day-to-day administrative responsibilities.

Territory

Coverall does not grant exclusive territories.

Crestcom International

6900 E. Belleview Ave., 1st Fl.
Greenwood Village, CO 80111
Tel: (888) 273-7826, (303) 267-8200
Fax: (303) 267-8207
Email: charles.parsons@crestcom.com
Website: www.crestcom.com
Charles Parsons, Vice President

For more than 25 years, Crestcom International franchisees have trained business people across the globe in the areas of management and leadership. Today, Crestcom has grown to become one of the training industry's most successful and widely used management and leadership programs among Fortune magazine's Top 100 Companies. Each month, thousands of business professionals across six continents participate in the Crestcom Bullet Proof Manager training. Crestcom's proprietary training is improving the way businesses motivate, communicate, and help managers succeed. Businesses turn to Crestcom to help transform managers into leaders and generate real business results. Crestcom's training program accommodates organizations of all sizes, from small to mid-sized businesses, to global multi-national organizations. Crestcom currently has franchise owners in over 62 countries and the Bullet Proof Manager training Program is available in 25 languages.

BACKGROUND:	IFA Member
Established: 1987;	First Franchised: 1992
Franchised Units:	192

Company-Owned Units:	0
Total Units:	192
Dist.:	US-31; CAN-14; O'seas-147
North America:	25 States, 4 Provinces
Density:	N/A
Projected New Units (12 Months):	30
Qualifications:	3, 3, 4, 4, 5, 3

FINANCIAL/TERMS:

Cash Investment:	$69.5K
Total Investment:	$85.3 – 104K
Minimum Net Worth:	N/A
Fees: Franchise -	$69.5K
Royalty - 35.5%;	Ad. - N/A
Financial Performance Representation:	No
Term of Contract (Years):	7/7
Avg. # of Employees:	0-2 FT, 0 PT
Passive Ownership:	Not Allowed
Encourage Conversions:	N/A
Area Develop. Agreements:	Yes
Sub-Franchising Contracts:	No
Expand in Territory:	Yes
Space Needs:	N/A

SUPPORT & TRAINING:

Financial Assistance Provided:	Yes (D)
Site Selection Assistance:	N/A
Lease Negotiation Assistance:	N/A
Co-operative Advertising:	No
Franchisee Assoc./Member:	Yes/Yes
Size of Corporate Staff:	15
Ongoing Support:	C,D,G,H
Training:	7 Days United States

SPECIFIC EXPANSION PLANS:

US:	All United States
Canada:	All Canada
Overseas:	All Countries

For more than 25 years, Crestcom International franchisees have trained business people across the globe in the areas of management and leadership. Today, Crestcom has grown to become one of the training industry's most successful and widely used management and leadership programs among Fortune magazine's Top 100 Companies. Each month, thousands of business professionals across six continents participate in the Crestcom Bullet

Proof Manager training. Crestcom's proprietary training is improving the way businesses motivate, communicate, and help managers succeed. Businesses turn to Crestcom to help transform managers into leaders and generate real business results. Crestcom's training program accommodates companies of all sizes, from small to mid-sized businesses, to global multi-national organizations. Crestcom has met the needs of some of the most successful businesses and brands around the world. The Bullet Proof Manager training session is a monthly business forum where leaders develop their skills, exchange ideas, and share what's working now. Participants can join the program at any time. The Bullet Proof Manager training program is a 12 month/one day per month program that covers 24 modules of management and leadership development. Managers from 75% of Fortune Magazine's "Most Admired Companies" have participated in the Bullet Proof Manager training. More than 98% of our clients have said Crestcom training equaled or exceeded their expectations. Companies of all sizes are seeing the effects on their bottom line; employees are realizing additional job satisfaction and realizing their full potential. To learn more about Crestcom franchise ownership please visit us at www.crestcomfranchise.com.

Operating Units	12/31/2011	12/31/2012	12/31/2013
Franchised	204	191	186
% Change	--	-6.37%	-2.62%
Company-Owned	0	0	0
% Change	--	--	--
Total	204	191	186
% Change	--	-6.37%	-2.62%
Franchised as % of Total	100%	100%	100%

Investment Required

The initial fee for a Crestcom Executive franchise is $69,500. Crestcom provides the following range of investments required to open your initial franchise. The range assumes that all items are paid for in cash. To the extent that you choose to finance any of these expense items, your front-end investment could be substantially reduced.

Item	Established Low Range	Established High Range
Initial Franchise Fee	$69,500	$69,500
Office Lease Costs	$0	$500
Equipment and Supplies	$725	$4,205
Insurance	$500	$1,800
Initial Training Expense	$1,120	$3,670
Seminar Expense	$0	$1,250
Legal and Accounting	$500	$1,500
Shipping Costs; Initial Inventory	$200	$700
Marketing Program	$7,800	$9,600
Additional Funds (3 months)	$5,000	$8,775
Total Initial Investment	$85,345	$101,500

Ongoing Expenses

Franchisees are required to pay ongoing royalty fees equal to 1.5% of gross revenues and a distribution fee of 34% of gross revenues.

What You Get: Training and Support

Franchisees will receive initial training consisting of approximately three days of franchise candidate training at company headquarters in Denver, CO, and three to four days of field training in Denver or another location. After six months new franchisees must also attend and complete the three-day Advanced Pro School training program, covering selling skills. Additionally, Crestcom will provide ongoing support regarding the daily operations of the franchise, as well as refresher training courses and seminars when deemed appropriate. Franchisees will also have access to the proprietary Crestcom Internet Support System to handle certain reporting functions for the business.

Territory

Crestcom does not grant exclusive territories, except in certain Area Developer territories.

CruiseOne

1201 W. Cypress Creek Rd., # 100
Ft. Lauderdale, FL 33309-1955
Tel: (888) 272-4964 (954) 958-3700
Fax: (954) 958-3697
Email: recruitment@wth.com
Website: www.cruiseonefranchise.com
Tim Courtney, Vice President Franchise Development

CRUISEONE is a nationwide, home-based cruise & travel franchise company representing all major cruise lines and tour operators. Franchisees are professionally trained in a 6-day comprehensive program. CruiseOne provides a heritage of excellence, unrivaled buying power, industry-leading technology solutions, pride of true business ownership, and access to a large corporate support team to help you grow. CruiseOne is a member of the International Franchise Association (IFA) and participates in the VetFran and MinorityFran initiatives offering incentives and rebates to encourage business ownership.

BACKGROUND: IFA Member
Established: 1991; First Franchised: 1992
Franchised Units: 945
Company-Owned Units: 0
Total Units: 945
Dist.: US-942; CAN-0; O'seas-3
 North America: 45 States
 Density: 60 in TX, 128 in FL, 75 in CA

Projected New Units (12 Months): 70
Qualifications: 3, 4, 2, 3, 5, 4

FINANCIAL/TERMS:
Cash Investment: $9.8K
Total Investment: $4.6 – 26.3K
Minimum Net Worth: N/A
Fees: Franchise - $9.8K
 Royalty - 3%; Ad. - .25%
Financial Performance Representation: No
Term of Contract (Years): 5
Avg. # of Employees: 1 FT, 0 PT
Passive Ownership: Allowed
Encourage Conversions: N/A
Area Develop. Agreements: No
Sub-Franchising Contracts: No
Expand in Territory: Yes
Space Needs: N/A

SUPPORT & TRAINING:
Financial Assistance Provided: Yes (I)
Site Selection Assistance: N/A
Lease Negotiation Assistance: N/A
Co-operative Advertising: Yes
Franchisee Assoc./Member: Yes/Yes
Size of Corporate Staff: 90
Ongoing Support: A,B,C,D,F,G,h,I
Training: 6 days Ft. Lauderdale, FL

SPECIFIC EXPANSION PLANS:
US: All United States
Canada: Yes
Overseas: Yes

Founded in 1992, CruiseOne's Franchise Model has revolutionized the cruise industry. Today, CruiseOne is part of World Travel Holdings (WTH), making us the world's largest distributor of cruise vacations with unrivaled buying power. Together, we create excellent cruise line relationships, innovative marketing programs, and a superior support model that provides our Franchise Owners with a set of tools unmatched by any other in the industry. Our Franchise Owners come from many different social and professional backgrounds, but they all have one thing in common - a passion for travel and a commitment to succeed! Each year, CruiseOne launches new marketing programs and enhances our proprietary technologies, while maintaining the personal service coveted by our Franchise Owners. Whether it's planning a family reunion cruise or a corporate meeting at sea, our Franchise Owners continue to set the pace by delivering our hallmark 'high tech with high touch' service. CruiseOne is large enough to lead the industry, while small enough to care about each and every Franchise Owner.

Operating Units	12/31/2011	12/31/2012	12/31/2013
Franchised	707	773	829
% Change	--	9.34%	7.24%
Company-Owned	0	0	0
% Change	--	--	--
Total	707	773	829
% Change	--	9.34%	7.24%
Franchised as % of Total	100%	100%	100%

Investment Required

The initial fee for a CruiseOne franchise can be $9,800, $3,195, or $495 depending on what level you have been designated. CruiseOne provides the following range of investments required to open your initial franchise. The range assumes that all items are paid for in cash. To the extent that you choose to finance any of these expense items, your front-end investment could be substantially reduced.

Item	Established Low Range	Established High Range
Initial Franchise Fee	$495	$9,800
Training Expense	$200	$250
Additional Signatories/Associates Training and Travel	$0	$1,245
Office Equipment and Furniture	$0	$1,500
Initial Office Supplies	$230	$545
Computer Hardware/Software Equipment	$0	$2,500
Insurance, Legal, and Accounting	$150	$1,000
Permits, Franchises, Bonds, & Memberships	$150	$650
Initial Promotion and Advertising	$2,400	$3,600
Criminal and Civil Background Check	$0	$100
Additional Funds (3 months)	$1,000	$5,000
Designated Credit Card	$0	$75
Total Estimated Investment	$4,625	$26,265

Ongoing Expenses

CruiseOne franchisees pay a 3% royalty fee of annual commissionable gross sales. Other fees include a monthly administrative service fee of $150.

Franchisee Satisfaction

A critical component of the due diligence process is that you, as a prospective franchisee, have a strong sense of existing franchisee satisfaction. Please review the franchisor's ratings below for this extremely important information.

How do you rate CruiseOne in terms of:	Rating*
Overall Communication Between Home Office Personnel and Franchisees	96%
Franchisor understands that if I am successful, they will be successful	94%
Ongoing Training and Support Supplied by Franchisor	96%

* Independent Audit of Existing Franchisees Who Rated CruiseOne as Excellent, Very Good, or Good

What You Get: Training and Support

The CruiseOne expert training team, with over 40 years of experience, will provide education on the core components of the cruise and travel industries while focusing on specific business building and operation skills to ensure success of the business. Franchisees will meet with our corporate team as well as many cruise line representatives who will introduce their products and personnel. Included with the training program are several tours of cruise ships, allowing firsthand experience of some of the industry's largest and newest ships. Unlike other organizations, CruiseOne will follow-up with franchisees within their first week home as part of our Boot-camp program which was developed by our Training Team. Your training liaison will guide you through those pivotal first steps from office set-up to business planning and all the way through marketing and selling cruise vacations.

Territory

CruiseOne does not grant exclusive territories.

Cruise Planners – American Express

CRUISE ⚓ PLANNERS [AMERICAN EXPRESS]

3300 University Dr., # 1
Coral Springs, FL 33065
Tel: (888) 582-2150
Fax: (866) 369-2791
Email: danhicks@cruiseplanners.com
Website: www.cruiseplannersfranchise.com
Dan Hicks, CP Franchise Development

CRUISE PLANNERS is a fun and rewarding industry with no travel experience necessary. We are an American Express Travel Service Representative, lending instant credibility to our franchise owners with a trusted, well-recognized brand in travel. Our home-based business model can be run either full time or part time.

BACKGROUND:
Established: 1994;
First Franchised: 1994
Franchised Units: 1,498
Company-Owned Units: 1
Total Units: 1,499
Dist.: US-1,499; CAN-0; O'Seas-0
North America: 47 States, 0 Provinces
Density: 368 in FL, 130 in CA, 121 in TX
Projected New Units (12 Months): N/A
Qualifications: N/A

FINANCIAL/TERMS:
Cash Investment: N/A
Total Investment: $2.1 – 22K
Minimum Net Worth: N/A
Fees: Franchise - $495 – 9,995
  Royalty - 1 – 3%; Ad. - 0
Financial Performance Representation: No
Term of Contract (Years): N/A
Avg. # of Employees: N/A
Passive Ownership: Allowed
Encourage Conversions: Yes
Area Develop. Agreements: No
Sub-Franchising Contracts: No
Expand in Territory: No
Space Needs: N/A

SUPPORT & TRAINING:
Financial Assistance Provided: Yes (D)
Site Selection Assistance: Yes
Lease Negotiation Assistance: Yes
Co-operative Advertising: No
Franchisee Assoc./Member: Yes/Yes
Size of Corporate Staff: N/A
Ongoing Support: A,B,C,D,E,F,G,H,I
Training: N/A

SPECIFIC EXPANSION PLANS:
US: N/A
Canada: N/A
Overseas: N/A

Since 1994, agents for Coral Springs, Florida-based Cruise Planners/American Express Travel Service have been connecting business and leisure travelers with the ideal cruise. Franchisees work from their homes, selling cruises full or part time. Cruise Planners/American Express is a low-cost franchise opportunity which yields high returns and requires no travel experience. Our home-based business model is a family of over 900 franchise owners and is one of the largest, privately owned, nationally recognized and continually awarded travel franchises in the country. We are an American Express Travel Service Representative Agency which lends instant credibility to our new franchise owners with a trusted, well-recognized brand. Our franchise is a low-investment, low-risk opportunity – no inventory to buy, no employees, no retail space, no construction, no time clock, and no mandatory monthly fees. We are a family business and you've joined a family of travel professionals when you buy a franchise with us. We have a home office staff of over 50 people whose sole responsibility is to ensure your success.

Operating Units	12/31/2011	12/31/2012	12/31/2013
Franchised	1,014	1,197	1,498
% Change	--	18.05%	25.15%
Company-Owned	1	1	1
% Change	--	0.0%	0.0%
Total	1,015	1,198	1,499
% Change	--	18.03%	25.13%
Franchised as % of Total	99.90%	99.92%	99.93%

Investment Required

The initial fee for a Cruise Planners franchise ranges from $495 to $9,995, depending on the franchisee's level of previous travel agent experience. Cruise Planners provides the following range of investments required to open your initial franchise. The range assumes that all items are paid for in cash. To the extent that you choose to finance any of these expense items, your front-end investment could be substantially reduced.

Item	Established Low Range	Established High Range
Initial Franchise Fee	$495	$9,995
Application and Processing Fee for Financing	$0	$200
Rent - 3 Months	$0	$3,000
Office Equipment, Furniture and Fixtures	$500	$2,500
Start-Up Marketing	$500	$1,500

Professional Fees	$100	$500
Initial Training Fee	$0	$495
Initial Training Expenses	$0	$150
Licenses and Permits	$150	$650
Miscellaneous Opening Costs	$100	$500
Additional Funds - 3 Months	$250	$2,500
Total Initial Investment	$2,095	$21,990

Ongoing Expenses

Cruise Planners franchisees pay a bimonthly royalty fee of 1-3% of gross commissionable revenues, depending on the commissionable rates paid by the travel supplier. Other fees include an annual maintenance fee of $0-2,000, and a technology services fee of $59 per person per month.

What You Get: Training and Support

The Cruise Planners training and business development team will guide you through all the start-up tasks from business cards to registering you with the cruise lines. It's a one-on-one process to prepare you to hit the ground running. Your Cruise Planners/American Express career continues with a comprehensive 6-day program in Coral Springs, FL, the heart of the cruise industry. It begins with an industry-wide tradeshow and a chance to meet members of the Home Office Team. Each day is filled with exclusively de-signed ship tours, training in the CP Cyberlab and product demonstrations from cruise line industry leaders. We've expanded our strong commitment to training and continuing education with the launch of our Cruise Planners University program. CPU is a total continuing education program made just for Cruise Planners Specialists. You'll find CPU opportunities at our annual convention, exclusive seminars at sea, live and on-demand webinars and our sales service center. Plus, both orientation and CPU are constructed to build accreditation towards CLIA (Cruise Lines International Association, Inc.) certification.

Territory

Cruise Planners does not grant exclusive territories.

Discovery Map International

P.O. Box 726
Waitsfield, VT 05673
Tel: (802) 316-4060
Fax: (802) 329-2353
Email: monica@discoverymap.com
Website: www.discoverymap.com
Monica Whitmore, Dir. Franchise Development

Headquartered in the Green Mountains of Vermont Discovery Map International, Inc. (DMI) has been creating and publishing beautifully illustrated, hand-drawn alternative advertising maps for over 30 years. In 1993 we were predominantly a Northeastern operation, but due to increasing demand and success, DMI (at that time called Resort Maps) expanded its reach by developing a franchise model for individual ownership and distribution of its maps of resort towns, vacation destinations and cities all over the U.S. and beyond. Today, that network of franchises has grown to 126 Discovery Map maps in publication in the US, the UK, Puerto Rico and Costa Rica, with several more in the process of being published. Nearly 25 million Discovery Map maps will be printed and distributed in 2012 and these figures continue to grow.

BACKGROUND: IFA Member
Established: 1981; First Franchised: 1993
Franchised Units: 124
Company-Owned Units: 0
Total Units: 124

Dist.:	US-122; CAN-1; O'seas-3
North America:	21 States, 1 Province
Density:	12 in VT, 10 in CO, 10 in MA
Projected New Units (12 Months):	N/A
Qualifications:	4, 3, 3, 3, 3, 4

FINANCIAL/TERMS:

Cash Investment:	$40K
Total Investment:	$35 – 45K
Minimum Net Worth:	$100K
Fees: Franchise -	$25K
Royalty - 10%;	Ad. - 1%
Financial Performance Representation:	Yes
Term of Contract (Years):	10/5/5
Avg. # of Employees:	N/A
Passive Ownership:	Not Allowed
Encourage Conversions:	N/A
Area Develop. Agreements:	Yes
Sub-Franchising Contracts:	No
Expand in Territory:	Yes
Space Needs:	N/A

SUPPORT & TRAINING:

Financial Assistance Provided:	No
Site Selection Assistance:	N/A
Lease Negotiation Assistance:	N/A
Co-operative Advertising:	No
Franchisee Assoc./Member:	Yes/No
Size of Corporate Staff:	10
Ongoing Support:	C,D,F,G,H,I
Training:	Franchise Owner's Home (varies);
	4 Days Waitsfield, VT; Field Training (varies)

SPECIFIC EXPANSION PLANS:

US:	All United States
Canada:	All Canada
Overseas:	Yes

With all the changes in media and technology, there is one thing that hasn't changed — tourists still love tourist maps. We've built a nationwide network of franchisees and dealers by fulfilling the real needs of travelers and advertisers alike. This is a home-based business that requires no special equipment (apart from a computer and smart phone), no employees, and has a low cost of entry. We look for ambitious self-starters who will sell advertising on our compelling print and web products. We want entrepreneurs who have drive and determination and who want to represent a useful and well-respected brand.

Operating Units	12/31/2011	12/31/2012	12/31/2013
Franchised	109	123	127
% Change	--	12.84%	3.25%
Company-Owned	3	6	7
% Change	--	100.0%	16.67%
Total	112	129	134
% Change	--	15.18%	3.88%
Franchised as % of Total	97.32%	95.35%	94.78%

Investment Required

The initial fee for a Discovery Map franchise is $25,000. Discovery Map provides the following range of investment items required to open your initial franchise. The range assumes that all items are paid for in cash. To the extent that you choose to finance any of these expense items, your front-end investment could be substantially reduced.

Item	Established Low Range	Established High Range
Franchise Fee	$25,000	$25,000
Map Layout and Production Services	$1,800	$2,500
Map Drawing	$1,800	$3,000

Ad Production Services	$2,000	$3,000
Expenses while Training	$500	$1,500
Office Equipment & Fixtures	$1,500	$2,600
Computer System	$800	$1,200
Licenses/Deposits	$100	$250
Supplies & Misc. Expense	$500	$1,000
Insurance	$250	$500
Sales Expense	$500	$750
Additional Funds	$500	$2,500
Total Initial Investment	$35,650	$43,800

Ongoing Expenses

Franchisees are required to pay ongoing royalty fees equal to 10% of total gross sales, except 25% of web ad sales, and advertising costs of 1% of total gross sales.

What You Get: Training and Support

Franchisees will participate in a three-day initial training program that will be conducted at company headquarters in Waitsfield, VT. Training will cover company history, administration, promotion, sales introduction, bookkeeping, and customer service. Discovery Map personnel will also be available to assist in the opening of your business if given proper advanced notice. Additionally, Discovery Map will provide up to five days of map mock-up development within your territory as well as provide additional time to prepare preliminary map drawing to be used by you.

Territory

Discovery Map International grants limited exclusive territories.

Express Oil Change

1880 Southpark Dr.
Birmingham, AL 35244
Tel: (888) 945-1771, (205) 945-1771
Fax: (205) 943-5779
Email: dlarose@expressoil.com
Website: www.expressoil.com
Don Larose, SVP Franchise Development

We are among the top ten fast oil change chains in the world. Per unit, sales out-pace our competitors by over 19%. Attractive, state-of-the-art facilities offer expanded, highly profitable services in addition to our ten minute oil change. We also provide transmission service, air conditioning service, brake repair, tire rotation and balancing and miscellaneous light repairs... Most extensive training and franchise support in the industry.

BACKGROUND: IFA Member
Established: 1979;   First Franchised: 1984
Franchised Units: 113
Company-Owned Units: 88
Total Units: 201
Dist.:   US-201; CAN-0; O'seas-0
     North America: 15 States
     Density: 90 in AL, 35 in GA, 20 in TN

Projected New Units (12 Months):	12
Qualifications:	5, 5, 1, 3, 3, 5
FINANCIAL/TERMS:	
Cash Investment:	$300 – 350K
Total Investment:	$1.3 – 1.6M
Minimum Net Worth:	$450K
Fees: Franchise -	$35K
Royalty - 5%;	Ad. - 0
Financial Performance Representation:	Yes
Term of Contract (Years):	10/10
Avg. # of Employees:	7 FT, 0 PT
Passive Ownership:	Allowed
Encourage Conversions:	Yes
Area Develop. Agreements:	Yes
Sub-Franchising Contracts:	No
Expand in Territory:	Yes
Space Needs:	22,000 SF
SUPPORT & TRAINING:	
Financial Assistance Provided:	Yes (I)
Site Selection Assistance:	Yes
Lease Negotiation Assistance:	Yes
Co-operative Advertising:	Yes
Franchisee Assoc./Member:	Yes/Yes
Size of Corporate Staff:	44
Ongoing Support:	A,B,C,D,E,F,G,H,I
Training:	Ongoing Closest Training Center;
	Ongoing Birmingham, AL; Ongoing On-Site
SPECIFIC EXPANSION PLANS:	
US:	South
Canada:	No
Overseas:	No

Founded 35 years ago in Birmingham, AL and now with over 200 locations across 15 states, Express Oil Change & Service Center is a leading automotive service center in the South. With its honed oil change process and a total-car-care mechanical department, Express Oil Change is committed to giving customers the quickest oil change without sacrificing the highest-quality service. The convenience of a quick oil change is expected to continue to draw customers away from long waits at automotive dealerships and mechanic shops, ensuring your franchise a secure spot in today's competitive market. Express Oil Change & Service Center stands on a firm foundation in a growing industry with a proven formula for success. To share its success, Express Oil Change seeks franchisees who possess the drive to succeed by delivering outstanding quality and service, proven business acumen, and the willingness and ability to invest.

Operating Units	12/31/2011	12/31/2012	12/31/2013
Franchised	106	109	112
% Change	--	2.83%	2.75%
Company-Owned	73	85	88
% Change	--	16.44%	3.53%
Total	179	194	200
% Change	--	8.38%	3.09%
Franchised as % of Total	59.22%	56.19%	56.0%

Investment Required

The initial fee for an Express Oil Change franchise is $35,000 for the first unit and $17,500 for each additional unit. Express Oil Change provides the following range of investments required to open your initial franchise. The range assumes that equipment and signage is leased and other items are paid for in cash. To the extent that you choose to finance any of these expense items, your front-end investment could be substantially reduced.

Item	Established Low Range	Established High Range
Initial Franchise Fee	$35,000	$35,000
Expenses While Training	$2,000	$5,000
Equipment	$150,000	$240,000
Inventory	$25,000	$45,000
Land	$550,000	$750,000
Building and Site Work	$550,000	$750,000
Organization, Loan Origination and Professional Fees	$40,000	$85,000

Opening Advertising	$10,000	$10,000
Additional Funds (3 Months)	$63,500	$143,500
Total Initial Investment	$1,425,500	$2,063,500

Ongoing Expenses

Express Oil Change franchisees pay royalty fees equal to 5% of gross sales and minimum advertising expenditures equal to 3% of gross sales.

Franchisee Satisfaction

A critical component of the due diligence process is that you, as a prospective franchisee, have a strong sense of existing franchisee satisfaction. Please review the franchisor's ratings below for this extremely important information.

How do you rate Express Oil Change in terms of:	Rating*
Franchisor Encourages High Standards of Quality Performance	100%
Opening Support Supplied by Franchisor	100%
Quality of Product/Service Received from Franchisor	97%

* Independent Audit of Existing Franchisees Who Rated Express Oil Change as Excellent, Very Good, or Good

What You Get: Training and Support

Express Oil Change provides comprehensive training to franchisees, managers and crew members. The initial classroom and field training includes an eight-week program for the franchisee or a designated manager, and two weeks for crew members at a store training center in Alabama. The program for franchisees and managers covers oil change procedures, mechanical training, store operation, inventory control, management, marketing, accounting, and human resources, while the training for crew members focuses on operational procedures. Express Oil Change franchisees also benefit from ExpressTrack, a proprietary management system which allows owners to easily track key indicators in their business, giving them real-time access to the elements in the operation that make the business work. A certified trainer will also spend at least five days at the franchisee's location during grand opening and as needed.

Territory

Express Oil Change grants exclusive territories.

Eye Level Learning Centers

105 Challenger Rd.
Ridgefield Park, NJ 07660
Tel: (888) 835-1212 x211
Email: xavier.kim@myeyelevel.com
Website: www.eyelevelfranchise.com
Xavier Kim, Vice President of Franchising

Eye Level is the key to self-directed learning. Eye Level nurtures problem solvers, critical thinkers, and lifelong learners. A premier supplemental education and enrichment program, Eye Level offers an innovative and effective teaching method in a fun and exciting learning environment, where self-directed learning, individualized academic coaching, and critical thinking are at the core of helping children improve and excel in their academic pursuits.

BACKGROUND:

	IFA Member
Established: 1976;	First Franchised: 1991
Franchised Units:	589
Company-Owned Units:	620
Total Units:	1,209
Dist.:	US-233; CAN-5; O'seas-975
North America:	26 States, 1 Province
Density:	36 in NY, 35 in NJ, 28 in IL
Projected New Units (12 Months):	50
Qualifications:	2, 2, 5, 2, 2, 1

FINANCIAL/TERMS:

Cash Investment:	$75K
Total Investment:	$68.1 – 135.1K
Minimum Net Worth:	$150K
Fees: Franchise -	$20K
Royalty -	$36-29/subject-student/month;
Ad. -	$1/subject-student
Financial Performance Representation:	No
Term of Contract (Years):	5

Avg. # of Employees:	N/A	Co-operative Advertising:	Yes
Passive Ownership:	Allowed	Franchisee Assoc./Member:	No
Encourage Conversions:	Yes	Size of Corporate Staff:	35
Area Develop. Agreements:	Yes	Ongoing Support:	A,B,C,D,E,F,G,H,I
Sub-Franchising Contracts:	No	Training:	3 Days Company Headquarters in
Expand in Territory:	No		Ridgefield Park, NJ; 3 Days in Field
Space Needs:	800 – 1,500 SF		
		SPECIFIC EXPANSION PLANS:	
SUPPORT & TRAINING:		US:	CA, TX, GA, FL, NY, NJ, CT, PA,
Financial Assistance Provided:	No		VA, NC, IL WI, MO, MA
Site Selection Assistance:	Yes	Canada:	Ontario
Lease Negotiation Assistance:	Yes	Overseas:	Australia, England

Eye Level is a systematic, individualized program that caters to students of all abilities utilizing a unique and proven learning method. This allows each child to have a customized starting point depending on their ability, regardless of his/her age and/or school grade. Each child's study progression will depend on the student's pace of learning. Eye Level was ranked #68 in Entrepreneur's Franchise 500 in 2015. With the support, services, and materials provided by its parent company Daekyo, Eye Level franchisees across the country have made their business ownership dreams a reality.

Operating Units	12/31/2011	12/31/2012	12/31/2013
Franchised	133	181	213
% Change	--	36.09%	17.68%
Company-Owned	2	2	4
% Change	--	0.0%	100.0%
Total	135	183	217
% Change	--	35.56%	18.58%
Franchised as % of Total	98.52%	98.91%	98.16%

Investment Required

The initial franchise fee for an Eye Level Learning Center is $20,000. Eye Level provides the following range of investments required to open your initial franchise. The rage assumes that all items are paid for in cash. To the extent that you choose to finance any of these expense items, your front-end investment could be substantially reduced.

Item	Established Low Range	Established High Range
Initial Franchise Fee	$20,000	$20,000
Rent	$1,500	$4,500
Security Deposit	$0	$5,000
Leasehold Improvements	$20,875	$60,000
Furniture, Fixtures, and Equipment	$2,500	$4,000
Professional Fees	$1,000	$3,000
Design and Architect Fees	$1,000	$3,000
Office Equipment, Computer, Opening Inventory, & Supplies	$2,000	$4,000
Business License and Permits	$100	$1,500
Grand Opening Marketing	$6,000	$6,000
Expenses While Training	$500	$4,000
Insurance (12 months)	$1,000	$1,500
Payroll Cost for Employees (3 months)	$1,620	$3,600
Additional Funds (3 months)	$10,000	$15,000
Total Initial Investment	$68,095	$135,100

Ongoing Expenses

Franchisees are required to pay continuing service and monthly royalty fees of $36-$29 per Subject Student, based on the total number of Subject Students enrolled, with a minimum royalty of $1,044 after one year of operation. Other fees include an enrollment royalty fee of $15 times the number of newly enrolled students for each reporting month, a Play Math continuing service and royalty fee of $30-$25 per Play Math student depending on the number of subjects, and a brand development fund of $1 per subject-student, among others.

What You Get: Training and Support

Franchisees must complete up to 85 hours of independent self-directed learning prior to being enrolled in a three-day centralized initial training program to take place in Ridgefield Park, NJ. An additional 16-36 hours of self-directed learning will also be required to complete before attending the three-day regional training program that will also take place in Ridgefield Park. Eye Level will continue to offer advice and guidance regarding the daily operations of the franchise, as well as conduct inspections and additional training programs when requested.

Territory

Eye Level Learning Centers grants limited protected territories.

Fantastic Sams

Fantastic Sams®
HAIR SALONS

500 Cummings Center, # 1100
Beverly, MA 01915
Tel: (877) 383-3831 (978) 232-5600
Fax: (888) 315-4437
Email: cgaudette@fantasticsams.com
Website: www.fantasticsamsfranchise.com
Cindy Gaudette, Project Manager, Franchise Sales

FANTASTIC SAMS is one of the world's largest full-service hair care franchises, with over 1,100 salons in North America. Our full-service salons offer quality, affordable hair care services for the entire family—including cuts, textures and color. When you join the FANTASTIC SAMS family of franchisees, you'll receive both local and national support through ongoing management training, educational programs and national conferences, as well as advertising and other benefits. No hair care experience required.

BACKGROUND: IFA Member

Established: 1974;	First Franchised: 1976
Franchised Units:	1,136
Company-Owned Units:	14
Total Units:	1,150
Dist.:	US-1,146; CAN-4; O'seas-0
North America:	43 States, 1 Province
Density:	200 in CA, 117 in MN, 100 in FL
Projected New Units (12 Months):	40
Qualifications:	5, 5, 1, 4, 1, 5

FINANCIAL/TERMS:

Cash Investment:	$75K
Total Investment:	$136.1 – 246.1K
Minimum Net Worth:	$300K
Fees: Franchise -	$25 – 40K
Royalty - Fixed Fee;	Ad. - $137.44
Financial Performance Representation:	No
Term of Contract (Years):	10/10
Avg. # of Employees:	8 FT, 0 PT
Passive Ownership:	Discouraged
Encourage Conversions:	Yes
Area Develop. Agreements:	Yes

Sub-Franchising Contracts:	No	Franchisee Assoc./Member:	No
Expand in Territory:	Yes	Size of Corporate Staff:	53
Space Needs:	1,000 – 1,200 SF	Ongoing Support:	C,D,E,G,H
		Training:	4 days salon fundamentals class;
SUPPORT & TRAINING:			ongoing in region
Financial Assistance Provided:	Yes (I)	**SPECIFIC EXPANSION PLANS:**	
Site Selection Assistance:	Yes	US:	All United States
Lease Negotiation Assistance:	Yes	Canada:	All Canada
Co-operative Advertising:	Yes	Overseas:	No

Dessange International: the beauty leader setting the standard for salon excellence in 30+ countries. This robust company includes a portfolio of three complementary brands reaching all segments of the hairdressing market: Dessange luxury brand, Camille Albane upscale, urban, trendsetting brand, and FANTASTIC SAMS full-service value brand. Fantastic Sams believes that every customer should be greeted with "honesty, integrity and responsiveness." The one-stop shop for women, men and children of all ages provides a wide range of quality services—haircuts and styles, up-dos, straightening, coloring, highlights, texturizing, beard and mustache trims, facial waxing and hair treatments at affordable prices without the need for appointments. In addition, FANTASTIC SAMS offers its own professional quality line of shampoos, conditioners, and styling aids. FANTASTIC SAMS serves over half a million guests per week in more than 1,100 salons in North America. With 40 years of business and franchising experience, it is one of the most recognized names in the hair care industry today.

Operating Units	12/31/2011	12/31/2012	12/31/2013
Franchised	1,086	1,079	1,048
% Change	--	-0.64%	-2.87%
Company-Owned	118	125	118
% Change	--	5.93%	-5.6%
Total	1,204	1,204	1,166
% Change	--	0.0%	-3.16%
Franchised as % of Total	90.20%	89.62%	89.88%

Investment Required

The fee for a single FANTASTIC SAMS franchise in a corporate-owned region is $30,000. FANTASTIC SAMS provides the following range of investments required to open your initial single franchise. The range assumes that all items are paid for in cash. To the extent that you choose to finance any of these expense items, your front-end investment could be substantially reduced.

Item	Established Low Range	Established High Range
Initial Franchise Fee	$30,000	$30,000
New Owner/SFC Training Fee	$0	$2,600
Expenses While Training	$1,500	$3,000
Leasehold Improvements	$30,000	$80,000
Rent	$1,600	$7,000
Utility Deposit	$500	$1,500
Initial Haircare Product Inventory (3 months)	$8,000	$14,000
Salon Equipment	$18,000	$25,000
Other Equipment, Fixtures, and Furnishings	$5,000	$10,000
Salon Supplies Non-Technical (3 months)	$2,500	$4,500
Salon Identity and Graphics Kit	$500	$1,500
Advertising (first 3 months)	$7,500	$15,000
Insurance	$1,000	$2,000
Additional Funds (3 Months)	$30,000	$50,000
Total Initial Investment	$136,100	$246,100

Ongoing Expenses

FANTASTIC SAMS franchisees pay ongoing fixed royalty fees (on average $375) per week, a national advertising fund fee of $137.44 per week and regional/local advertising fund fees, when applicable.

NOTE: The fees noted above are for corporate-owned regions. Fees in other regions may differ, so please consult the specific FDD for the territory you are interested in.

What You Get: Training and Support

Owner and manager classes consist of a minimum of four days of training and are held three to four times a year. Hairstylist classes are held throughout the year at designated facilities. The owner and manager training covers the history of the Fantastic Sams system, salon operations, accounting system, inventory control, financial management, human resources, product knowledge, customer and employee relations, advertising/marketing, and more. The hairstylist training includes hairstyling techniques, the FANTASTIC SAMS system, and sales training. Regional seminars are also provided periodically. A staff of over 50 professional instructors offer ongoing support in operations, products, and promotions. National conferences play a key role in motivating franchisees, allowing them to network and gain more training. The Fantastic Sams name is given fresh exposure annually through coordinated efforts in national and regional advertising campaigns.

Territory

FANTASTIC SAMS does not grant exclusive territories.

FASTSIGNS

More than fast. More than signs.®

2542 Highlander Wy.
Carrollton, TX 75006

Tel: (800) 827-7446, (214) 346-5679
Fax: (866) 422-4927
Email: mark.jameson@fastsigns.com
Website: www.fastsigns.com
Mark Jameson, Executive Vice President of Franchise Support & Development

Signage has never been more important. Right now, businesses are looking for new and better ways to compete. Industries are revamping to meet compliance standards and advertisers are expanding their reach into new media, like digital signage, QR codes and mobile websites. Join the franchise that's leading the next generation of business communication. Now more than ever, businesses look to FASTSIGNS® for innovative ways to connect with customers in a highly competitive marketplace. Our high standards for quality and customer service have made FAST-SIGNS the most recognized brand in the industry, driving significantly more traffic to the Web than any other sign company.

BACKGROUND: IFA Member
Established: 1985; First Franchised: 1986
Franchised Units: 571
Company-Owned Units: 0
Total Units: 571
Dist.: US-507; CAN-26; O'seas-40
  North America: 50 States, 8 Provinces
  Density: 58 in TX, 36 in FL, 45 in CA
Projected New Units (12 Months): 45
Qualifications: 5, 5, 1, 3, 4, 5

FINANCIAL/TERMS:
Cash Investment: $80K
Total Investment: $178.2 – 289.5K

Minimum Net Worth: $250K
Fees: Franchise - $37.5K
  Royalty - 6%; Ad. - 2%
Financial Performance Representation: Yes
Term of Contract (Years): 20/20
Avg. # of Employees: 2-3 FT, 0 PT
Passive Ownership: Discouraged
Encourage Conversions: Yes
Area Develop. Agreements: Yes
Sub-Franchising Contracts: No
Expand in Territory: Yes
Space Needs: 1,200-1,500 SF

SUPPORT & TRAINING:
Financial Assistance Provided: Yes (I)
Site Selection Assistance: Yes
Lease Negotiation Assistance: Yes
Co-operative Advertising: No
Franchisee Assoc./Member: Yes/Yes
Size of Corporate Staff: 110
Ongoing Support: C,D,E,G,H,I
Training: 2 weeks Dallas, TX; 1 week on-site;
  1 week local center

SPECIFIC EXPANSION PLANS:
US: All United States
Canada: All Canada except Quebec as Master/
  Area Developer Only
Overseas: UK, South America, Africa, Europe,
  Asia, New Zealand, Mexico

FASTSIGNS is a pioneer and leader in the signs and graphics industry, combining advanced technology with innovative ideas to design and produce signs for businesses and organizations of all types and sizes. FAST-SIGNS offers consulting, design, production, file transfer, delivery, and installation for a full range of sign and graphic products. Since 1985, the company has grown to a network spanning across the globe. FASTSIGNS has been ranked among the top in Entrepreneur's Annual 500 for over 15 years named #1 in the Business Services Category by Franchise Business Review for 8 years in a row, a World-Class Franchise by the Franchise Research Institute for 8 years in a row, and has received the Canadian Franchise Association's Franchisees' Choice Designation for 10 years in a row.

Operating Units	12/31/2011	12/31/2012	12/31/2013
Franchised	451	463	485

% Change	--	2.66%	4.75%
Company-Owned	0	0	0
% Change	--	--	--
Total	451	463	485
% Change	--	2.66%	4.75%
Franchised as % of Total	100%	100%	100%

Investment Required

The initial fee for a FASTSIGNS franchise is $37,500. FASTSIGNS provides the following range of investments required to open your initial franchise. The range assumes that all items are paid for in cash. To the extent that you choose to finance any of these expense items, your front-end investment could be substantially reduced.

Item	Established Low Range	Established High Range
Initial Franchise Fee	$37,500	$37,500
Leasehold Improvements	$16,350	$54,528
Furniture & Fixtures	$7,688	$10,978
Deposits	$600	$9,150
Telephone & Networking	$3,750	$5,329
Decor and Graphics	$1,651	$1,855
Tools, Supplies, and Substrate Cutter	$6,304	$8,558
Production Equipment	$37,160	$39,470
POS Computer	$5,837	$6,133
Signage	$3,875	$11,843
Initial Inventory	$2,928	$3,915
Architectural/Engineering	$0	$7,283
Initial Advertising	$12,500	$12,500

Expenses While Training	$6,001	$9,320
Administrative Supplies	$1,468	$1,831
Business Licenses and Permits	$275	$1,875
Insurance Deposits and Premiums (3 Months)	$650	$900
Professional Fees	$0	$1,750
Mobile Device, Digital Sign Kiosk, Digital Sign Demo Kit and Media Player	$3,670	$4,780
Working Capital (12 months)	$30,000	$60,000
Total Initial Investment	$178,207	$289,498

Ongoing Expenses

FASTSIGNS franchisees pay a monthly service fee equal to 3% of gross sales the first year, then 6% of gross sales thereafter. Franchisees also pay an ad fee equal to 1% of gross sales the first year, then 2% of gross sales thereafter. Other fees may include an advertising cooperative fee equal to a maximum of 2% of gross sales and a technology fee not to exceed $150 per month.

Franchisee Satisfaction

A critical component of the due diligence process is that you, as a prospective franchisee, have a strong sense of existing franchisee satisfaction. Please review the franchisor's ratings below for this extremely important information.

How do you rate FASTSIGNS in terms of:	Rating*
Overall Communication Between Home Office Personnel and Franchisees	99%
Initial Training Supplied by Franchisor	97%
Franchisor Encourages High Standards of Quality Performance	97%

* Independent Audit of Existing Franchisees Who Rated FASTSIGNS as Excellent, Very Good, or Good

What You Get: Training and Support

The new franchisee (or one of the controlling principals), a computer graphic designer, and a visual communications specialist are provided with an initial training program, which includes two weeks of classroom instruction at company headquarters in Carrollton, TX, as well as at least 32 hours of optional, in-store training. For owners, training topics include sales, marketing, and administrative and financial management; for the computer graphics designer and visual communications specialist, training topics include sales, product knowledge, POS, product fulfillment, and other related subjects. Ongoing support for franchisees includes support from a FASTSIGNS Business Consultant and a FASTSIGNS Marketing Services Manager and optional additional managing and operations advisory assistance by means of written materials, toll-free telephone service, electronic communication, or at the FASTSIGNS office. FASTSIGNS also holds an annual convention, sales summit, and two vendor shows.

Territory

FASTSIGNS grants protected territories encompassing an area with a minimum of 4,000 businesses.

FirstLight HomeCare

9435 Waterstone Blvd., # 190
Cincinnati, OH 45249
Tel: (877) 570-0002, (513) 400-5136
Fax: (513) 830-5003
Email: bmcpherson@firstlighthomecare.com
Website: www.firstlightfranchise.com
Bill McPherson, Executive Director

FIRSTLIGHT HOMECARE offers comprehensive, in-home, non-medical and personal care services to seniors, new mothers, adults with disabilities, and others needing assistance. FIRSTLIGHT's founders bring more than 132 years of franchising experience and over 92 years of health-care and senior services experience, creating the core of FIRSTLIGHT's foundation. FIRSTLIGHT franchisees are passionate and caring and strive to provide exceptional service. Owning a FIRSTLIGHT franchise offers the benefits of traditional business ownership with less risk and provides an established business system along with other advantages.

BACKGROUND:

	IFA Member
Established: 2009;	First Franchised: 2010
Franchised Units:	124
Company-Owned Units:	0
Total Units:	124
Dist.:	US-110; CAN-1; O'seas-0
North America:	25 States, 1 Province

Density:	13 in OH, 6 in FL, 6 in IL
Projected New Units (12 Months):	30
Qualifications:	5, 5, 1, 3, 4, 5

FINANCIAL/TERMS:

Cash Investment:	$60K
Total Investment:	$85.2 – 128.6K
Minimum Net Worth:	$150K
Fees: Franchise -	$38K
Royalty - 5%;	Ad. - 1%
Financial Performance Representation:	Yes
Term of Contract (Years):	10/10
Avg. # of Employees:	2 FT, 6-50+ PT
Passive Ownership:	Allowed
Encourage Conversions:	Yes
Area Develop. Agreements:	Yes
Sub-Franchising Contracts:	No
Expand in Territory:	Yes
Space Needs:	600 SF

SUPPORT & TRAINING:

Financial Assistance Provided:	Yes (I)
Site Selection Assistance:	Yes
Lease Negotiation Assistance:	N/A
Co-operative Advertising:	Yes
Franchisee Assoc./Member:	Yes/Yes
Size of Corporate Staff:	13
Ongoing Support:	C,D,E,G,H,I
Training:	8 days and ongoing Cincinnati, OH

SPECIFIC EXPANSION PLANS:

US:	All United States except HI
Canada:	Yes
Overseas:	No

The successful business owner in home healthcare has a bright future. With the impact of the aging baby boomers and improving medical technologies, the demand for home care services in the United States is staggering. Home health care businesses are providing skilled medical, non-medical, or both types of services to cope with a rapidly aging population. FirstLight HomeCare meets this increasing demand with high quality, comprehensive, in-home, non-medical, and personal care services to seniors, new mothers, disabled adults, and others needing assistance. FirstLight HomeCare's values-driven approach includes groundbreaking, industry-leading tools for clients and their families that sets FirstLight apart from the competition.

Operating Units	12/31/2011	12/31/2012	12/31/2013
Franchised	31	52	81
% Change	--	67.64%	55.77%
Company-Owned	0	0	0
% Change	--	--	--
Total	31	52	81
% Change	--	67.74%	55.77%
Franchised as % of Total	100%	100%	100%

Investment Required

The initial fee for a FirstLight HomeCare franchise is $38,000. FirstLight HomeCare provides the following range of investments required to open your initial franchise. The range assumes that all items are paid for in cash. To the extent that you choose to finance any of these expense items, your front-end investment could be substantially reduced.

Item	Established Low Range	Established High Range
Initial Fee	$38,000	$38,000
Expenses while Training	$3,025	$6,050
Business Premises	$0	$3,600
Start-Up Supples and Inventory	$300	$900
Employment Screening	$256	$384
Equipment, Signage, Graphics	$250	$2,450
Advertising, Marketing, and Promotions	$3,600	$4,500
Grand Opening Marketing	$2,500	$3,000
Other Paid Expenses Expenses	$950	$4,500

Business Permits, Licenses and Fees	$0	$10,000
Insurance	$2,200	$4,400
Computer Equipment	$2,200	$2,900
Additional Funds (3 to 6 months)	$32,000	$47,975
Total Initial Investment	$85,281	$128,659

Ongoing Expenses

Franchisees are required to pay ongoing royalty fees equal to the greater of 5% of gross revenues or $250 per month for the first 15 months, followed by 5% of gross revenues or the minimum performance standard gross revenue amount thereafter.

What You Get: Training and Support

Franchisees will be enrolled in an initial training program that consists of approximately one to two weeks of classroom training covering administration and business start-up, human resources, technology, marketing, and financial planning. FirstLight HomeCare may also provide opening field support assistance when deemed necessary, continuing advice and consultation, and merchandising and marketing data when available.

Territory

FirstLight HomeCare grants protected territories.

Five Star Painting

1010-1020 N. University Parks Dr.
Waco, TX 76707
Tel: (800) 583-8003, (254) 745-2500
Fax: (254) 745-2501
Email: mike.hawkins@dwyergroup.com
Website: www.fivestarpaintingfranchise.com
Mike Hawkins, VP Franchise Development

Buying a Five Star Painting franchise isn't an investment in a new job, but a new lifestyle. It's an opportunity to be your own boss and make positive changes in the lives of the customers you service—changing your own life in the process. At Five Star we take great pride in meeting the needs of the ever-changing painting world and offer an exceptional franchise opportunity to advance your career. Five Star Painting is now a Dwyer Group-owned franchise company.

BACKGROUND:

	IFA Member
Established: 2000;	First Franchised: 2005
Franchised Units:	66
Company-Owned Units:	1
Total Units:	67
Dist.:	US-61; CAN-7; O'seas-1
North America:	36 States, 2 Provinces

Density:	16 in TX, 9 in UT, 4 in NV
Projected New Units (12 Months):	50
Qualifications:	4, 3, 2, 2, 3, 4

FINANCIAL/TERMS:

Cash Investment:	$40.5 – 86.6K
Total Investment:	$25 – 70K
Minimum Net Worth:	$20 – 40K
Fees: Franchise -	$20 – 40K
Royalty - 5%;	Ad. - 4.5%
Financial Performance Representation:	No
Term of Contract (Years):	10/10
Avg. # of Employees:	Start up 3 FT
Passive Ownership:	Not Allowed
Encourage Conversions:	N/A
Area Develop. Agreements:	No
Sub-Franchising Contracts:	No
Expand in Territory:	Yes
Space Needs:	N/A

SUPPORT & TRAINING:

Financial Assistance Provided:	Yes (D)
Site Selection Assistance:	N/A
Lease Negotiation Assistance:	N/A
Co-operative Advertising:	Yes
Franchisee Assoc./Member:	No
Size of Corporate Staff:	8
Ongoing Support:	b,C,d,G,H,I
	1 Week Springville, UT

SPECIFIC EXPANSION PLANS:

US:	All United States
Canada:	All Canada
Overseas:	All Countries

Over a decade ago the first Five Star Painting crew started a business. It consisted of 5 life-long friends who wanted to have the freedom to be their own boss and the ability to reach their potential. Now there are over 100 Five Star Painting franchises operating in both the USA, Canada, Mexico, and Brazil. Every franchise is locally owned and operated and committed to making sure that every job is clean, on time, and on budget. Five Star Painting offers its franchisees access to custom and unique software, a 24/7 sales & support center, high end marketing, training, and management support. Customers of a Five Star Painting Franchise receive a Five Star job without a five star price. As one of the fastest growing franchises in the service industry, Five Star Painting works with industry leaders to deliver business opportunities to entrepreneurs committed to a high level of customer service.

Operating Units	12/31/2011	12/31/2012	12/31/2013
Franchised	78	91	103
% Change	--	16.67%	13.19%
Company-Owned	2	2	2
% Change	--	--	--
Total	80	93	105
% Change	--	16.25%	12.9%
Franchised as % of Total	97.50%	97.85%	98.10%

Investment Required

The initial fee to open a Five Star Painting franchise is $40,000. Five Star Painting provides the following range of investments required to open your initial franchise. The range assumes that all items are paid for in cash. To the extent that you choose to finance any of these expense items, your front-end investment could be substantially reduced.

Item	Established Low Range	Established High Range
Franchise Fee	$30,000	$40,000
Advertising	$5,000	$5,000
Contractor License	$0	$250
Lease and Utilities Deposits and Payments	$0	$1,000
Franchise Premises Rent	$0	$1,500
Supplies and Equipment Inventory	$0	$7,000

Office Setup	$500	$1,500
Computer Equipment	$500	$1,500
Expenses While Training	$500	$4,000
Cell Phone	$50	$250
Clothing and Uniforms	$0	$250
Car Signs/Decals	$100	$1,500
Licenses and Bonds	$0	$1,500
Vehicle	$0	$35,000
Insurance (6 months)	$360	$1,500
Micellaneous Opening Costs	$200	$600
Additional Funds (6 months)	$6,000	$10,000
Total Initial Investment	$43,210	$112,350

Ongoing Expenses

Franchisees are required to pay ongoing royalty fees equal to 5% of gross revenue for up to $1,000,000 or 4% of gross revenue for over $1,000,000, or a minimum of $12,000 per year. Other fees include a national advertising fee of up to 2.5% of gross revenue, a local advertising requirement of 7.5% of annual gross revenue, and Executive Program fees.

What You Get: Training and Support

Franchisees will be enrolled in a five-day initial training course that will be held at company headquarters in Spanish Fork, UT. Five Star Painting will continue to offer ongoing advice and supervision regarding the daily operations of the franchise, as well as administer the advertising program and hold additional training courses when necessary.

Territory

Five Star Painting grants exclusive territories that typically consist of 100,000 households.

Fresh Coat Painters

10700 Montgomery Rd., # 300
Cincinati, OH 45242
Tel: (513) 483-3296
Email: bboecker@franchisesupport.net
Website: www.freshcoatpainters.com
Beth Boecker, Dir. Franchise Sales Administration

Ranked "Top 75 Low-Cost Franchise" and "Top 100 Homebased Franchise" in 2013 by Entrepreneur magazine. With 5 strong profit centers, you'll grow and manage your organization while the painters you hire do the painting. This is a great home-based opportunity for mid-managers and executives in the booming $100 billion home services industry. Own this exciting, year-round, recession-resistant business with low start-up costs, low overhead and high profit margin potential.

BACKGROUND: IFA Member
Established: 2004; First Franchised: 2005
Franchised Units: 116
Company-Owned Units: 0
Total Units: 116
Dist.: US-114; CAN-1; O'seas-0
  North America: 30 States, 1 Province
  Density: 12 in TX, 9 in OH, 8 in Florida
Projected New Units (12 Months): 60

Qualifications: 3, 4, 1, 2, 2, 4

FINANCIAL/TERMS:
Cash Investment: $44.4 – 71K
Total Investment: $44.4 – 71K
Minimum Net Worth: $50K
Fees: Franchise - $39.9 – 45.9K
  Royalty - 6%; Ad. - 2%
Financial Performance Representation: Yes
Term of Contract (Years): 10/10/10
Avg. # of Employees: 2 FT, 4 PT
Passive Ownership: Discouraged
Encourage Conversions: No
Area Develop. Agreements: Yes
Sub-Franchising Contracts: No
Expand in Territory: Yes
Space Needs: N/A

SUPPORT & TRAINING:
Financial Assistance Provided: Yes (D)
Site Selection Assistance: N/A
Lease Negotiation Assistance: N/A
Co-operative Advertising: No
Franchisee Assoc./Member: No
Size of Corporate Staff: 50
Ongoing Support: B,C,G,H,I
Training: 5 Days Cincinnati, OH

SPECIFIC EXPANSION PLANS:
US: All United States
Canada: All Canada
Overseas: All Countries

As a residential and commercial painting expert, Fresh Coat provides high-quality and affordable services in more than 100 major North American cities. All Fresh Coat painters are experienced professionals who are carefully screened, bonded and insured to ensure that their clients are protected. Only premium, low-odor and eco-friendly paints are used. While residential clients enjoy a two-year warranty, commercial clients benefit from an automatic six-month retouch program which garners high customer satisfaction and retention. Fresh Coat employs an extensive marketing and branding program, as well as comprehensive training to help franchisees start off strong. A Fresh Coat franchise is a home-based business that requires low start-up costs.

Operating Units	12/31/2011	12/31/2012	12/31/2013
Franchised	53	65	96
% Change	--	22.64%	47.69%
Company-Owned	0	0	0
% Change	--	--	--
Total	53	65	96
% Change	--	22.64%	47.69%
Franchised as % of Total	100%	100%	100%

Investment Required

The initial fee for a Fresh Coat franchise ranges from $39,900 to $45,900 depending on financing options and territory size. Fresh Coat provides the following range of investments required to open your initial franchise. The range assumes that all items are paid for in cash. To the extent that you choose to finance any of these expense items, your front-end investment could be substantially reduced.

Item	Established Low Range	Established High Range
Initial Franchise Fee	$39,900	$45,900
Furniture and Equipment	$0	$1,000
Computer System	$1,000	$3,000
Travel and Living Expenses While Training	$500	$1,500
Initial Rent, Telephone, Bank, Licensing Fees, and Other Deposits	$0	$2,000
Insurance	$2,000	$6,000
Pre-Opening Promotion	$3,000	$4,000
Compliance with Regulations	$450	$1,350
Technology/Software Licensing Fee	$500	$1,200

Additional Funds (3 Months)	$2,000	$10,000
Monthly Office Rental Payment	$0	$1,000
Total Initial Investment	$49,350	$76,950

Ongoing Expenses

Fresh Coat franchisees pay royalties equal to 6% of gross revenues with a monthly minimum of $300. Other fees include a national branding fee of 2% of gross revenues with a monthly minimum of $250, and a local cooperative advertising contribution of up to 3% of gross revenues.

What You Get: Training and Support

Fresh Coat's Jump Start Program is a preliminary training phase that franchisees engage in at home, helping them to study the operations manual, prepare a business plan, open a bank account, obtain insurance, and schedule training dates. A five-day initial training program is then provided for two employees at corporate headquarters in Cincinnati, OH. Training covers the areas of database management, human resources, financial management, hiring, scheduling, equipment, customer service, and marketing. Fresh Coat maintains a website, provides assistance with finding suppliers and offers ongoing assistance with marketing and promotional materials. Fresh Coat also holds franchise meetings to discuss sales techniques, proven strategies, and to introduce new management tools and marketing programs.

Territory

Fresh Coat grants protected territories.

Furniture Medic

 FURNITURE MEDIC®

3839 Forest Hill-Irene Rd.
Memphis, TN 38125-2502
Tel: (800) 230-2360, (901) 597-8600
Fax: (901) 597-8660
Email: cbeck@furnituremedic.com
Website: www.furnituremedicfranchise.com
Chris Beck, Franchise Sales Manager

FURNITURE MEDIC is a division of The ServiceMaster Company. It is the largest furniture and wood repair and restoration company in the world with over 300 franchises. Furniture Medic has unique products and processes which enable much of the work to be done on-site, reducing costs and saving time for its residential and commercial customers. Financing is provided for the initial franchise fees, start-up equipment and vehicles to qualified candidates through ServiceMaster Acceptance Company.

BACKGROUND: IFA Member
Established: 1990;   First Franchised: 1992
Franchised Units: 334
Company-Owned Units: 0
Total Units: 334
Dist.:   US-302; CAN-51; O'seas-80
   North America: 47 States
   Density: 21 in VA, 38 in FL, 18 in IL
Projected New Units (12 Months): 30

Qualifications: 4, 4, 2, 3, 3, 5

FINANCIAL/TERMS:
Cash Investment: $20 – 25K
Total Investment: $54.1 – 70.4K
Minimum Net Worth: $75K
Fees: Franchise - $29.9K
   Royalty - 7%/$250 Min.;   Ad. - 1%/$50 Min.
Financial Performance Representation: No
Term of Contract (Years):   5/5
Avg. # of Employees: 1 FT, 1 PT
Passive Ownership: Allowed
Encourage Conversions: Yes
Area Develop. Agreements: No
Sub-Franchising Contracts: No
Expand in Territory: Yes
Space Needs: N/A

SUPPORT & TRAINING:
Financial Assistance Provided: Yes (D)
Site Selection Assistance: N/A
Lease Negotiation Assistance: No
Co-operative Advertising: Yes
Franchisee Assoc./Member: Yes/Yes
Size of Corporate Staff: 21
Ongoing Support: A,B,G,h,I
Training: 3 Weeks Memphis, TN

SPECIFIC EXPANSION PLANS:
US: Most metropolitan markets in US
Canada: All Canada
Overseas: All Countries

As one of the world's largest on-site wood and furniture repair and restoration companies, Furniture Medic owes its success to its commitment to providing customers with unsurpassed, quality service. Utilizing advanced technology, Furniture Medic specializes in enhancement, refinishing, and restoration for antiques, specialty items, millwork, paneling, doors and banisters, cabinetry and mantels, hardwood floors, and upholstery for both residential and commercial customers. Since 1992, it has grown to a network of more than 361 franchises throughout North America and Europe. The company has been named as the #1 furniture repair and restoration franchise by the Entrepreneur magazine for 10 years running. Furniture Medic—along with ServiceMaster Clean, Amerispec, Merry Maids, Terminix, and American Home Shield—is part of the ServiceMaster family, providing a wide array of home maintenance, commercial cleaning, and restoration services.

Operating Units	12/31/2011	12/31/2012	12/31/2013
Franchised	218	206	203
% Change	--	-5.5%	-1.46%
Company-Owned	0	0	0
% Change	--	--	--
Total	218	206	203
% Change	--	-5.5%	-1.46%
Franchised as % of Total	100%	100%	100%

Investment Required

The fee for a Furniture Medic franchise is $29,900. Furniture Medic may offer discounts to existing franchisees, ServiceMaster affiliates and employees, women, minorities and to those who have served in the military. Furniture Medic provides the following range of investments required to open your initial franchise. The range assumes that all items are paid for in cash. To the extent that you choose to finance any of these expense items, your front-end investment could be substantially reduced. Furniture Medic's affiliate, SMAC, offers financing for the initial franchise fee and opening product equipment package.

Item	Estimated Low Range	Estimated High Range
Initial Franchise Fee	$29,900	$29,900
Training Related Expenses	$1,065	$3,125
Opening Package	$13,000	$13,000
Sales Tax, Shipping and Handling of Opening Package	$2,000	$2,000
iPad	$900	$2,000

Insurance - General Liability and Vehicle	$2,500	$4,500
Insurance - Workers' Compensation	$700	$2,000
Internet Connection	$45	$150
Misc. Opening Costs	$200	$1,500
Service Vehicle	$2,000	$4,000
Van Detail Package	$150	$462
Advertising Fund Contribution (3 months)	$300	$300
Additional Start-Up Funds (3 months)	$2,000	$6,000
Initial Marketing	$100	$3,000
Total Initial Investment	$54,130	$70,373
Total Initial Investment	$54,130	$70,373

Ongoing Expenses

Furniture Medic franchisees pay royalty fees equal to the greater of $250 per month or 7% gross sales, a national advertising fund fee equal to the greater of $100 per month or 2% of gross sales, and monthly software fees.

What You Get: Training and Support

The initial training consists of a Pre-Academy program of roughly 50 hours, a two-week, hands-on training session at the FM training center in Memphis, TN, and a one-week Post-Academy training covering advanced topics. The program covers business plans, marketing, record keeping, technical skills, and more. After graduation from the Academy, franchisees may opt to participate in a mentoring program that pairs experienced franchisees with new owners in the same general service area. The purpose of the mentoring program is to press new skill sets into use while developing finesse in customer acquisition. Franchisees also benefit from around-the-clock telephone support and comprehensive marketing strategies that target brand awareness.

Territory

Furniture Medic does not grant exclusive territories, but a protected area containing at least 100,000 people will be granted.

Glass Doctor

GLASSDOCTOR.
HOME • AUTO • BUSINESS
We fix your panes!®

1020 N. University Parks Dr.
Waco, TX 76707
Tel: (800) 224-9489, (254) 745-2464
Email: mike.hawkins@dwyergroup.com
Website: www.leadingtheserviceindustry.com/Glass-Doctor.aspx
Mike Hawkins, Vice President of Franchise Sales

From windows to windshields to storefronts, Glass Doctor can handle any glass repair or replacement need. Glass Doctor also offers custom glass services, such as tub and shower enclosures, window replacement, entry door glass and mirrors. Established in 1962 with one shop in Seattle, WA, today Glass Doctor offers complete glass repair, replacement and services to the residential, automotive, and commercial markets. Glass Doctor began franchising in 1977 and joined The Dwyer Group, Inc., an international franchisor of service industry companies, in 1998. Now there are more than 170 Glass Doctor franchise owners across the US and Canada. New franchisees are trained at the nation's only full-service glass training facility, Glass Doctor University, at company headquarters in Waco, Texas. The Dwyer Group family of companies also includes Aire Serv Heating and Air Conditioning, Mr. Appliance, Mr. Electric, Mr. Rooter, The Ground Guys, and Rainbow International Restoration and Cleaning.

BACKGROUND: IFA Member
Established: 1962; First Franchised: 1977
Franchised Units: 174
Company-Owned Units: 0
Total Units: 174
Dist.: US-163; CAN-11; O'seas-0
  North America: 46 States, 3 Provinces
  Density: 15 in TX, 12 in FL, 11 in CA
Projected New Units (12 Months): 30
Qualifications: 4, 4, 2, 2, 3, 5

FINANCIAL/TERMS:
Cash Investment: $90 – 100K
Total Investment: $108K+
Minimum Net Worth: Varies
Fees: Franchise - $28K/100K Pop.
  Royalty - 5-7%; Ad. - 2%
Financial Performance Representation: Yes
Term of Contract (Years): 10/10
Avg. # of Employees: 4 FT, 0 PT
Passive Ownership: Not Allowed
Encourage Conversions: Yes
Area Develop. Agreements: No
Sub-Franchising Contracts: No
Expand in Territory: Yes
Space Needs: 1,500 SF

SUPPORT & TRAINING:
Financial Assistance Provided: Yes (I)
Site Selection Assistance: No
Lease Negotiation Assistance: No
Co-operative Advertising: Yes
Franchisee Assoc./Member: Yes/No

Size of Corporate Staff:	20
Ongoing Support:	A,B,C,D,E,F,G,H,I
Training:	5 Days optional Auto Glass Tech Basic/Certification; 4 Hours Online Training; 9 Days Basic Franchisee Training Waco, TX

SPECIFIC EXPANSION PLANS:	
US:	All United States
Canada:	Yes
Overseas:	No

Glass Doctor is the largest fully franchised residential, business, and auto-glass franchise company in North America, and combines all the benefits of a local business with the strength of a 50-year-old national brand name. In 2012, Entrepreneur magazine ranked Glass Doctor #1 in the Franchise 500 home-service category. As a Glass Doctor franchisee, you will be equipped with marketing and operations support, the World Class Frontline Service System to give your customers the best possible experience, vendor rebates and incentives, and training in our Code of Values to keep your business focused on what matters most. Your business will benefit from the instant brand recognition and consumer loyalty that comes with being part of an industry leader.

Operating Units	12/31/2011	12/31/2012	12/31/2013
Franchised	174	167	163
% Change	--	-4.02%	-2.4%
Company-Owned	0	0	0
% Change	--	--	--
Total	174	167	163
% Change	--	-4.02%	-2.4%
Franchised as % of Total	100%	100%	100%

Investment Required

The initial fee to purchase a Glass Doctor franchise is $28,000 plus $280 per 1,000 population for additional territory. Glass Doctor provides the following range of investments required to open your initial franchise. The range assumes that all items are paid for in cash. To the extent that you choose to finance any of these expense items, your front-end investment could be substantially reduced.

Item	Established Low Range	Established High Range
Initial Franchise Fee	$28,000	$28,000 + $280 per 1,000 add'l pop.
Vehicle	$3,500	$60,000
Equipment, Supplies, & Inventory	$20,000	$55,000
Insurance	$2,000	$6,000
Advertising & Promotional	$4,000	$20,000
Expenses while Training	$2,500	$5,000
Deposits, Permits, & Licenses	$2,000	$5,000
Professional Fees	$300	$5,000
Real Estate	$4,000	$15,000
Local Marketing Spending for Marketing Start-up Phase	$7,500	$15,000
Additional Funds (3 months)	$35,000	$75,000
Total Initial Investment	$108,800	$289,000 + add'l franchise fee

Ongoing Expenses

Franchisees are required to pay ongoing license fees ranging from 5% to 7% of gross sales, a MAP fee equal to 2% of gross sales, a TAFS fee equal to 2% of gross sales, and local and cooperative marketing spending.

What You Get: Training and Support

Franchisees will be enrolled in an initial training program that may include a Phase I program of 2.5 days via webinar/video-conferencing, and a Phase II program consisting of 10 days classroom training at company headquarters in Waco, TX. Additionally, franchisees may be required to complete one to five days of field training at a franchised business. Glass Doctor will continue to provide ongoing advice and assistance regarding the operations of the franchise, as well as develop and administer promotional and advertising programs and hold refresher training courses when deemed necessary.

Territory

Glass Doctor grants exclusive territories with populations of approximately 100,000 to 1,500,000.

Griswold Home Care

HOME CARE

Exceptional Service for Over 30 Years

120 West Germantown Pike, # 200
Plymouth Meeting, PA 19462
Tel: (888) 777-7630, (215) 402-0200 x110
Fax: (215) 261-1733
Email: mike@griswoldhomecare.com
Website: www.griswoldhomecare.com
Mike Magid, Vice President of Franchise Development

Griswold Home Care is dedicated to providing Extraordinary Home Care at Affordable Rates. We refer Caregivers for older adults, people recovering from illness or surgery, and people with long-term disabilities. Caregiver services include personal care, homemaking, companionship, incidental transportation and other services to Clients wishing to remain safe and independent. We operate a model that is completely unique in the industry. We also offer the largest protected territories and lowest ongoing fees.

BACKGROUND:

	IFA Member
Established: 1982;	First Franchised: 1984
Franchised Units:	235
Company-Owned Units:	9
Total Units:	244
Dist.:	US-244; CAN-0; O'seas-0
North America:	30 States
Density:	19 in NJ, 15 in OH, 22 in PA

Projected New Units (12 Months):	56
Qualifications:	5, 4, 2, 3, 4, 5

FINANCIAL/TERMS:

Cash Investment:	$75K
Total Investment:	$95 – 121K
Minimum Net Worth:	$275K
Fees: Franchise -	$49.5K
Royalty - 4%;	Ad. - 0.5% avg.
Financial Performance Representation:	Yes
Term of Contract (Years):	10/5
Avg. # of Employees:	3-5 (in office) FT
Passive Ownership:	Allowed
Encourage Conversions:	No
Area Develop. Agreements:	No
Sub-Franchising Contracts:	No
Expand in Territory:	Yes
Space Needs:	Minimum 150 SF

SUPPORT & TRAINING:

Financial Assistance Provided:	No
Site Selection Assistance:	No
Lease Negotiation Assistance:	N/A
Co-operative Advertising:	Yes
Franchisee Assoc./Member:	Yes/Yes
Size of Corporate Staff:	23
Ongoing Support:	C,D,G,H,I
Training:	10 days corporate office;
	1-2 days franchisee location

SPECIFIC EXPANSION PLANS:

US:	Yes
Canada:	Yes
Overseas:	No

Experience the benefits of business ownership for you and your family while making a difference in your community. Griswold Home Care is dedicated to providing "Extraordinary Home Care at Affordable Rates." We refer caregivers for older adults, people recovering from illness or surgery, and people with long-term disabilities. Caregiver services include personal care, homemaking, companionship, incidental transportation, and other services to clients wishing to remain safe and independent. Griswold Home Care strives to achieve this balance of superior quality and affordability, and the company is recognized as the world's oldest, non-medical home care company. Our winning business model cuts overhead costs, allowing franchisees to keep rates low to attract more clients, and to insure the highest industry wages to attract the best caregivers.

Operating Units	12/31/2011	12/31/2012	12/31/2013
Franchised	141	183	235
% Change	--	29.79%	28.42%
Company-Owned	11	11	9
% Change	--	0.0%	-18.18%
Total	152	194	244
% Change	--	27.63%	25.77%
Franchised as % of Total	92.76%	94.33%	96.31%

Investment Required

The initial fee for a Griswold Home Care franchise with a population the greater of 250,000 individuals or 25,000 senior citizens (aged 65 and older) is $49,500. Larger territories can be purchased for an additional $0.10 per person up to a total territory population of 300,000. Griswold Home Care provides the following range of investments required to open your initial franchise. The range assumes that all items are paid for in cash. To the extent that you choose to finance any of these expense items, your front-end investment could be substantially reduced.

Item	Established Low Range	Established High Range
Initial Franchise Fee	$49,500	$49,500
Expenses Whil Training	$1,500	$3,000
Local Lift-Off Program	$12,500	$12,500
Office Lease	$0	$5,000
Office Equipment	$2,500	$4,000
First Year Computer Software Fee	$1,400	$1,400
Signage	$0	$1,000
Opening Office Supplies and Inventory	$0	$750
Insurance	$1,125	$1,800
Printed Materials and Shipping	$0	$200
License, Permit Registration or Certificate Costs	$0	$2,000
Additional Funds (6 to 18 months)	$30,000	$40,000
Total Initial Investment	$98,525	$121,150

Ongoing Expenses

Franchisees are required to pay monthly royalty fees equal to 4%, a general marketing fee equal to 0.5%, and a software fee minimum of $100 per month.

What You Get: Training and Support

Griswold Home Care provides training that is unparalleled in the industry: 30-45 days of pre-training preparation, up to ten days at our Homecare Academy in suburban Philadelphia, PA, a twelve-week post training program, annual conferences, regional conferences, ongoing webinars and workshops, and more. Because we operate company units, we truly understand the business.

Territory

Griswold Home Care grants exclusive territories.

The Grounds Guys

GroundsGuys®
LANDSCAPE MANAGEMENT

1020 N. University Parks Dr.
Waco, TX 76707
Tel: (800) 638-9851, (254) 245-2554
Email: patrick.hyland@groundsguys.com
Website: www.leadingtheserviceindustry.com/The-Grounds-Guys-LLC.aspx
Patrick Hyland, Franchise Development Team Leader

The Grounds Guys is one of the fastest growing landscape management companies in the U.S. The Grounds Guys portfolio of services includes: landscape management, lawn and grounds care, irrigation, outdoor lighting, and snow and ice removal services for both residential and commercial clients. The proprietary systems help franchisees find new customers, gain market share over local competition, and operate a profitable and sustainable landscape business. The Grounds Guys is part of The Dwyer Group family of companies, which also includes Mr. Rooter, Aire Serv, Mr. Electric, Mr. Appliance, Glass Doctor and Rainbow International.

BACKGROUND: IFA Member
Established: 2010;   First Franchised: 2010
Franchised Units: 149
Company-Owned Units: 0
Total Units: 149
Dist.:   US-149; CAN-0; O'seas-0
  North America: 32 States

Density:	8 in TX, 8 in FL, 5 in NC
Projected New Units (12 Months):	55
Qualifications:	4, 2, 2, 2, 3, 5

FINANCIAL/TERMS:

Cash Investment:	$40K+
Total Investment:	$50 – 140K
Minimum Net Worth:	$100K
Fees: Franchise -	$28.5K/100K Pop.
Royalty - 7%;	Ad. - 2%
Financial Performance Representation:	No
Term of Contract (Years):	10/10
Avg. # of Employees:	N/A
Passive Ownership:	Not Allowed
Encourage Conversions:	Yes
Area Develop. Agreements:	No
Sub-Franchising Contracts:	No
Expand in Territory:	Yes
Space Needs:	N/A

SUPPORT & TRAINING:

Financial Assistance Provided:	Yes (D)
Site Selection Assistance:	Yes
Lease Negotiation Assistance:	Yes
Co-operative Advertising:	Yes
Franchisee Assoc./Member:	Yes/Yes
Size of Corporate Staff:	N/A
Ongoing Support:	A,B,C,D,E,F,G,H,I
Training:	39 Hours Classroom Training Waco, TX; 5 Days Classroom Training Waco, TX

SPECIFIC EXPANSION PLANS:

US:	Yes
Canada:	No
Overseas:	No

The Grounds Guys is a full-service grounds care company. Our established systems allow us to deliver industry-leading lawn care and landscape solutions to commercial and residential clients. Built on a family tradition of caring, The Grounds Guys are driven by a passion to exceed the expectations of our customers. With The Grounds Guys proprietary landscape franchise management systems, our landscape franchisees can learn how to find new customers, gain market share over local competition, and operate a profitable and sustainable landscape franchise. The Grounds Guys' portfolio of services includes landscape management, lawn and grounds care, irrigation, outdoor lighting, and snow and ice removal services for both residential and commercial clients.

Operating Units	12/31/2011	12/31/2012	12/31/2013
Franchised	33	70	117
% Change	--	112.12%	67.14%
Company-Owned	0	0	0
% Change	--	--	--
Total	33	70	117
% Change	--	112.12%	67.14%
Franchised as % of Total	100%	100%	100%

Investment Required

The initial fee to purchase a Grounds Guys franchise is $28,500 plus $285 per 1,000 population for additional territory. The Grounds Guys provides the following range of investments required to open your initial franchise. The range assumes that all items are paid for in cash. To the extent that you choose to finance any of these expense items, your front-end investment could be substantially reduced.

Item	Established Low Range	Established High Range
Initial Franchise Fee	$28,500	$28,500 + $285 per add'l 1,000 pop.

Software Fee	$1,440	$1,440
Vehicle	$4,000	$50,000
Equipment, Supplies, & Inventory	$16,300	$36,300
Insurance	$1,200	$5,000
Advertising & Promotional	$6,000	$25,000
Expenses while Training	$2,250	$4,850
Deposits, Permits, & Licenses	$50	$1,000
Professional Fees	$250	$5,000
Real Estate	$0	$3,000
Additional Funds (3 months)	$5,000	$30,000
Local Marketing Spending for Marketing Start-up Phase	$7,500	$15,000
Total Initial Investment	$66,170	$190,670 + add'l franchise fee

Ongoing Expenses

Franchisees are required to pay ongoing license fees equal to 7% of gross sales, a MAP fee equal to 2% of gross sales, and local marketing and telemarketing spending, among other fees.

What You Get: Training and Support

Franchisees will be enrolled in an initial training program that may include a Phase I program of 2.5 days via webinar/video-conferencing, and a Phase II program consisting of 5-8 days classroom training at company headquarters in Waco, TX. Additionally, franchisees may be required to complete 1-5 days of field training at a franchised business. The Grounds Guys will continue to provide ongoing advice and assistance regarding the operations of the franchise, as well as develop and administer promotional and advertising programs and hold refresher training courses when deemed necessary.

Territory

The Grounds Guys grants exclusive territories with populations of approximately 100,000 to 1,500,000.

The Growth Coach

THE GROWTHCOACH™
Business and Sales Coaching

10700 Montgomery Rd., # 210
Cincinnati, OH 45242
Tel: (888) 292-7992
Email: bboecker@franchisesupport.net
Website: www.thegrowthcoach.com
Beth Boecker, Dir. Franchise Sales Administration

The Growth Coach is the leader in business and sales coaching as well as one of the most affordable franchises in the industry. Change the direction of your life by taking control of your future. Utilize your skills, experience and passion to help others succeed and finally love what you do. The Growth Coach works with small business owners, franchise owners, self-employed professionals, sales teams and managers to drive success in business and find balance in life through our proven and proprietary Strategic Mindset Coaching Process.

BACKGROUND:	IFA Member
Established: 2002;	First Franchised: 2002
Franchised Units:	120
Company-Owned Units:	0
Total Units:	120
Dist.:	US-143; CAN-2; O'seas-9
North America:	40 States, 2 Provinces

Density:	11 in TX, 12 in OH, 12 in FL
Projected New Units (12 Months):	60
Qualifications:	3, 3, 1, 3, 3, 5

FINANCIAL/TERMS:

Cash Investment:	$7 – 36.9K
Total Investment:	$52.1 – 82K
Minimum Net Worth:	$50K
Fees: Franchise -	$39.9 – 45.9K
Royalty - 10%	Ad. - 2%
Financial Performance Representation:	No
Term of Contract (Years):	10/10/10
Avg. # of Employees:	1 FT, 0 PT
Passive Ownership:	Allowed
Encourage Conversions:	Yes
Area Develop. Agreements:	Yes
Sub-Franchising Contracts:	No
Expand in Territory:	Yes
Space Needs:	N/A

SUPPORT & TRAINING:

Financial Assistance Provided:	Yes (D)
Site Selection Assistance:	N/A
Lease Negotiation Assistance:	N/A
Co-operative Advertising:	No
Franchisee Assoc./Member:	No
Size of Corporate Staff:	50
Ongoing Support:	C,D,E,G,H,I
Training:	8 Business Days Cincinnati, OH

SPECIFIC EXPANSION PLANS:

US:	All United States
Canada:	All Canada
Overseas:	All Countries

The Growth Coach helps business professionals reach their full potential—in their person and professional lives. Through their revolutionary system—The Strategic Mindset—The Growth Coach has been able to help their client work smarter enabling them to earn more, work less, and enjoy a richer life.

Operating Units	12/31/2011	12/31/2012	12/31/2013
Franchised	130	124	105
% Change	--	-4.62%	-15.32%
Company-Owned	0	0	0
% Change	--	--	--
Total	130	124	105
% Change	--	-4.62%	-15.32%
Franchised as % of Total	100%	100%	100%

Investment Required

The initial franchise fee varies depending on whether the Growth Coach finances a portion of it and/or the number of businesses in your territory, but ranges from $39,900 to $45,900. The Growth Coach provides the following range of investments required to open your initial franchise. The range assumes that all items are paid for in cash. To the extent that you choose to finance any of these expense items, your front-end investment could be substantially reduced.

Item	Estimated Low Range	Estimated High Range
Initial Franchise Fee	$39,900	$45,900
Furniture and Equipment	$500	$1,000
Computer System	$1,000	$3,000
Travel and Living Expenses While Training	$750	$1,500

Initial Rent, Telephone, Bank, and Other Deposits	$350	$2,000
Additional Funds (6 months)	$5,000	$18,000
Grand Opening Promotion	$1,000	$4,500
Lead Generation Program	$3,000	$3,000
Technology/Software Licensing Fee	$125	$125
Monthly Office Rental Payment	$0	$1,000
Insurance	$500	$2,000
Total Initial Investment	$52,125	$82,025

Ongoing Expenses

The royalty fee for The Growth Coach is 10% of gross revenues, with a minimum of $750 per month. Franchisees are also responsible for a national branding fee of 2% of gross revenues per month, with a $350 minimum, and a local cooperative advertising fee of up to 3% of gross revenues.

What You Get: Training and Support

New franchisees are provided with a week-long training program at company headquarters in Cincinnati, OH that will cover marketing activities, sales processes, group facilitation and coaching, and financial management. The Growth Coach will also continue to provide assistance and guidance regarding the operation of the franchise as deemed necessary.

Territory

The Growth Coach offers exclusive territories that will contain a maximum of 10,000 businesses.

Hand & Stone Massage and Facial Spa

MASSAGE | FACIALS | WAXING

200 Horizon Dr., # 203
Hamilton, NJ 08691
Tel: (609) 587-9800
Email: rmcquillan@handandstone.com
Website: www.handandstone.com
Robert McQuillan, VP Franchise Development

Hand and Stone Massage and Facial Spa offers massage, facial, and hair removal services, as well as facial products at one convenient retail location. Hand and Stone offers a recurring revenue model that allows this membership-based business to produce a predictable income stream for the franchisee.

BACKGROUND:
Established: 2004;	First Franchised: 2006
Franchised Units:	179
Company-Owned Units:	1
Total Units:	180
Dist.:	US-170; CAN-10; O'seas-0
North America:	20 States, 1 Province
Density:	33 in NJ, 23 in FL, 20 in PA
Projected New Units (12 Months):	0
Qualifications:	N/A

FINANCIAL/TERMS:
Cash Investment:	N/A
Total Investment:	$393.5 – 488.6K
Minimum Net Worth:	N/A
Fees: Franchise -	$39K
Royalty - 5%;	Ad. - 5%
Financial Performance Representation:	Yes
Term of Contract (Years):	N/A
Avg. # of Employees:	N/A
Passive Ownership:	Allowed
Encourage Conversions:	Yes
Area Develop. Agreements:	Yes
Sub-Franchising Contracts:	No
Expand in Territory:	No
Space Needs:	N/A

SUPPORT & TRAINING:
Financial Assistance Provided:	Yes (D)
Site Selection Assistance:	Yes
Lease Negotiation Assistance:	Yes
Co-operative Advertising:	No
Franchisee Assoc./Member:	Yes/Yes
Size of Corporate Staff:	0
Ongoing Support:	A,B,C,D,E,G,H,I
Training:	

SPECIFIC EXPANSION PLANS:
US:	No
Canada:	No
Overseas:	No

Hand and Stone Massage and Facial Spa offers massage, facial, and hair removal services, as well as facial products at one convenient retail location. Hand and Stone offers a recurring revenue model that allows this membership-based business to produce a predictable income stream for the franchisee. Our ability to offer more products and services than our competition gives us an edge in the marketplace.

Operating Units	12/31/2011	12/31/2012	12/31/2013
Franchised	65	95	141

% Change	--	46.15%	48.42%
Company-Owned	2	2	2
% Change	--	0.0%	0.0%
Total	67	97	143
% Change	--	44.78%	47.42%
Franchised as % of Total	97.01%	97.94%	98.60%

Investment Required

The initial franchise fee to purchase a Hand and Stone franchise is $39,000. Hand and Stone provides the following range of investments required to open your initial franchise. The range assumes that all items are paid for in cash. To the extent that you choose to finance any of these expense items, your front-end investment could be substantially reduced.

Item	Established Low Range	Established High Range
Initial Franchise Fee	$39,000	$39,000
Real Estate/Rent	$11,733	$17,067
Utility Deposits	$500	$500
Leasehold Improvements	$173,800	$214,400
Furniture, Fixtures & Equipment	$62,993	$81,557
Computer/POS System	$16,608	$16,608
Insurance	$1,250	$1,500
Office Equipment and Supplies	$9,363	$9,751
Camera/Music System	$6,287	$7,036
Initial Inventory	$10,590	$12,227
Travel Expenses	$1,000	$2,000
Signage	$3,671	$9,171
Grand Opening	$5,000	$10,000

Licenses, Permits and Architectural Fees	$7,500	$8,500
Legal & Accounting	$4,250	$4,250
Additional Funds (6 Months)	$40,000	$55,000
Total Initial Investment	$393,545	$488,567

Ongoing Expenses

Hand and Stone franchisees pay a weekly royalty fee equal to 5% of gross sales and a weekly marketing fund contribution of 1% of gross sales. Additional fees include a weekly local advertising fee of 4% of gross sales, telephone directory advertising fees, and computer software maintenance and support fees.

What You Get: Training and Support

Hand and Stone provides an initial training program for the Designated Manager and up to three additional assistants. The training takes place at an operating spa or at company headquarters in Hamilton, New Jersey. Lasting for approximately two weeks, the training covers all business and administrative aspects of running a Hand and Stone franchise, including sales and marketing methods, financial controls, maintenance of quality standards, customer service techniques, record keeping, and on-the-job training. Hand and Stone also provides a two-day initial massage protocol training program for the franchise's new Lead Therapist.

Territory

Hand and Stone grants protected territories.

Home Helpers

Making Life Easier*

10700 Montgomery Rd., # 300
Cincinnati, OH 45242
Tel: (513) 413-4899
Email: bboecker@franchisesupport.net
Website: www.homehelpershomecare.com
Beth Boecker, Dir. Franchise Sales Adminitration

Home Helpers was ranked "#1 Senior Care Franchise" in North America and "Best of the Best" by Entrepreneur magazine five years in a row! This is a rewarding business providing medical, non-medical and personal care for: seniors, new moms, those recuperating from illness or injury, and those with lifelong challenges.

BACKGROUND:
Established: 1996;   IFA Member
                          First Franchised: 1997
Franchised Units: 655
Company-Owned Units: 0
Total Units: 655
Dist.:   US-655; CAN-0; O'seas-0
  North America: 43 States
  Density: 27 in PA, 31 in IL, 36 in CA
Projected New Units (12 Months):   50
Qualifications: 3, 3, 1, 2, 3, 4

FINANCIAL/TERMS:
Cash Investment: $44.9K
Total Investment: $64.5 – 104.9K
Minimum Net Worth: $0K
Fees: Franchise - $44.9K
Royalty - 6-3% Varies;   Ad. - $350/month or 2%
Financial Performance Representation: Yes
Term of Contract (Years):   10/10/10
Avg. # of Employees: 1 FT, 33 PT
Passive Ownership: Discouraged
Encourage Conversions: Yes
Area Develop. Agreements: Yes
Sub-Franchising Contracts: No
Expand in Territory: Yes
Space Needs: N/A

SUPPORT & TRAINING:
Financial Assistance Provided: Yes (I)
Site Selection Assistance: N/A
Lease Negotiation Assistance: N/A
Co-operative Advertising: Yes
Franchisee Assoc./Member: No
Size of Corporate Staff: 50
Ongoing Support: C, D, G, H, I
Training: 5 business days Cincinnati, OH

SPECIFIC EXPANSION PLANS:
US: All United States
Canada: All Canada
Overseas: All Countries

With the senior care industry booming and projected to grow steadily to $193 billion by 2030, now is the perfect time to invest in a Home Helpers franchise, ranked the #1 senior care franchise in North America for 5 straight years by Entrepreneur magazine, among other awards. Combine your motivation to succeed and your passion for helping others with our proven system and you can enjoy the freedom and lifestyle you deserve.

Operating Units	12/31/2011	12/31/2012	12/31/2013
Franchised	311	318	324
% Change	--	2.25%	1.89%

Company-Owned	0	0	0
% Change	--	--	--
Total	311	318	324
% Change	--	2.25%	1.89%
Franchised as % of Total	100%	100%	100%

Investment Required

The initial fee to purchase a Home Helpers franchise is $44,900 in cash, or $50,900 with financing, for a territory of up to 175,000 people. Larger territories will cost $500 for every 1,000 additional people. Home Helpers provides the following range of investments required to open your initial franchise. The range assumes that all items are paid for in cash. To the extent that you choose to finance any of these expense items, your front-end investment could be substantially reduced.

Item	Established Low Range	Established High Range
Initial Franchise Fee	$44,900	$50,900
Furniture and Equipment	$500	$1,000
Computer System	$2,000	$4,000
Expenses While Training	$750	$1,500
Initial Deposits (Rent, Telephone, Bank)	$0	$2,000
Additional Funds (3 Months)	$10,000	$20,000
Pre-opening Promotion	$3,000	$4,000
Technology/Software Licensing Fee	$1,350	$1,500
Licensing Fee	$0	$15,000
Monthly Office Rental Payment	$0	$1,000
Insurance	$2,000	$4,000
Total Initial Investment	$64,500	$104,900

Ongoing Expenses

Franchisees must pay ongoing royalty fees equal to 6% down to 3% of gross revenues, with monthly minimums. Other fees include a national branding fee equal to 2% of gross revenue with a monthly minimum of $350, and local cooperative advertising of up to 3% of gross revenues.

What You Get: Training and Support

Franchisees will be enrolled in an initial training program of approximately one week to take place in Cincinnati, OH. Topics covered include business planning, client services, human resources management, and financial management. Home Helpers will continue to provide ongoing assistance via telephone, email, office visits, and web-based programs as deemed necessary.

Territory

Home Helpers grants exclusive territories.

HouseMaster Home Inspections

HouseMaster®

Home Inspections. Done Right. Since 1979.®

850 Bear Tavern Rd., # 303
Ewing, NJ 08628
Tel: (800) 526-3930, (732) 823-4087
Fax: (802) 419-3434
Email: kim.fanus@housemaster.com
Website: www.franchise.housemaster.com
Kim Fanus, Director of Franchise Development

HouseMaster has been helping entrepreneurs from all educational and business backgrounds realize their dreams for the past 35 years, and has collectively performed over 3 million inspections. It is our motto to go above and beyond in supporting our franchisees; providing training, comprehensive business planning, solid marketing programs, operations support, resources and coaching in all areas of the business. Franchisee and customer satisfaction alike, along with the highest level of quality service available are why HouseMaster continues to be the recognized authority on everything home inspection.

BACKGROUND:	IFA Member
Established: 1971;	First Franchised: 1979
Franchised Units:	320
Company-Owned Units:	5
Total Units:	325
Dist.:	US-286; CAN-34; O'seas-0
North America:	45 States, 8 Provinces
Density:	23 in NJ, 20 in NY, 18 in FL
Projected New Units (12 Months):	40
Qualifications:	4, 3, 2, 2, 5, 5

FINANCIAL/TERMS:	
Cash Investment:	$60.1 – 107.9K
Total Investment:	$60.1 – 107.9K
Minimum Net Worth:	$80K
Fees: Franchise -	$42.5K
Royalty - 7.5%;	Ad. - 2.5%
Financial Performance Representation:	Yes
Term of Contract (Years):	5/5
Avg. # of Employees:	Varies FT, Varies PT
Passive Ownership:	Not Allowed

Encourage Conversions:	N/A
Area Develop. Agreements:	Yes
Sub-Franchising Contracts:	No
Expand in Territory:	Yes
Space Needs:	N/A

SUPPORT & TRAINING:	
Financial Assistance Provided:	Yes (I)
Site Selection Assistance:	N/A
Lease Negotiation Assistance:	N/A
Co-operative Advertising:	Yes
Franchisee Assoc./Member:	Yes/Yes
Size of Corporate Staff:	12
Ongoing Support:	A,B,C,D,E,G,h,I
Training:	2 weeks Medford, NJ

SPECIFIC EXPANSION PLANS:	
US:	All United States
Canada:	All Canada
Overseas:	No

HouseMaster has been helping entrepreneurs from all educational and business backgrounds realize their dreams for the past 35 years, and has collectively performed over 3 million inspections. It is our motto to go above and beyond in supporting our franchisees; providing training, comprehensive business planning, solid marketing programs, operations support, resources and coaching in all areas of the business. Franchisee and customer satisfaction alike, along with the highest level of quality service available are why HouseMaster continues to be the recognized authority on everything home inspection.

Operating Units (in the U.S. and its Territories)	12/31/2011	12/31/2012	12/31/2013
Franchised	308	279	280
% Change	--	-9.42	0.36%
Affiliate-Owned	9	6	6
% Change	--	-33.33%	0.0%
Total	317	285	286

% Change	--	-10.09%	0.35%
Franchised as % of Total	97.16%	97.89%	97.90%

Investment Required

The initial fee for a HouseMaster franchise is $42,500. HouseMaster provides the following range of investments required to open your initial franchise. The range assumes that all items are paid for in cash. To the extent that you choose to finance any of these expense items, your front-end investment could be substantially reduced.

Item	Established Low Range	Established High Range
Initial Franchise Fee/Deposit Remittance Fee	$42,500	$42,500
Training Expenses	$500	$3,000
Licensing Compliance Costs	$0	$15,000
Marketing Materials and Supplies	$3,000	$6,000
Office Equipment, Furniture	$0	$2,000
Computer System	$150	$4,850
Rent	$0	$750
Prepaid Expenses	$250	$2,500
General Liability Insurance	$500	$2,500
Errors and Omissions Insurance	$2,500	$3,500
Legal Services	$1,000	$2,500
Conference Travel Expenses	$1,000	$3,000
Vehicle andVehicle Branding	$2,700	$5,800
Grand Opening Promotion Expense	$1,000	$3,000
Additional Funds (3 Months)	$6,000	$11,000
Total Initial Investment	$61,100	$107,900

Ongoing Expenses

Franchisees are required to pay royalties equal to 7.5% of the first $125,000 in gross sales per year; 7% on $125,001-$250,000; 6.5% on $250,001-$500,000; 6% on $500,001-$1,000,000; 5.5% on $1,000,001-$1,500,000; and 5% on gross sales over $1,500,000. Other ongoing fees include a marketing contribution that ranges from 2-2.5% of gross sales and a technology fee of $150 per month.

What You Get: Training and Support

New franchisees will complete a month of pre-classroom and business preparedness training prior to attending two weeks of marketing, operations and technical training through the National Institute of Building Inspectors in New Jersey. Additionally, HouseMaster will provide ongoing marketing and operations support, as well as continuing training opportunities, annual recertification testing, and national/regional conferences with educational sessions.

Territory

HouseMaster grants exclusive territories.

Intelligent Office

Intelligent Office®
Work Anywhere...Professionally

1515 Wynkoop St., # 360
Denver, CO 80202
Tel: (800) 800-4987, (303) 417-2100
Fax: (303) 448-8882
Email: tscalzotto@intelligentoffice.com

Website: www.intelligentoffice.com
Tonia Scalzotto, Director of Franchise Development

This highly evolved alternative to the traditional office provides a prestigious address, anywhere communications and a live receptionist for businesses, corporate executives and professionals, releasing them from the limitations and expense of a traditional or home office. INTELLIGENT OFFICE offers private offices, conference rooms and professional office services on an as-needed basis and at only a fraction of the cost of a traditional office.

BACKGROUND:	IFA Member	Encourage Conversions:	No
Established: 1995;	First Franchised: 1999	Area Develop. Agreements:	Yes
Franchised Units:	40	Sub-Franchising Contracts:	No
Company-Owned Units:	5	Expand in Territory:	No
Total Units:	45	Space Needs:	3,000 – 5,000 SF
Dist.:	US-45; CAN-18; O'seas-0		
North America:	19 States, 1 Province	**SUPPORT & TRAINING:**	
Density:	11 in ON, 7 in DC, 4 in VA	Financial Assistance Provided:	No
Projected New Units (12 Months):	18	Site Selection Assistance:	Yes
Qualifications:	5, 1, 1, 1, 1, 5	Lease Negotiation Assistance:	Yes
		Co-operative Advertising:	Yes
FINANCIAL/TERMS:		Franchisee Assoc./Member:	Yes/Yes
Cash Investment:	$150K	Size of Corporate Staff:	10
Total Investment:	$314.5 – 524.3K	Ongoing Support:	A,B,C,D,E,G,H,I
Minimum Net Worth:	$1M	Training:	1 Week Denver, CO; 1 Week On-Site;
Fees: Franchise -	$59K		2 Weeks Online
Royalty - 5%;	Ad. - $1,550/Mo.		
Financial Performance Representation:	Yes	**SPECIFIC EXPANSION PLANS:**	
Term of Contract (Years):	20/20	US:	All United States
Avg. # of Employees:	2 FT, 1 PT	Canada:	All Canada
Passive Ownership:	Allowed	Overseas:	All Countries

Intelligent Office Centers offer the next-generation of virtual officing and communications solutions, providing individuals and businesses with tele-communications, office space and office support services. Unlike traditional "executive suites" or office sharing arrangements, Intelligent Office Centers offer dedicated and non-dedicated office space, and "virtual" officing that provide specific telecommunications services that are not dependent on the physical location of the office.

Operating Units	12/31/2011	12/31/2012	12/31/2013
Franchised	29	33	32
% Change	--	13.79%	-3.03%
Company-Owned	4	5	5
% Change	--	25.0%	0.0%
Total	33	38	37
% Change	--	15.15%	-2.63
Franchised as % of Total	87.88%	86.84%	86.49%

Investment Required

The fee for an Intelligent Office franchise is $30,000. Intelligent Office provides the following range of investments required to open your initial franchise. The range assumes that all items are paid for in cash. To the extent that you choose to finance any of these expense items, your front-end investment could be substantially reduced.

Item	Established Low Range	Established High Range
Initial Franchise Fee	$30,000	$30,000
Marketing and Training Fee	$29,000	$29,000
Space Design and Plan; Other Architectural Services	$13,000	$15,000
Project Management Fee	$15,000	$15,000
Leasehold Improvements	$10,000	$86,000
Fixture Purchases	$59,000	$72,000
Furniture and Artwork	$47,000	$62,000
Office Equipment, Supplies and Plants	$6,200	$6,600
Security Deposits, Utility Deposits and Business Licenses	$5,000	$10,000
Additional Funds (6 months)	$102,500	$152,750
Total Initial Investment	$316,700	$478,350

Ongoing Expenses

Intelligent Office franchisees pay royalty fees equal to 5% of monthly gross revenue, a telephone technology fee based on gross revenues, with a minimum of $1,965 per month, and a data IP technology fee of $1,550 per month, among others.

What You Get: Training and Support

Prior to the initial training program, franchisees will complete approximately 60 hours of pre-training materials, including audio, visual, and written instructional materials. During the initial training program, franchisees undergo a total of approximately four days of classroom training at Intelligent Office's headquarters in the Denver, CO area and five days of on-the-job training. Topics include phone sales training, technical training, corporate culture, business services, marketing and system development.

Territory

Intelligent Office grants protected territories.

The Interface Financial Group - IFG 50/50

THE INTERFACE
FINANCIAL GROUP
50 / 50
Funding Small Business Together

7910 Woodmont Ave., # 1430
Bethesda, MD 20814
Tel: (800) 387-0860, (905) 475-5701
Fax: (240) 559-1213
Email: ifg@interfacefinancial.com
Website: www.interfacefinancial.com
David Banfield, President

Franchisees buy quality accounts receivable from client companies at a discount to provide short-term working capital to expanding businesses.

BACKGROUND:	IFA Member
Established: 1972;	First Franchised: 1990
Franchised Units:	54
Company-Owned Units:	0
Total Units:	54
Dist.:	US-45; CAN-2; O'seas-7
North America:	34 States, 6 Provinces
Density:	7 in FL, 2 in ON
Projected New Units (12 Months):	14
Qualifications:	1, 5, 2, 3, 1, 1

FINANCIAL/TERMS:	
Cash Investment:	$50K or less
Total Investment:	$50 – 100K
Minimum Net Worth:	$100 – 150K
Fees: Franchise -	$34.5K
Royalty - 8%;	Ad. - N/A
Financial Performance Representation:	No
Term of Contract (Years):	10/5

Avg. # of Employees:	N/A	Lease Negotiation Assistance:	N/A
Passive Ownership:	Not Allowed	Co-operative Advertising:	No
Encourage Conversions:	N/A	Franchisee Assoc./Member:	Yes/Yes
Area Develop. Agreements:	No	Size of Corporate Staff:	13
Sub-Franchising Contracts:	No	Ongoing Support:	D,G
Expand in Territory:	No	Training:	6 Days Total (2 days on-site)
Space Needs:	N/A		
		SPECIFIC EXPANSION PLANS:	
SUPPORT & TRAINING:		US:	All United States
Financial Assistance Provided:	No	Canada:	All Canada
Site Selection Assistance:	N/A	Overseas:	Australia and UK

The INTERFACE FINANCIAL GROUP is part of a trillion dollar industry that teaches franchisees how to be successful. Decades of experience in franchising give Interface the knowledge and expertise needed when venturing the world of franchising. Interface strives to give their clients control over their business and their lives through INTERFACE'S uniquely designed program. Please note that in 2014 the INTERFACE FINANCIAL GROUP re-branded as IFG 50/50 and currently has 45 units in the United States.

Operating Units	12/31/2011	12/31/2012	12/31/2013
Franchised	144	139	139
% Change	--	-3.47%	0.0%
Company-Owned	0	0	0
% Change	--	--	--
Total	144	139	139
% Change	--	-3.47%	0.0%
Franchised as % of Total	100%	100%	100%

Investment Required

The initial franchise fee for IFG 50/50 is $34,500. The INTERFACE FINANCIAL GROUP provides the following range of investments required to open your initial franchise. The range assumes that all items are paid for in cash. To the extent that you choose to finance any of these expense items, your front-end investment could be substantially reduced.

Item	Estimated Low Range	Estimated High Range
Initial Franchise Fee	$34,500	$34,500
Expenses While Traveling	$500	$1,000
Equipment	$800	$1,300
Initial Promotion	$1,000	$1,000
Additional Funds	$50,000	$100,000
Total Estimated Investment	$86,800	$137,800

Ongoing Expenses

Franchisees are responsible for a royalty fee of 8% of gross profits and a monthly maintenance fee of $150. The franchisee must also spend at least $1,000 for local promotional items within the first 90 days of opening the franchised business.

What You Get: Training and Support

Interface will provide a mandatory initial training program within six weeks of signing the franchise agreement. Training is split between the Interface corporate headquarters and your specific franchise location.

Territory

Interface doesn't grant exclusive territories as the franchise does not need to be in a specific location.

Jani-King International

16885 Dallas Pkwy.
Addison, TX 75001-5215
Tel: (800) 526-4546, (972) 991-0900
Fax: (972) 239-7706
Email: tlooney@janiking.com
Website: www.janiking.com
Ted Looney, Vice President of Franchising

JANI-KING INTERNATIONAL is the world's largest commercial cleaning franchisor, with locations in 14 countries and over 120 regions in the U. S. and abroad. Our franchise opportunity includes initial customer contracts, training, continuous local support, administrative and accounting assistance, an equipment leasing program and national advertising. If you are searching for a flexible business opportunity, look no further.

BACKGROUND:

	IFA Member
Established: 1969;	First Franchised: 1974
Franchised Units:	10,000
Company-Owned Units:	22
Total Units:	10,022
Dist.:	US-12,153; CAN-351; O'seas-528
North America:	39 States, 7 Provinces
Density:	500 in TX, 900 in FL, 900 in CA

Projected New Units (12 Months):	1
Qualifications:	2, 2, 1, 2, 2, 3

FINANCIAL/TERMS:

Cash Investment:	$2.9 – 33K
Total Investment:	$8.2 – 74K
Minimum Net Worth:	$2.9 – 33K
Fees: Franchise -	$8 – 33K
Royalty - 10%;	Ad. - 1%
Financial Performance Representation:	No
Term of Contract (Years):	20/20
Avg. # of Employees:	N/A
Passive Ownership:	Discouraged
Encourage Conversions:	N/A
Area Develop. Agreements:	Yes
Sub-Franchising Contracts:	Yes
Expand in Territory:	Yes
Space Needs:	N/A

SUPPORT & TRAINING:

Financial Assistance Provided:	No
Site Selection Assistance:	N/A
Lease Negotiation Assistance:	N/A
Co-operative Advertising:	No
Franchisee Assoc./Member:	Yes/Yes
Size of Corporate Staff:	65
Ongoing Support:	A,B,C,D,G,H,I
Training:	2+ weeks local regional office

SPECIFIC EXPANSION PLANS:

US:	All United States
Canada:	All Canada
Overseas:	All Countries

Jani-King is one of the world's leading commercial cleaning franchise companies with more than 12,000 authorized franchise owners worldwide. Through a network of more than 115 regional offices, Jani-King contracts commercial cleaning services, while the work is performed by franchisees who own and operate their own business. Since 1974, Jani-King has been a leader in franchising. Entrepreneur magazine recognizes Jani-King as one of the Top 10 Franchise companies, ranking it as the #3 Commercial Cleaning Franchise for 2010 and the #2 Low-Cost Franchise for 2010. Jani-King's top rankings are a direct reflection of the opportunity and support provided by Jani-King International and Jani-King regional offices around the world.

A Jani-King franchise offers aspiring new business owners the chance to begin their business with an initial client base to service, and a well-organized support system that helps new franchisees achieve a desired level of success.

Operating Units	12/31/2011	12/31/2012	12/31/2013
Franchised	8,948	8,028	7,481
% Change	--	-10.28%	-6.81%
Company-Owned	21	22	21
% Change	--	4.76%	-4.55%
Total	8,969	8,050	7,502
% Change	--	-10.25%	-6.81%
Franchised as % of Total	99.77%	99.73%	99.72%

Investment Required

The fee for a Jani-King franchise ranges from $16,250 to $142,750, including an initial finder's fee. The fee may be higher depending on the plan chosen. Jani-King provides the following range of investments required to open your initial franchise. The range assumes that all items are paid for in cash. To the extent that you choose to finance any of these expense items, your front-end investment could be substantially reduced.

Item	Established Low Range	Established High Range
Initial Franchise Fee and Initial Finder's Fee	$8,600	$16,250
Real Estate	$0	$5,000
Supplies	$600	$800
Equipment	$1,812	$5,781
Security Deposits, etc.	$100	$1,000
Business Entity Establishment Fees	$100	$1,000

Additional Funds (For initial 120 day period)	$800	$8,500
Total Initial Investment	$12,012	$38,331

Ongoing Expenses

Jani-King franchisees pay royalty fees equal to 10% of monthly gross revenue (subject to monthly minimums), an accounting fee equal to 3% of monthly gross revenue and an advertising fee equal to 2.0% of monthly gross revenues.

What You Get: Training and Support

Jani-King offers a level of training, business development and administrative support that is unparalleled in the cleaning industry. Jani-King's local regional offices provide franchisees with initial training in the operation of a franchise business. The program provides training in Jani-King's methods and practices of professional cleaning services, management and industry-specific training. Training also includes classroom lectures and discussions, actual demonstrations, printed manuals, video presentations, formal instruction and practical hands-on training. Home study materials, additional training seminars and refresher courses are available to help keep franchisees informed of the latest trends and technology in the industry. Jani-King supports franchisees on an ongoing basis by providing advice, business development support and technical support through its regional offices. Each office has a marketing staff whose goal is to provide new business to Jani-King franchisees and ensure the satisfaction of clients. The regional offices also provide franchisees with complete customer invoicing and other administrative support. Local operations teams are available 24 hours a day and perform routine inspections of each account. Jani-King franchisees have a vested interest in the work they perform because satisfaction is what drives their business.

Territory

Jani-King does not grant exclusive territories.

Jan-Pro Cleaning Systems

Measurable Cleaning. Guaranteed Results.™

2520 Northwinds Pkwy., # 375
Alpharetta, GA 30009
Tel: (866) 355-1064, (678) 336-1780
Fax: (678) 336-1782
Email: scott.thompson@premiumfranchisebrands.com
Website: www.jan-pro.com
Scott Thompson, Vice President of Franchise Development

Jan-Pro provides one of today's exceptional business opportunities, allowing you to enter one of the fastest-growing industries by safely becoming your own boss through the guidance and support of an established franchise organization.

BACKGROUND: IFA Member
Established: 1991; First Franchised: 1992
Franchised Units: 10,842
Company-Owned Units: 0
Total Units: 10,842
Dist.: US-9,235; CAN-793; O'seas-64
　North America: 39 States, 5 Provinces
　Density: 858 in GA, 695 in FL, 1,316 in CA
Projected New Units (12 Months): 2,000
Qualifications: 3, 2, 1, 1, 1, 1

FINANCIAL/TERMS:
Cash Investment: $1 – 30K
Total Investment: $2.8 – 44K
Minimum Net Worth: $50K
Fees: Franchise - $1 – 30K
　Royalty - 10%; Ad. - 0%
Financial Performance Representation: No
Term of Contract (Years): 5/5
Avg. # of Employees: 0 FT, 0 PT
Passive Ownership: Not Allowed
Encourage Conversions: Yes
Area Develop. Agreements: Yes
Sub-Franchising Contracts: Yes
Expand in Territory: Yes
Space Needs: 0 SF

SUPPORT & TRAINING:
Financial Assistance Provided: Yes (D)
Site Selection Assistance: Yes
Lease Negotiation Assistance: Yes
Co-operative Advertising: No
Franchisee Assoc./Member: Yes/No
Size of Corporate Staff: 15
Ongoing Support: A,B,C,D,E,F,G,H,I
Training: 5 Weeks Regional and Local

SPECIFIC EXPANSION PLANS:
US: All United States
Canada: All Canada
Overseas: All Countries except England and Ireland

Jan-Pro offers professional-quality cleaning services using the latest technology at the best possible price. The commercial cleaning franchise utilizes a decentralized management structure, which is one of the underlying factors for the company's success and robust growth. While unit franchise owners are responsible for serving clients, master franchise owners (of which there are currently 133) act as regional managers who award and manage unit franchises and bring in new clients. Jan-Pro provides comprehensive training and support, leaving master and unit franchisees free to manage and operate effectively. With over $300 million in sales and more than 10,000 franchisees nationwide, Jan-Pro is a major force in the nearly $140 billion commercial cleaning industry.

Regional Master Franchise Operating Units	12/31/2011	12/31/2012	12/31/2013
Franchised	84	81	80
% Change	--	-3.57%	-1.23%
Company-Owned	0	0	0
% Change	--	--	--
Total	84	81	80
% Change	--	-3.57%	-1.23%
Franchised as % of Total	100%	100%	100%

Investment Required

The fee for a Jan-Pro Cleaning Systems franchise ranges from $75,000-$600,000 depending on the population of the franchisee's territory. Jan-Pro provides the following range of investments required to open your initial franchise. The range assumes that all items are paid for in cash. To the extent that you choose to finance any of these expense items, your front-end investment could be substantially reduced.

Item	Established Low Range	Established High Range
Initial Franchise Fee	$75,000	$600,000
Real Estate	$1,500	$5,000
Initial Supplies	$1,500	$2,000
Equipment and Office Furniture	$7,500	$19,000
Licenses, Permits, Deposits, and Other Prepaid Expenses	$1,000	$3,000
Insurance	$1,000	$3,000
Training	$3,000	$5,000

Legal Fees and Registration Expenses	$1,500	$10,000
Computer Hardware and Software	$2,750	$5,000
Initial Advertising Expenses	$3,000	$5,000
Additional Funds (3 Months)	$75,000	$100,000
Total Initial Investment	$172,750	$757,000

Ongoing Expenses

Jan-Pro Regional Master franchisees pay contract services fees equal to 4% of gross monthly revenue, monthly advertising fees equal to $150, and sales royalty fees equal to 10% of the total initial franchise fees. Account upgrade fees and financing charges are paid by unit franchisees. Additional fees payable by the franchisee include computer-related service fees and national accounts support fees equal.

What You Get: Training and Support

Initial training for master franchisees is located at Jan-Pro headquarters in Alpharetta, GA, and consists of four weeks of classroom and on-the-job training. Topics include franchise sales, recruiting, office management and procedures, contract sales, and cleaning methods and procedures. Jan-Pro's tried and true support system continues after initial training, with ongoing regional support and meetings. Jan-Pro also provides assistance with site selection, as well as regularly updated training manuals, videos, and presentations.

Territory

Jan-Pro grants exclusive territories to Regional Master Franchisees containing a minimum of 500,000 daytime population.

Kiddie Academy

KIDDIE 🎓 ACADEMY.
EDUCATIONAL CHILD CARE

3415 Box Hill Corporate Center Dr.
Abington, MD 21009
Tel: (800) 554-3343, (410) 515-5436
Fax: (410) 569-2729
Email: gwhite@kiddieacademy.com
Website: www.kiddieacademyframchising.com
Greg White, Vice President Franchise Development

We offer comprehensive training and support without additional cost. KIDDIE ACADEMY's step-by-step program assists with staff recruitment, training, accounting support, site selection, marketing, advertising and curriculum. A true turn-key opportunity that provides ongoing support so you can focus on running a successful business.

BACKGROUND: IFA Member
Established: 1981; First Franchised: 1992
Franchised Units: 125
Company-Owned Units: 0
Total Units: 125
Dist.: US-125; CAN-0; O'seas-0
North America: 22 States
Density: 19 in NJ, 19 in NY, 16 in CA
Projected New Units (12 Months): 20
Qualifications: 4, 4, 2, 3, 2, 4

FINANCIAL/TERMS:
Cash Investment: $175K
Total Investment: $372.7 – 702K
Minimum Net Worth: $450K
Fees: Franchise - $120K
Royalty - 7%; Ad. - 2%
Financial Performance Representation: Yes
Term of Contract (Years): 15/15
Avg. # of Employees: N/A
Passive Ownership: Not Allowed
Encourage Conversions: Yes
Area Develop. Agreements: No
Sub-Franchising Contracts: No
Expand in Territory: Yes
Space Needs: 7,000-10,000 SF

SUPPORT & TRAINING:
Financial Assistance Provided: Yes (I)
Site Selection Assistance: Yes
Lease Negotiation Assistance: Yes
Co-operative Advertising: Yes
Franchisee Assoc./Member: No
Size of Corporate Staff: 45
Ongoing Support: B,C,D,E,G,H,I
Training: Ongoing staff training;
1 Week Director Training, Corp. HQ;
1 Weeks Owner Training, Corp. HQ

SPECIFIC EXPANSION PLANS:
US: All United States
Canada: No
Overseas: No

Since its launch more than 30 years ago, KIDDIE ACADEMY has become a leader in early child education with locations coast to coast. At the center of KIDDIE ACAdEMY's educational philosophy is an age-appropriate curriculum based on the individual needs of each child. Kiddie Academy's Life Essentials program emphasizes taking advantage of learning opportunities throughout a child's normal daily routine, a learning approach that sets Kiddie Academy apart from ordinary nursery schools. Along with healthy eating habits and character development, KIDDIE ACADEMY provides well-rounded, enriching, and educationally focused care that parents everywhere constantly seek.

Operating Units	12/31/2011	12/31/2012	12/31/2013
Franchised	92	106	112
% Change	--	15.22%	5.66%
Company-Owned	2	2	2
% Change	--	0.0%	0.0%
Total	94	108	114
% Change	--	14.89%	5.56%
Franchised as % of Total	97.87%	98.15%	98.25%

Investment Required

The initial fee for a KIDDIE ACADEMY franchise is $20,000. KIDDIE ACADEMY provides the following range of investments required to open your initial franchise. The range assumes that all items are paid for in cash. To the extent that you choose to finance any of these expense items, your front-end investment could be substantially reduced. Please note that the figures below represent expenses for a leased franchise location.

Item	Established Low Range	Established High Range
Initial Fees	$120,000	$120,000
Lease Deposit	$10,000	$85,000
Professional Fees and Loan Fees	$18,000	$70,000
Kitchen Equipment and Supplies	$14,000	$22,000
Supplies/Equipment for Inside of Academy, Playground and Online Training Component	$75,000	$145,000
Outdoor Fixed Playground Equipment	$39,000	$57,000
Computer Hardware and Software and Classroom Technology	$20,000	$25,000

Office and Lobby Furniture, Office Equipment and Supplies, and Telephone System	$8,000	$14,000
Indoor and Outdoor Signage	$10,000	$18,000
Expenses While Training	$1,000	$5,000
Transportation Vehicles and Equipment	$0	$5,000
Insurance and Utility Deposits	$2,500	$5,000
Business Licenses	$200	$1,000
Start-Up Marketing and Advertising Expenses	$30,000	$30,000
Additional Funds (3 Months)	$25,000	$100,000
Total Initial Investment	$372,700	$702,000

Ongoing Expenses

Kiddie Academy franchisees pay a royalty fee equal to 7% of gross revenues and an advertising and brand building fund contribution equal to 2% of gross revenues.

What You Get: Training and Support

Kiddie Academy offers an initial four-week franchisee training program, as well as a five-day program for site directors that will be held at corporate headquarters near Baltimore, MD and in the surrounding area. Additional on-site training, covering day-to-day management and operations, is provided prior to grand opening. Assistance with obtaining all childcare facility licenses required by local governmental agencies and purchasing necessary children's learning and play equipment is also provided. Kiddie Academy also provides ongoing assistance with educational materials and marketing of the academy, as well as on-site support visits and evaluations when deemed necessary.

Territory

Kiddie Academy grants protected territories.

KidzArt |

301 Main Plaza, # 3376
New Braunfels, TX 78130
Tel: (888) 813-2287, (517) 784-5000
Fax: (517) 338-5300
Email: sure$kidzart.com
Website: www.kidzart.com
Sue Bartman, President

KidzArt's drawing-based fine arts programs emphasize creativity, individuality and building confidence for all ages groups. You don't have to be an artist to own and operate a KidzArt franchise! While art education is all but eliminated from many schools around the country, KidzArt is providing a viable solution with after school fine arts programs, as well as programs that serve all ages. KidzArt programs and locations are simple to establish and businesses love to partner with us. Our rave reviews and national recognition from parents, teachers, educational administrators and community leaders will support you in your efforts. With KidzArt your opportunities are endless. And that's just the beginning.

BACKGROUND:	IFA Member
Established: 1998;	First Franchised: 2002
Franchised Units:	74
Company-Owned Units:	0
Total Units:	74

Dist.:	US-74; CAN-0; O'seas-0
North America:	29 States
Density:	10 in AZ, 9 in CA, 4 in NC
Projected New Units (12 Months):	N/A
Qualifications:	3, 5, 2, 3, 4, 5

FINANCIAL/TERMS:	
Cash Investment:	$50 – 70K
Total Investment:	$17.8 – 39.3K
Minimum Net Worth:	$200K
Fees: Franchise -	$32K
Royalty - 8%/$250 Min.;	Ad. - 1%
Financial Performance Representation:	No
Term of Contract (Years):	10/10
Avg. # of Employees:	2 FT, 4-15 PT
Passive Ownership:	Allowed
Encourage Conversions:	No
Area Develop. Agreements:	No
Sub-Franchising Contracts:	No
Expand in Territory:	No
Space Needs:	N/A

SUPPORT & TRAINING:	
Financial Assistance Provided:	No
Site Selection Assistance:	Yes
Lease Negotiation Assistance:	N/A
Co-operative Advertising:	No
Franchisee Assoc./Member:	Yes/Yes
Size of Corporate Staff:	7
Ongoing Support:	C,D,E,G,h,I
Training:	4 Days New Braunfels, TX

SPECIFIC EXPANSION PLANS:	
US:	All States Exc. Registration
Canada:	No
Overseas:	No

In the early 1990s, longtime friends, Shell Herman and Chris Cruikshank shared a common vision: to build a successful business enterprise that would lift the spirit, enliven the soul, and reward the participants and the communities where they lived. The result: KidzArt. From the Picassos-in-training to those who think they'll never get it, art becomes approachable and much more fun than ever imagined with KidzArt. KidzArt is a business that offers an opportunity to be successful and creative while doing what you love for a living. In July 2002, KidzArt realized a major benchmark, becoming fully franchised. In 2004, they were named one of Entrepreneur Magazine's Top 500 Franchises. Today KidzArt is ranked by Entrepreneur Magazine as the Number One Art franchise in the country.

Operating Units	12/31/2011	12/31/2012	12/31/2013
Franchised	60	60	63
% Change	--	0.0%	5.0%
Company-Owned	0	0	1
% Change	--	--	--
Total	60	60	64
% Change	--	0.0%	6.67%
Franchised as % of Total	100%	100%	98.43%

Investment Required

The initial fee to purchase a KidzArt franchise is $39,900 or $24,900 for a Club Scientific franchise. KidzArt provides the following range of investments required to open your initial franchise. The range assumes that all items are paid for in cash. To the extent that you choose to finance any of these expense items, your front-end investment could be substantially reduced. Please note that the figures below represent expenses for a standard KidzArt franchise.

Item	Established Low Range	Established High Range
Franchise Fee	$39,900	$39,900

Initial Training	$1,000	$2,500
Certified Instructor Training	$0	$500
Initial Art Inventory Fee	$820	$820
Initial Marketing Materials Fee	$575	$575
Initial Website Fee and Web Hosting Fee	$500	$500
Initial Registration Setup Fee and Monthly Registration Fee	$510	$510
Video Camera	$0	$600
Local Advertising	$100	$500
Insurance	$150	$250
Miscellaneous Opening Costs	$2,000	$4,500
Additional Funds (3 Months)	$500	$2,500
Total Initial Investment	$46,055	$52,755

Ongoing Expenses

Franchisees are required to pay ongoing royalty fees equal to 8% of monthly gross revenues with a minimum royalty of $300 per month for the first year of the franchise term, and $400 per month thereafter. Other fees include an advertising fee equal to 1% of gross revenue with a minimum of $25 per month and various technology fees.

What You Get: Training and Support

Franchisees will be enrolled in a week-long initial training program to take place at company headquarters in Jackson, MI which will cover teaching art, working with children, art materials, management, sales, and operating procedures. KidzArt will continue to offer advice and guidance concerning the franchise, as well as conduct visits by field representatives and annual conferences when appropriate.

Territory

KidzArt grants exclusive territories with a population of 15,000 qualifying households. You may expand your territory by paying $0.40 per additional qualifying household.

Kinderdance International

Education Through Dance

INTERNATIONAL
"Established in 1979"
1333 Gateway Dr., # 1003
Melbourne, FL 32901
Tel: (800) 554-2334, (321) 984-4448
Fax: (321) 984-4490
Email: karenmaltese@kinderdance.com
Website: www.kinderdance.com
Karen Maltese, VP Franchise Development

KINDERDANCE is the original Developmental Dance, Motor Skills, Gymnastics, Music and Fitness Program, blended with academics, specifically designed for boys and girls age 2 to 12. KINDERDANCE franchisees are trained to teach 5 developmentally unique "Education Through Dance and Motor Development" programs: KINDERDANCE, KINDERGYM, KINDERTOTS), KINDERCOMBO, as well as KINDERMOTION, which are designed for boys and girls ages 2-12. Children learn the basics of ballet, tap, gymnastics, motor development and creative dance, as well as learning numbers, colors, shapes and songs. No studio or dance experience required. Franchisees teach at child care centers and other viable locations.

BACKGROUND:	IFA Member
Established: 1979;	First Franchised: 1985
Franchised Units:	125
Company-Owned Units:	2
Total Units:	127

Dist.:	US-123; CAN-2; O'seas-10
North America:	38 States, 1 Province
Density:	8 in TX, 14 in FL, 12 in CA
Projected New Units (12 Months):	20
Qualifications:	2, 2, 1, 2, 2, 5

FINANCIAL/TERMS:	
Cash Investment:	$12 – 40K
Total Investment:	$15 – 46K
Minimum Net Worth:	N/A
Fees: Franchise -	$12 – 40K
Royalty - 6-15%;	Ad. - 3%
Financial Performance Representation:	Yes
Term of Contract (Years):	5/5
Avg. # of Employees:	2 FT, 1-2+ PT
Passive Ownership:	Not Allowed
Encourage Conversions:	Yes
Area Develop. Agreements:	Yes
Sub-Franchising Contracts:	No
Expand in Territory:	Yes
Space Needs:	N/A

SUPPORT & TRAINING:	
Financial Assistance Provided:	Yes (D)
Site Selection Assistance:	N/A
Lease Negotiation Assistance:	N/A
Co-operative Advertising:	Yes
Franchisee Assoc./Member:	Yes/Yes
Size of Corporate Staff:	8
Ongoing Support:	A,B,C,D,E,F,G,H,I
Training:	6+ days Melbourne, FL and On-Site

SPECIFIC EXPANSION PLANS:	
US:	All United States
Canada:	All Canada
Overseas:	Europe, Asia, New Zealand, South America, Mexico, Australia

KINDERDANCE is designed for children ages 2 to 12. The KINDER-DANCE system incorporates dance, motor development, gymnastics, fitness, and education concepts. The program has emphasized building self-confidence and self-esteem in young children since its creation in 1981.

Operating Units	12/31/2011	12/31/2012	12/31/2013
Franchised	125	117	118
% Change	--	-6.4%	0.85%
Company-Owned	2	2	2
% Change	--	0%	0%
Total	127	119	120
% Change	--	-6.3%	0.84%
Franchised as % of Total	98.43%	98.32%	98.33%

Investment Required

A KINDERDANCE franchise is available for purchase at three different levels: $12,000 for a Bronze franchise, $20,000 for a Silver franchise, and $30,000 for a Gold franchise. Kinderdance provides the following range of investments required to open your initial franchise. The range assumes all items are paid for in cash. To the extent that you choose to finance any of these expense items, your front-end investment could be substantially reduced. The estimated initial investment required for KINDERDANCE franchises have been broken down by the three different program levels.

Item	Established Low Range	Established High Range
Bronze Franchise		
Initial Franchise Fee	$12,000	$12,000
Initial Inventory	$125	$125
Expenses While Training	$425	$1,000
Insurance	$400	$600
Additional Funds	$2,000	$4,000

Total Initial Investment	$14,950	$17,725
Silver Franchise		
Initial Franchise Fee	$20,000	$20,000
Initial Inventory	$275	$275
Expenses While Training	$450	$1,000
Insurance	$400	$600
Additional Funds	$2,000	$4,000
Total Initial Investment	$23,100	$25,875
Gold Franchise		
Initial Franchise Fee	$30,000	$30,000
Initial Inventory	$500	$500
Area Representative Fee (optional)	$10,000	$10,000
Expenses While Training	$450	$1,000
Insurance	$400	$600
Additional Funds	$2,000	$4,000
Total Initial Investment	$33,350	$36,100

Ongoing Expenses

In addition to the estimated initial fees, the franchisee is responsible for paying other ongoing fees. The royalty fee is dependent on the type of franchise program you have: bronze franchises pay a minimum of $100 per month or 12% of gross revenues; silver franchises pay a minimum of $200 per month or 7-10% of gross revenues; gold franchises pay $300 per month or 6-7% of gross sales. Franchises are also responsible for paying an advertising contribution equaling 3% of monthly gross sales, as well as $500 per employee for training.

What You Get: Training and Support

During initial training, in Melbourne, FL, KINDERDANCE will instruct trainees on the basic KINDERDANCE programs and operation of a KIN-

DERDANCE business for five to seven days. Training is provided by Kinderdance, but the trainees are responsible for taking care of all other related costs such as food, lodgings, etc. Kinderdance charges an additional training fee for training more than one person for Silver franchises and more than two people for Gold franchises. Kinderdance also hosts an annual conference which provides advanced training in Kinderdance, Kindergym, Kindermotion, and Kindercombo. Kinderdance does not charge for this annual conference, but the franchisee is responsible for paying all other expenses.

Territory

The Bronze program is limited to 10 locations in a non-exclusive area. The Silver is limited to 20 locations in a non-exclusive area. Bronze and Silver (franchisees) are not allowed to hire and train teachers. We do not grant exclusive territories, but we do warrant that we will not appoint more than 1 Silver or Bronze Level franchise per each unit of 100,000 population, or portion of it, in your Territory. The Gold program allows you to operate a Kinderdance Business solely in the Territory.

Kitchen Tune-Up

kitchen**tune·up**®
Remodeling your expectations.

813 Circle Dr.
Aberdeen, SD 57401
Tel: (800) 333-6385, (605) 225-4049
Fax: (800) 308-4206
Email: craig@kitchentuneup.com
Website: www.kitchentuneup.com
Craig Green, Franchise Director

The housing downturn hasn't hurt the "mini-remodeling" market! We're recession proof. Join Kitchen Tune-Up, the number one ranked kitchen and bath remodeling franchise. You will serve the growing home remodeling industry and enjoy the convenience of working from your home. Retail location business models are also available if you prefer to have a store front. We have been offering franchise opportunities since 1988. We offer "Kitchen Solutions for Any Budget": cabinet & wood restoration, cabinet refacing, custom cabinetry, custom storage solutions and more. If you are looking for the freedom of owning your own business, are driven to succeed and enjoy meeting and helping people, this may be the ideal opportunity for you.

BACKGROUND:	IFA Member
Established: 1975;	First Franchised: 1988
Franchised Units:	104
Company-Owned Units:	0
Total Units:	104

Dist.:	US-102; CAN-2; O'seas-0
North America:	38 States, 2 Provinces
Density:	11 in FL, 10 in CO, 10 in IL
Projected New Units (12 Months):	40
Qualifications:	4, 5, 1, 3, 2, 4

FINANCIAL/TERMS:

Cash Investment:	$50 – 55K
Total Investment:	$83 – 91K
Minimum Net Worth:	$150K
Fees: Franchise -	$25K
Royalty - Varies;	Ad. - $300/mo
Financial Performance Representation:	Yes
Term of Contract (Years):	10/10
Avg. # of Employees:	2-3 FT, 1 PT
Passive Ownership:	Not Allowed
Encourage Conversions:	Yes
Area Develop. Agreements:	Yes
Sub-Franchising Contracts:	No

Expand in Territory:	Yes
Space Needs:	500 – 2,500 SF

SUPPORT & TRAINING:

Financial Assistance Provided:	Yes (D)
Site Selection Assistance:	Yes
Lease Negotiation Assistance:	No
Co-operative Advertising:	Yes
Franchisee Assoc./Member:	Yes/Yes
Size of Corporate Staff:	14
Ongoing Support:	A,B,D,e,G,h,I
Training:	9 Days Home Office; 2-3 Weeks Pre-Training; 4 Days In-the-Field Training

SPECIFIC EXPANSION PLANS:

US:	All States
Canada:	Masters Only
Overseas:	No

Kitchen Tune-Up is one of the top-ranked kitchen and bath remodeling franchises. Established in 1975, Kitchen Tune-Up has been franchising since 1988 and providing services such as on-site wood restoration, repair services, replacing cabinets and hardware, closet and shelf organizers, and more.

Operating Units	12/31/2011	12/31/2012	12/31/2013
Franchised	155	155	178
% Change	--	0.0%	14.84%
Company-Owned	0	0	0
% Change	--	--	--
Total	155	155	178
% Change	--	0.0%	14.84%
Franchised as % of Total	100%	100%	100%

Investment Required

The initial fee to purchase a Kitchen Tune-Up franchise is $39,995. Kitchen Tune-Up provides the following range of investments required to open your initial franchise. The range assumes that all items are paid for in cash. To the extent that you choose to finance any of these expense items, your front-end investment could be substantially reduced.

Item	Established Low Range	Established High Range
Initial Franchise Fee	$39,995	$39,995
Expenses while Training	$1,000	$2,000
Vehicle	$500	$1,600
Misc. Tools and Office Supplies	$350	$3,000
Misc. Opening Costs	$200	$1,500
Insurance	$1,000	$3,000
Advertising (3months)	5% of gross revenue	10% of gross revenue
Additional Funds (3 months)	$2,500	$4,000
Lead Safe	$300	$300
Total Initial Investment	$45,845	$55,395

*This deposit reserves the proposed franchised area until franchisee completes the standard training program. On completion of training, this deposit is then applied to the initial franchise fee.

Ongoing Expenses

Franchisees are required to pay ongoing royalty fees equal to 7% of gross revenue or at least $300 per month, as well as a recommended local marketing expenditure of 5-10% of gross revenue.

What You Get: Training and Support

Franchisees will receive 5 days of in-person classroom and practical training in Aberdeen, SD, followed by 3-4 days of field training no later than 60 days following the completion of classroom training. The franchisee will also participate in Kitchen Tune-Up's Twelve Week Action Plan which is meant to reinforce and supplement various facets of the training program. Franchisees are also required to attend the annual International Reunion and Training Seminar. Kitchen Tune-Up will continue to provide general consultation and advice regarding the operation of the franchise, as well as additional training as deemed necessary.

Territory

Kitchen Tune-Up grants exclusive territories except in certain metropolitan areas.

Kumon North America

KUM○N®

MATH. READING. SUCCESS.

300 Frank W. Burr Blvd., # 6
Teaneck, NJ 07666
Tel: (866) 633-0740, (201) 928-0444
Fax: (201) 692-3130
Email: tkuczek@kumon.com
Website: www.kumonfranchise.com
Thomas Kuczek, Vice President of Franchising

Premiere supplemental education franchise where you'll find success, one child at a time.

BACKGROUND: IFA Member
Established: 1958; First Franchised: 1958
Franchised Units: 1,975
Company-Owned Units: 25
Total Units: 2,000
Dist.: US-1,492; CAN-328; O'seas-23,590
North America: 50 States, 9 Provinces
Density: 110 in TX, 93 in NY, 241 in CA
Projected New Units (12 Months): 120
Qualifications: 3, 3, 3, 5, 4, 4

FINANCIAL/TERMS:
Cash Investment: $70K

Total Investment: $72.2 – 149.3K
Minimum Net Worth: $150K
Fees: Franchise - $1K, Materials: $1K
  Royalty - $32-$36/subj./mo.; Ad. - N/A
Financial Performance Representation: Yes
Term of Contract (Years): 5
Avg. # of Employees: 1 FT, 1-3 PT
Passive Ownership: Not Allowed
Encourage Conversions: N/A
Area Develop. Agreements: No
Sub-Franchising Contracts: No
Expand in Territory: No
Space Needs: 1,000 SF

SUPPORT & TRAINING:
Financial Assistance Provided: No
Site Selection Assistance: Yes
Lease Negotiation Assistance: No
Co-operative Advertising: Yes
Franchisee Assoc./Member: Yes/Yes
Size of Corporate Staff: 400
Ongoing Support: C,D,E,F,G,H,I
Training: Kumon University Teaneck, NJ and
  local region; 13-16 days total start-up

SPECIFIC EXPANSION PLANS:
US: All United States
Canada: All Canada
Overseas: All Countries

Kumon is one of the largest and most established franchises in the world, and is a leader in the after-school enrichment programs industry. With nearly 365,000 students enrolled in over 1,500 centers in North America, Kumon tailors highly effective after-school math and reading programs specializing in individualized, self-paced learning. Services cater to both students who need extra help and advanced students who need a challenge. The individualized programs provide students a richer and more successful learning experience, fostering the confidence that is necessary to accomplish more on their own. Kumon is looking for achievement-oriented franchisees who love to work with children. A background in education is not necessary, as Kumon provides all the training and support you will need in order to run a successful business and help children with their goals in education.

Operating Units	12/31/2011	12/31/2012	12/31/2013
Franchised	1,423	1,475	1,468
% Change	--	3.65%	-0.47%
Company-Owned	26	25	28
% Change	--	-3.85%	12.0%
Total	1,449	1,500	1,496
% Change	--	3.52%	-0.27%
Franchised as % of Total	98.21%	98.33%	98.13%

Investment Required

The initial fee for a Kumon franchise is $1,000. Kumon provides the following range of investments required to open your initial franchise. The range assumes that all items are paid for in cash. To the extent that you choose to finance any of these expense items, your front-end investment could be substantially reduced.

Item	Established Low Range	Established High Range
Training Agreement Deposit Fee	$500	$500

Expenses While Training	$5,385	$9,700
Initial Franchise Fee	$1,000	$1,000
Initial Purchase of Materials	$1,000	$1,000
Architect Design	$0	$9,500
Leasehold Improvements	$30,000	$65,000
Security Deposit (if required)	$0	$4,500
Rent	$1,500	$4,500
Furniture, Equipment, Primary Sign, and Supplies	$9,000	$19,000
Notebook Computer	$600	$1,400
Professional Fees	$1,000	$3,000
Liability Insurance	$449	$449
Business License, Name Registration	$100	$200
Lead Management Telephone System	$340	$340
Recommended Reading List	$2,545	$2,545
Fingerprinting, Criminal Background Check	$18	$60
Payroll Cost for Assistants	$3,750	$4,125
New Center Marketing	$2,000	$5,000
Additional Funds (3 Months)	$13,500	$18,000
Total Initial Investment	$72,187	$149,319

Ongoing Expenses

Kumon franchisees pay an initial enrollment fee of $15 for each newly enrolled student, and monthly royalty fees equal to $36 times the number of full-paying students enrolled and $18 times the number of partially exempt and/or prorated tuition students during the Temporary License Period. After completion of the Temporary License Period, franchisees pay monthly royalty fees equal to $32 times the number of full-paying students enrolled and $16 times the number of partially exempt and/or prorated tuition students. Kumon franchisees also pay insurance fees of $4.32 per math student per year.

What You Get: Training and Support

Before awarding a franchise, Kumon requires applicants to complete two semesters of training, the first lasting 4-5 months and the second taking approximately five days of classroom training to complete. Completion of the first semester of the Instructor Development Program includes training at a Kumon Branch Office, training at the Kumon Regional Office for the region where you are located, In-Center training at an existing Kumon Center, on-line training, homework assignments, study of curriculum and worksheets, and two or four trips to Kumon University, Teaneck, New Jersey to attend the classroom portion of the training. The second semester requires travel to Kumon University, Teaneck, New Jersey following opening for two additional courses. Kumon offers continuous support to franchisees both in program administration and center growth and development by providing follow-up training and monthly instructor meetings at branch offices. Kumon reviews student materials to keep learning methods updated and efficient. Kumon marketing efforts have become increasingly aggressive to support current franchisees in their efforts to reach as many potential students as possible.

Territory

Kumon does not grant exclusive territories.

LearningRx

train the brain. get smarter. guaranteed.

5085 List Dr., # 200
Colorado Springs, CO 80919
Tel: (866) 679-1569, (719) 955-6708
Fax: (719) 522-0434
Email: sales@learningrx.com
Website: www.learningrx-franchise.com
Jordan Vaughan, Franchise Development Coordinator

LearningRx is a personal one-on-one Brain Training franchise leading the Brain Training industry with unmatched training results. LearningRx improves skills like memory, attention, and processing speed and has programs that can help people of all ages with ADHD, autism, dyslexia, brain injury, etc. Studies show that 88% of learning/processing problems are caused by one or more weak cognitive skills, and LearningRx is the expert in assessing and improving these skills. One on one brain training and our proprietary methodology make LearningRx the answer to remediation and enhancement for all ages.

BACKGROUND:

	IFA Member
Established: 1986;	First Franchised: 2003
Franchised Units:	91
Company-Owned Units:	2
Total Units:	93
Dist.:	US-93; CAN-0; O'seas-0
North America:	28 States

Density:	16 in TX, 7 in MN, 7 in VA
Projected New Units (12 Months):	20
Qualifications:	3, 3, 3, 3, 4, 4

FINANCIAL/TERMS:

Cash Investment:	$65 – 75K
Total Investment:	$109 – 209K
Minimum Net Worth:	$250K
Fees: Franchise -	$25 – 35K
Royalty - 10%;	Ad. - 2.5%
Financial Performance Representation:	Yes
Term of Contract (Years):	10/10
Avg. # of Employees:	3 FT, 20 PT
Passive Ownership:	Not Allowed
Encourage Conversions:	N/A
Area Develop. Agreements:	Yes
Sub-Franchising Contracts:	No
Expand in Territory:	Yes
Space Needs:	1,200 – 1,800 SF

SUPPORT & TRAINING:

Financial Assistance Provided:	No
Site Selection Assistance:	Yes
Lease Negotiation Assistance:	No
Co-operative Advertising:	No
Franchisee Assoc./Member:	No
Size of Corporate Staff:	20
Ongoing Support:	A,C,G,H
Training:	2 Weeks plus On-Site

SPECIFIC EXPANSION PLANS:

US:	Yes
Canada:	No
Overseas:	No

LearningRx is one of the top educational and child franchises in the nation. We change lives every day through the incredible power of brain training. Our programs are designed to target weak cognitive skills and help anyone from age 4 to 94 to achieve guaranteed results. Our goal is to ensure that people of all ages can receive the help they need to train their brains, get smarter, and be successful in life. For almost 30 years, and with the help of tens of thousands of students, LearningRx's founders improved the programs to become #1 in results. Our franchises are owned and operated by individuals from all over the professional spectrum, from audiologists to psychologists; from entrepreneurs to moms and dads with kids of their own. If purpose, meaning, helping others, and making a difference are important to you, then LearningRx might be the right business for you.

Operating Units	12/31/2011	12/31/2012	12/31/2013
Franchised	74	79	88
% Change	--	6.76%	11.39%
Company-Owned	2	2	2
% Change	--	0.0%	0.0%
Total	76	81	90
% Change	--	6.58%	11.11%
Franchised as % of Total	97.37%	97.53%	97.78%

Investment Required

The initial fee for a LearningRx franchise is $25,000 for an area with a population of up to 75,000 people, or $35,000 for an area with a population between 75,000 and 200,000 people. LearningRx provides the following range of investments required to open your initial franchise. The range assumes that all items are paid for in cash. To the extent that you choose to finance any of these expense items, your front-end investment could be substantially reduced.

Item	Established Low Range	Established High Range
Initial Franchise Fee	$25,000	$35,000
Initial Training and Material Fee	$10,000	$10,000
Travel and Living Expenses	$3,000	$4,000
Rent or Real Estate and Improvements	$3,000	$20,000
Furniture and Fixtures	$5,000	$15,000
Signage	$2,000	$6,000

Misc. Opening Costs	$3,000	$5,000
Opening Inventory	$3,000	$5,000
Advertising (6 months)	$30,000	$45,000
Insurance Policies	$1,000	$3,000
Computer Equipment & Proprietary Software	$4,000	$6,000
Additional Funds (3 months)	$20,000	$55,000
Total Initial Investment	$109,000	$209,000

Ongoing Expenses

Franchisees pay monthly royalties equal to 10% of gross revenues, a marketing development fund of 2.5% of gross revenues per month, and backbone advertising fund of up to $4,000 of gross revenues per month. Additional fees include advertising cooperatives, computer equipment maintenance fees, and a technology fee.

What You Get: Training and Support

LearningRx franchisees, their designated manager, and up to two additional employees will be enrolled in an initial training course conducted at company headquarters in Colorado Springs, CO. The program will cover all aspects of the LearningRx business model, including accounting, marketing, skills testing, ThinkRx, ReadRx, MathRx, ComprehendRx, and Liftoff procedures, and personnel. LearningRx will also provide up to four days of initial on-site training at franchise's location. LearningRx will also offer continuing advisory services by phone or in-person on request, as well as marketing and promotional materials assistance.

Territory

LearningRx grants exclusive territories.

Liberty Tax Service

Total Units:	4,438
Dist.:	US-4,175; CAN-263; O'seas-0
North America:	50 States, 10 Provinces
Density:	N/A
Projected New Units (12 Months):	500
Qualifications:	2, 4, 2, 1, 3, 5

FINANCIAL/TERMS:

Cash Investment:	$57.8 – 71.9K
Total Investment:	$57.8 – 71.9K
Minimum Net Worth:	$50K
Fees: Franchise -	$40K
Royalty - 14%;	Ad. - 5%
Financial Performance Representations:	No
Term of Contract (Years):	5/5
Avg. # of Employees:	4-6 FT, 2 PT
Passive Ownership:	Discouraged
Encourage Conversions:	No
Area Develop. Agreements:	Yes
Sub-Franchising Contracts:	No
Expand in Territory:	Yes
Space Needs:	400+ SF

1716 Corporate Landing Pkwy.
Virginia Beach, VA 23454
Tel: (877) 285-4237, (757) 493-8855
Fax: (800) 880-6432
Email: sales@libtax.com
Website: www.libertytaxfranchise.com
David Tarr, Director of Franchise Development

LIBERTY TAX SERVICE is one of the fastest-growing international tax services ever, and has been ranked on Entrepreneur magazine's annual "Franchise 500" every year since 1998. Any given year, there is a ready market of taxpayers, and as the tax laws change frequently, many taxpayers are turning to professional preparers to complete that annual task. LIBERTY's growth is fueled by a proven operating system that has been fine-tuned by the leadership and field support staff's more than 600 total years of experience. As a result, no prior tax experience is required to put this system to work. Founder/CEO John Hewitt has worked 45 tax seasons, including 12 years with H&R Block. Accounting Today magazine has named Hewitt one of the accounting profession's Top 100 Most Influential People - 11 times! The International Franchise Association has honored Hewitt as its "Entrepreneur of the Year."

SUPPORT & TRAINING:

Financial Assistance Provided:	Yes (I)
Site Selection Assistance:	Yes
Lease Negotiation Assistance:	Yes
Co-operative Advertising:	No
Franchisee Assoc./Member:	No
Size of Corporate Staff:	520
Ongoing Support:	A,B,C,D,E,F,G,H,I
Training:	5 days Virginia Beach, VA - initial, intermediate, advanced; 3 days various cities - intermediate, advanced

BACKGROUND:

	IFA Member	
Established: 1997;	First Franchised: 1997	
Franchised Units:		4,222
Company-Owned Units:		216

SPECIFIC EXPANSION PLANS:

US:	All United States
Canada:	Yes
Overseas:	No

Founded in 1997, Liberty Tax Service has experienced explosive growth in the past 17 years. With over 4,400 offices opened, Liberty Tax Service has been growing more than three times faster than any other tax preparation company. Throughout this decade, Liberty Tax Service has demonstrated significant gains in an industry formerly dominated by tax giant H&R Block and, during the 21st century, Liberty has grown by more tax returns than both Jackson Hewitt and H&R Block combined. Liberty Tax Service is ranked as the #1 tax franchise on Entrepreneur magazine's "Franchise 500" in 2011, and is the only tax franchise on the Forbes 2012 "Top 20 Franchises for the Buck." Liberty Tax franchise costs are significantly less than most franchises due to its seasonal work force and low inventory costs. Its proven system, comprehensive training program as well as one-on-one, ongoing assistance provides an excellent opportunity for people seeking a small business opportunity.

Operating Units (In the U.S. and its Territories)	12/31/2011	12/31/2012	12/31/2013
Franchised	3,545	3,809	3,931
% Change	--	7.45%	3.2%
Company-Owned	36	80	244
% Change	--	122.22%	205.0%
Total	3,581	3,889	4,175
% Change	--	8.6%	7.35%
Franchised as % of Total	98.99%	97.94%	94.16%

Investment Required

The fee for a Liberty Tax franchise is $40,000. Liberty Tax Service provides the following range of investments required to open your initial franchise. The range assumes that all items are paid for in cash. To the extent that you choose to finance any of these expense items, your front-end investment could be substantially reduced.

Item	Established Low Range	Established High Range
Initial or Resale Franchise Fee	$40,000	$40,000
Initial Advertising	$5,000	$7,500

Expenses While Training	$100	$2,500
Equipment and Furniture	$3,000	$5,000
Signs	$500	$1,000
Rent	$3,000	$6,000
Payroll	$3,000	$5,000
Insurance	$200	$400
Additional Funds (3 Months)	$3,000	$4,500
Total Initial Investment	$57,800	$71,900

Estimated Franchise Start-Up and Operating Costs for Canada
(Note: Some costs are variable depending on your local area)

Item	Established Low Range	Established High Range
Initial Franchise Fee	$25,000	$25,000
Initial Advertising	$5,000	$7,500
Expenses While Training	$100	$2,500
Equipment and Furniture	$2,000	$5,000
Signs	$500	$2,500
Lease/Leasehold Improvements	$3,000	$6,000
Payroll	$3,000	$5,000
Insurance	$200	$400
Additional Funds (3 Months)	$3,000	$4,500
Total Initial Investment	$41,800	$58,400

Ongoing Expenses

Liberty Tax Service franchisees pay royalty fees equal to 14% of gross receipts with the following minimums: $5,000 for first year, $8,000 for second year, and $11,000 for third year and beyond. Additional fees payable by the franchisee include kiosk rentals during tax season and marketing training sessions.

What You Get: Training and Support

Training consists of two phases. First, Liberty Tax Services provides a comprehensive, minimum five-day Effective Operations Training (EOT) course in Virginia Beach, VA that instructs franchisees on the basics of operating an income tax preparation office. Other subjects include accounting, marketing, hiring and staffing, management, customer services, budgeting, and software applications. This course is followed by a one-day hands-on training at designated franchisee locations across the country and covers topics on preparing and processing tax returns, delivering bank products, guerilla marketing, and office procedures. For one to three days every year, an advanced training session is conducted across the country or via the Internet to update franchisees on new tax laws, software, and marketing programs. Franchisees also benefit from a support system of employees who have a combined total of 600 years of industry experience.

Territory

Liberty Tax Service grants exclusive territories.

Liquid Capital

5525 N. MacArthur Blvd., # 535
Irving, TX 75038
Tel: (844) 547-8434
Fax: (866) 611-8886
Email: mpeterson@liquidcapitalcorp.com
Website: www.lcfranchise.com
Michael Peterson, Director of Franchise Sales

Factoring is the funding of B2B receivables. It is a $2.9 Trillion global industry. The Liquid Capital competitive advantage is the relationship a client enjoys with the franchisee Typically a franchisee has 8-12 clients, who generally will factor their receivables for 2 to 3 years. Liquid Capital is a low overhead, high return, home based business that provides a franchisee with a great life style with high earning potential. Liquid Capital will loan its franchisees up to 6 times their investment.

BACKGROUND: IFA Member
Established: 1999; First Franchised: 2000
Franchised Units: 79

Company-Owned Units:	2	Area Develop. Agreements:	No
Total Units:	81	Sub-Franchising Contracts:	No
Dist.:	US-49; CAN-29; O'seas-5	Expand in Territory:	No
North America:	32 States, 6 Provinces	Space Needs:	N/A
Density:	9 in AB, 6 in FL, 3 in IL		
Projected New Units (12 Months):	12	**SUPPORT & TRAINING:**	
Qualifications:	5, 5, 2, 4, 2, 3	Financial Assistance Provided:	Yes (D)
		Site Selection Assistance:	N/A
FINANCIAL/TERMS:		Lease Negotiation Assistance:	N/A
Cash Investment:	$200K – 1M	Co-operative Advertising:	Yes
Total Investment:	$200K – 1M	Franchisee Assoc./Member:	Yes/Yes
Minimum Net Worth:	$250K	Size of Corporate Staff:	20
Fees: Franchise -	$50K	Ongoing Support:	A,G,H,I
Royalty - 8%;	Ad. - $500/Mo.	Training:	5 days Toronto, Canada
Financial Performance Representation:	Yes		
Term of Contract (Years):	10/10	**SPECIFIC EXPANSION PLANS:**	
Avg. # of Employees:	1 FT, 0 PT	US:	All United States
Passive Ownership:	Not Allowed	Canada:	All Canada
Encourage Conversions:	N/A	Overseas:	Yes

Liquid Capital™ is an international commercial finance company with more offices across North America than any other factoring firm. This extensive geographic network of local offices allows them to be the only commercial finance firm able to provide clients with an unmatchable level of individual client service and satisfaction. Well-recognized for their specialty of providing clients with accounts receivable financing, Liquid Capital™ also has the ability to fund purchase orders, or provide credit and trade insurance. For over a decade, the company has successfully combined the strengths of a top-tier finance corporation with a personalized approach to full-service funding through local professionals who know the community and understand business. Liquid Capital™ principals are consistently recognized for the prompt, friendly service and personal attention expected from financing executives who live in the communities in which they do business.

US Numbers

Operating Units	12/31/2011	12/31/2012	12/31/2013
Franchised	37	40	43
% Change	--	8.11%	7.5%

Company-Owned	1	1	1
% Change	--	0.0%	0.0%
Total	38	41	44
% Change	--	7.89%	7.32%
Franchised as % of Total	97.37%	97.56%	97.73%

Canada Numbers

Operating Units	12/31/2010	12/31/2010	12/31/2011
Franchised	26	28	28
% Change	--	7.7%	0.0%
Company-Owned	1	1	1
% Change	--	0.0%	0.0%
Total	27	29	29
% Change	--	7.4%	0.0%
Franchised as % of Total	96.3%	96.55%	96.55%

Investment Required

The fee for a single territory Liquid Capital™ franchise is $50,000. If you qualify for the multi-territory program, the initial franchise fee is $130,000 for the first three territories and $40,000 for each additional territory. Liquid Capital™ provides the following range of investments required to open your initial franchise. The range assumes that all items are paid for in cash. To the extent that you choose to finance any of these expense items, your front-end investment could be substantially reduced. Please note that the figures below represent expenses for a single territory franchise.

Item	Established Low Range	Established High Range
Initial Franchise Fee	$50,000	$50,000
Office Supplies	$500	$1,000

Lease	$0	$2,000
Furniture, Fixtures, and Equipment	$0	$12,000
Signage	$0	$2,000
Computer Hardware and Software	$2,500	$9,000
Insurance	$1,000	$1,500
Initial Training	$600	$2,600
Professional Services	$1,500	$5,000
Additional Funds (3 months)	$2,100	$10,000
Total Initial Investment	$58,200	$95,100

Ongoing Expenses

Liquid Capital™ franchisees pay a continuing royalty fee equal to 8% of gross revenue. Additional ongoing fees include a marketing fund contribution of $500 per month, back office services fees, exchange fees, and insurance fees.

Franchisee Satisfaction

A critical component of the due diligence process is that you, as a prospective franchisee, have a strong sense of existing franchisee satisfaction. Please review the franchisor's ratings below for this extremely important information.

How do you rate Liquid Capital™ in terms of:	Rating*
Overall Quality of the Franchisor	100%

Ability to Communicate Directly and Effectively with Senior Management	100%
Helpfullness of Franchisor's Field Representative	100%

* Independent Audit of Existing Franchisees Who Rated Liquid Capital™ as Excellent, Very Good, or Good

What You Get: Training and Support

Liquid Capital™ provides approximately five days of comprehensive training at its corporate headquarters in Toronto that covers all aspects of factoring, accounts receivable management, security issues, and credit-related matters. The Liquid Capital Factoring Advisory Team, a group of highly experienced factoring specialists, also mentors principals on an ongoing basis. In addition, a strong corporate infrastructure and back-office administrative support system streamlines operations for principals while providing them with a myriad of resources.

Onboarding Program

Liquid Capital franchisees spend their first 90 in an intense ongoing training program that we call our Onboarding program. With this program, they work directly with our Network Marketing Coach on a weekly basis to plan their week's strategies and events, and receive coaching, guidance and direction. The final step in the program is a market visit by a Liquid Capital executive to meet with existing and prospective candidates and referral sources.

Territory

Liquid Capital™ grants protected territories.

The Little Gym

Serious Fun.

7001 N. Scottsdale Rd., # 1050
Scottsdale, AZ 85253
Tel: (888) 228-2878, (480) 948-2878
Fax: (480) 948-2765
Email: leo@thelittlegym.com
Website: www.thelittlegym.com
Leo Smart, Director of Franchise Development

The Little Gym helps children ages 4 months through 12 years build the confidence and skills needed at each stage of childhood. Our trained instructors nurture happy, confident kids through a range of programs including parent/child classes, gymnastics, karate, dance and sports skills development, plus enjoyable extras like camps, Parents' Survival Nights and Awesome Birthday Bashes. Each week, progressively structured classes and a positive learning environment create opportunities for children to try new things and build self-confidence, all with a grin that stretches from ear to ear.

BACKGROUND:
Established: 1976;	IFA Member
	First Franchised: 1992
Franchised Units:	294
Company-Owned Units:	0
Total Units:	294
Dist.:	US-205; CAN-11; O'seas-78
North America:	36 States, 6 Provinces

Density:	29 in TX, 17 in NJ, 14 in CA
Projected New Units (12 Months):	15
Qualifications:	4, 4, 1, 3, 4, 5

FINANCIAL/TERMS:
Cash Investment:	$75 – 100K
Total Investment:	$145.8 – 366K
Minimum Net Worth:	$150 – 250K
Fees: Franchise -	$29.5 – 49.5K
Royalty - 8%;	Ad. - 1%
Financial Performance Representation:	Yes
Term of Contract (Years):	10/10
Avg. # of Employees:	2-3 FT, 4-8 PT
Passive Ownership:	Allowed
Encourage Conversions:	N/A
Area Develop. Agreements:	Yes
Sub-Franchising Contracts:	Yes
Expand in Territory:	No
Space Needs:	2,500-3,600 SF

SUPPORT & TRAINING:
Financial Assistance Provided:	Yes (I)
Site Selection Assistance:	Yes
Lease Negotiation Assistance:	Yes
Co-operative Advertising:	No
Franchisee Assoc./Member:	No
Size of Corporate Staff:	32
Ongoing Support:	C,D,E,h
Training:	7 days various locations;
	14 days Scottsdale, AZ

SPECIFIC EXPANSION PLANS:
US:	All United States except South Dakota
Canada:	All Canada
Overseas:	All Countries

The Little Gym introduces a program of experiential learning and child physical development for children from four months through 12 years old. Lessons are designed to build kids' self-esteem through a progressively structured class schedule and a positive learning environment. At The Little Gym, the environment is fun, but the purpose is serious.

Operating Units	12/31/2011	12/31/2012	12/31/2013
US Franchised	208	203	203

% Change	--	-2.4%	0.0%
Company-Owned	2	0	0
% Change	--	-100.0%	--
Total	210	203	203
% Change	--	-3.33%	0.0%
Franchised as % of Total	99.05%%	100%	100%

Investment Required

The initial fee for a Little Gym franchise is $69,500 for standard territories, although small market territories may also be purchased for an initial fee of $49,500. The Little Gym provides the following range of investments required to open your initial franchise. The range assumes that all items are paid for in cash. To the extent that you choose to finance any of these expense items, your front-end investment could be substantially reduced.

Item	Established Low Range	Established High Range
Initial Franchise Fee	$25,000	$69,500
Start Up Equipment and Inventory	$59,000	$69,000
Signs, Fixtures, Tenant Improvements	$7,000	$114,000
Furnishings, Equipment, Supplies	$8,000	$14,000
Initial Sales Promotion	$10,000	$18,000
Security Deposits and Other Prepaid Expenses	$4,000	$15,000
Expenses While Training	$5,000	$10,000
Insurance Premiums	$2,500	$3,500
Misc. Payments Before Operations	$4,000	$11,000

Additional Funds (3 months)	$35,000	$70,000
Total Initial Investment	$159,500	$394,000

Ongoing Expenses

Franchisees are responsible for paying a monthly royalty fee equal to 8% of gross revenue, as well as marketing fees; the general marketing fund is equal to 1% of monthly gross revenue and the local advertising fee is equal to the greater of 4% of gross monthly revenue or $1,250 minimum on an average annualized basis. Other additional fees include a proprietary software maintenance fee of $65 per month, loyalty program fees, and an automated communication touchpoint system fee.

What You Get: Training and Support

Little Gym offers a training program consisting of four parts; Business Startup Training, Boot Camp I, Boot Camp II, and Internship Training — and ranges between three to four weeks long. While The Little Gym will pay for the initial training program, the franchisee is responsible for all related expenses including travel, lodging, meals, etc. You may also be required to attend individual training which costs up to $250 per day per person or to attend additional group training sessions costing up to $250 per day per person.

Territory

The Little Gym grants exclusive territories with a few exceptions.

MAACO |

440 S. Church St., # 700
Charlotte, NC 28202
Tel: (800) 275-5200, (704) 444-8206
Fax: (704) 372-4826
Email: travis.miller@drivenbrands.com
Website: www.maacofranchise.com
Travis Miller, SVP Franchise Development & Sales

There are over 400 MAACO franchise centres in Canada, the U.S. and Puerto Rico. Between them, these franchises repair and paint over 800,000 vehicles a year. Thousands of car owners as well as local and national fleet administrators rely upon their local MAACO centre to maintain their vehicles' appearance. In 2013, MAACO was ranked #1 in Automotive Appearance Services in Entrepreneur magazine's annual Franchise 500.

BACKGROUND:

	IFA Member
Established: 1972;	First Franchised: 1972
Franchised Units:	458
Company-Owned Units:	5
Total Units:	463
Dist.:	US-439; CAN-23; O'seas-1
North America:	27 States, 6 Provinces
Density:	19 in ON, 6 in AB, 3 in BC
Projected New Units (12 Months):	50

Qualifications:	3, 4, 1, 2, 4, 5
FINANCIAL/TERMS:	
Cash Investment:	$140K
Total Investment:	$250 – 300K
Minimum Net Worth:	$300K
Fees: Franchise -	$35K
Royalty - 8%;	Ad. - $850/Wk.
Financial Performance Representation:	Yes
Term of Contract (Years):	15/5
Avg. # of Employees:	6-10 FT, 0 PT
Passive Ownership:	Discouraged
Encourage Conversions:	Yes
Area Develop. Agreements:	Yes
Sub-Franchising Contracts:	No
Expand in Territory:	Yes
Space Needs:	7,000 SF
SUPPORT & TRAINING:	
Financial Assistance Provided:	Yes (I)
Site Selection Assistance:	Yes
Lease Negotiation Assistance:	Yes
Co-operative Advertising:	No
Franchisee Assoc./Member:	Yes/Yes
Size of Corporate Staff:	100
Ongoing Support:	A,B,C,D,E,F,G,H,I
Training:	4-6 weeks in store; 4 weeks
	Charlotte, NC; Ongoing as required in store
SPECIFIC EXPANSION PLANS:	
US:	Yes
Canada:	All Canada
Overseas:	No

Poised as a leader in the colossal automotive aftercare industry, MAACO offers considerable stable and profitable entrepreneurial opportunities. Since 1972, MAACO has served communities throughout the United States and abroad, providing reliable, superior auto paint and auto body repair services to over 16.5 million vehicles throughout its history. Today, MAACO operates nearly 500 franchises that service approximately 650,000 vehicles per year. Moreover, the automotive aftercare market is one of the fastest growing industries in the U.S., representing a nearly $290 billion industry in 2010. With new car sales declining and more people choosing to retain their vehicles for longer periods of time, the automotive collision and cosmetic repair industry possesses considerable potential for explosive growth in the next few years. Franchisees benefit from unparalleled brand recognition and the stability of a company with an impressive 45% of the U.S. market share within the industry. MAACO offers a reliable business model, complete with an exceptional, comprehensive training program. Additionally, by working with MAACO, franchisees have the chance to build a family-oriented business with comfortable operating hours and a substantial, stable income potential.

Operating Units	12/31/2011	12/31/2012	12/31/2013
Franchised	431	416	436
% Change	--	-3.48%	4.81%
Company-Owned	2	1	1
% Change	--	-50.0%	0.0%
Total	433	417	437
% Change	--	-3.7%	4.8%
Franchised as % of Total	98.54%	99.76%	99.77%

Investment Required

The initial fee for a MAACO franchise is $35,000. MAACO provides the following range of investments required to open your initial franchise. The range assumes that all items are paid for in cash. To the extent that you choose to finance any of these expense items, your front-end investment could be substantially reduced.

Item	Established Low Range	Established High Range
Initial Franchise Fee	$17,500	$35,000
Initial Training/Opening Fee	$5,000	$5,000
Initial Advertising	$15,000	$30,000
Equipment	$2,071	$143,165
Opening Inventory/Supplies	$7,124	$19,582

Stationary & Promotional Materials	$338	$376
Signage	$3,510	$13,240
Miscellaneous Opening Costs	$20,000	$45,000
Initial Software License Fee	$0	$5,000
Initial Computer Hardware	$1,400	$4,500
Additional Funds (3 Months)	$8,600	$150,000
Total Initial Investment	$80,543	$450,863

Ongoing Expenses

MAACO franchisees pay royalty fees equal to 9% of gross sales, a minimum advertising contribution of $850 per week, and a national marketing fee of $70 per week.

What You Get: Training and Support

Franchisees attend a mandatory three-week intensive training program conducted at the MAACO training center in Charlotte, NC. The training focuses on management methods and techniques, including local advertising, marketing, POS system, merchandising, painting equipment, safety regulations, personnel management, customer relations, sales, and facilities maintenance. Following this initial training, MAACO offers additional on-site assistance for approximately two to four weeks throughout the grand opening process. Continuing assistance and support includes marketing, with MAACO supplying advertising programs and promotional materials. MAACO conducts occasional inspections and evaluations of the franchise center regarding operational success and efficiency, and offers feedback and guidance accordingly. Franchisees further benefit from ongoing online training classes, interactive help websites, meetings, and conventions.

Territory

MAACO does not grant exclusive territories.

The Maids

The Maids®

Referred for a reason.

9394 W. Dodge Rd., # 140
Omaha, NE 68114
Tel: (800) 843-6243, (402) 558-5555
Fax: (402) 558-4112
Email: rcordova@maids.com
Website: www.themaidsfranchise.com
Ronn Cordova, Vice President of Development

Distinguished as the number one residential cleaning franchise in 2007, 2008, 2009, 2011, 2012, and 2014 by Entrepreneur Magazine's Top 500, THE MAIDS is the quality leader in the industry. THE MAIDS provides the most comprehensive package of training, support, and exclusive territory in the industry. We provide extensive training, including 7 weeks of pre-training and 9 days of classroom and 4 days of field training. With THE MAIDS, you can build a great business and achieve the lifestyle you desire, all with nights, weekends and holidays off. We are looking for people who want an executive experience. With THE MAIDS, you are working ON the business, not IN the business. THE MAIDS ideal franchise candidate will have good management and business skills, and most importantly, great people skills.

BACKGROUND: IFA Member
Established: 1979; First Franchised: 1980
Franchised Units: 1,114
Company-Owned Units: 35
Total Units: 1,149
Dist.: US-1,117; CAN-32; O'seas-0

North America:	42 States, 4 Provinces
Density:	94 in TX, 83 in FL, 103 in CA
Projected New Units (12 Months):	80
Qualifications:	5, 4, 1, 3, 1, 5

FINANCIAL/TERMS:

Cash Investment:	$60 – 65K
Total Investment:	$97 – 123K
Minimum Net Worth:	$250K
Fees: Franchise -	$12.5K + $.95 per QHH
Royalty - 3.9-6.9%;	Ad. - 2%
Financial Performance Representation:	Yes
Term of Contract (Years):	20/20
Avg. # of Employees:	2 FT, 4 PT
Passive Ownership:	Discouraged
Encourage Conversions:	Yes
Area Develop. Agreements:	Yes
Sub-Franchising Contracts:	No
Expand in Territory:	Yes
Space Needs:	1,000 - 1,200 SF

SUPPORT & TRAINING:

Financial Assistance Provided:	No
Site Selection Assistance:	Yes
Lease Negotiation Assistance:	No
Co-operative Advertising:	Yes
Franchisee Assoc./Member:	No
Size of Corporate Staff:	35
Ongoing Support:	A,B,C,D,E,F,G,h,I
Training:	9 days Corporate training - Omaha, NE; 2-3 days power training - franchisee location; 7 weeks foundation training (pre-training)

SPECIFIC EXPANSION PLANS:

US:	All United States
Canada:	All except Saskatchewan and Quebec
Overseas:	No

The multi-billion dollar home services industry is booming due to busy dual-career families, increased corporate demands, and long commutes. In this climate, maid service is no longer a luxury; it is a time management tool for leisure-starved households. A leader in its field, The Maids has been recognized as the fastest growing residential cleaning franchise by Entrepreneur magazine for the past four years. Offering the broadest service package and the highest quality cleaning services, The Maids enjoys excellent customer loyalty that draws from primarily affluent families with high disposable income. In allowing ownership of large markets, The Maids franchise system offers franchisees the greatest opportunity in the home services industry.

Operating Units	12/31/2011	12/31/2012	12/31/2013
Franchised	1,072	1,069	1,110
% Change	--	-0.28%	3.84%
Company-Owned	26	29	31
% Change	--	11.54%	6.9%
Total	1,098	1,098	1,141
% Change	--	0.0%	3.92%
Franchised as % of Total	97.63%	97.36%	97.28%

Investment Required

The fee for a Maids franchise is $12,500, plus an initial territory fee of $0.95 for each potential customer in the Designated Market Area. The Maids provides the following range of investments required to open your initial franchise. The range assumes that all items are paid for in cash. To the extent that you choose to finance any of these expense items, your front-end investment could be substantially reduced.

Item	Established Low Range	Established High Range
Initial Franchise Fee	$12,500	$12,500
Territory Fee	$28,500	$28,500
Initial Equipment and Supply Package	$17,500	$18,500
Initial Software License	$2,895	$4,895
Office Security Deposit	$700	$1,000
Computer Hardware	$3,000	$4,000

Office Fixtures, Decorations and Furniture	$1,500	$2,500
Auto Painting/Wrap	$750	$1,500
Telephone Deposit	$100	$200
Insurance Deposit	$2,200	$3,200
Signs	$500	$1,000
Washer and Dryer	$800	$1,000
Start-Up Professional Services	$500	$1,500
Expenses During Corporate Training	$4,900	$8,050
Additional Funds (3 Months)	$20,800	$35,550
Total Initial Investment	$97,145	$123,895

Ongoing Expenses

The Maids franchisees pay continuing license fees ranging from 3.9% to 6.9% of gross revenues (2.4% to 6.9% for conversions), advertising fees equal to 2% of gross revenues (1% to 2% for conversions), and required local advertising expenditures equal to at least $1.20 per potential customer, per year. Additional fees payable by the franchise include a national convention registration fee, an annual software membership fee, and a technology fee of up to 1% of weekly gross revenues.

What You Get: Training and Support

The Maids training is one of the most intensive and advanced in the franchise community. Training includes an initial program to help ensure a successful opening, comprehensive corporate training, site visits by trainers and business coaches to streamline operations, and ongoing web-based training at no additional charge. The Maids' marketing staff and business coaches provide comprehensive marketing support throughout opening and operations. The Maids helps franchisees build an initial marketing plan and provides ongoing consulting, ad design, public relations, and direct mail support. The Maids also assigns a franchise business coach to provide franchisees with one-on-one counsel and support in all facets of business growth and management.

Territory

The Maids grants exclusive territories.

Massage Heights

MASSAGE HEIGHTS®

13750 US Hwy. 281 N., #230
San Antonio, TX 78232
Tel: (210) 402-0777
Email: bfranson@massageheights.com
Website: www.massageheights.com
Bret Franson, Director of Franchise Development

Massage Heights' mission is to help all types of people incorporate convenient, high-quality, rejuvenating massage into their healthy lifestyles. Massage Heights fosters a culture of excellence and gives our franchisees the tools and the opportunities to grow and succeed. We are strongly positioned to outpace the competition with an aggressive growth strategy, strong leadership, a unique position in the marketplace, a membership-based business model, our distinctive Retreat design, and the upside potential of multiple revenue streams, including Membership fees, add-ons, and Massage Heights branded retail products.

BACKGROUND:

Established: 2005;	First Franchised: 2005
Franchised Units:	119
Company-Owned Units:	2
Total Units:	121
Dist.:	US-116; CAN-5; O'seas-0
North America:	21 States, 1 Province

Density:	42 in TX, 16 in CA, 8 in IA
Projected New Units (12 Months):	N/A
Qualifications:	N/A

FINANCIAL/TERMS:

Cash Investment:	N/A
Total Investment:	$235.1 – 595.9K
Minimum Net Worth:	N/A
Fees: Franchise -	$42K
Royalty - 5%;	Ad. - 2%
Financial Performance Representation:	Yes
Term of Contract (Years):	N/A
Avg. # of Employees:	N/A
Passive Ownership:	Allowed
Encourage Conversions:	Yes
Area Develop. Agreements:	No
Sub-Franchising Contracts:	No
Expand in Territory:	No
Space Needs:	N/A

SUPPORT & TRAINING:

Financial Assistance Provided:	Yes (D)
Site Selection Assistance:	Yes
Lease Negotiation Assistance:	Yes
Co-operative Advertising:	No
Franchisee Assoc./Member:	Yes/Yes
Size of Corporate Staff:	N/A
Ongoing Support:	A,B,C,D,E,F,G,H,I
Training:	N/A

SPECIFIC EXPANSION PLANS:

US:	No
Canada:	No
Overseas:	No

Massage Heights began in San Antonio, Texas in 2004. Today, we have dozens of locations open with aggressive growth planned throughout the U.S. Our mission is to help all types of people incorporate convenient, high-quality, rejuvenating massage into their healthy lifestyles. Our business is built on a membership model that helps make massages more affordable, while still providing the level of service you'd expect at a five-star resort. Massage Heights fosters a culture of excellence and gives our franchisees the tools and the opportunities to grow and succeed. We are strongly positioned to outpace the competition with an aggressive growth strategy, strong leadership, a unique position in the marketplace, a membership-based business model, our distinctive Retreat design, and the upside potential of multiple revenue streams, including Membership fees, add-ons, and Massage Heights branded retail products.

Operating Units	12/31/2011	12/31/2012	12/31/2013
Franchised	67	77	93
% Change	--	14.93%	20.78%
Company-Owned	3	2	2
% Change	--	-33.33%	0.0%
Total	70	79	95
% Change	--	12.86%	20.25%
Franchised as % of Total	95.71%	97.47%	97.89%

Investment Required

The initial fee to purchase a Massage Heights franchise is $42,000. Massage Heights provides the following range of investments required to open your initial franchise. The range assumes that all items are paid for in cash. To the extent that you choose to finance any of these expense items, your front-end investment could be substantially reduced.

Item	Established Low Range	Established High Range
Franchise Fee	$42,000	$42,000

Retreat Development Package	$107,000	$128,000
Security Deposit	$3,500	$9,600
Lease Rent (3 months)	$10,500	$42,500
Leasehold Improvements	$10,000	$217,600
Exterior Signage	$4,300	$8,000
Equipment	$12,300	$14,600
Computer Hardware and Software	$9,000	$13,000
Business Licenses and Permits	$150	$1,500
Professional Fees	$3,300	$14,750
Initial Inventory	$9,400	$13,750
Insurance	$1,000	$5,000
Expenses while Training	$1,500	$3,000
Start-up Advertising Expense	$20,000	$22,000
Telecommunications Services and Advertising	$150	$800
Additional Expenditures for Facial Services	$7,850	$9,600
Lease Negotiation Fee	$0	$4,500
Site Evaluation Assistance Fee	$0	$5,000
Demographic/Physiographic Analysis	$1,000	$1,000
Additional Funds (3 months)	$15,000	$50,000
Total Initial Investment	$257,950	$606,200

Ongoing Expenses

Franchisees are required to pay ongoing royalty fees equal to 5% of gross revenues, national advertising fees of up to 3% of gross revenue, and a monthly software maintenance fee of $500.

What You Get: Training and Support

Franchisees will be enrolled in an initial training program to take place at company headquarters in San Antonio, TX and consists on four separate five-day periods with both classroom and on-the-job training. Massage Heights also provides an On-Site Assistance program that consists of up to five days of training and assistance at your franchise location. Massage Heights will continue to offer advice and guidance regarding the operation of the franchise, as well as administer the advertising fund and provide additional training when deemed necessary.

Territory

Massage Heights does not grant exclusive territories.

Mathnasium Learning Centers

5120 W. Goldleaf Circle, # 300
Los Angeles, CA 90056
Tel: (877) 531-6284, (323) 421-8000
Fax: (310) 943-2111
Email: franchise@mathnasium.com
Website: www.mathnasium.com/franchising

Mathnasium Learning Centers is an excellent blend of a rewarding business opportunity and making a difference in children's lives. We make math make sense for kids, giving them the tools to catch up, maintain, and get ahead.

BACKGROUND:	
Established: 2002;	First Franchised: 2003
Franchised Units:	525
Company-Owned Units:	10
Total Units:	535
Dist.:	N/A
Projected New Units (12 Months):	N/A
Qualifications:	N/A

FINANCIAL/TERMS:	
Cash Investment:	$40K
Total Investment:	$99.8 – 139.4K
Minimum Net Worth:	N/A
Fees: Franchise -	$40K
Royalty - 10% and $500/mo.;	Ad. - 2% and $250/mo.
Financial Performance Representation:	No
Term of Contract (Years):	5/5

Avg. # of Employees:	N/A	Co-operative Advertising:	No
Passive Ownership:	Allowed	Franchisee Assoc./Member:	Yes/Yes
Encourage Conversions:	N/A	Size of Corporate Staff:	160
Area Develop. Agreements:	No	Ongoing Support:	A,B,C,D,E,F,G,H,I
Sub-Franchising Contracts:	No	Training:	Ongoing Online Training; 1 Week HQ
Expand in Territory:	No		in Los Angeles, CA; Apprenticeship
Space Needs:	N/A		at existing location
SUPPORT & TRAINING:		**SPECIFIC EXPANSION PLANS:**	
Financial Assistance Provided:	No	US:	All United States
Site Selection Assistance:	Yes	Canada:	All Canada
Lease Negotiation Assistance:	No	Overseas:	Europe

Mathnasium is an international chain of year-round learning centers where children go to improve their math skills. Each franchised center utilizes the Mathnasium Method, an individually personalized educational curriculum created through over 35 years of classroom experience and research. Entrepreneurs recognize Mathnasium as a dynamic and rewarding business opportunity that gives them the chance to make a difference in a child's life every time they come to work. Each Mathnasium franchise is the product of a collaborative exchange between the Mathnasium corporate team and the local franchisee, combining our extensive franchising and education experience with the entrepreneur's business acumen, passion for education, and desire to succeed. Mathnasium has been making a difference in the lives of children since we opened our first center in 2003. Today, we have over 300 thriving centers in the United States along with open centers now on four continents... and we are continuing to grow.

Operating Units	12/31/2011	12/31/2012	12/31/2013
Franchised	285	337	409
% Change	--	18.25%	21.36%
Company-Owned	1	3	8
% Change	--	200%	166.67%
Total	286	340	417
% Change	--	18.88%	22.65%
Franchised as % of Total	99.65%	99.12%	98.08%

Investment Required

The initial fee for a Mathnasium franchise is $40,000. Mathnasium provides the following range of investment items required to open your initial franchise. The range assumes that all items are paid for in cash. To the extent that you choose to finance any of these item, your front-end investment could be substantially reduced.

Item	Established Low Range	Established High Range
Franchise Fee	$40,000	$40,000
Expenses while Training	$1,500	$2,500
Rent	$6,000	$12,000
Paint, Carpet, & Tenant Improvements	$2,500	$5,000
Furniture, Signs, Equipment, & Supplies	$15,000	$18,000
Insurance	$1,000	$2,500
Business License, Name Registration	$250	$1,000
Professional Services	$1,500	$2,000
Phone and Utilities	$500	$1,000
Video Surveillance	$1,500	$5,000
Early Stage Advertising	$15,000	$20,000
Additional Funds (4 months)	$15,000	$30,000
Total Initial Investment	$99,750	$139,000

Ongoing Expenses

Franchisees are required to pay ongoing monthly royalties starting at 10% of monthly gross receipts plus a base royalty fee of $500 per month. Other fees include a monthly marketing fee of $250 plus 2% of gross receipts and a technology license fee currently at $75 per month.

What You Get: Training and Support

Franchisees will be enrolled in an initial training program that will last at least five days, covering systems and tools, marketing, Mathnasium management system, daily operations, and an education review. Franchisees will also participate in a 4 to 5 day apprenticeship in a Mathnasium Mentor Center. Mathnasium will continue to provide assistance regarding franchise operations and additional services, programs, or products that you develop.

Territory

Mathnasium grants exclusive territories.

Meineke

440 S. Church St.
Charlotte, NC 28202
Tel: (800) 275-5200, (704) 444-8206
Fax: (704) 377-9904
Email: dave.schaefers@meineke.com
Website: www.meinekefranchise.com
Dave Schaefers, VP Franchise Development

MEINEKE has been offering superior automotive repair services at discount prices for over 40 years. We are a nationally-recognized brand with a proven system. Brand recognition, comprehensive training and ongoing technical and operational support are some of the benefits enjoyed by MEINEKE franchisees.

BACKGROUND:	IFA Member
Established: 1972;	First Franchised: 1972
Franchised Units:	979
Company-Owned Units:	0
Total Units:	979
Dist.:	US-884; CAN-51; O'seas-44
North America:	46 States, 5 Provinces
Density:	40 in ON, 4 in AB, 3 in NL
Projected New Units (12 Months):	45
Qualifications:	4, 4, 1, 2, 3, 4

FINANCIAL/TERMS:	
Cash Investment:	$110K
Total Investment:	$200 – 250K
Minimum Net Worth:	$250K
Fees: Franchise -	$30K
Royalty - 5-8%;	Ad. - 8%
Financial Performance Representation:	Yes
Term of Contract (Years):	15/15
Avg. # of Employees:	6-10 FT, 0 PT
Passive Ownership:	Discouraged
Encourage Conversions:	Yes
Area Develop. Agreements:	Yes
Sub-Franchising Contracts:	No

Expand in Territory:	Yes	Size of Corporate Staff:	110
Space Needs:	8,000 SF	Ongoing Support:	A,B,C,D,E,G,H,I
		Training:	4 Weeks Charlotte, NC
SUPPORT & TRAINING:			
Financial Assistance Provided:	Yes (I)	**SPECIFIC EXPANSION PLANS:**	
Site Selection Assistance:	Yes	US:	All United States
Lease Negotiation Assistance:	Yes	Canada:	All Canada
Co-operative Advertising:	No	Overseas:	All Countries
Franchisee Assoc./Member:	Yes/Yes		

Forty-two years ago, Sam Meineke began his first store in Houston, TX with a single product line and a simple concept: provide quality products and workmanship at a fair price. That concept, along with the application of new technology and strategies, has made Meineke Car Care Centers one of the most recognized and trusted automotive franchise brands in North America. Today, the automotive franchise has nearly 1,000 centers world-wide and has successfully evolved into a one-stop automotive business that consumers are looking for. The Meineke franchise represents a great opportunity as more people are holding on to older cars longer, driving the demands for professional repair and maintenance services. The U.S. automotive aftermarket repair and service business is approaching $320 billion in annual sales.

Operating Units	12/31/2011	12/31/2012	12/31/2013
Franchised	844	837	773
% Change	--	-0.83%	-7.65%
Company-Owned	7	6	4
% Change	--	-14.29%	-33.33%
Total	851	843	777
% Change	--	-0.94%	-7.83%
Franchised as % of Total	99.18%	99.29%	99.49%

Investment Required

The fee for a Meineke franchise is $30,000. Meineke provides the following range of investments required to open your initial franchise. The range assumes that all items are paid for in cash. To the extent that you choose to finance any of these expense items, your front-end investment could be substantially reduced. Please note the figures below represent expenses for a 6 Bay Location. Franchisees can also purchase a 5 Bay Location, with a Total Initial Investment of $183,494.61 to $422,125.32, or a 4 Bay Location with a Total Initial Investment of $173,450.61 to $330,720.21.

Item	Established Low Range	Established High Range
Initial Franchise Fee	$7,500	$30,000
Expenses While Training	$1,875	$2,700
Real Estate Rent and Security Deposit	$4,800	$21,000
Opening Inventory	$2,000	$20,000
Equipment, Signs, Tools, etc.	$104,442.23	$163,080.08
Freight	$1,500	$3,500
POS Software, Computer Hardware	$7,363	$9,871.94
Center Supplies	$11,959.38	$11,959.38
Insurance	$200	$6,294
Initial Marketing	$500	$17,000
Legal/Accounting Expenses	$500	$12,000
Pre-paid Expenses	$100	$75,000
Additional Funds (3 months)	$40,000	$80,000
Total Initial Investment	$182,739.61	$452,405.40

Ongoing Expenses

Meineke franchisees pay a royalty fee equal to the greater of an annual minimum of $20,800 or a fee ranging from 3-7% of gross revenue, depending on the types of services or products provided. Other fees include an advertising fund contribution equal to 1.5% of gross revenue generated from tire sales, towing services and inspections, and 8% of all other gross revenue.

What You Get: Training and Support

An initial training program is conducted every month at the Meineke University in Charlotte, NC and lasts a maximum of 17 days; and the length for each trainee depends on the trainee's job function(s). Training covers a vast number of areas, including advertising and marketing strategies, human resources, computer software, customer relations and hands on repairs. Ongoing support with advertising and training is also provided.

Territory

Meineke grants protected territories.

Molly Maid

3948 Ranchero Dr.
Ann Arbor, MI 48108
Tel: (734) 822-6800
Email: april.scarlett@servicebrands.com
Website: www.mollymaid.com
April Scarlett, Manager of Franchise Development

For more than 25 years, Molly Maid has offered bonded, insured residential maids who pride themselves in quality home cleaning services that create "me time" for our hardworking homeowners. Last year, Molly Maid franchisees performed 1.46 million "cleans" and 90% were from repeat customers. We also have a 97% customer retention rate.

BACKGROUND:

Established: 1979;	First Franchised: 1979
Franchised Units:	455

Company-Owned Units:	0
Total Units:	455
Dist.:	US-455; CAN-0; O'seas-0
North America:	44 States
Density:	N/A
Projected New Units (12 Months):	N/A
Qualifications:	N/A
FINANCIAL/TERMS:	
Cash Investment:	N/A
Total Investment:	$150 – 175K
Minimum Net Worth:	N/A
Fees: Franchise -	$14.9K
Royalty - 3-6.5%;	Ad. - $250/mo
Financial Performance Representation:	Yes
Term of Contract (Years):	N/A
Avg. # of Employees:	N/A
Passive Ownership:	Allowed
Encourage Conversions:	Yes
Area Develop. Agreements:	No
Sub-Franchising Contracts:	No
Expand in Territory:	No
Space Needs:	N/A

SUPPORT & TRAINING:		Ongoing Support:	A,B,C,D,E,F,G,H,I
Financial Assistance Provided:	Yes (D)	Training:	N/A
Site Selection Assistance:	Yes		
Lease Negotiation Assistance:	Yes	**SPECIFIC EXPANSION PLANS:**	
Co-operative Advertising:	No	US:	No
Franchisee Assoc./Member:	Yes/Yes	Canada:	No
Size of Corporate Staff:	N/A	Overseas:	No

Molly Maid originated in Canada in 1979, but our story begins in 1984 when David McKinnon, a service industry franchisee, acquired the rights to expand the brand into the United States. David headquartered Molly Maid in Ann Arbor, Michigan, where he assembled his development and support teams. Today, there are more than 450 Molly Maid residential cleaning franchises across the United States. Throughout the years, we've created lasting relationships with more than 17 million customers in 40 states. In addition, there are more than 180 Molly Maid franchises in Canada, The U.K., Portugal, and Japan. You'll never be happier about your financial future. You'll invest in a business where the top 25% of Molly Maid franchise owners average $1.2 million in annual revenues. You won't be chasing new customers either. Last year, Molly Maid franchisees performed 1.46 million "cleans" and 90% were from repeat customers, and we also have a 97% customer retention rate. Customers will welcome you into their homes, thank you for a job well done, and invite you back.

Operating Units	12/31/2011	12/31/2012	12/31/2013
Franchised	436	439	450
% Change	--	0.69%	2.51%
Company-Owned	0	0	0
% Change	--	--	--
Total	436	439	450
% Change	--	0.69%	2.51%
Franchised as % of Total	100%	100%	100%

Investment Required

The initial fee for a Molly Maid franchise is $14,900, along with an initial package fee of $10,095 and a territory fee equal to $1 per target household value in your territory which typically ranges from $30,000 to $45,000 for a standard size market and $20,000 to $30,000 for a mid-size market. Molly Maid provides the following range of investments required to open you initial franchise. The range assumes that all items are paid for in cash. To the extent you choose to finance any of these expense items, your front-end investment could be substantially reduced.

Item	Established Low Range	Established High Range
Initial Licensing Fee	$14,900	$14,900
Territory Fee	$20,000	$45,000
Initial Package Fee	$10,095	$10,095
Auto Lease Deposit and 3 months Lease Expense	$3,000	$5,500
Leasehold Improvements	$0	$2,000
Real Estate, Utility Deposits, and 3 months Rent	$4,000	$6,000
Furniture, Fixtures, and Equipment	$2,500	$3,500
Permits and Licenses	$100	$1,000
Insurance Deposit and 3 months Insurance Expense	$2,200	$5,300
Expenses While Training	$4,000	$5,000
Additional Funds (3 months)	$25,000	$33,000
Total Initial Investment	$85,795	$131,295

Ongoing Expenses

Franchisees are required to pay ongoing royalty fees equal to a percentage based on a calendar year sliding scale of 6.5% to 3% of gross sales. Other fees include a national marketing fee of $250 per month, local marketing of $1 per target household value per year, and technology and internet connection fees.

What You Get: Training and Support

Franchisees will be enrolled in a six to eight week Right Start training program, which consists of numerous pre-opening activities to take place in your hometown. Franchisees will next participate in a ten day initial training program that includes both classroom and on-the-job training to take place in Ann Arbor MI and one of our Owner Training Centers. Molly Maid will continue to provide continuing support regarding the ongoing operation of the business, and additional training when needed.

Territory

Molly Maid grants exclusive territories.

Money Mailer

12131 Western Ave.
Garden Grove, CA 92841
Tel: (888) 446-4648 (714) 889-4694
Fax: (800) 819-4322
Email: djenkins@moneymailer.com
Website: www.franchise.moneymailer.com
Dennis Jenkins, VP Franchising Licensing

Money Mailer has re-invented marketing for local businesses. Franchisees become local marketing experts and each operating unit is an in-house ad agency resource for local, community-based businesses in a protected territory. Millions have been invested in targeting technology, digital media components and a game-changing product upgrade to our core offering so franchisees can now show clients how to reach their best prospects in the mail, on the Internet, on mobile devices and social media. Lead generation is provided and there are no royalties for the entire first year. Training and support is unrivaled. An aggressive launch package allows for extremely fast startup, 8 weeks after completion of Money Mailer University. Immediately following MM University the franchisee's personal Coach spends several weeks in the territory to help ensure a successful Grand Opening. Once a campaign is finalized it is sent to Money Mailer for printing, mailing and digital placements.

BACKGROUND:	IFA Member
Established: 1979;	First Franchised: 1980
Franchised Units:	197
Company-Owned Units:	40
Total Units:	237
Dist.:	US-237; CAN-0; O'seas-0

North America:	38 States	Expand in Territory:	Yes
Density:	44 in CA, 25 in IL, 21 in NJ	Space Needs:	Standard Home Office
Projected New Units (12 Months):	45		
Qualifications:	3, 4, 1, 3, 4, 5	**SUPPORT & TRAINING:**	
		Financial Assistance Provided:	Yes (I)
FINANCIAL/TERMS:		Site Selection Assistance:	N/A
Cash Investment:	$50K	Lease Negotiation Assistance:	N/A
Total Investment:	$58K	Co-operative Advertising:	Yes
Minimum Net Worth:	$200K	Franchisee Assoc./Member:	Yes/Yes
Fees: Franchise -	$50K	Size of Corporate Staff:	125
Royalty - $250/10K Mailed; Ad. - $.50/ad sold		Ongoing Support:	A,B,C,D,G,H,I
Financial Performance Representation:	Yes	Training:	20 days Field Training in Territory;
Term of Contract (Years):	10/10		2 Weeks Corporate Headquarters
Avg. # of Employees:	Owner/operator first year		
Passive Ownership:	Not Allowed	**SPECIFIC EXPANSION PLANS:**	
Encourage Conversions:	No	US:	Yes
Area Develop. Agreements:	No	Canada:	No
Sub-Franchising Contracts:	No	Overseas:	No

Money Mailer, ranked #1 for advertising services by Entrepreneur Magazine, has been a leader in the $53 Billion Direct Marketing industry for over 33 years. As a recognized leader in direct marketing with a history of success, Money Mailer franchisees and their staffs have helped local business owners increase market share. Our targeted, hyper-local approach allows businesses to reach prospects with offers in the mail, online, on mobile devices, and through social media. Our record results are being driven by two powerful trends: the consumers' need to save money and the local business owners' need for marketing expertise to build market share under constantly changing economic conditions.

Operating Units	12/31/2011	12/31/2012	12/31/2013
Franchised	194	190	197
% Change	--	-2.06%	3.68%
Company-Owned	43	41	40
% Change	--	-4.65%	-2.44%
Total	237	231	237
% Change	--	-2.53%	2.6%
Franchised as % of Total	81.86%	82.25%	83.12%

Investment Required

The initial fee for a Money Mailer franchise depends on the number of mailing zones (approximately 10,000 households) in your mailing territory: it is $50,000 for 4-7 zones, $75,000 for 8-14 zones, $100,000 for 15-20 zones, or $5,000 per zone for 21 or more zones. Money Mailer provides the following range of investments required to open your initial franchise. The range assumes that all items are paid for in cash. To the extent that you choose to finance any of these expense items, your front-end investment could be substantially reduced.

Item	Established Low Range	Established High Range
Franchise Fee	$50,000	$100,000
Rent, Security Deposit, Telephone, etc.	$100	$1,750
Training	$4,000	$6,000
Insurance	$500	$1,500
Computer and Other Equipment	$2,000	$3,000
Fax Machine and Mobile Phone	$200	$1,000
Office Supplies including business cards, advertising agreements, letterhead	$250	$750
Additional Funds (1-4 months)	$1,000	$5,000
Total Initial Investment	$58,050	$119,000

Ongoing Expenses

Franchisees are required to pay royalty fees based on duplicated zones in annual mailing plans, with a maximum of $300 per zone if you are in good standing or $350 per zone if you are not in good standing. Other ongoing fees include a national marketing fee of $0.50 per spot as well as shared mailing production services and materials provided.

Franchisee Satisfaction

A critical component of the due diligence process is that you, as a prospective franchisee, have a strong sense of existing franchisee satisfaction. Please review the franchisor's ratings below for this extremely important information.

How do you rate Money Mailer in terms of:	Rating*
Overall Communication between Home Office Personnel and Franchisees	94%
Initial Training Suppied by Franchisor	90%
Franchisor Responds in a Timely Way to Questions and Minor Problems	90%

* Independent Audit of Existing Franchisees Who Rated Money Mailer as Excellent, Very Good, or Good

What You Get: Training and Support

Franchisees will be enrolled in an initial Money Mailer University training program that includes up to two weeks of classroom training, four to eleven weeks of field training depending on the size of your territory, and ongoing refresher training when necessary. Money Mailer will also make available shared mailing production materials and services, as well as allow franchisees to participate in a start-up benefits program for those who qualify.

Territory

Money Mailer grants exclusive territories.

Mosquito Squad

2924 Emerywood Parkway, # 101
Richmond, VA 23294
Tel: (800) 722-4668, (804) 353-6999 x101
Fax: (804) 358-1878
Email: rwhite@outdoorlivingbrands.com
Website: www.mosquitosquadfranchise.com
Rob White, Vice President of Development

Mosquito Squad is North America's fastest growing outdoor living franchise concept with an incredible, high-margin recurring revenue stream. Since joining the Outdoor Living Brands' franchise lineup in 2009, Mosquito Squad has been experiencing explosive franchise unit and consumer sales growth. Clients want to take back their backyards by combating annoying insect bites and protecting their families and pets from the dangerous diseases such as Lyme Disease, Encephalitis and West Nile Virus.

BACKGROUND: IFA Member
Established: 2004; First Franchised: 2005
Franchised Units: 142
Company-Owned Units: 0
Total Units: 142
Dist.: US-142; CAN-0; O'seas-0
North America: 29 States
Density: 10 in MI, 10 in NY, 13 in NC

Projected New Units (12 Months): 25
Qualifications: 5, 5, 1, 3, 3, 4

FINANCIAL/TERMS:
Cash Investment: $50K
Total Investment: $35 – 75K
Minimum Net Worth: $100K
Fees: Franchise - $25K
Royalty - $400 – 1,900/mo.;   Ad. - $100 – 400/mo.
Financial Performance Representation: Yes
Term of Contract (Years): 7/7
Avg. # of Employees: 1 FT, 2 PT
Passive Ownership: Discouraged
Encourage Conversions: Yes
Area Develop. Agreements: Yes
Sub-Franchising Contracts: No
Expand in Territory: Yes
Space Needs: N/A

SUPPORT & TRAINING:
Financial Assistance Provided: Yes (D)
Site Selection Assistance: N/A
Lease Negotiation Assistance: N/A
Co-operative Advertising: No
Franchisee Assoc./Member: No
Size of Corporate Staff: 30
Ongoing Support: b,C,D,E,F,G,h,I
Training: 4-5 days depending on class size in Richmond, VA

SPECIFIC EXPANSION PLANS:
US: All United States
Canada: No
Overseas: No

Mosquito Squad is proud to be North America's first, best, and most trusted choice in eliminating mosquitoes, ticks, and the diseases they can bring to families and communities. We are the leading national brand with the most locations, largest footprint, and largest client base in the category. No one has eliminated more mosquitoes and ticks— it's not even close! Our founders are industry pioneers and created many of the programs utilized by the entire industry category, including our competitors. With over 140 franchises in operation and many more on the way, Mosquito Squad has grown at an incredible rate of 296% over the last three years as recognized by Inc. Magazine. And we enjoy the strongest market share in the industry, by far.

Operating Units	12/31/2011	12/31/2012	12/31/2013
Franchised	87	111	142
% Change	--	27.59%	27.93%
Company-Owned	0	0	0
% Change	--	--	--
Total	87	111	142
% Change	--	27.59%	27.93%
Franchised as % of Total	100%	100%	100%

Investment Required

The initial franchise fee for a Mosquito Squad franchise is $25,000 for a standard territory, and $10,000 for a micro market territory. Mosquito Squad provides the following range of investments required to open your initial franchise. The range assumes that all items are paid for in cash. To the extent that you choose to finance any of these expense items, your front-end investment could be substantially reduced.

Item	Established Low Range	Established High Range
Initial Franchise Fee	$0	$25,000
Expenses While Training	$500	$1,000

Tools and Equipment	$800	$1,700
Computer Hardware and Software	$800	$2,000
Inventory	$1,200	$3,000
Trade Show Booth	$2,500	$2,500
Storage Facility for Inventory and Equipment	$0	$375
Vehicle	$0	$2,250
Vehicle Signage	$1,300	$1,800
Initial Marketing Expenses	$5,000	$15,000
Additional Funds (3 months)	$2,500	$7,500
Total Initial Investment	$14,600	$62,125

Ongoing Expenses

Mosquito Squad franchisees pay a monthly brand licensing fee that increases yearly, ranging from $400-$1,900 for standard territories and $300-$900 for micro market territories. Additional fees include a monthly national branding and marketing fee and a software fee. There is also a required annual minimum marketing spend of $25,000 per territory.

Franchisee Satisfaction

A critical component of the due diligence process is that you, as a prospective franchisee, have a strong sense of existing franchisee satisfaction. Please review the franchisor's ratings below for this extremely important information.

How do you rate Mosquito Squad in terms of:	Rating*
Overall Communication Between Home Office Personnel and Franchisees	99%
Franchisor Responds in Timely Manner to Questions/ Minor Problems	97%
Helpfulness of Franchisor's Field Representatives	94%

* Independent Audit of Existing Franchisees Who Rated Mosquito Squad as Excellent, Very Good, or Good

What You Get: Training and Support

Mosquito Squad franchisees will receive a 4.5 day training course at their corporate office in Richmond, VA which will cover a vast array of topics including on-site installations, marketing, and technology training. The Mosquito Squad team is fully committed to whatever it takes to support you and your goals as a franchisee. You'll have access to responsive support from a smart, professional staff in all of the key disciplines you'll need. This includes lead generation, marketing support, customer acquisition and retention, training and technology, and a franchise partner network.

Territory

Mosquito Squad grants exclusive territories.

Mr. Appliance Corporation

1010-1020 N. University Parks Dr.
Waco, TX 76707
Tel: (800) 290-1422, (254) 245-2462
Email: brandon.haire@dwyergroup.com
Website: www.mrappliance.com
Brandon Haire, Director of Franchise Development

Mr. Appliance is North America's largest appliance repair franchise system. Established in 1996, its franchises provide full-service residential and light commercial appliance repair. Mr. Appliance has more than 150 locations throughout the United States and Canada and is consistently ranked among the top home service franchises by Entrepreneur magazine and other industry experts. Mr. Appliance is a subsidiary of The Dwyer Group, Inc. For more information, visit www.mrappliance.com.

BACKGROUND:	IFA Member
Established: 1996;	First Franchised: 1996
Franchised Units:	185
Company-Owned Units:	0
Total Units:	185
Dist.:	US-161; CAN-5; O'seas-0
North America:	41 States, 4 Provinces
Density:	18 in TX, 17 in CA, 10 in FL
Projected New Units (12 Months):	50

Qualifications:	4, 4, 2, 2, 3, 5
FINANCIAL/TERMS:	
Cash Investment:	$40 – 90K
Total Investment:	$47.4 – 99.1K+
Minimum Net Worth:	Varies
Fees: Franchise -	$27K+
Royalty - 7%;	Ad. - 2%
Financial Performance Representation:	Yes
Term of Contract (Years):	10/10
Avg. # of Employees:	Varies
Passive Ownership:	Not Allowed
Encourage Conversions:	Yes
Area Develop. Agreements:	No
Sub-Franchising Contracts:	No
Expand in Territory:	Yes
Space Needs:	N/A
SUPPORT & TRAINING:	
Financial Assistance Provided:	Yes (D)
Site Selection Assistance:	N/A
Lease Negotiation Assistance:	N/A
Co-operative Advertising:	Yes
Franchisee Assoc./Member:	No
Size of Corporate Staff:	20
Ongoing Support:	A,C,D,E,F,G,H,I
Training:	1 Week & Ongoing Waco, TX
SPECIFIC EXPANSION PLANS:	
US:	All United States
Canada:	All Canada
Overseas:	Master Franchise Only

Mr. Appliance Corporation is one of the largest and fastest-growing full service appliance repair companies in the world. We service all types and brands of home appliances and commercial equipment. Mr. Appliance franchises across North America service all types of brands of home appliances and commercial equipment. Our professional franchise system will help you find new customers, gain market share over your local competition, and take your business to a new level of prosperity. As a Mr. Appliance franchisee, you will be equipped with marketing and public relations support, vendor rebates and incentives, and a dedicated franchise consultant to keep you on the right track. We'll provide ongoing training in our World Class Frontline Service System, designed to give your customers the best possible experience, and our Code of Values to keep your business focused on what matters most. With over 160 other franchise owners to share best practices, you won't be alone.

Operating Units	12/31/2011	12/31/2012	12/31/2013
Franchised	146	140	152
% Change	--	-4.11%	8.57%
Company-Owned	0	0	0
% Change	--	--	--
Total	146	140	152
% Change	--	-4.11%	8.57%
Franchised as % of Total	100%	100%	100%

Investment Required

The initial fee to purchase a Mr. Appliance franchise is $27,000 plus $270 per 1,000 population for additional territory. Mr. Appliance provides the following range of investments required to open your initial franchise. The range assumes that all items are paid for in cash. To the extent that you choose to finance any of these expense items, your front-end investment could be substantially reduced.

Item	Established Low Range	Established High Range
Initial Franchise Fee	$27,000	$27,000 + $270 per add'l 1,000 pop.
Vehicle	$2,250	$29,220
Equipment, Supplies, & Inventory	$5,900	$11,400
Insurance	$1,000	$2,000

Advertising & Promotional	$2,200	$6,000
Expenses while Training	$3,000	$5,500
Deposits, Permits, & Licenses	$0	$1,000
Professional Fees	$0	$5,000
Additional Funds (3 months)	$6,000	$12,000
Local Marketing Spending for Marketing Start-up Phase	$7,500	$15,000
Total Initial Investment	$54,850	$114,120 + add'l franchise fee

Ongoing Expenses

Franchisees are required to pay ongoing license fees equal to 7% of gross sales, a MAP fee equal to 2% of gross sales, a TAFS fee equal to 2% of gross sales, and local and cooperative advertising spending.

What You Get: Training and Support

Franchisees will be enrolled in an initial training program that may include a one-week Phase I program via webinar/video-conferencing, and a Phase II program consisting of 5 days of classroom training at company headquarters in Waco, TX. Phase III training will occur via telephone and is comprised of tasks and learning related to setting up the business. Additionally, franchisees will be required to complete one to five days of field training at a franchised business. Mr. Appliance will continue to provide ongoing advice and assistance regarding the operations of the franchise, as well as develop and administer promotional and advertising programs and hold refresher training courses when deemed necessary.

Territory

Mr. Appliance grants exclusive territories with a population of approximately 100,000 to 1,500,000.

Mr. Electric Corp.

1020 N. University Parks Dr.
Waco, TX 76707
Tel: (800) 805-0575, (254) 759-5861
Email: ronnie.musick@dwyergroup.com
Website: www.mrelectric.com
Ronnie Musick, Franchise Development Director

Established in 1994, Mr. Electric is a global franchise organization providing electrical installation and repair services. Recognized by Entrepreneur magazine among its "Franchise 500," Mr. Electric franchisees provide these services to both residential and commercial customers at 160 locations worldwide. Mr. Electric is part of The Dwyer Group family of companies, which also includes Rainbow International, Mr. Rooter, Aire Serv, Mr. Appliance, The Grounds Guys, and Glass Doctor.

BACKGROUND:

	IFA Member
Established: 1994;	First Franchised: 1994
Franchised Units:	174
Company-Owned Units:	0
Total Units:	174
Dist.:	US-146; CAN-28; O'seas-71
North America:	42 States, 1 Province
Density:	12 in TX, 12 in FL, 7 in OH
Projected New Units (12 Months):	30

Qualifications: 4, 3, 4, 2, 3, 5

FINANCIAL/TERMS:

Cash Investment:	$75K+
Total Investment:	$73.4 – 171K+
Minimum Net Worth:	$150K
Fees: Franchise -	$28K/100K Pop.
Royalty - 6-8%;	Ad. - 2%
Financial Performance Representation:	Yes
Term of Contract (Years):	10/10
Avg. # of Employees:	4 FT, 1 PT
Passive Ownership:	Not Allowed
Encourage Conversions:	Yes
Area Develop. Agreements:	No
Sub-Franchising Contracts:	No
Expand in Territory:	Yes
Space Needs:	N/A

SUPPORT & TRAINING:

Financial Assistance Provided:	Yes (D)
Site Selection Assistance:	N/A
Lease Negotiation Assistance:	N/A
Co-operative Advertising:	Yes
Franchisee Assoc./Member:	No
Size of Corporate Staff:	20
Ongoing Support:	A,B,C,D,E,F,G,H,I
Training:	2.5 Business Days Corporate Office; 5 Business Days On-Site in Business

SPECIFIC EXPANSION PLANS:

US:	All United States
Canada:	Yes
Overseas:	Most Latin America and Asian Countries

Established in 1994, Mr. Electric is a global franchise organization providing electrical installation and repair services. Recognized by Entrepreneur magazine among its "Franchise 500," Mr. Electric franchisees provide these services to both residential and commercial customers at 160 locations worldwide. Mr. Electric is part of The Dwyer Group family of companies, which also includes Rainbow International, Mr. Rooter, Aire Serv, Mr. Appliance, The Grounds Guys, and Glass Doctor.

Operating Units	12/31/2011	12/31/2012	12/31/2013
Franchised	131	130	130
% Change	--	-0.76%	0.0%
Company-Owned	0	0	0
% Change	--	--	--
Total	131	130	130
% Change	--	-0.76%	0.0%
Franchised as % of Total	100%	100%	100%

Investment Required

The initial franchise fee for a Mr. Electric Corp. franchise is $28,000, plus $280 per 1,000 population for additional territory. Mr. Electric Corp. provides the following range of investments required to open your initial franchise. The range assumes that all items are paid for in cash. To the extent that you choose to finance any of these expense items, your front-end investment could be substantially reduced.

Item	Established Low Range	Established High Range
Initial Franchise Fee	$28,000	$28,000 + $280 per 1,000 additional pop.
Vehicle	$2,200	$27,000
Equipment, Supplies & Inventory	$11,000	$17,000
Insurance	$1,200	$2,500
Advertising & Promotional	$5,000	$35,000
Expenses While Training	$3,000	$7,000
Deposits, Permits & Licenses	$1,000	$2,500
Professional Fees	$0	$5,000
Additional Funds (3 Months)	$25,000	$50,000

Local Marketing Spending for Marketing Start-up Phase	$7,500	$15,000
Total Initial Investment	$83,900	$189,000 + any additional franchise fee

Ongoing Expenses

Mr. Electric Corp. franchisees pay a weekly license fee of 6-8% of gross sales, a weekly MAP fee of 2% of gross sales, and an advertising cooperative fee of up to 2% of gross sales. Additional fees include software training and support fees, call center fees, and training fees.

What You Get: Training and Support

Mr. Electric Corp. offers a two-part training program for new managers and franchisees. Phase I consists of 16 hours of classroom training, provided via webinar or video conferencing. Topics covered include marketing, public relations basics, building your budget, and understanding your franchise agreement. Phase II of the training program combines both classroom and hands-on training methods, and takes place at the company offices in Waco, Texas. The second phase generally lasts about 5 days. Lastly, all trainees must complete 1-5 days of field training at a Mr. Electric franchised business selected by the company.

Territory

Mr. Electric Corp. does not grant exclusive territories.

Mr. Rooter

1010-1020 N. University Parks Dr.
Waco, TX 76707
Tel: (800) 298-6855, (254) 759-5820
Email: sam.thurman@dwyergroup.com
Website: www.mrrooter.com
Sam Thurman, Franchise Development Team Leader

Established in 1970, Mr. Rooter is an all-franchised, full-service plumbing and drain cleaning company with approximately 300 franchises worldwide. Recognized by Entrepreneur magazine among its "Franchise 500" and Franchise Times Top 200, Mr. Rooter franchisees provide services to both residential and commercial customers. Mr. Rooter began franchising in 1974 and is part of The Dwyer Group family of companies, which also includes Rainbow International, Aire Serv, Mr. Electric, Mr. Appliance, The Grounds Guys, and Glass Doctor.

BACKGROUND:

	IFA Member
Established: 1970;	First Franchised: 1974
Franchised Units:	241
Company-Owned Units:	0
Total Units:	241
Dist.:	US-212; CAN-27; O'seas-2
North America:	48 States, 7 Provinces
Density:	32 in CA, 18 in TX, 15 in OH

Projected New Units (12 Months):	25
Qualifications:	4, 3, 3, 2, 3, 5

FINANCIAL/TERMS:

Cash Investment:	$40 – 79K
Total Investment:	$68.4 – 162.6K+
Minimum Net Worth:	$100K
Fees: Franchise -	$30K/100K pop. + $300/1K add'l pop.
Royalty - 5-7%;	Ad. - 2%
Financial Performance Representation:	Yes
Term of Contract (Years):	10/10
Avg. # of Employees:	Varies
Passive Ownership:	Allowed
Encourage Conversions:	Yes
Area Develop. Agreements:	No
Sub-Franchising Contracts:	No
Expand in Territory:	Yes
Space Needs:	N/A

SUPPORT & TRAINING:

Financial Assistance Provided:	Yes (D)
Site Selection Assistance:	N/A
Lease Negotiation Assistance:	N/A
Co-operative Advertising:	Yes
Franchisee Assoc./Member:	No
Size of Corporate Staff:	25
Ongoing Support:	A,C,D,E,G,H
Training:	5 Days Waco, TX

SPECIFIC EXPANSION PLANS:

US:	Uncovered Areas
Canada:	Selected Areas
Overseas:	No

Established in 1970, Mr. Rooter is an all-franchised, full-service plumbing and drain cleaning company with approximately 300 franchises worldwide. Recognized by Entrepreneur magazine among its "Franchise 500" and Franchise Times Top 200, Mr. Rooter franchisees provide services to both residential and commercial customers. Mr. Rooter began franchising in 1974 and is part of The Dwyer Group family of companies, which also includes Rainbow International, Aire Serv, Mr. Electric, Mr. Appliance, The Grounds Guys, and Glass Doctor.

Operating Units	12/31/2011	12/31/2012	12/31/2013
Franchised	224	222	212
% Change	--	-0.89%	-4.5%
Company-Owned	0	0	0
% Change	--	--	--
Total	224	222	212
% Change	--	-0.89%	-4.5%
Franchised as % of Total	100%	100%	100%

Investment Required

The initial franchise fee for a Mr. Rooter franchise is $31,000, plus $310 per 1,000 population for additional territory. Mr. Rooter provides the following range of investments required to open your initial franchise. The range assumes that all items are paid for in cash. To the extent that you choose to finance any of these expense items, your front-end investment could be substantially reduced.

Item	Established Low Range	Established High Range
Initial Franchise Fee	$31,000	$31,000 + $310 per 1,000 additional pop.
Vehicle	$2,975	$29,250
Equipment, Supplies & Inventory	$10,000	$40,000
Insurance	$1,400	$2,700
Advertising & Promotional	$10,000	$25,000
Expenses While Training	$2,250	$4,850
Deposits, Permits & Licenses	$0	$1,000
Professional Fees	$0	$5,000
Additional Funds (3 months)	$15,000	$35,000

Local Marketing Spending for Marketing Start-up Phase	$7,500	$15,000
Total Initial Investment	$80,125	$188,880 + add'l franchise fee

Ongoing Expenses

Mr. Rooter franchisees pay weekly license fees of 5-7% of gross sales, a weekly MAP fee of 2% of gross sales, and a $50 monthly call center fee. Additional fees include the training fee and the systems accounts/administrative fee.

What You Get: Training and Support

Mr. Rooter offers a two-part training program for new managers and franchisees. Phase I involves three hours of classroom training, provided via webinar, video, or over the phone. Topics covered include website overview, budget planning, and office setup. Phase II of the training program combines both classroom and hands-on training methods, and takes place at the company offices in Waco, Texas. The second phase generally lasts about 5 days. Lastly, all trainees must complete 1-5 days of field training at a Mr. Rooter franchised business selected by the company.

Territory

Mr. Rooter grants exclusive territories.

Padgett Business Services®

400 Blue Hill Dr., # 201
Westwood, MA 02090
Tel: (877) 729-8725, (781) 251-9410
Fax: (781) 251-9520
Email: cclark@smallbizpros.com
Website: www.smallbizpros.com
Carol Clark, Franchise Development Coordinator

America's top-rated and fastest-growing tax and accounting franchise - serving the fastest-growing segment of the economy - America's small business owners. Initial training. Specialized software. Ongoing support.

BACKGROUND: IFA Member
Established: 1966;   First Franchised: 1975
Franchised Units: 385
Company-Owned Units: 0
Total Units: 385
Dist.:   US-268; CAN-117; O'seas-0
  North America: 43 States, 7 Provinces
  Density: 38 in QC, 67 in ON, 26 in GA
Projected New Units (12 Months):   50
Qualifications: 3, 3, 4, 4, 2, 4

FINANCIAL/TERMS:
Cash Investment: $100K
Total Investment: $100K
Minimum Net Worth: $100K
Fees: Franchise - $38K +18K Training
  Royalty - 9-4.5%;   Ad. - 0%
Financial Performance Representation: Yes
Term of Contract (Years):   10/10
Avg. # of Employees: 1 FT, 2 PT
Passive Ownership: Not Allowed
Encourage Conversions: Yes
Area Develop. Agreements: No
Sub-Franchising Contracts: No
Expand in Territory: Yes
Space Needs: 200-400 SF

SUPPORT & TRAINING:
Financial Assistance Provided: No
Site Selection Assistance: N/A
Lease Negotiation Assistance: N/A
Co-operative Advertising: No
Franchisee Assoc./Member: Yes/Yes
Size of Corporate Staff: 40
Ongoing Support: C,D,G,H,I
Training: 3 (2 day) tax seminar;
                          2 weeks Athens, GA

SPECIFIC EXPANSION PLANS:
US: All United States
Canada: All Canada
Overseas: No

Padgett Business Services® is America's top-rated and fastest-growing tax and accounting franchise. With a network of almost 400 offices in the United States and Canada, Padgett is one of the largest privately-owned small business services firms in the country, providing a wide array of financial services including tax planning and preparation, payroll services, financial reporting, business consultation, and other services pertinent to small businesses. Padgett franchisees help other entrepreneurs reach their full potential by building strong relationships with clients and running their businesses more effectively and efficiently. With plans to open 200 franchised units in the next five years, Padgett Business Services® is actively recruiting new franchise owners to help build on their proven formula of success. Initial training, specialized software, and ongoing support for franchisees ensure they are equipped with the tools needed to successfully branch out and reach their goals.

Operating Units	12/31/2011	12/31/2012	12/31/2013
Franchised	297	277	269
% Change	--	-6.73%	-2.89%
Company-Owned	0	0	0
% Change	--	--	--
Total	297	277	269
% Change	--	-6.73%	-2.89%
Franchised as % of Total	100%	100%	100%

Investment Required

The fee for a Padgett Business Services® franchise is $56,000. This fee is divided into a $1,000 application fee, a $37,000 initial license fee and a $18,000 training fee. Padgett Business Services provides the following range of investments required to open your initial franchise. The range assumes that all items are paid for in cash. To the extent that you choose to finance any of these expense items, your front-end investment could be substantially reduced.

Item	Established Low Range	Established High Range
Application Fee	$1,000	$1,000
Initial License Fee	$37,000	$37,000
Initial Training Fee	$18,000	$18,000
Expenses While Training	$2,000	$2,000
Equipment and Fixtures	$3,500	$3,500
Marketing	$27,900	$27,900

Initial Software Fee	$3,000	$3,000
Office Supplies	$2,000	$2,000
Initial Insurance	$800	$800
Rent, Telephone, Postage, etc.	$1,200	$1,200
Other Expenses	$2,375	$2,375
Additional Funds (3 Months)	$1,200	$1,200
Total Initial Investment	$99,975	$99,975

Ongoing Expenses

Padgett Business Services® franchisees pay royalty fees equal to the greater of 9% of gross receipts or a fixed amount, ranging from $50 to $750 per month depending on how long the franchisee has been in business. Franchisees also may pay advertising contributions equal to up to 2% of gross receipts.

What You Get: Training and Support

New franchisees receive two weeks of training in Athens, GA in the Padgett Marketing and Operations System before opening their own franchise, and an additional course after six months of operation. Step-by-step courses and seminars are held on all major aspects of the business. Additionally, Padgett Business Services® offers franchisees free ongoing professional training several times a year, where they can polish their knowledge, learn about developments in the industry, and network with each other at annual tax seminars and marketing conferences. Padgett provides its franchisees with telephone support, web support, and has a franchisee-staffed Advisory Board where franchisees can voice ideas and opinions to the Padgett support team. Padgett supplies marketing plans, professionally designed programs, and ready-made sales materials that create qualified business leads. Padgett's research and development team provides timely computer updates, new methods of client development, and workable solutions to many day-to-day problems.

Territory

Padgett Business Services® does not grant exclusive territories.

Pillar to Post Home Inspectors

PILLARTOPOST
HOME INSPECTORS

14502 N. Dale Mabry Hwy., # 200
Tampa, FL 33618
Tel: (877) 963-3129, (214) 794-7497
Email: brian.wieters@pillartopost.com
Website: www.pillartopost.com
Brian Wieters, Vice President Franchise Sales

Pillar To Post is North America's leading home inspection franchise. We have been named a Top 50 Franchise for franchisee satisfaction in 2013, 2014, and 2015 by Franchise Business Review, #1 Home Inspection franchise for 2013, 2014, and 2015 by Entrepreneur Magazine, as well as a Top Low Cost Franchise, Top Home Based Franchise, and among the Best of the Best listings with Entrepreneur magazine in 2013, 2014, and 2015.

BACKGROUND: IFA Member
Established: 1994;   First Franchised: 1994
Franchised Units: 435
Company-Owned Units: 0
Total Units: 435
Dist.:   US-358; CAN-77; O'seas-0
North America: N/A
Density: 22 in FL, 20 in PA, 17 in CA
Projected New Units (12 Months):   100

Qualifications: 3, 3, 3, 3, 3, 3

FINANCIAL/TERMS:
Cash Investment: $10 – 36.5K
Total Investment: $31.5 – 36.5K
Minimum Net Worth: N/A
Fees: Franchise - $16.9K
  Royalty - 7%;   Ad. - 4%
Financial Performance Representation: Yes
Term of Contract (Years):   5/5x5
Avg. # of Employees: N/A
Passive Ownership: Not Allowed
Encourage Conversions: Yes
Area Develop. Agreements: No
Sub-Franchising Contracts: No
Expand in Territory: No
Space Needs: N/A

SUPPORT & TRAINING:
Financial Assistance Provided: Yes (D)
Site Selection Assistance: N/A
Lease Negotiation Assistance: N/A
Co-operative Advertising: No
Franchisee Assoc./Member: N/A
Size of Corporate Staff: N/A
Ongoing Support: A,B,C,D,E,F,G,H,I
Training: 2 Weeks Toronto, ON

SPECIFIC EXPANSION PLANS:
US: All States
Canada: All Canada
Overseas: No

331

Pillar To Post is the #1 North American Home Inspection Franchise with more than 400 locations in North America. We are part of an elite group of real estate partners that select us as their preferred home inspection company. Our brand is trusted and reliable and we are committed to providing our franchisees with training, tools, and marketing to help them grow their business year over year. If you like to earn money based on your individual performance, while setting your own hours that are suitable to your own schedule and lifestyle, then you've come to the right place.

Operating Units	12/31/2011	12/31/2012	12/31/2013
Franchised	261	277	325
% Change	--	6.13%	17.33%
Company-Owned	0	0	0
% Change	--	--	--
Total	261	277	325
% Change	--	6.13%	17.33%
Franchised as % of Total	100%	100%	100%

Investment Required

The initial fee to purchase a Pillar to Post franchise is $35,900 to $45,900 for a Tier 1 exclusive territory, $29,900 for a Tier 2 exclusive territory, or $19,900 for a Tier 3 exclusive territory. Pillar to Post provides the following range of investments required to open your initial franchise. The range assumes that all items are paid for in cash. To the extent that you choose to finance any of these expense items, your front-end investment could be substantially reduced.

Item	Established Low Range	Established High Range
Initial Franchise Fee	$19,900	$45,900
Expenses while Training	$500	$1,000
Pillar to Post Tool Bundle	$3,000	$3,000

Local Tool/Equipment Purchases	$750	$750
Computer Equipment and Software	$4,000	$6,000
Office Equipment, Furniture, and Supplies	$1,000	$1,000
Foundations for Success Marketing Bundle	$1,500	$1,500
Foundations for Success Automated Marketing Campaign	$2,000	$3,500
Pillar to Post Attire	$300	$300
Various Account Set Up Fees and Organization Dues	$600	$600
Errors, Omissions and Other Insurance Premiums (3 months)	$1,000	$2,000
Additional Funds (3 months)	$1,800	$5,000
Total Initial Investment	$36,350	$70,550

Ongoing Expenses

Franchisees are required to pay ongoing royalty fees equal to 7% of gross revenues, or a minimum of $260 per month, as well as a brand fee equal to 4% of gross revenues, subject to a $150 monthly minimum.

What You Get: Training and Support

Franchisees will be enrolled in an initial training program of up to two weeks to take place at corporate headquarters in Toronto, ON. Topics covered include the inspection process, plumbing system, electrical system, report writing, and marketing. After successful completion of the training program, franchisees must also participate in practice inspections, reviews of those inspections, and other conference calls/webinars. Pillar to Post may require additional training and education, as well as administer a promotional and advertising program.

Territory

Pillar to Post grants exclusive territories.

Pop-A-Lock

1018 Harding St., # 101
Lafayette, LA 70503
Tel: (877) 233-6211, (337) 233-6211
Fax: (337) 233-6655
Email: michaelkleimeyer@systemforward.com
Website: www.popalock.com/franchising
Michael Kleimeyer, Director of Franchise Development

POP-A-LOCK is America's largest locksmith, car door unlocking, and roadside assistance service. We provide fast, professional, guaranteed service using our proprietary tools and opening techniques. We offer an outstanding community service through our industry.

BACKGROUND:

	IFA Member
Established: 1991;	First Franchised: 1994
Franchised Units:	302
Company-Owned Units:	0
Total Units:	302
Dist.:	US-359; CAN-25; O'seas-31
North America:	40 States, 1 Province
Density:	39 in TX, 42 in CA, 33 in FL
Projected New Units (12 Months):	113

Qualifications:	4, 5, 1, 3, 3, 4

FINANCIAL/TERMS:

Cash Investment:	$120K+
Total Investment:	$99.8 – 133.4K + $15.5K/ add. franchise (min. 4 franchises)
Minimum Net Worth:	$250 – 400K
Fees: Franchise -	Min. $62K
Royalty - 6%;	Ad. - 1%
Financial Performance Representation:	Yes
Term of Contract (Years):	10/10
Avg. # of Employees:	2 FT, 1 PT
Passive Ownership:	Allowed
Encourage Conversions:	N/A
Area Develop. Agreements:	Yes
Sub-Franchising Contracts:	No
Expand in Territory:	Yes
Space Needs:	N/A

SUPPORT & TRAINING:

Financial Assistance Provided:	Yes (I)
Site Selection Assistance:	N/A
Lease Negotiation Assistance:	N/A
Co-operative Advertising:	Yes
Franchisee Assoc./Member:	Yes/Yes
Size of Corporate Staff:	15
Ongoing Support:	A,b,C,D,E,F,G,h,I
Training:	5-15 days Lafayette, LA; add'l local

SPECIFIC EXPANSION PLANS:

US:	All United States
Canada:	Edmonton, Winnepeg, Regina
Overseas:	Mexico, Middle East, Australia

POP-A-LOCK was established in 1991 to provide unlocking services for automobile doors. Since then, they have grown to serve a wide range of locksmith services for business, home, or auto. POP-A-LOCK is the market leader in the mobile security industry. The company started franchising in 1994 and currently has more than 4,000 service centers nationwide. Pop-A-Lock provides mobile security services with all new modern technologies, proprietary tools, and opening techniques to ensure secure access. They also provide emergency services like the Emergency Car Door Unlocking (EDU) Program when human life is in danger, such as when a child is locked inside a car. This free Pop-A-Lock service has rescued over 280,000 children from locked vehicles since the company began its journey.

Operating Units	12/31/2011	12/31/2012	12/31/2013
Franchised	165	243	415
% Change	--	47.27%	70.78%
Company-Owned	0	0	0
% Change	--	--	--
Total	165	243	415
% Change	--	47.27%	70.78%
Franchised as % of Total	100%	100%	100%

Investment Required

The initial franchise fee for a POP-A-LOCK franchise is $15,500 for an exclusive territory population of 125,000. (Multiple territories may be awarded, based on exclusive population density.) POP-A-LOCK provides the following range of investments required to open your initial franchise. The range assumes that all items are paid for in cash. To the extent that you choose to finance any of these expense items, your front-end investment could be substantially reduced.

Item	Established Low Range	Established High Range
Franchise Fee	$15,500	$15,500

Pop-A-Lock Tool Kits	$1,400	$1,400
Printed Materials	$1,500	$2,640
CDU (Technical) Training	$1,600	$1,600
Travel and Living Expenses While Training	$3,520	$3,520
Equipment- Communication	$600	$600
Equipment- Roadside Service	$600	$600
Locksmith Service Training	$1,950	$1,950
Locksmith Service Equipment	$16,995	$34,000
Equipment- Office (Computer System)	$3,000	$3,000
Telephone Directory Display Advertisement	$578	$6,642
Initial Advertising (12 months)	$15,000	$15,000
Miscellaneous Opening Costs	$800	$1,200
Additional Funds (12 months)	$33,000	$41,000
Vehicle Identification	$1,600	$2,400
Mentor Program	$2,350	$2,350
Total Initial Investment	$99,993	$133,402

Ongoing Expenses

POP-A-LOCK franchisees pay ongoing royalty fees equal to 6% of monthly gross sales, an advertising and marketing fee equal to 1% of gross sales, and a local advertising fee of $15,000 for the first year.

Franchisee Satisfaction

A critical component of the due diligence process is that you, as a prospective franchisee, have a strong sense of existing franchisee satisfaction. Please review the franchisor's ratings below for this extremely important information.

How do you rate Pop-A-Lock in terms of:	Rating*
Overall Communication Between Home Office Personnel and Franchisees	96%
Franchisor and I are Committed to Positive, Long-Term Relationship	95%
Franchisor Encourages High Standards of Quality Performance	94%

* Independent Audit of Existing Franchisees Who Rated Pop-A-Lock as Excellent, Very Good, or Good

What You Get: Training and Support

The POP-A-LOCK Franchisee Training Program introduces the various facets of operating one of their franchises, including operations, standards, human resources, administration, accounting, and advertising and marketing. New Franchisee training is conducted at the corporate offices in Lafayette, LA for a minimum of four days. This program is followed by technical training, which demonstrates how to use POP-A-LOCK's proprietary equipment and techniques to open vehicles and is conducted at the national training facility in Lafayette, LA. Franchise compliance specialists will periodically contact or visit each franchise location to perform a field inspection. POP-A-LOCK regularly posts updated vehicle information and lock diagrams for the Confidential Manual to a secure website for downloadable updates. The franchisee and technicians will also be able to contact a research and development specialist 24 hours a day, seven days a week in the event there is a need for technical assistance to open a vehicle in the field.

Territory

POP-A-LOCK grants exclusive territories.

Pridestaff

PRIDESTAFF®

7535 N. Palm Ave., # 101
Fresno, CA 93711
Tel: (800) 774-3316, (559) 432-7780
Fax: (559) 432-4371
Email: pturner@pridestaff.com
Website: www.pridestaff.com
Paula W. Turner, EVP/Chief Operating Officer

We specialize in supplemental staffing (temporary help), outsourcing and full-time placement. PRIDESTAFF fills administrative, clerical, customer service, data entry, word processing and light industrial positions. The staffing industry is one of the fastest-growing industries in the United States.

BACKGROUND:

Established: 1974;	First Franchised: 1994
Franchised Units:	40
Company-Owned Units:	3
Total Units:	43
Dist.:	US-32; CAN-0; O'seas-0
North America:	13 States
Density:	12 in CA, 4 in AZ, 4 in IL
Projected New Units (12 Months):	N/A
Qualifications:	N/A

FINANCIAL/TERMS:

Cash Investment:	$75 – 100K
Total Investment:	$80.4 – 126.9K
Minimum Net Worth:	N/A
Fees: Franchise -	$12.5K
Royalty - 65% Gross Margin;	Ad. - N/A
Financial Performance Representation:	No
Term of Contract (Years):	10/5/5/5
Avg. # of Employees:	2 FT, 0 PT
Passive Ownership:	Allowed
Encourage Conversions:	No
Area Develop. Agreements:	No
Sub-Franchising Contracts:	No
Expand in Territory:	Yes
Space Needs:	1,200 SF

SUPPORT & TRAINING:

Financial Assistance Provided:	Yes (D)
Site Selection Assistance:	Yes
Lease Negotiation Assistance:	Yes
Co-operative Advertising:	No
Franchisee Assoc./Member:	No
Size of Corporate Staff:	16
Ongoing Support:	A,C,D,E,G,H,I
Training:	1 Week Branch Office; 1 Week Fresno, CA

SPECIFIC EXPANSION PLANS:

US:	All United States
Canada:	No
Overseas:	No

In 1978, George Rogers had a vision, a dream to create a new type of staffing organization—one that offered the resources and expertise of a national firm with the spirit, dedication, and personal service of smaller, entrepreneurial firms. The result is PrideStaff, a national staffing organization delivering innovative solutions to the challenges employers face every day. Through a combination of strong leadership at the national and local level, PrideStaff has consistently delivered exceptional service to franchisees, clients, and field associates. With businesses increasingly demanding more "just-in-time" solutions to their hiring needs, and the US Department of Labor forecasting increasing talent shortages over the next 20 years or more, the staffing industry is poised for significant long-term growth. And PrideStaff franchisees will be at the forefront of capitalizing on that job growth.

Operating Units	12/31/2011	12/31/2012	12/31/2013
Franchised	36	41	46
% Change	--	13.89%	12.2%
Company-Owned	3	3	3
% Change	--	0.0%	0.0%
Total	39	44	49
% Change	--	12.82%	11.36%
Franchised as % of Total	91.31%	93.18%	93.88%

Investment Required

The initial fee for a PrideStaff franchise is $35,000. PrideStaff provides the following range of investments required to open your initial franchise. The range assumes that all items are paid for in cash. To the extent that you finance any of these items, your front-end investment could be substantially reduced.

Item	Established Low Range	Established High Range
Initial Franchise Fee	$35,000	$35,000
Business Premises	$3,600	$6,000
Leasehold Improvements	$0	$12,000
Utility Deposits	$0	$1,500

Furnishings	$3,000	$13,500
Business Equipment	$5,000	$6,000
First Year Skills Testing Software License Fee	$83	$1,000
Computer System	$9,100	$10,100
Signs	$4,000	$5,000
Expenses While Training	$5,000	$6,500
Permits, Memberships, Subscriptions	$500	$1,000
Business Insurance Premiums	$1,600	$2,200
Initial Supplies	$500	$1,000
Additional Funds (270-360 days)	$67,609	$95,100
Total Initial Investment	$134,992	$195,900

Ongoing Expenses

Franchisees pay ongoing royalty fees equal to the greater of 35% of gross margin or 6% of net billings, plus 21% of direct hire and conversion fees. Other ongoing payments include an advertising fee of 0.25% of gross billings, an annual skills testing software fee of $1,000, and a Staffing Software fee of $95 per user per month.

What You Get: Training and Support

PrideStaff's competitive difference is marked by specially developed business management, marketing, training, and promotional programs. To ensure consistent quality, franchisees are provided with leading computerized software programs for the evaluation, training, and selection of Field Associates. Franchisees tap into PrideStaff's planned approach to the recruiting process that maximizes access to passive job candidates. Franchisees have access to PrideStaff's internal applicant tracking and skill matching system, which uses state of the art technology to expedite the order fulfillment process and provide flexible reporting capabilities. PrideStaff's award winning direct marketing system provides a step-by-step process for attracting the attention of staffing decision makers and creating opportunities to close business, plus a quality assurance and continuous improvement process guarantees client satisfaction. Through PrideStaff's corporate intranet, onsite sales and operations training, and the annual PAC conference, franchisees are provided with the most up-to-date techniques to maximize the effectiveness of their sales and servicing activities.

Territory

PrideStaff grants exclusive territories.

Pronto Insurance

805 Media Luna Rd., # 400
Brownsville, TX 78520
Tel: (855) 687-7088, (956) 574-7088
Fax: (956) 574-9076
Email: franchise@prontoinsurance.com
Website: www.prontoinsurance.com
Carlos A. Varela, Franchise Sales & Development Manager

Pronto Insurance is an insurance and financial service provider based in south Texas. Founded in 1997, Pronto developed a unique approach to the insurance business and has been revolutionizing the industry ever since. Through aggressive marketing, brand awareness, and highly competitive pricing, Pronto has quickly become an industry leader in Texas and now has the strength of over 130 branded agencies throughout the state. Personal property and liability insurance is a multi-billion dollar industry in Texas and the demand for affordable products has never been greater. Pronto offers a unique retail approach to

our consumers, who need reasonably priced insurance and financial products. Pronto prides itself in providing fast and efficient service. Our slogan "Pronto, It's our name and our promise"™ speaks for itself. As a Pronto Franchise owner, you will have the power of our brand and the expertise to guide you along the way.

BACKGROUND:	IFA Member
Established: 1997;	First Franchised: 2009
Franchised Units:	33
Company-Owned Units:	98
Total Units:	131
Dist.:	US-131; CAN-0; O'seas-0
North America:	1 State
Density:	131 in TX
Projected New Units (12 Months):	15
Qualifications:	3, 4, 1, 2, 4, 5

FINANCIAL/TERMS:	
Cash Investment:	$50 – 60K
Total Investment:	$60 – 100K
Minimum Net Worth:	$200K
Fees: Franchise -	$15 – 25K
Royalty - 0%;	Ad. - $500 or 1% of sales
Financial Performance Representation:	Yes

Term of Contract (Years):	5/5	Lease Negotiation Assistance:	Yes
Avg. # of Employees:	2-3 FT, 0 PT	Co-operative Advertising:	Yes
Passive Ownership:	Discouraged	Franchisee Assoc./Member:	Yes/Yes
Encourage Conversions:	Yes	Size of Corporate Staff:	500
Area Develop. Agreements:	Yes	Ongoing Support:	A,B,C,D,E,G,H,I
Sub-Franchising Contracts:	No	Training: 3 weeks Brownsville, TX; OR 2 weeks	
Expand in Territory:	Yes	Various locations throughout Texas	
Space Needs:	800 – 1,200 SF		
		SPECIFIC EXPANSION PLANS:	
SUPPORT & TRAINING:		US:	Yes, TX
Financial Assistance Provided:	Yes (I)	Canada:	No
Site Selection Assistance:	Yes	Overseas:	No

Pronto Insurance has more than 14 years of experience operating large numbers of highly-successful insurance agencies in the state of Texas. It has developed a competitive product line and an effective business model that consistently outperforms the competition. Pronto Insurance strives to provide peace of mind to the value-focused consumer through convenient insurance and financial products. A Pronto franchisee receives the advantage of brand recognition as well as extensive training and expert support in operations, marketing, and human resources. This affordable franchise is one-of-a-kind and unique in the industry. There is no need to invest in high-cost equipment, large inventories, or a large staff like the majority of franchises. Franchisees simply equip an office in a retail location, hire a few employees, and are on their way to running a Pronto Insurance franchise.

Operating Units	12/31/2011	12/31/2012	12/31/2013
Franchised	17	21	27
% Change	--	23.53%	28.57%
Company-Owned	92	95	93
% Change	--	3.26%	-2.11%
Total	109	116	120
% Change	--	6.42%	3.45%
Franchised as % of Total	15.60%	18.10%	22.50%

Investment Required

The franchise fee for a Pronto Insurance agency store is $20,000. Pronto Insurance also has an Area Development Program available. Pronto Insurance provides the following range of investments required to open your initial franchise. The range assumes that all items are paid for in cash. To the extent that you choose to finance any of these expense items, your front-end investment could be substantially reduced.

Item	Established Low Range	Established High Range
Initial Franchise Fee	$15,000	$25,000
Business Licenses & Permits	$150	$300
Leasehold Improvements	$5,000	$15,000
Fixtures, Furnishings & Equipment	$10,000	$20,000
Computer System	$1,800	$2,400
Architect/Engineering Fees	$150	$250
Rent, Security Deposits and Utility Deposits	$2,400	$4,000
Other Professional Fees	$100	$200
Insurance Deposit	$225	$400
Initial Inventory of Operating Supplies	$250	$350
Expenses While Training	$500	$1,200
Grand Opening Advertising	$5,000	$5,000
Additional Funds (3 Months)	$10,000	$15,000
Total Initial Investment	$50,575	$89,100

Ongoing Expenses

Pronto Insurance collects all gross franchise revenue earned by the franchise, and pays franchisees a sales commission equal to 12% of all insurance premium revenue and 90% of all tax preparation fee revenue, with a minimum of $150 retained each month. Additional fees include an advertising obligation of the greater of $500 per month or 1% of gross franchise revenue and a quality control evaluation fee not to exceed $500 per year.

What You Get: Training and Support

Pronto Insurance has developed a comprehensive training program that teaches franchisees every aspect of the insurance business model. This model can be broken down into the following: selling policies, providing excellent customer service, managing employees, and bookkeeping. Franchisees are also provided with the Pronto Insurance proprietary software needed to track and maintain a book of business. The Managing General Agency at Pronto Insurance corporate headquarters provides the support that franchisee customers need when dealing with a claim or policy care. Local Pronto staff also offers ongoing support for franchisees by taking care of their clients.

Territory

Pronto Insurance does not grant exclusive territories.

Rainbow International Restoration & Cleaning

Rainbow-International-LLC.aspx
Lewis Burch, Senior Director of Development

1020 N. University Parks Dr.
Waco, TX 76707
Tel: (800) 280-9963, (254) 745-2403
Email: lewis.burch@rainbowintl.com
Website: www.leadingtheserviceindustry.com/

Established in 1981, Rainbow International Restoration & Cleaning is a global franchise organization providing residential and commercial restoration and cleaning services. Recognized by Entrepreneur magazine among its "Franchise 500," Rainbow International franchisees offer a broad range of damage restoration services (ranging from water, smoke and fire damage to carpet and upholstery cleaning and deodorization) to 330 locations worldwide. The new Rapid Structural Drying Network of Rainbow International has established a network of elite water loss mitigation franchises across the United States. Rainbow International is part of The Dwyer Group family of companies, which also includes Mr. Rooter, Aire Serv, Mr. Electric, Mr. Appliance, The Grounds Guys, and Glass Doctor.

BACKGROUND: IFA Member
Established: 1980; First Franchised: 1981
Franchised Units: 309
Company-Owned Units: 0
Total Units: 309
Dist.: US-285; CAN-21; O'seas-3
  North America: 47 States, 2 Provinces
  Density: 30 in TX, 12 in OH, 9 in CA
Projected New Units (12 Months): 58
Qualifications: 4, 3, 1, 1, 3, 5

FINANCIAL/TERMS:
Cash Investment: $50K+
Total Investment: $115.7 – 189.1K
Minimum Net Worth: $250K
Fees: Franchise - $28K/100K Pop.
  Royalty - 3-7%; Ad. - 2%

Financial Performance Representation: Yes
Term of Contract (Years): 10/10
Avg. # of Employees: 8 FT
Passive Ownership: Not Allowed
Encourage Conversions: Yes
Area Develop. Agreements: No
Sub-Franchising Contracts: No
Expand in Territory: Yes
Space Needs: N/A

SUPPORT & TRAINING:
Financial Assistance Provided: Yes (D)
Site Selection Assistance: Yes
Lease Negotiation Assistance: No
Co-operative Advertising: Yes
Franchisee Assoc./Member: Yes/Yes
Size of Corporate Staff: 25
Ongoing Support: C,D,E,G,H,I
Training: 1 Day Classroom Training Waco, TX; 15 Days On-Site

SPECIFIC EXPANSION PLANS:
US: All United States
Canada: No
Overseas: No

Established in 1981, Rainbow International Restoration & Cleaning is a global franchise organization providing residential and commercial restoration and cleaning services. Recognized by Entrepreneur magazine among its "Franchise 500," Rainbow International franchisees offer a broad range of damage restoration services (ranging from water, smoke and fire damage to carpet and upholstery cleaning and deodorization) to 330 locations worldwide. The new Rapid Structural Drying Network of Rainbow International has established a network of elite water loss mitigation franchises across the United States. Rainbow International is part of The Dwyer Group family of companies, which also includes Mr. Rooter, Aire Serv, Mr. Electric, Mr. Appliance, The Grounds Guys, and Glass Doctor.

Operating Units	12/31/2011	12/31/2012	12/31/2013
Franchised	264	275	277
% Change	--	4.17%	0.73%

Company-Owned	0	0	0
% Change	--	--	--
Total	264	275	277
% Change	--	4.17%	0.73%
Franchised as % of Total	100%	100%	100%

Investment Required

The initial franchise fee for a Rainbow International franchise is $28,000, plus $280 per 1,000 population for additional territory. Rainbow International provides the following range of investments required to open your initial franchise. The range assumes that all items are paid for in cash. To the extent that you choose to finance any of these expense items, your front-end investment could be substantially reduced.

Item	Established Low Range	Established High Range
Initial Franchise Fee	$28,000	$28,000 + $280 per 1,000 additional pop.
Vehicle	$2,000	$39,000
Equipment, Supplies & Inventory	$70,000	$78,000
Insurance	$7,500	$15,000
Advertising & Promotional	$1,500	$4,000
Expenses While Training	$5,500	$9,000
Deposits, Permits & Licenses	$1,675	$3,100
Professional Fees	$2,500	$5,000
Additional Funds (6-9 Months)	$30,000	$60,000
Local Marketing Spending for Marketing Start-up Phase	$7,500	$15,000

Total Initial Investment	$156,175	$256,100 + additional franchise fee

Ongoing Expenses

Rainbow International franchisees pay a weekly license fee of 3-7% of gross sales, a weekly MAP fee of 2% of gross sales, and an advertising cooperative fee of up to 2% of gross sales. Additional fees include a training fee and the annual convention fee.

What You Get: Training and Support

Rainbow International offers a two-part training program for new managers and franchisees. Phase I involves three hours of classroom training, provided via webinar, video, or over the phone. Topics covered include website overview, budget planning, and office setup. Phase II of the training program combines both classroom and hands-on training methods, and takes place at the company offices in Waco, Texas. The second phase generally lasts about 15 days. Lastly, all trainees must complete 1-5 days of field training at a Rainbow International franchised business selected by the company. Rainbow International also offers optional training courses in specific fields such as: air duct training, mold remediation training, and EPA lead safe training.

Territory

Rainbow International grants exclusive territories.

ServiceMaster Clean

ServiceMASTER Clean ®

3839 Forest Hill Irene Rd.
Memphis, TN 38125
Tel: (800) 255-9687, (901) 597-7500
Fax: (901) 597-7580
Email: mpearce@smclean.com
Website: www.servicemasterfranchise.com
Michael Pearce, Chief Development Officer

SERVICEMASTER CLEAN is a division of The ServiceMaster Company. With over 60 years of franchising experience and over 4,000 franchises, SERVICEMASTER CLEAN continues to grow each year and offers franchise opportunities in three distinct categories: 1) Commercial Cleaning services 2) Floor Care services & 3) Disaster Restoration services. Financing is provided for the initial franchise fee, start-up equipment & vehicles to qualified candidates through ServiceMaster Acceptance Co.

BACKGROUND:

Established: 1947;	IFA Member
	First Franchised: 1952
Franchised Units:	4,450
Company-Owned Units:	0
Total Units:	4,450
Dist.:	US-3,082; CAN-176; O'seas-1,360
North America:	50 States, 10 Provinces

Density:	231 in CA, 198 in IL, 152 in OH
Projected New Units (12 Months):	150
Qualifications:	5, 3, 2, 2, 3, 5

FINANCIAL/TERMS:

Cash Investment:	$12K
Total Investment:	$49.6 – 180.6K
Minimum Net Worth:	$75K
Fees: Franchise -	$24.9 – 67K
Royalty - 5-10%;	Ad. - 1%
Financial Performance Representation:	Yes
Term of Contract (Years):	5/5
Avg. # of Employees:	3 FT, 2 PT
Passive Ownership:	Not Allowed
Encourage Conversions:	Yes
Area Develop. Agreements:	No
Sub-Franchising Contracts:	Yes
Expand in Territory:	Yes
Space Needs:	N/A

SUPPORT & TRAINING:

Financial Assistance Provided:	Yes (D)
Site Selection Assistance:	No
Lease Negotiation Assistance:	No
Co-operative Advertising:	Yes
Franchisee Assoc./Member:	Yes/Yes
Size of Corporate Staff:	200
Ongoing Support:	A,B,C,D,F,G,H,I
Training:	1 week on-site; 2 weeks Memphis, TN

SPECIFIC EXPANSION PLANS:

US:	All United States
Canada:	All Canada
Overseas:	All Countries

ServiceMaster Clean is part of the ServiceMaster family of companies and is an expert in residential and commercial cleaning and disaster restoration. With over 60 years of franchise experience, ServiceMaster Clean can teach franchisees how to successfully run a business with the knowledge, support, and resources of the ServiceMaster Clean family. With an annual revenue of almost $4 billion, the ServiceMaster family is a stable and profitable investment for any franchisee.

Operating Units	12/31/2011	12/31/2012	12/31/2013
Franchised	3,038	3,044	3,077
% Change	--	0.2%	1.08%
Company-Owned	0	0	5
% Change	--	--	--
Total	3,038	3,044	3,082
% Change	--	0.2%	1.25%
Franchised as % of Total	100%	100%	99.84%

Investment Required

The initial fee for a ServiceMaster Clean franchise varies depending on the type of services your franchise will offer. There are different categories of service such as disaster restoration services, floor care services, and janitorial services. ServiceMaster Clean provides the following range of investments required for your initial franchise. The range assumes that all items are paid for in cash. To the extent that you choose to finance any of these expense items, your front-end investment could be substantially reduced. Please note that the figures below represent expenses for a disaster restoration services franchise.

Item	Established Low Range	Established High Range
Initial Franchise Fee	$61,900	$67,000
Opening Package	$66,280	$66,280
Vehicle - Purchase	$3,000	$4,000
Vehicle Graphics	$975	$1,500
Insurance	$6,200	$7,450
Expenses While Training	$600	$1,000
The Institute of Inspection, Cleaning and Restoration Certification	$65	$260

Computer Hardware and Software	$6,500	$7,000
High Speed Internet Connection	$300	$1,000
Advertising (3 months)	$1,200	$6,400
Misc. Opening Costs	$1,000	$7,200
Additional Funds (3 months)	$12,000	$18,500
Total Initial Investment	$153,705	$180,580

Ongoing Expenses

There is a monthly royalty fee equal to the greater of $250 or 10% of gross service sales. There is also a national advertising fee fund equal to the greater of $200 or 1% of gross service sales.

What You Get: Training and Support

The training program varies depending on what type of franchise service you are opening. For example, Disaster Restoration training consists of roughly 155 hours - 42 hours of on-the job training, 30-50 hours of self-study, and 101 hours of classroom training.

Territory

ServiceMaster Clean does not grant exclusive territories.

SERVPRO

Fire & Water - Cleanup & Restoration™

801 Industrial Dr.
Gallatin, TN 37066
Tel: (800) 826-9586, (615) 451-0200
Fax: (615) 451-1602
Email: lwilliams@servpronet.com
Website: www.servpro.com
Laura Williams, Franchise Expansion Division Manager

A completely diversified cleaning and restoration business, with multiple income opportunities. The insurance restoration market (fire, smoke and water damages) is our main focus. We also specialize in commercial and residential cleaning. SERVPRO teaches effective management, marketing and technical skills. We are seeking qualified individuals with the desire to own their own business and become part of the SERVPRO team. If you want to be the best, join the best team. Call 1-800-826-9586.

BACKGROUND:

Established: 1967;	First Franchised: 1969
Franchised Units:	1,649
Company-Owned Units:	0
Total Units:	1,649
Dist.:	US-1,641; CAN-8; O'seas-0
North America:	48 States, 5 Provinces
Density:	191 in CA, 93 in FL, 100 in TX

Projected New Units (12 Months):	64
Qualifications:	3, 4, 1, 3, 4, 4

FINANCIAL/TERMS:

Cash Investment:	$80K+
Total Investment:	$138.6 – 187.2K
Minimum Net Worth:	$150K
Fees: Franchise -	$44K
Royalty - 3-10%;	Ad. - 3%
Financial Performance Representation:	No
Term of Contract (Years):	5/5
Avg. # of Employees:	5-10 FT, 2-4 PT
Passive Ownership:	Allowed
Encourage Conversions:	Yes
Area Develop. Agreements:	No
Sub-Franchising Contracts:	No
Expand in Territory:	No
Space Needs:	1,500+ SF

SUPPORT & TRAINING:

Financial Assistance Provided:	Yes (D)
Site Selection Assistance:	Yes
Lease Negotiation Assistance:	No
Co-operative Advertising:	Yes
Franchisee Assoc./Member:	No
Size of Corporate Staff:	401
Ongoing Support:	C,D,E,G,H,I
Training:	2.5 weeks Gallatin, TN; 1 week franchisee's location

SPECIFIC EXPANSION PLANS:

US:	All United States
Canada:	All Canada except Quecbec
Overseas:	No

SERVPRO is one of the most highly ranked and rated restoration franchises in America and Canada. SERVPRO specializes in removing the damages caused by fire, smoke, soot, water, mold, natural disasters, etc.

Operating Units	12/31/2011	12/31/2012	12/31/2013
Franchised	1,611	1,624	1,641
% Change	--	0.81%	1.05%
Company-Owned	0	0	0

% Change	--	--	--
Total	1,611	1,624	1,641
% Change	--	0.81%	1.05%
Franchised as % of Total	100%	100%	100%

Investment Required

The initial fee for a SERVPRO franchise is $44,000 for territories with populations of approximately 50,000 to 80,000. In certain exceptional circumstances, a larger territory may be allowed with an additional $489 charged per 1,000 people over the maximum population. SERVPRO provides the following range of investments required to open your initial franchise. The range assumes that all items are paid for in cash. To the extent that you choose to finance any of these expense items, your front-end investment could be substantially reduced.

Item	Estimated Low Range	Estimated High Range
Initial Franchise Fee	$44,000	$44,000 +
Vehicle	$600	$29,000
Equipment and Products Package	$64,000	$64,000
Supplies	$3,850	$8,500
Insurance	$3,000	$3,750
Advertising and Promotional	$250	$1,500
Expensing while Training, Training	$550	$1,900
Deposits, Permits, Licenses	$700	$2,550
Accounting Services, Online Tax Table Service and QuickBooks Pro Training	$600	$1,500
Xactimate Estimating and Pricing Software and Training	$1,000	$2,500

Additional Funds (3 months)	$20,000	$25,000
Real Estate	$0	$3,000
Total Initial Investment	$138,550	$187,200 +

Ongoing Expenses

SERVPRO franchisees pay royalty fees ranging from 3-10% of monthly gross volume with a minimum payment of $100. There is also a fixed fee that wavers between $45 - $115 based on monthly gross volume. In addition, there is an advertising fee of .5% of monthly gross volume plus 2.5% of annual gross volume on a calendar year basis, not including gross volumes from subcontract services.

What You Get: Training and Support

The SERVPRO training system consists of a five step Business Development Program: Prerequisite Progress which includes preparing your business prior to classroom training; Prerequisite Consultation consisting of an onsite Trainer visit; New Franchise Training Program, a 15 day classroom session; Business Setup, 5 days of onsite Trainer visits; and finally Business Consultation consisting of six onsite Trainer visits.

Territory

SERVPRO does not grant exclusive territories.

ShelfGenie

ShelfGenie®
EVERYTHING WITHIN REACH™

5500 Interstate North Pkwy., # 250
Atlanta, GA 30328
Tel: (877) 434-3643, (770) 955-4377
Fax: (320) 923-8858
Email: franchise@shelfgenie.com
Website: www.shelfgenie.com
Gillian Harper, Chief Development Officer

Want to glide into a fabulous business opportunity? We're looking for a select group of franchise owners, who want to provide great products and services to clients in their own protected territories. As a franchise owner with ShelfGenie, you'll have a wealth of resources that take away many of the administrative headaches of running your business (phone calls, manufacturing, and installations) along with advanced technologies that help you make informed management decisions.

BACKGROUND:	
Established: 2001;	IFA Member
	First Franchised: 2008
Franchised Units:	126
Company-Owned Units:	28
Total Units:	154
Dist.:	US-150; CAN-4; O'seas-0
North America:	26 States, 1 Province
Density:	16 in TX, 12 in FL, 7 in CA

Projected New Units (12 Months):	25
Qualifications:	3, 3, 1, 3, 4, 5
FINANCIAL/TERMS:	
Cash Investment:	$80 – 128K
Total Investment:	$80 – 128K
Minimum Net Worth:	$150K
Fees: Franchise -	$45K
Royalty - 5%;	Ad. - 2%
Financial Performance Representation:	Yes
Term of Contract (Years):	5/5
Avg. # of Employees:	0 FT, 4 PT
Passive Ownership:	Not Allowed
Encourage Conversions:	Yes
Area Develop. Agreements:	No
Sub-Franchising Contracts:	No
Expand in Territory:	No
Space Needs:	N/A
SUPPORT & TRAINING:	
Financial Assistance Provided:	Yes (I)
Site Selection Assistance:	No
Lease Negotiation Assistance:	No
Co-operative Advertising:	Yes
Franchisee Assoc./Member:	No
Size of Corporate Staff:	35
Ongoing Support:	C,D,E,F,G,H
Training:	8 days Atlanta, GA
SPECIFIC EXPANSION PLANS:	
US:	All United States
Canada:	All Canada
Overseas:	No

ShelfGenie manufactures Glide-Out™ shelving solutions that are custom built to fit virtually any existing cabinet, pantry, or furniture. Glide-Out™ shelves are ideal for homeowners due to their durability, affordability, utility in their increased accessibility, as well as the fact that they are environmentally friendly and made in the USA. ShelfGenie target client demographics include both "Luxury Purchasers" desiring to make affordable upgrades to their homes, as well as "Necessity Purchasers" who are adapting to smaller homes or desiring greater accessibility due to disability or age. This range of clients, in addition to the growth that the home remodeling industry has been experiencing, means that even in today's challenging economy, ShelfGenie franchisees are doing exceptionally well.

Operating Units	12/31/2011	12/31/2012	12/31/2013
Franchised	99	123	111
% Change	--	24.24%	-9.76%
Company-Owned	20	9	22
% Change	--	-55.0%	144.44%
Total	119	132	133
% Change	--	10.92%	0.76%
Franchised as % of Total	83.19%	93.18%	83.46%

Investment Required

The initial fee for a ShelfGenie franchise is $45,000. ShelfGenie provides the following range of investments required to open your initial franchise. The range assumes that all items are paid for in cash. To the extent that you choose to finance any of these expense items, your front-end investment could be substantially reduced.

Item	Established Low Range	Established High Range
Initial Franchise Fee	$45,000	$45,000
Leasehold Improvements	$0	$1,000
Vehicles	$0	$25,000
Furniture and Fixtures	$0	$15,000
Technology and Office Equipment/Supplies	$500	$2,000
Other Equipment	$1,000	$1,250
Business Licenses and Permits	$100	$1,000
Professional Fees	$2,000	$5,000
Insurance	$500	$2,500
Training Expenses	$1,000	$3,500
Initial Marketing	$15,000	$15,000

Additional Funds (3 Months)	$5,000	$15,000
Total Initial Investment	$70,100	$131,250

Ongoing Expenses

ShelfGenie franchisees pay a weekly royalty fee of 5% of gross revenues, as well as a weekly marketing contribution fee of 2% of gross revenues. Additional fees include a local advertising minimum spending requirement and a business services fee.

What You Get: Training and Support

The ShelfGenie support team provides franchisees with assistance in both opening and operation, including up to eight days of comprehensive start-up training at the home office in Atlanta, GA. This initial training is followed by on-site start up assistance, periodic field visits, and ongoing remote support from experienced ShelfGenie representatives. ShelfGenie also provides a confidential operations manual detailing day-to-day operations and professionally designed consumer marketing materials. ShelfGenie franchisees are given access to the ShelfGenie Business Support Center customer calling center for assistance with customer service, as well as a proprietary web-based business management system.

Territory

ShelfGenie does not grant exclusive territories.

Snip-its

Kids. Haircuts. Parties. Fun.

6409 City West Pkwy. # 205-A
Eden Prairie, MN 55344
Tel: (877) 764-7487, (952) 288-2222
Fax: (952) 288-2235
Email: inquiry@snipits.com
Website: www.snipitsfranchise.com
Kim Ellis, Vice President Franchise Development

Snip-its has changed the dynamic of children's hair-care by turning what has traditionally been considered a mundane and often unpleasant experience into a fun-filled adventure. The Snip-its custom interior features an original cast of cartoon characters, interactive computer play stations, the Magic Box, and a complete line of haircare products formulated just for kids. These, along with our proprietary point of sale, proven marketing system, and specially trained stylists represent one of the most innovative franchise opportunities available. With more than 65 locations nationwide, Snip-its' franchise program is a unique franchise opportunity with great earning potential.

BACKGROUND:

	IFA Member
Established: 1995;	First Franchised: 2003
Franchised Units:	64
Company-Owned Units:	1
Total Units:	65
Dist.:	US-65; CAN-0; O'seas-0

North America:	25 States
Density:	13 in TX, 10 in MA, 4 in NY
Projected New Units (12 Months):	12
Qualifications:	5, 5, 1, 4, 2, 5

FINANCIAL/TERMS:

Cash Investment:	$100K
Total Investment:	$120.3 – 255.4K
Minimum Net Worth:	$500K
Fees: Franchise -	$25K
Royalty - 6%;	Ad. - 2%
Financial Performance Representation:	Yes
Term of Contract (Years):	10/5
Avg. # of Employees:	8 FT, 2 PT
Passive Ownership:	Allowed
Encourage Conversions:	No
Area Develop. Agreements:	Yes
Sub-Franchising Contracts:	No
Expand in Territory:	No
Space Needs:	1,200 SF

SUPPORT & TRAINING:

Financial Assistance Provided:	No
Site Selection Assistance:	Yes
Lease Negotiation Assistance:	Yes
Co-operative Advertising:	Yes
Franchisee Assoc./Member:	No
Size of Corporate Staff:	9
Ongoing Support:	a,B,C,D,E,F,G,h
Training:	1 week Minneapolis, MN; 1 week onsite

SPECIFIC EXPANSION PLANS:

US:	East Coast and Southwest
Canada:	No
Overseas:	No

Snip-its has changed the dynamic of children's haircare by turning what has traditionally been considered a mundane and often unpleasant experience into a fun-filled adventure. The Snip-its custom interior features an original cast of cartoon characters, interactive computer play stations, the Magic Box, and a complete line of haircare products formulated just for kids. These, along with our proprietary point of sale, proven marketing system, and specially trained stylists, represent one of the most innovative franchise opportunities available. With more than 60 locations nationwide, Snip-its' franchise program is a unique franchise opportunity with great earning potential.

Operating Units	12/31/2011	12/31/2012	12/31/2013
Franchised	58	63	64
% Change	--	8.62%	1.59%
Company-Owned	3	1	1
% Change	--	-66.67%	0.0%
Total	61	64	65
% Change	--	4.92%	1.56%
Franchised as % of Total	95.08	98.44%	98.46%

Investment Required

The initial fee for a Snip-its franchise is $25,000. Snip-its provides the following range of investment items required to open your initial franchise. The range assumes that all items are paid for in cash. To the extent that you choose to finance any of these expense items, your front-end investment could be substantially reduced.

Item	Established Low Range	Established High Range
Initial Fee	$18,750	$25,000
Security Deposit and Rent	$4,000	$16,333
Staff Recruiting	$150	$1,000
Expenses while Training	$100	$2,100
Architecture Fees	$3,000	$5,500
Base Construction and Lease-hold Improvements	$27,000	$65,000
Millwork	$18,000	$27,000
"Snipification" of Salon	$16,000	$30,000
Computers, Software, and Set-up	$4,000	$6,000

Exterior Signage	$4,000	$6,000
Furniture	$2,800	$5,500
Audio Visual Equipment	$1,500	$4,500
Initial Inventory and Salon Supplies	$3,500	$13,000
Shipping	$1,500	$4,000
Insurance	$500	$1,500
Professional Services	$500	$3,000
Grand Opening Advertising	$10,000	$15,000
Additional Funds (3 months)	$5,000	$25,000
Total Initial Investment	$120,300	$255,433

Ongoing Expenses

Franchisees are required to pay ongoing royalty fees equal to 5% of gross sales for the first year, and 6% of gross sales for the balance of the term, as well as a marketing contribution and marketing fund equal to 1.5% of gross sales for the first year, and 2% of gross sales for the balance of the term.

What You Get: Training and Support

Snip-its offers an initial training program that consists of approximately 2 weeks of classroom and on-the-job training at company headquarters in Eden Prairie, MN. Topics that will be covered include: customer service, products and services, management, retail operations, human resources, and finance. Snip-its will also provide assistance in developing a Grand Opening Advertising Program, as well as ongoing advice and guidance, including additional training programs when deemed necessary.

Territory

Snip-its grants protected territories.

Spherion Staffing Services

One Overton Park 3625 Cumberland Blvd., # 600
Atlanta, GA 30339
Tel: (800) 903-0082, (404) 964-5508
Email: billtasillo@spherion.com
Website: www.spherion.com
Bill Tasillo, Vice President Market Expansion

Spherion Staffing Services franchise opportunities provide individuals a chance to join an exciting and rewarding industry. For more than 68 years, we've placed millions of workers in flexible, temp-to-hire and direct-hire jobs spanning nearly every industry and skill set. For seven consecutive years, Spherion has been named a world-class franchise opportunity by the Franchise Research Institute. What does this mean? Spherion franchisees confidentially participated in a third-party, unbiased survey to gain an inside perspective of what it is like to be a franchise owner for the company. Spherion achieved exceptional scores across the board! Our franchisees have a long history of contributing their talent, commitment and passion to building our brand, strengthening the system and enjoying the satisfaction and rewards that come from being part of a winning team. Our company and our industry have stood the test of time.

BACKGROUND: IFA Member
Established: 1946;   First Franchised: 1956
Franchised Units: 146
Company-Owned Units: 0
Total Units: 146

Dist.:	US-146; CAN-0; O'seas-0
North America:	32 States
Density:	14 in FL, 11 in CA, 21 in OH
Projected New Units (12 Months):	15
Qualifications:	5, 4, 1, 3, 4, 4

FINANCIAL/TERMS:

Cash Investment:	$100 – 170K
Total Investment:	$98 – 164K
Minimum Net Worth:	$100K
Fees: Franchise -	$25K
Royalty - 3-6%/25%;	Ad. - 0.25%
Financial Performance Representation:	Yes
Term of Contract (Years):	10/5
Avg. # of Employees:	3 FT, 0 PT
Passive Ownership:	Allowed
Encourage Conversions:	Yes
Area Develop. Agreements:	No
Sub-Franchising Contracts:	No
Expand in Territory:	Yes
Space Needs:	1,000 SF

SUPPORT & TRAINING:

Financial Assistance Provided:	No
Site Selection Assistance:	Yes
Lease Negotiation Assistance:	No
Co-operative Advertising:	Yes
Franchisee Assoc./Member:	No
Size of Corporate Staff:	30+
Ongoing Support:	A,B,C,D,E,G,H,I
Training:	120 hours in-office instruction; Ongoing additional self-paced instruction

SPECIFIC EXPANSION PLANS:

US:	Targeted cities in US
Canada:	No
Overseas:	No

Spherion Staffing Services is a leading recruiting and staffing provider that specializes in placing administrative, clerical, customer service and light industrial candidates in temporary and full-time opportunities. As an industry pioneer for more than 68 years, Spherion has sourced, screened and placed millions of individuals in virtually every industry through a network of offices across the United States. Spherion offers companies a unique combination of personalized customer service backed by the resources, knowledge and geographic breadth of a $2 billion dollar workforce leader. We help clients find the right talent to meet their workforce goals. Each local office is individually owned and operated by a team of staffing specialists who are known throughout the community.

Operating Units	12/31/2011	12/31/2012	12/31/2013
Franchised	148	146	146
% Change	--	-1.35%	0.0%
Company-Owned	0	0	0
% Change	--	--	--
Total	148	146	146
% Change	--	-1.35%	0.0%
Franchised as % of Total	100%	100%	100%

Investment Required

The fee for a for a Spherion franchise is $25,000. Spherion provides a 25% discount off the franchise fee for military veterans or those with 5+ years of staffing industry experience. Spherion provides the following range of investments required to open your initial franchise. The range assumes that all items are paid for in cash. To the extent that you choose to finance any of these expense items, your front-end investment could be substantially reduced.

Item	Established Low Range	Established High Range
Initial Franchise Fee	$25,000	$25,000
Computer System	$3,650	$5,750
Real Property	$1,400	$3,000
Leasehold Improvements, Furniture, and Fixtures	$7,500	$15,500
Equipment	$4,650	$10,500

Opening Advertising	$1,050	$5,150
Training Expenses	$1,050	$3,100
Start-Up Supplies	$510	$1,050
Insurance	$2,100	$7,850
Utility Expenses	$160	$1,100
Professional Fees	$1,050	$5,200
Business Franchises	$160	$1,100
Hardware Installation	$720	$1,100
Additional Funds (12 months)	$51,500	$82,500
Total Initial Investment	$100,400	$167,800

Ongoing Expenses

Spherion franchisees contribute to a national brand awareness fund and pay a computer system support fee, among others that help to enhance the brand and operations.

Franchisee Satisfaction

A critical component of the due diligence process is that you, as a prospective franchisee, have a strong sense of existing franchisee satisfaction. Please review the franchisor's ratings below for this extremely important information.

How do you rate Spherion Staffing Services in terms of:	Rating*
Overall Quality of the Franchisor	100%
Ongoing Training and Support Supplied by Franchisor	100%

Helpfulness of Franchisor's Field Representatives	100%

* Independent Audit of Existing Franchisees Who Rated Spherion Staffing Services as Excellent, Very Good, or Good

What You Get: Training and Support

Spherion bills clients, pays employees, and provides the software applications and cutting-edge technology that connect the franchisee to the corporate network, eliminating many operating costs associated with running the business. Some of the highlights include a dedicated and experienced field support team, extensive training programs, in-depth mentoring and coaching programs, centralized recruiter tools and helpful resources, comprehensive pre-opening procedures, centralized sales and marketing tools, national sales programs, web-based technology and tools, 100% financing for temporary payroll, client invoicing, accounting support, and a call center for operations and technical help. Once the franchisee is in business, Spherion will provide continued assistance and services, including standardized sales and promotional programs, campaigns and materials; preparing and paying the weekly payroll for temporary employees, including payroll taxes and other direct labor costs, preparing and delivering invoices to the customer for full-time placements and for services performed by temporary employees, and provide all other management information services and equipment previously discussed. This year, Spherion franchisees received unprecedented support in connection with compliance with the Affordable Care Act and substantial steps were taken to make this process as painless as possible for the franchisees both now and for the future.Franchisees will also receive advice and guidelines in handling customer collections, arranging and paying for accrued expenses relating to insurance, and a mailing list of current and prospective customers, full-time placement applicants, and temporary employees.

Territory

Spherion grants exclusive and non-exclusive territories.

Sport Clips

SportClips HAIRCUTS

IT'S GOOD TO BE A GUY

P.O. Box 3000-266
Georgetown, TX 78627
Tel: (800) 872-4247, (512) 869-1201
Fax: (512) 868-4601
Email: karen.young@sportclips.com
Website: www.sportclipsfranchise.com
Karen Young, Franchise Recruitment Manager

Our fun, sports-themed, men's and boys' haircutting concept is so unique it has made us the fastest-growing haircutting franchise in the country. This is a great recession-resistant business that's all cash, no receivables, and no industry experience is necessary. Better yet, you keep your current job while building your SPORT CLIPS business for the future.

BACKGROUND:

	IFA Member
Established: 1993;	First Franchised: 1995
Franchised Units:	1,178
Company-Owned Units:	29
Total Units:	1,207
Dist.:	US-1,196; CAN-11; O'seas-0
North America:	45 States, 1 Province
Density:	104 in CA, 82 in IL, 174 in TX
Projected New Units (12 Months):	180
Qualifications:	4, 5, 1, 1, 3, 5

FINANCIAL/TERMS:

Cash Investment:	$100K
Total Investment:	$158.3 – 316.5K
Minimum Net Worth:	$300K
Fees: Franchise-	$25 – 59.5K
Royalty - 6%;	Ad. - $300-450/Wk.
Financial Performance Representation:	Yes
Term of Contract (Years):	5/5
Avg. # of Employees:	6-8 FT
Passive Ownership:	Discouraged
Encourage Conversions:	No
Area Develop. Agreements:	Yes
Sub-Franchising Contracts:	No
Expand in Territory:	Yes
Space Needs:	1,200 SF

SUPPORT & TRAINING:

Financial Assistance Provided:	Yes (D)
Site Selection Assistance:	Yes
Lease Negotiation Assistance:	Yes
Co-operative Advertising:	Yes
Franchisee Assoc./Member:	No
Size of Corporate Staff:	98
Ongoing Support:	C,D,E,F,G,H,I
Training:	1 week locally for manager; 1 week local; 5 days Georgetown, TX for franchisee

SPECIFIC EXPANSION PLANS:

US:	All United States
Canada:	Yes
Overseas:	No

The haircutting industry is worth nearly $50 billion, but the majority of hair salon franchises are tailored towards women. SPORT CLIPS is designed to fill a niche in the hair industry by providing great haircutting experiences for men, including an exciting sports-themed environment where customers can watch sports while getting their hair cut. This innovative concept has made Sport Clips a highly successful, fast-growing franchise opportunity, with more than 1,200 locations in 45 states. Since 1993, the SPORT CLIPS team of experts has refined every aspect of the franchise, and it has paid off; SPORT CLIPS is consistently awarded accolades as one of the top franchise opportunities, including Entrepreneur magazine's Top 50 fastest growing franchises and Forbes ranks Sport Clips as one of the Top 5 Best Franchises to Buy.

Operating Units	12/31/2011	12/31/2012	12/31/2013
Franchised	819	976	1,123
% Change	--	19.17%	15.06%
Company-Owned	22	25	28
% Change	--	13.64%	12.0%
Total	841	1,001	1,151
% Change	--	19.02%	14.99%
Franchised as % of Total	97.38%	97.50%	97.57%

Investment Required

The fee for a SPORT CLIPS franchise is $59,500. SPORT CLIPS provides the following range of investments required to open your initial license. The range assumes that all items are paid for in cash. To the extent that you choose to finance any of these expense items, your front-end investment could be substantially reduced.

Item	Established Low Range	Established High Range
Initial Franchise Fee	$25,000	$59,500
Expenses While Training	$1,000	$2,000
Opening Inventory	$4,000	$6,000
Fixtures and Equipment	$35,000	$45,000
Leasehold Improvements	$35,000	$100,000
Supplemental Services Fee	$3,000	$5,000
Professional Fees	$1,000	$5,000
Permits and Licenses	$1,000	$3,500
Lease Deposit	$0	$5,000
Signage	$4,000	$8,000

Miscellaneous Opening Costs	$3,000	$5,000
Insurance	$1,300	$2,500
Grand Opening Advertising	$20,000	$20,000
Additional Funds (6 Months)	$25,000	$50,000
Total Initial Investment	$158,300	$316,500

*Except for the initial franchise fee (which reflects the cost for 3 stores), the amounts in the chart above reflect the estimated cost to open one store.

Ongoing Expenses

SPORT CLIPS franchisees pay royalty fees equal to 6% of net sales, weekly advertising fees equal to the greater of 5% of net sales or $300, and a weekly local advertising co-op fee of up to $300. Other fees payable by the franchisee include a weekly training fee and a monthly computer software maintenance fee.

What You Get: Training and Support

Initial training begins with comprehensive classroom and on-the-job instruction at corporate headquarters in Georgetown, TX, and covers all facets of running a SPORT CLIPS business: business operations, team development, marketing, and SPORT CLIPS standards. Franchisees also receive hands-on training at their area developer's pilot store. Sport Clips continues to support franchisees after store opening with ongoing training and responsive phone support. Sport Clips provides local, regional, and national advertising programs, and partners with national and local sports teams and NASCAR to promote individual store locations.

Territory

Sport Clips grants exclusive territories only for the initial five-year term of the franchise agreement.

Spring-Green Lawn Care

SPRING-GREEN.
Your **Neighborhood** Lawn Care Professional.

11909 Spaulding School Dr.
Plainfield, IL 60585
Tel: (800) 777-8608, (815) 230-1302
Fax: (815) 436-9056
Email: nbabyar@spring-green.com
Website: www.springgreenfranchise.com
Nancy Babyar, Franchise Development Manager

SPRING-GREEN delivers lawn and tree care services nationwide. Our service is centered on the beautification of middle class and affluent neighborhoods and communities. Our customers include both residential and commercial establishments. SPRING-GREEN services include lawn, tree and shrub fertilization as well as disease and perimeter pest control. SPRING-GREEN has been beautifying the environment for more than 35 years as your national lawn care team.

BACKGROUND:

	IFA Member
Established: 1977;	First Franchised: 1977
Franchised Units:	94
Company-Owned Units:	26
Total Units:	120
Dist.:	US-120; CAN-0; O'seas-0
North America:	26 States
Density:	15 in WI, 10 in NC, 31 in IL
Projected New Units (12 Months):	7
Qualifications:	4, 3, 1, 3, 2, 4

FINANCIAL/TERMS:

Cash Investment:	$40K
Total Investment:	$82.9 – 94.2K
Minimum Net Worth:	$160K
Fees: Franchise -	$30K
Royalty - 10-8%;	Ad. - 2%
Financial Performance Representation:	Yes
Term of Contract (Years):	10/10
Avg. # of Employees:	N/A
Passive Ownership:	Allowed
Encourage Conversions:	Yes
Area Develop. Agreements:	Yes
Sub-Franchising Contracts:	No
Expand in Territory:	No
Space Needs:	N/A

SUPPORT & TRAINING:

Financial Assistance Provided:	Yes (I)
Site Selection Assistance:	N/A
Lease Negotiation Assistance:	N/A
Co-operative Advertising:	No
Franchisee Assoc./Member:	Yes/Yes
Size of Corporate Staff:	22
Ongoing Support:	C,D,E,F,G,h,i
Training:	1 Week Training at Corp. HQ; 2 Days Field Training

SPECIFIC EXPANSION PLANS:

US:	All except AK, AZ, CA, CT, NY, NV, ND, HI, MA, MO, ME, MS, NM, RI
Canada:	No
Overseas:	No

Founded in 1977, Plainfield, Illinois-based Spring-Green Lawn Care has been delivering both traditional and organic lawn and tree care services nationwide for over 35 years. Its service is centered on the beautification of residential and commercial customers in middle-class and affluent neighborhoods and communities. Spring-Green is an attractive opportunity for candidates who do not want to be tied to a storefront operation, retail hours, or set appointments. Franchisees enjoy a lifestyle of being in an outdoor-based business with recurring revenues that allow the business to continue to scale. Spring-Green currently has franchises operating in 26 states and projections call for continued growth in the coming years.

Operating Units	12/31/2011	12/31/2012	12/31/2013
Franchised	94	94	99
% Change	--	0.0%	5.32%
Company-Owned	26	26	26
% Change	--	0%	0%
Total	120	120	125
% Change	--	0.0%	4.17%
Franchised as % of Total	78.33%	78.33%	79.20%

Investment Required

The initial fee for a Spring-Green franchise is $30,000 for a geographic territory containing 40,000 single family dwelling units (SFDUs), with an additional cost of $0.50 for each SFDU over 40,000 to the maximum of 60,000 SFDUs. Spring-Green provides the following range of investments required to open your initial franchise. The range assumes that equipment and signage is leased and other items are paid for in cash. To the extent that you choose to finance any of these expense items, your front-end investment could be substantially reduced.

Item	Established Low Range	Established High Range
Initial Franchise Fee	$30,000	$40,000
Vehicles, Equipment and Fixtures	$4,374	$5,744
Technology Equipment and Software	$2,063	$2,063
Opening Inventory and Supplies	$4,000	$4,000
Initial Marketing Campaign Fee	$25,000	$25,000
Training Expenses	$1,226	$1,226

Miscellaneous Opening Costs	$2,000	$2,000
Additional Funds (3 Months)	$15,000	$15,000
Total Initial Investment	$83,663	$95,033

Ongoing Expenses

Spring-Green's franchisees pay ongoing royalty fees of 8-10% of gross sales, advertising fund contributions of 2% of gross sales, and regional advertising fees of up to 2% of gross sales, among others.

Franchisee Satisfaction

A critical component of the due diligence process is that you, as a prospective franchisee, have a strong sense of existing franchisee satisfaction. Please review the franchisor's ratings below for this extremely important information.

How do you rate Spring-Green Lawn Care in terms of:	Rating*
Overall Communication Between Home Office Personnel and Franchisees	91%
Helpfulness of Franchisor's Field Representatives	93%
Ongoing Training and Support Supplied by Franchisor	90%

* Independent Audit of Existing Franchisees Who Rated Spring-Green Lawn Care as Excellent, Very Good, or Good

What You Get: Training and Support

Initial training includes up to one week of classroom training and at least two days of on-the-job training covering topics such as marketing and sales, commercial services, equipment and computer operations, and safety. As you leave your initial training program, a member of the support team will begin your in-field training, helping with staff development, computer support, and in-field marketing support. You can expect daily communication, conference calls with your peers and multiple field visits your first and second year. Ongoing support is provided in the following areas: hiring and staff development, technology and financial assistance, agronomic support, equipment, and marketing. Spring-Green believes that the collective knowledge of its franchise owners can propel the franchise organization faster than anyone can accomplish individually. Therefore, throughout the year Spring-Green will offer franchise owners the opportunity to meet with their peers and discuss relevant topics surrounding the Spring-Green business.

Territory

Spring-Green grants limited exclusive territories.

Tutor Doctor

"We Make House Calls!"

2070 Codlin Crescent, # 1
Toronto, ON M9W 7J2
Tel: (877) 988-8679, (416) 646-0364
Fax: (416) 646-0366
Email: opportunity@tutordoctor.com
Website: www.tutordoctoropportunity.com
Fiorella Alva, Franchise Development Assistant Manager

Tutor Doctor allows you to join a fast-growth, recession resistant industry while making a difference in your community. Our franchisees, who manage a team of professional tutors, benefit from our successful one-to-one tutoring model that provides at-home service to students of all ages. This eliminates the need for high overhead costs associated with a traditional bricks and mortar businesses. With around 400 franchises in 14 countries, there has never been a better opportunity to join our team! 83% of Tutor Doctor franchisees come from backgrounds other than Education. In fact, 25% of Tutor Doctor's franchise community has a background in Financial Services, IT, Manufacturing, and HealthCare. If you want to be part of a growing network of diverse franchisees who make money while making a difference, join the Tutor Doctor Family!

BACKGROUND:		Sub-Franchising Contracts:	No
	IFA Member	Expand in Territory:	No
Established: 2000;	First Franchised: 2003	Space Needs:	N/A
Franchised Units:	400		
Company-Owned Units:	0	**SUPPORT & TRAINING:**	
Total Units:	400	Financial Assistance Provided:	Yes (I)
Dist.:	US-235; CAN-98; O'seas-67	Site Selection Assistance:	N/A
North America:	33 States, 5 Provinces	Lease Negotiation Assistance:	N/A
Density:	40 in CA, 61 in ON, 28 in BC	Co-operative Advertising:	No
Projected New Units (12 Months):	138	Franchisee Assoc./Member:	No
Qualifications:	3, 4, 1, 4, 4, 3	Size of Corporate Staff:	30
		Ongoing Support:	A,b,C,D,G,h,I
FINANCIAL/TERMS:		Training:	30 days Pre-Training & Road
Cash Investment:	$62.5 – 100.7K	to Toronto - Online; 7 Days In-Home Training	
Total Investment:	$62.5 – 100.7K	Toronto, Canada; 24 Weeks Jump-Start & Mentor-	
Minimum Net Worth:	$100K	ship - Online & Parachuting	
Fees: Franchise -	From $39.7K		
Royalty - 8% or $300;	Ad. - 2%	**SPECIFIC EXPANSION PLANS:**	
Financial Performance Representation:	Yes	US:	All United States
Term of Contract (Years):	10/5	Canada:	All Canada Except Quebec
Avg. # of Employees:	1 FT	Overseas:	Australia, New Zealand, UK,
Passive Ownership:	Discouraged	Mexico, Brazil, South Africa, Other countries	
Encourage Conversions:	Yes	under evalution	
Area Develop. Agreements:	Yes		

If we compare the Tutor Doctor's services to the traditional center-based tutoring operations, the superiority of the in-home, one-on-one tutoring model becomes obvious. The Tutor Doctor Platform matches a highly qualified tutor with a student in the privacy and comfort of their own home. Students prefer this stress-free approach to learning as they can progress at their own pace and are free from peer pressure and the embarrassment they often feel in traditional learning environments. By removing the intimidation and fear of failure, students suddenly become comfortable, confident and eager to learn. Unlike many tutoring programs that require parents to bring their child to a tutoring center, at Tutor Doctor we provide students with affordable, professional, one-on-one, individualized tutoring services in the comfort of their own home. By working collaboratively with students, parents and teachers, Tutor Doctor tutors provide the best supplemental, personalized instruction along with the motivation and confidence needed to help students succeed. With a growing market need, and such a superior service offering, it isn't difficult to see why parents and students find the Tutor Doctor offering so refreshing. Named the #1 at-home tutoring franchise worldwide by Entrepreneur Magazine and Child's Magazine's Parents

Choice Award in 2010 and 2011, Tutor Doctor is quickly expanding and becoming the standard in the tutoring industry.

Operating Units	12/31/2011	12/31/2012	12/31/2013
Franchised	177	229	227
% Change	--	29.38%	-0.87%
Company-Owned	0	0	0
% Change	--	--	--
Total	177	229	227
% Change	--	29.38%	-0.87%
Franchised as % of Total	100%	100%	100%

Investment Required

The initial fee for a Tutor Doctor franchise ranges from $39,700 for a local territory franchise to $54,700 for a national territory franchise. Tutor Doctor provides the following range of investments required to open your initial franchise. The range assumes that all items are paid for in cash. To the extent that you choose to finance any of these expense items, your front-end investment could be substantially reduced.

Item	Established Low Range	Established High Range
Initial Franchise Fee	$39,700	$54,700
Mentoring Program	$4,000	$4,000
Rent Deposit, Pre-Paid Rent, Utility and Phone Deposits	$0	$500
Insurance Initial Payment	$1,300	$3,000
Computer and Software	$1,000	$5,000
Printing	$1,500	$1,500
Market Advertising and Promotion	$3,000	$13,000

Phone and Fax	$500	$500
Training	$2,000	$2,000
Additional Funds (3 months)	$5,000	$10,000
Professional Fees	$1,500	$3,000
Field Training	$2,000	$2,000
Smart Car	$1,000	$1,500
Total Initial Investment	$62,500	$100,700

Ongoing Expenses

There are other fees to consider such as a monthly royalty fee equal to the greater of 8% of gross revenues or the minimum royalty which ranges from $300 for a local territory franchise to $700 for an international territory franchise. You must also pay $1,000 per month toward lead generations and a national/international branding fee equal to 2% of gross revenue.

What You Get: Training and Support

Tutor Doctor will offer an initial 40-hour training program that will take place in Toronto, Canada and will cover operations, marketing/sales, human resources, and personal and professional development. Franchisees will also participate in a two-phase mentoring program, in which you will shadow a mentor at their business for three days during phase one, and will receive direct support at your place of business by a mentor over a period of three to nine months during phase two. Tutor Doctor will continue to provide assistance regarding the daily operations of the franchise, as well as additional training when deemed necessary.

Territory

Tutor Doctor does not grant exclusive territories, however, the territories are protected in that franchisees can not market or solicit customers in each other's territories.

Vanguard Cleaning Systems

VANGUARD
Cleaning Systems

655 Mariners Island Blvd., # 303
San Mateo, CA 94404
Tel: (800) 564-6422, (650) 287-2400
Fax: (650) 591-1545
Email: elast@vanguardcleaning.com
Website: www.vanguardcleaning.com
Eric Last, Franchise Development Director

The Vanguard Cleaning Systems franchise organization has 2,821 independently owned and operated franchised businesses in North America. Through a master franchise network of 59 regional offices, Vanguard Cleaning Systems franchisees provide cleaning services for more than 15,000 commercial customers.

BACKGROUND:
	IFA Member
Established: 1984;	First Franchised: 1984
Franchised Units:	2,821
Company-Owned Units:	0
Total Units:	2,821
Dist.:	US-2,247; CAN-193; O'seas-0
North America:	31 States, 3 Provinces
Density:	413 in CA

Projected New Units (12 Months):	852
Qualifications:	2, 2, 3, 1, 3, 5

FINANCIAL/TERMS:
Cash Investment:	$2.5 – 30.8K
Total Investment:	$8.5 – 37.9K
Minimum Net Worth:	$2.5 – 30.8K
Fees: Franchise -	$7.2 – 34.2K
Royalty - 10%;	Ad. - N/A
Financial Performance Representation:	No
Term of Contract (Years):	10/10
Avg. # of Employees:	0 FT, 1 PT
Passive Ownership:	Not Allowed
Encourage Conversions:	Yes
Area Develop. Agreements:	Yes
Sub-Franchising Contracts:	Yes
Expand in Territory:	Yes
Space Needs:	N/A

SUPPORT & TRAINING:
Financial Assistance Provided:	Yes (D)
Site Selection Assistance:	N/A
Lease Negotiation Assistance:	N/A
Co-operative Advertising:	No
Franchisee Assoc./Member:	No
Size of Corporate Staff:	9
Ongoing Support:	A,C,D,G,H,I
Training:	2 weeks+ at local regional office

SPECIFIC EXPANSION PLANS:
US:	All United States
Canada:	All Canada
Overseas:	No

The Vanguard Cleaning Systems franchise organization has a network of over 2,800 franchisees who provide high-quality janitorial services for over 15,000 commercial cleaning accounts. Since 1984, Vanguard Cleaning Systems franchisees have provided a wide range of specialized janitorial services—general office cleaning, carpet cleaning, hard surface floor care, window washing, power washing, and green cleaning—to many different commercial facilities including office complexes, industrial buildings, medical offices, schools, and more. Vanguard Cleaning Systems regions provide their franchisees with an initial business system program and customer service support. Franchisees can choose to grow their business at their own pace, allowing for a steady revenue base at start-up and lower risk.

Operating Units	12/31/2011	12/31/2012	12/31/2013
Franchised	2,247	2,480	2,671
% Change	--	10.37%	7.7%
Company-Owned	0	0	0
% Change	--	--	--
Total	2,247	2,480	2,671
% Change	--	10.37%	7.7%
Franchised as % of Total	100%	100%	100%

Investment Required

The fee for a Vanguard Cleaning Systems franchise ranges from $8,000 to $34,000, although financing may be available. Vanguard Cleaning Systems provides the following range of investments required to open your initial franchise. The range assumes that all items are paid for in cash. To the extent that you choose to finance any of these expense items, your front-end investment could be substantially reduced.

Item	Established Low Range	Established High Range
Franchise Fee	$3,094.66	$32,130
Equipment and Supplies	$800	$1,300
Licenses and Permits	$100	$1,500
Insurance	$200	$600
Additional Funds (3 months)	$200	$300
Total Initial Investment	$4,394.66	$35,830

Ongoing Expenses

Vanguard Cleaning Systems franchisees pay ongoing royalty fees of 10% of gross revenues, business support service fees of 5.0% of gross revenues, as well as marketing fees.

What You Get: Training and Support

Vanguard Cleaning Systems regions provides franchisees with an initial educational program that includes DVD instruction, web-based/e-learning, and commercial cleaning information. Vanguard Cleaning Systems regions supports franchisees on an ongoing basis, and regional office staff are available to answer any questions about customer cleaning needs or to provide technical assistance.

Territory

Vanguard Cleaning Systems regions do not grant exclusive territories for unit franchises.

Window Genie

We Clean Windows and a Whole Lot More!

40 W. Crescentville Rd.
Cincinnati, OH 45246
Tel: (800) 700-0022, (513) 541-3351
Email: rik@windowgenie.com
Website: www.windowgeniefranchise.com
Richard Nonelle, CEO

The home services leader, specializing in 3 distinct categories: Window Cleaning, Window Tinting, and Pressure Washing. With protected territories and tremendous market appeal, Window Genie is perfectly positioned to service time-starved homeowners.

BACKGROUND: IFA Member
Established: 1994; First Franchised: 1998
Franchised Units: 168
Company-Owned Units: 0
Total Units: 168
Dist.: US-168; CAN-0; O'seas-0
  North America: 28 States
  Density: 19 in GA, 20 in FL, 15 in NC
Projected New Units (12 Months): 35
Qualifications: 4, 4, 1, 3, 3, 5

FINANCIAL/TERMS:
Cash Investment: $75K
Total Investment: $85 – 150K
Minimum Net Worth: $150K
Fees: Franchise - $32K
  Royalty - 7%; Ad. - $300/Mo.
Financial Performance Representation: Yes

Term of Contract (Years):	10/5	Lease Negotiation Assistance:	N/A
Avg. # of Employees:	7 FT, 2 PT	Co-operative Advertising:	No
Passive Ownership:	Not Allowed	Franchisee Assoc./Member:	No
Encourage Conversions:	Yes	Size of Corporate Staff:	8
Area Develop. Agreements:	No	Ongoing Support:	C,D,E,F,G,H,I
Sub-Franchising Contracts:	No	Training: 5 Days Corporate, Cincinnati, OH;	
Expand in Territory:	Yes	5 Days on-site	
Space Needs:	N/A		
		SPECIFIC EXPANSION PLANS:	
SUPPORT & TRAINING:		US:	All United States
Financial Assistance Provided:	No	Canada:	Yes
Site Selection Assistance:	N/A	Overseas:	No

Window Genie is a well-established cleaning franchise offering three different home care services that add beauty and value to customers' homes. As the number of empty-nest households in the country grows, the market for home cleaning services is expected to continue to increase as well. This is a business whose potential has yet to be realized on the national level, leaving tremendous opportunity. As a Window Genie franchisee, you will learn to set-up and run a business from a team of professionals who know and understand the business. It is an opportunity designed around managing people and building a successful business.

Operating Units	12/31/2011	12/31/2012	12/31/2013
Franchised	44	46	62
% Change	--	4.55%	34.78%
Company-Owned	0	0	0
% Change	--	--	--
Total	44	46	62
% Change	--	4.55%	34.78%
Franchised as % of Total	100%	100%	100%

Investment Required

The fee for a Window Genie franchise is $32,000 for up to 50,000 households. Additional households in geographic areas contiguous to the Base Marketing Area may be purchased for fifty cents ($0.50) per household. The total number of households may not exceed 100,000 households. Window Genie provides the following range of investments required to open your initial franchise. The range assumes that all items are paid for in cash. To the extent that you choose to finance any of these expense items, your front-end investment could be substantially reduced. Please note that the figures below represent expenses for a Unit Franchise.

Item	Established Low Range	Established High Range
Initial Franchise Fee	$32,000	$57,000
Start-Up Equipment & Supply Package	$25,000	$25,000
Office Package	$0	$1,500
Initial Training	$600	$1,300
Opening Advertising	$3,000	$9,000
Security, Utility Deposits, etc.	$1,200	$2,200
Vehicle	$0	$1,500
Real Estate	$0	$500
Additional Funds (3 months)	$28,000	$41,000
Total Initial Investment	$89,800	$139,000
Real Estate	$0	$500
Additional Funds (3 months)	$28,000	$41,000
Total Initial Investment	$81,250	$131,100

Ongoing Expenses

Window Genie unit franchisees pay an ongoing royalty fee of 7% of gross revenue and a national marketing fee of at least $300 per month. Additional fees include a quarterly local marketing requirement and a technology fee of $269 per month.

What You Get: Training and Support

Window Genie offers a complete package of support that is based on the established Window Genie system. New franchisees will begin with five days of training at the corporate office in Cincinnati, OH, where franchisees will be taught operations, service procedures, marketing/sales, and administration. Continuing support will always be available by phone and at the annual convention.

Territory

Window Genie grants exclusive territories.

Alphabetical Listing of Franchisors

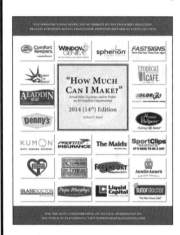

DEFINITIVE FRANCHISOR DATABASE AVAILABLE FOR RENT

SAMPLE FRANCHISOR PROFILE

EXPRESS EMPLOYMENT PROFESSIONALS
9701 Boardwalk Blvd.
Oklahoma City, OK 73162-5145, U.S.A.

800/LocalTelephone #:	(877) 652-6400 (405) 840-5000
Fax #:	(405) 717-5665
EMail:	david.lewis@expresspros.com
Internet Address:	www.expressfranchising.com
# Franchised Units:	692
# Company-Owned Units:	1
# Total Units:	693
Company Contact/Title:	Mr. David Lewis, Vice President Franchising
Contact Salutation:	Mr. Lewis
President/Title:	Mr. Robert A. Funk, Chief Executive Officer
President Salutation:	Mr. Funk
IFA Member:	International Franchise Association
CFA Member:	Canadian Franchise Association

KEY FEATURES

•	Number of Active North American Franchisors	~3,000
•	% US	~80%
•	% Canadian	~20%
•	Idividual contacts included with optional Custom Database	~13,000
•	Data Fields (See Above)	~30
•	Industry Categories	29
•	% With Number of Total Operating Units	90%
•	Guaranteed Accuracy — $0.50 Rebate/Returned Bad Address	
•	Converted to Any Popular Database or Contact Management Program	
•	Initial Front-End Cost	$1,000/$2,000
•	Quarterly Up-Dates	$150/$250
•	Mailing Labels Only — One-Time Use	$600

For more information, please contact
Source Book Publications
1814 Franklin St., Suite 603, Oakland, CA 94612
(888) 612-9908 or (510) 839-5471 or fax (510) 839-2104